D0896474

17—   X

# LIES TOLD UNDER OATH

THE PUZZLING STORY OF THE
PFANSCHMIDT MURDERS AND OF THE
SURVIVING SON—VICTIM OR VILLAIN?

# LIES TOLD UNDER OATH

## BETH LANE

iUniverse, Inc.
Bloomington

**Lies Told Under Oath**
**The Puzzling Story of the Pfanschmidt Murders and of the Surviving Son—Victim or Villain?**

Copyright © 2012 by Beth Lane

All rights reserved. No part of this book may be used or reproduced by any means, graphic, electronic, or mechanical, including photocopying, recording, taping or by any information storage retrieval system without the written permission of the publisher except in the case of brief quotations embodied in critical articles and reviews.

iUniverse books may be ordered through booksellers or by contacting:

iUniverse
1663 Liberty Drive
Bloomington, IN 47403
www.iuniverse.com
1-800-Authors (1-800-288-4677)

Because of the dynamic nature of the Internet, any web addresses or links contained in this book may have changed since publication and may no longer be valid. The views expressed in this work are solely those of the author and do not necessarily reflect the views of the publisher, and the publisher hereby disclaims any responsibility for them.

Any people depicted in stock imagery provided by Thinkstock are models, and such images are being used for illustrative purposes only.

Certain stock imagery © Thinkstock.

ISBN: 978-1-4620-7630-7 (sc)
ISBN: 978-1-4620-7631-4 (hc)
ISBN: 978-1-4620-7633-8 (e)

Library of Congress Control Number: 2011962705

Printed in the United States of America

iUniverse rev. date: 02/01/2012

This book is dedicated to two special people:

Lynn Miller Snyder, without whom it would still be an idea.

And most of all, to my mother, Kathleen Miller House,

without whom it would not have seen print.


Thank you!

"Innocent or guilty, that boy has got a wonderful lot of nerve."

—Tom Post, jury foreman, Macomb, Illinois, 1914

# Contents

## Section I
## Events of September 1912–February 1913

# Section II
## The Trial, March 1913

# Section III
## Days of Defeat and Strategy

# Cast of Characters

## The Pfanschmidt Family

Ray Pfanschmidt

Charles Pfanschmidt—Ray's father (murdered September 28, 1912)

Mathilda (Tilde or Tillie) Pfanschmidt—Ray's mother (murdered September 28, 1912)

Blanche Pfanschmidt—Ray's sister (murdered September 28, 1912)

Charles C. Pfanschmidt (a.k.a C. C.)—Ray's grandfather, father of Charles Pfanschmidt

Emma Kaempen—schoolteacher boarding with the family (murdered September 28, 1912)

E. W. Charles Kaempen—Emma's father

Emil Kaempen—Emma's brother

Esther Reeder—Ray's fiancée

Daniel Reeder—Esther's father

Fred and Mary Pfanschmidt—Ray's uncle and aunt

Walter Pfanschmidt—Fred's son, Ray's cousin

Henry Geisel—Ray's uncle; his wife, Mary, was sister to Charles Pfanschmidt

Henry Niekamp—Ray's uncle; his wife, Hannah, was sister to Charles Pfanschmidt

Walter Herr—Ray's uncle; his wife, Minnie, was sister to Charles Pfanschmidt

Elizabeth Petrie—Ray's widowed aunt, housekeeper for C. C., sister to Charles Pfanschmidt

Howard Petrie—Ray's cousin, son of Elizabeth Petrie

Walter O. Cook—Ray's uncle; his wife, Ida, was sister to Charles Pfanschmidt

William Abel—Ray's uncle, brother of Mathilda Pfanschmidt

Fred Knollenberg—Ray's uncle; his wife, Louisa, was sister to Charles Pfanschmidt

## Neighbors and Employees

Henry Kaufman—closest neighbor of the Pfanschmidt farm

August (Gus) Kaufman—son of Henry

John, Will, and Clarence Kaufman—brothers of Gus, sons of Henry

Ben, Ed, and Moritz Lier (a.k.a. Liehr, Lehr)—brothers, and neighbors of the farm

John Lier—part-time Pfanschmidt hired hand, brother to Ben, Ed, and Moritz Lier

Henry Schreck—neighbor of the farm

Ben Holeman (Holman)—Ray's friend and foreman at "the works"

The Eakins (a.k.a. Aikins) family—where Ben Holman boarded

Silba (a.k.a. Zeba, Ziba) Lawrence—Ray's second foreman

Joseph L. Frese (a.k.a. Freese, Freze)—storekeeper, owner of "the works" and Ray's employer

Claude (a.k.a. Clark) Hubbard—handyman working for J. L. Frese

Charles H. Achelpohl—Grandfather C. C. Pfanschmidt's friend

Casper Mast—neighbor of Daniel Reeder

Roy Peter—neighbor of the Pfanschmidt farm

E. W. Peter—neighbor of the Pfanschmidt farm

## Attorneys and Court Officials

Judge Guy H. Williams—presiding judge

Wm. H. Govert—Ray's attorney and father of attorney G. W. Govert

George W. Govert—Ray's attorney

Emery Lancaster—Ray's attorney

John T. (Tony) Gilmer—outgoing-state's attorney in 1912

Fred G. Wolfe—incoming-state's attorney (1912) and lead prosecutor

John E. Wall—private attorney for the prosecution retained by Charles Kaempen

## Law Enforcement and Detectives

Peter B. Lott—Quincy police chief

Joseph Lipps—Adams county sheriff

William Schaeffer—sheriff's deputy

Fred Scharnhorst—deputy

George Coens (a.k.a. Coons)—deputy

George Koch—private detective, later Adams county sheriff

H. G. Strumpfer—bloodhound handler and Illinois state fire marshal

A. H. Bogardus Jr.—Illinois state fire marshal

Robert Bumster (a.k.a. Bumpster)—police detective

C. W. Tobie—private detective from the Burns Agency

Arthur G. Lund (a.k.a. Lunt)—detective from the Burns Agency

Herbert F. Young—owner of Young's Secret Service Company of Chicago, Illinois

Richard W. Farley—private detective from the Young Agency

Monk Frye—jailor at the Quincy jail

Loftus—Iowa sheriff sent by the Iowa governor

Barden—police detective from Chicago

Bates—police detective from Chicago

George Hutmacker (a.k.a. Hutmacher)—civilian

Plank—civilian

John Fogal (a.k.a. Fogel)—civilian

## Doctors
Dr. Ludwig Hektoen—blood expert from Chicago

Dr. Thomas B. Knox—Quincy physician

Dr. Charles Erickson—Quincy physician

Dr. H. O. Collins—city physician for Quincy

Dr. Charles D. Center—Quincy physician

# List of Images

# Introduction

"Did you know our great-grandfather was an eyewitness in an axe-murder trial?" My cousin tossed this offhand remark in my direction and waited.

"He was *blind*!" The words tumbled out before I thought about it. "How could a blind man possibly be an 'eyewitness' to anything, much less a murder?" I thought it a reasonable question.

She simply shrugged and said that his name was listed in an old newspaper article about the trial.

Within days I was immersed in old accounts, digging through the basement and the creepy subbasement of the present-day Quincy, Illinois, courthouse for the Coroner's Inquest transcript, eventually traveling to the state capital to read the trial transcript itself. The Pfanschmidt case involved a most sensational crime, both resembling and falling hard on the heels of the infamous Villisca, Iowa, axe murders.[1] In the Pfanschmidt Illinois case, four people were murdered—mother, father, daughter, and a schoolteacher who boarded with the family. The only surviving son, Ray, was suspected by the newspapers and convicted by public opinion even before being arrested and tried for the murders. Forensics of the day were crude or nonexistent, and the courtroom drama was intense.

---

[1] In June of 1912, eight bodies (six children and two adults) were found bludgeoned to death in the home of the Moore family of Villisca, Iowa. The crime remains unsolved.

By the time I figured out that my great-grandfather ("Pa" as we called the gentle old man named Fred Schnellbecker who sat out his days in a rocker by his window) was *not* the eyewitness, the story would not let go.

The saga of Ray's trials, which follows here, is presented as you might have heard it from a seat in the courtroom audience. Witnesses appear and speak in their own words, as they appeared at that time and in the order of the proceedings.

Testimony is taken from the official transcripts or period newspaper accounts. When several witnesses testified to the same evidence or opinion, a synopsis is given. The presentation of the prosecution's case in particular is often confusing, but the original sequence remains intact, for the very strategy of the prosecution and the ultimate verdict in this trial tell a story of their own. The contest between the prosecution and the defense attorneys was passionate, repetitive, hard to follow, but always fascinating. As when watching two heavyweight fighters in a long bout trading flat-footed punches, there is no time to look away, for you might miss a knockout blow.

Remember that judicial rules and procedures were different in 1912. In the course of the trial, the defense and the prosecution made innumerable objections. With some witnesses, the attorneys objected to every statement. At one point in the official transcript, the court reporter noted that he would no longer insert the entire wording of every objection and exception, as they were so numerous as to be cumbersome. Sometimes the judge simply instructed the court reporter to note an identical objection after every single question to a witness. Other times the judge ignored an objection. Both sides were fighting for what they saw as justice.

This crime and its resulting three sensational trials caused a change in the Illinois laws of inheritance, are still cited as precedence in trials involving bloodhound evidence, and created changes in regulations governing terms of the circuit courts.

It all began this way …

# Section I

# Events of September 1912–February 1913

# Chapter 1

~

# Illusions of Peace

### Saturday, September 28, 1912

The peaceful Illinois prairie kept deadly secrets that autumn Saturday. A white-frame farmhouse sat silently, concealed by its orchard. Chickens lazily scratched the dirt in the garden, and the leaves of carefully tended fruit trees stirred in an erratic breeze. Horses stomped and whickered in the barn but could not be heard from the nearby road. Neither the lively Pfanschmidt family, who owned and tended the place, nor their boarder, the new schoolteacher, was anywhere to be seen.

It appeared to early morning passersby that the family had gone to the city for the day.

Just a mile down the road, a little rock building known as Hibner School also rested silently, locked and shuttered at the edge of the fields as the buggy of mail carrier William Long clopped by. The stone walls of the one-room school drank in the pale sunshine; the wood stove, cold and still, awaited the teacher's match come Monday.

Mr. Long thought about the newly hired teacher, Emma Kaempen, and wondered how the plain-faced young city woman would fare in the country. Usually on Saturday mornings, Miss Kaempen arranged to make the hour and a half ride back to her family on the Payson/Quincy stagecoach. Or sometimes she would tie a rag on the mailbox and the neighboring farmer, Mr. Kaufman, would stop for her on his way to deliver his eggs and butter to the Quincy stores. That thirteen-mile journey spanned more than miles; it crossed boundaries of attitude and culture.

At the Pfanschmidt farm on this fall morning there was no flag on the mailbox, so the neighbor went on his way without stopping.

Mailman Long left the newspaper in the box by the road, since no one was waiting to gather it. Neither blonde, pretty Blanche nor her smiling mother, Mathilda, was there. There was no friendly wave from Blanche's father, Charles, usually hard at work in the fields. Mr. Long didn't expect to see the only other member of the family, a grown son named Ray, who worked in town.

All day the empty windows of the two-story farm house gazed blankly toward the road. There was, however, an odd odor tossed about by the unpredictable breeze. Woodcutter Roy Peter, passing the farm about 7:00 a.m., thought someone might have disposed of cholera hogs. This dreadful disease had been about the area recently, and the only sure way to stop its spread was to burn the diseased carcasses. Whatever the source, the smell was decidedly unpleasant.

That day, the neighbor's son, Gus Kaufman, chopped corn and cut weeds up near the Payson Road, just a hundred yards from the Pfanschmidt home. He saw only a quiet, peaceful farm. It was an uneventful day for him, the last such for a long time.

As the light wind changed direction, rippling the corn stalks in the fields, the nose-wrinkling smell appeared and dissipated, never revealing its source. Toward sunset, when the damp air quieted the breeze and made all odors more distinctive, the stench grew stronger. At least that's how it seemed to neighbor Peter as he made his return trip past the farm that evening.

Later still, about ten o'clock, a little shower settled the dust on the roads before the darkened farmhouse.

# Chapter 2

# Fire!

## Sunday, September 29, 1912

By two o'clock Sunday morning flames were staining the sky, bouncing dirty red among the clouds.

At the Schreck farm, a mile north of the Pfanschmidt place, a shrill noise disturbed a sleeping woman, who then roused her husband. Groggy, Henry Schreck stumbled to the loudly ringing wall phone. Calls in the dead of night were never good news, especially the single long peal of alarm spilling out of the crank phone.

He was galvanized awake by one word that first penetrated his sleep-shrouded brain: "Fire!" followed by, "Pfanschmidts!"

Rubbing his eyes, Henry peered toward the neighbors but saw only an angry red reflection in the sky. He jerked his shoulders into a denim shirt and pulled on pants as he made his way out the door, ignoring anxious questions from his wife.

Crossing to the wooden windmill, he forced his stiff and tired body to clamber up high enough for a decent view over the trees. But even from this vantage he could not tell if the flames were consuming a barn or the house.

Scrambling down, he threw a bridle on the closest horse in the barn and galloped bareback across the fields. The horse, unwilling to approach the flames, shied at some distance from the farmstead. Henry, figuring it was quicker to proceed on foot than to fight the rearing horse, jumped down. His horse spun in a circle and trotted back toward the safety of home.

"Charles! Tilde!" Henry bellowed the names of his friends against the awful clawing roar of the flames. His cries went unanswered.

The chimney bricks and the tin roof of the house had already collapsed, nearly leveling the two-story home. Henry circled the house. Only the fire spoke, using crashes and crackles and showers of sparks.

Scant minutes later, the four Lier brothers arrived from their farm to the north. John, the eldest, had left Quincy a few hours earlier, just after midnight Saturday and dozed as his horses carried the buggy home in the early hours of Sunday morning. He had been unhitching his team when the wind carried the scent of fire and jolted him awake. He roused his brothers, and they hurried through the night, following the beacon of the flames.

Another neighbor, Gus Kaufman, breathlessly arrived on foot just as Ben was tying the Liers' horses to the back side of the barn, out of sight of the terrifying flames.

"Where's Charles and Tilde?" he rasped.

"Don't know," replied Henry. "Best get on the telephone and try and find them. Maybe they're to town." The bleakness in his eyes belied his hopeful words.

John Wand was the next neighbor to arrive. His watch, illuminated by the blaze, showed 2:20 a.m. He angled his wagon across the drive, sealing off the lane where it ran closest to the house. He knew others would be arriving soon, the countryside roused by the efficient party-line alarms pealing through the night.

The house was now completely engulfed. The northwest corner was the last to be wrapped in the red-orange embrace of the fire. In short order, the timber frame was completely consumed by the fire's fierce hunger. Only a stove pipe protruded drunkenly from what used to be the kitchen. It leaned away from the silent dinner bell sitting forlornly atop its post in the backyard. The place smelled of ash and despair.

"They must not have been home," a voice said with the quiet determination of hope. "There was a porch roof both of those bedrooms gave on to. If they'd of been home they could have got out."

"Yeah," agreed a second voice. "Smoke couldn't have got 'em all. They must be in town."

"Go call Geisel—he might know where they are." Henry Geisel was the missing farmer's brother-in-law and lived just south of Quincy. Perhaps the family had spent the night there.

Phone calls were made in a flurry from a neighbor's house. The telephone party lines sang out their long and short rings, demanding answers. Since everyone on a party line listened in on calls rousing the countryside in the dead of night, news spread at the speed of speech.

John Lier gestured to Schreck. "Henry, I checked the barn. There's four horses in there, and they were awful thirsty. I don't think they were fed or watered yesterday. That big one was so skittish it climbed into the manger."

Henry saw there was still more. Lier continued: "The buggy's there too settin' in the runway of the barn with a bag of sugar in it. And there's a wagon loaded with oats."

Almost in unison, shoulders slumped in defeat. Eyes searched the ground, vainly seeking some remaining hope for their friends. The men milled around in predawn, smoky-tasting gloom. Unequipped to fight the blaze, they waited while the unhampered fire burned the darkness for another interminable hour or two, until Henry Geisel finally arrived.

"We'd better pull the roof off," was all he said.

Geisel exhorted and ordered and organized the growing crowd into forming a bucket line from the cistern. Their efforts were surely no threat to the furnace raging through the ruins of the house, but it provided an outlet for the frustration and fear of the watchers. As the pale gray light erased the darkness, Moritz and Ben Lier climbed the telephone poles to harvest wires to use to drag the hot metal lid from the house.

Fred Schnellbecker and Ed Wand, from two neighboring farms, left the growing crowd of spectators and headed to the barnyard with a coal oil lamp to tend to the cows that would need to be milked—fire or not.

But there were no cows to be found. It was another oddity to add to the growing number of unexplained and disturbing things amiss in the orderly homestead.

"Look at this." In the flickering light from the lamp, Fred pointed to the ground in the barnyard. "Looks like someone was here last night after the rain. There's a track cuts through the crust."

"Turned sharp on itself," muttered Ed. "Can't see where it stopped though."

"Don't look like a rubber tire track, does it?"

Ed answered with a negative shake of his head. "Nope. Must have been steel tires to make tracks that sharp."

Methodically working at the house ruins, the men used pitchforks to puncture the heat-brittle metal that had been the roof. Easing phone wire through the holes, they made loops to pull away the protesting strips. Uncovered embers flared flame red as the morning air reached them, but cistern water quenched their brief return and cooled them to ashes.

"Let's check the kitchen first. Maybe this thing started from a stove." John Lier and three men moved to the northeast side of the debris and began working at the roof, laying bare the flattened room below.

Soon two stoves were exposed to the dawn. One, an old-style cooking stove had collapsed into itself from the heat. The remains of a newer-model coal oil range had been warped by the fire, solder melting off some of the tubes. There was no sign of explosion from either one. It seemed they were not to blame.

"Look at this." One of the men held up a strange, contorted object. "Must of been a fork." He dropped it with a muted clatter onto a pile of silver-plated cutlery, now twisted by the heat and stripped of its shiny exterior. Little was now recognizable except metal and earthenware.

The flooring of the east room had collapsed. It exposed a forlorn jumble of goods lying on the cement cellar floor below, much of it home-canned jars of garden vegetables that Mathilda and Blanche had worked hard to put up against the winter. John Lier, poking through the debris, prodded at a charred mass not quite a yardstick long.

When he flipped it over, the underside revealed a scrap of blue hickory shirt and undershirt saved from the fire by what should have been the left hip. The lump had once been somebody.

"Where's his head?" gagged a voice as the stench released by turning the body rose to engulf them.

"Dig for the rest of him. Be careful!" John's voice cracked. It would prove to be a fruitless search. There were no arms, or legs, or head to be found. On the west side of the home, the search was faring no better.

Ben and the Wand boy had their backs to the fire, straining to wrest a long strip of roof iron free, but they whirled as one upon hearing a strangled cry.

"Who is that? Where's the body?" These words flew from a horrified Henry Miller, driver of a mule team freight wagon who had arrived before daylight. He had followed the red glow of firelight in the clouds for some time as he ferried his load from the little town of New Canton toward Quincy, and he had been among the first to arrive. All three men were mesmerized by the bizarre head that seemed to pop up out of the ruins, sightless eyes blazing at them.

"There's the rest." Ben pointed toward a torso that had a stump of a neck and most of one leg missing.

"There's more." The numb quiet that had fallen allowed the anguished tones to carry over the shriek of metal as the last two roof panels were dragged away with a groan. There on the remains of a smoldering mattress two bodies lay side-by-side. They were eventually identified by their braided hair.

# Chapter 3

~

# Dawn of Ashes

## Sunday, September 29, 1912

As Sunday morning dragged on, the hushed and curious crowd at the fire grew until it reached into the hundreds. By some estimates more than a thousand people, which included most of the population of the township and many others from farther away, visited the site before sundown. Farmers, friends, and the curious came to see and to mourn their own.

The growing light revealed the ruin of what had been a south-facing two-story, white-frame home, with a porch spanning the front and shutters decorating the windows. Behind the house two barns still stood, a chicken house, granary, and windmill outlining a small barnyard with a garden nearest the home. An orchard of fruit trees grew to the south of the house on land bordering the Payson Road. The field west of the house was sown with wheat, and corn stood, almost ready to harvest, off to the east. This was the second year the Pfanschmidts had tried the new crop—wheat—losing most of it to the scourge of Hessian flies that first year. Charles had said that if it did not produce well that year, he would not plant it again.

At daybreak some men fenced off the curious tracks in the barnyard with a makeshift barrier of twine strung on boxes and boards, between the granary on the south and the chicken house on the north. Two battered wooden boxes were set over the impressions of horseshoe tracks to protect them from being disturbed by wandering visitors and scratching chickens.

Ray Pfanschmidt, son of the missing Charles and Mathilda and brother to Blanche, arrived as the tin roof was coming off amid groans and clanks. Alone in his tent at his job site north of Quincy, he had been awakened by his uncle, Henry Niekamp, and then taken in a futile rush to his grandfather's home in the German south part of the city. On the way he was told that his family had most likely perished inside his burned home. He numbly requested that the coroner be called, and collecting his aunt, Elizabeth Petrie, drove his little sorrel team of horses as fast as it would go all the eleven long miles to the farmstead. He arrived sometime before 7:00 a.m. Ray, not yet twenty-one years old, was a very handsome and ambitious young man. His fiancée, Esther Reeder, would arrive by midmorning to console him and share the horror.

The sheriff, the coroner, and other relatives of the Pfanschmidts began to arrive. The schoolteacher's father, Charles Kaempen, reached the fire about half past seven in Mr. Ed Buerkin's auto. Mr. Kaempen's own auto had picked that morning to decline to start.

In the midst of shock, speculation, and grieving, the wheels of officialdom began to search for answers. The Quincy chief of police pulled up in a motor car driven by a young man named Hiedbreder, accompanied by two employees of the State Street Bank. In an attempt to identify the buggy that created those tracks in the barnyard, Police Chief Lott and Ed Buerkin measured the distance between the lines it left in the dirt, using a piece of binder twine they found in the hay barn. Lifting the wooden box they inspected the shoe print left by the "off horse" pulling the buggy.[2]

Where the lane entered the farm, Lott and Buerkin examined the track of the buggy as it came from the direction of Quincy and continued without a break or a stop in a tight circle all around the barnyard and out again, leaving the driveway and turning back to the north toward the city.

---

[2] The "off" horse, when someone is seated in the buggy, is the horse on the right in a two-horse team. The "near" horse is to the driver's left.

Ray, the last surviving member of his family, wandered about the grounds of his home in a sort of daze. To observers, his actions seemed disjointed and random. Ray noticed a burned and dented gasoline can out of place near what had once been the front door. He pointed it out to someone but later would not remember who he had spoken to. It would turn out to be Deputy Scharnhorst of Quincy.

Finally, Ray's fiancée, Esther Reeder, arrived under the protective gaze of her father, Daniel. The Reeder and the Pfanschmidt families had been friends as well as future in-laws. The Reeders also arrived in auto—this one driven by Casper Mast.

Ray politely escorted Esther and her father to the ruins and pointed out his mother's body on one mattress, his sister and the teacher on the other, and said there was little left of his father. To Daniel Reeder, Ray seemed nervous but normal. For Ray, it was difficult to know how to act or what to do when all answers were absent. The rigorous rules of comportment did not seem to cover this situation, leaving Ray only his stoic German heritage to draw upon. Eventually he introduced Esther to some Payson friends and then left her to resume his wandering about the grounds.

Young Pfanschmidt appeared disconnected from events around him, as though the unreality of it all was overwhelming. His aunt would later testify that she found him crying in the granary; his neighbors said he quite uncharacteristically asked for a shot of whiskey, which they provided. Some Payson folks said he was rather nonchalant in pointing out the bodies of his parents and sister as they lay charred in the wreckage of their home; others heard him say to take the fence down around the tracks—that they weren't needed anymore.

By about ten in the morning, Hermann Stoermer, a Quincy undertaker, had arrived. He removed the bodies from where they lay in the ruins, wrapped them in canvas, placed them in body baskets,[3] and transported them in a horse-drawn ambulance to be autopsied. He also bundled up

---

[3] Human-sized, woven baskets used at the time for transporting bodies to mortuaries.

the bedding on which they had been found. The autopsies would reveal a frightening story.

Even before Ray and Esther left the fire scene, family lawyers were sent for, and the call had gone out to the state capitol of Springfield to send the bloodhounds as well. If there was a trail to be followed, perhaps the four-legged detectives could be of some use. C. C. Pfanschmidt, patriarch of the family and Ray's grandfather, wanted answers. He would stand the expense for the dogs.

Ray remained distant and seemed completely unaware that his behavior was in any way unusual. Others, especially the authorities observing him, had begun to have dangerous ideas about his apparent lack of grief.

# Chapter 4

# Autopsy

## Sunday Afternoon, September 29, 1912

The remains of the dead were hauled eleven miles in the Freiberg funeral ambulance. Once in Quincy, they were delivered to the back room of the Stoermer Funeral Home to await official inspection. It came quickly.

The bodies of two of the women were laid out on tables, while the bedding and the torso remained bundled in canvas. Mathilda Abel Pfanschmidt, wife of Charles, was born on July 27, 1866. She had been a big woman, happy and willing to pitch in whenever needed. The smaller of the two bodies, Ray's sister, Blanche, had just celebrated her fifteenth birthday. She was a bright, good-looking, friendly girl who was interested in music. Mathilda and Blanche had faithfully made the long trip to Quincy every Wednesday for Blanche's lessons at the music academy. Between lessons she would practice on the family piano in the parlor.

The third woman's remains still lay in a body basket. Emma Louise Kaempen was born to Louise and Charles Kaempen at their home on S. Sixteenth Street in Quincy on June 19, 1893. Her father was a prominent contractor in partnership with Edwin Buerkin. Emma left behind four brothers and two sisters. It was an accident of circumstance that had put her in harm's way.

A month or so earlier, neighbor Mrs. Henry Kaufman decided that she would not be able to keep her pledge to board the new teacher. Mrs. Kaufman had recently borne a son and reluctantly admitted that she was not able to handle both a new baby and a boarder. Rural school districts commonly provided housing for their teachers, who usually were young, unmarried women. Offering to board the new teacher was a community service that Mathilda was willing and happy to offer. So it was agreed at the last moment that Emma would be domiciled at the Pfanschmidts. Because of that, she died.

The doctors who gathered for the grim examination were Thomas B. Knox, MD; Dr. C. D. Center; Dr. H. O. Collins, city physician; and Charles Erickson, MD. Also in attendance were witnesses: detective George Koch; undertaker Joe Freiburg; State's Attorney John Gilmer; and Emma's brother and father, Emil and Charles Kaempen.

The examination began about three o'clock in the afternoon, around twelve hours after the fire had been discovered. It was conducted in a room with no ventilation system. The bodies were "crispy" in some places and still hot. Steam from their internal organs drifted upward as the doctors worked.

The procedure started with one of the female bodies laid out on the table. This one was missing most of the skull; the extremities had partially burned away, leaving bone extending from the arms and legs where flesh from feet and hands was lost. On the face, the nose and the lips had vanished, exposing the front teeth, and flashing a gold filling. By her two braids, this body was identified as Blanche Pfanschmidt.

Scrutinizing the ticking and feathers of the mattress that had been beneath this body, they were seen to be saturated with a substance Dr. Knox believed to be blood. The fluid had penetrated the mattress covering and stuffing to a depth of at least half an inch. It would later be called a "copious" amount of blood.

A basket cradled the body of the young woman believed to be Emma Kaempen. The right side of her face was burned away, but the left side was intact, protected by the pillow and mattress on which she lay. Above her left eye and through the superior maxilla above her mouth were clean breaks from a sharp instrument. Her teeth, loosened by blows or from the fire, fell free as they were touched. Her mouth was filled with baked blood. The skin of her abdomen had burned away, leaving her intestines exposed. To make things harder on the witnesses, her left leg was extended, her right leg drawn up in a macabre dance-like pose. Undershirt and nightgown pieces from under her body were stained with blood, as was the pillow. A single braid of light-brown hair was preserved below her shoulders.

No blisters were seen on any remaining patch of skin. To the doctors, these horrible wounds—clotted blood and lack of blistering—proclaimed murder before the fire. Since the body identified as Emma had an almost complete skull that bore evidence of several fatal cutting wounds, the doctors would come to wonder if perhaps the fire had destroyed evidence of other similar head wounds.

The second table held a headless woman's body wearing two dark braids from the shoulders down. Again her extremities were burned away, but the undershirt and nightgown exhibited a considerable amount of staining. The fire had caused this body to draw its arms closely up against her sides and behind her back. Both feet and parts of her hands were destroyed or missing.

The final and smallest cadaver was all that remained of Charles Pfanschmidt, a "jovial" man who loved fine horses and was active in local politics, although he never held office. This body remnant was one side of the trunk from about the middle of the waist down almost to the knee. There was a clear cut up through the center of the body. The only unburned fabric adhering to the lump of flesh was a palm-sized portion of undershirt and blue hickory cloth[4] beneath what once had been a hip.

---

[4] This type of cloth is listed in the 1927 Sears Catalogue as "Standard Hickory: Especially durable. Strong, heavy weight hickory shirting, priced for real economy.... Suitable too for men's medium weight overalls." The twenty-four-inch wide material in indigo blue with white pinstripes sold for eighteen cents a yard. —Information courtesy of Pat Nichols's collections.

As the doctors worked, they carefully clipped, tagged, and preserved pieces of the mattress, the clothing, and the braids from the bodies. Hermann Stoermer would burn the remaining bedding.

These bodies told of deaths that did not seem accidental. The next day's headlines in the *Herald* would accurately sum up the prevailing view of the situation: "Community in Gloom at Worst Crime in County's History."

At about the same time that the bodies left for Quincy, Ray also left the burned-out farm. He went to the Reeder home at about noon, where Esther prepared some dinner for the three of them. After eating, Mr. Reeder, not being one to waste daylight, rose from the table and went into his orchard to pick apples and think his thoughts.

Sometime after two o'clock, Ray, having first looked in the wrong orchard, found his prospective father-in-law a quarter mile south of the Reeder home. Ray approached and asked permission to take Esther to "the works," as he called his camp, to check on his things and his work crew.

As Mr. Reeder would later recount that conversation, he admitted reluctance to have Esther out and about with Ray. The conversation, as Reeder later remembered, went like this:

Mr. Reeder: "Ray, I don't like much to have her go."

Ray: "Why not?"

Mr. Reeder: "Don't you know that you are strongly suspicioned?"

Ray: "Me? Under suspicion of killing my father?"

Mr. Reeder: "Yes. I could tell from the actions of the people there. Maybe you did not notice it on account of your excitement, and they have nobody to suspicion, and who's the gainer but you?"

Ray was said to have replied: "My goodness alive!"

Ray and Mr. Reeder eventually agreed that Esther could go to the camp at Twelfth and Cedar on condition that it was a quick trip and that they would return before dark. Reeder figured Ray could get up there and back in two hours or so—it being about a twelve-mile roundtrip.

During this conversation, Esther remained in the buggy out of sight where the road ran over low ground, and out of earshot as well. She later said that when Ray returned to the buggy, he looked odd.

The pair would finally return four hours later—after sunset and just before true dark.

Sunday night, Ray slept in an upstairs bedroom at the Reeder's home south of Quincy. Mr. Reeder slept not at all, by his own report. When Ray left the farm early the next morning, he would never really be back again. From that point on, relations between Ray and his fiancée's father were cool at best. They were, however, better than those Ray would maintain with his grandfather, C. C. Pfanschmidt.

# Chapter 5

# A Look at Ray Pfanschmidt

Who was the young man at the center of this vortex of tragedy and intense speculation? Who was Ray Pfanschmidt? Some things were easily known. Others were recalled or revealed as the story unfolded.

Ray was born in March of 1892. He had beautiful blue eyes, light brown hair that hung in curls to his shoulders, and a face that would have been at home in an old master's painting. Yet even in his short-pants picture, his pose is cocky. He leans against an ornate wicker prop in the photo studio, right foot crossed over left, and his left hand hangs by its thumb from his pants pocket. His shoes are shined, his shirt bright white, and a red silk scarf is knotted jauntily at his throat. He looks at the camera, leaning slightly forward. It is as if he was deciding whether—or not—to allow his beautiful little mouth to explain something to you. "Self-Possessed" would certainly apply as a caption for the picture of this child.

*Ray Pfanschmidt as a young boy*

Photo courtesy of Helen Peter

Blanche Phanschmidt

*Blanche Pfanschmidt as a child*

Photo courtesy Helen Peter

This portrait of Ray's sister, Blanche, presumably taken at the same time as the picture of her brother, shows a younger and more relaxed child. Her curls are not as perfect as Ray's; her dress, while beautiful in its lacy whiteness, is at odd angles in the photo; her necklace is off-kilter, and her blue eyes are obviously looking at someone next to the camera. She too is a lovely child, more open, wider of face, her open lips not quite smiling.

## *Front Row: Ray Pfanschmidt, Blanche Peter*
## *Back Row: Claude Peter, Blanche Pfanschmidt,*
## *Emma Kaempen, and Esther Reeder*

Photo courtesy Helen Peter

In a photo taken most likely just before this tragedy, Ray's curls are cut short and he looks tanned. He has grown to be five feet, ten and a quarter inches tall and is slight of frame. His shirt is just as white but the cuffs are turned up to the elbows, and his trademark narrow red tie is tucked into his shirt, hiding the bottom. He sits on a wagon with his sister, Blanche, and Emma Kaempen, Esther Reeder, and Claude and Blanche Peter. The four women wear attractive white dresses, white stockings, and white shoes, their hair carefully done up. It is a casual snapshot taken at what looks to be a social gathering at a neighboring home. There are buggies in the background, one of which may be Ray's. Ray sits slightly isolated, turned and looking away from the camera, his arms crossed and resting on his knees.

There was more to learn about Ray however, and much more came to light during the investigations. From the beginning, it was apparent that Ray thought highly of himself, as do most young men at that age. He enjoyed fast horses and speedy buggies. His team of small bays pulled a 'Velie' brand buggy, which was undercut at the front wheels to allow for a short turning radius. This buggy was fast and more maneuverable than other designs. There were only a handful of these buggies in the area.

Ray was also ambitious. He took up the profession of blaster or dynamiter, hired his own crew, and began his own business at age twenty. This was the reason that he was camping at a work site on the north edge of Quincy, where he had contracted to move dirt by blasting for a railroad siding and coal yard. In fact, Ray referred to himself as "Dynamite Pfanschmidt," not exactly a modest nickname in any era.

Ray was also progressive, forward thinking, not afraid of debt, and proud of his appearance and reputation. At a time when shock and fear were rampant and Ray had lost his entire immediate family, he held his emotions close inside and showed the world very little. Even among the traditionally reserved people who shared and treasured their stoic German heritage, Ray remained a puzzle.

This did not make him a sympathetic figure.

# Chapter 6

~

# A Plague of Rumors Monday

### Monday, September 30, 1912

The days after the fire were anxious ones indeed in the community. Wherever nervous neighbors gathered, speculations flew. Wherever people were alone, bodies were startled by the slightest sound, and anxious glances were thrown about. The phone lines buzzed. In an era when four or five families shared one telephone party line, theories, questions, and accusations flew across the farmland and city blocks, into grocery stores, and barber shops grabbed, expanded, and propounded the smallest details, overheard or imagined, into living, breathing stories. Everyone knew everything and nothing.

On this cool fall Monday, the village of Payson tried and failed to go about its daily business, and a variety of business it was indeed. The settlement had begun in 1839 and grew into a prosperous town by the early 1900s. Its early settlers arrived mostly from New England and kept many ties and much of the hard-working, conservative, republican mindset from that area. They were later joined by other immigrants, most notably from Germany.

These prairie pioneers threw themselves into agriculture and horticulture and entrepreneurial endeavors. The area around Payson tried its hand at producing everything from silk (producing enough raw silk to supply local dressmakers) to concord grape, peach, apple, apricot, cherry, and pear orchards that surrounded the village. Grain crops, cattle, hogs, chickens, guinea fowl, plus a few goats and sheep were also raised on the surrounding family farms.

The village had a large central park—a grassy area with shade trees and room for large gatherings like the Old Settler's Parade and Celebration held every August. State Street, running east and west, divided the open space into two equal parts. A local history of Payson[5] lists the following businesses as active in the town at that time: tinsmiths, carpenters, four blacksmith shops employing eight people, a variety store, shoe store, shoe and harness repair shop, grocery stores, clothing stores, at least two millinery shops, bakery, butcher shop, barber shop, ice-cream parlor, undertaking establishments, photographic gallery, skating rink, wagon shops, drugstore, pork-packing plant, early hotels, a cabinet maker, and three insurance agents. Most businesses were operated from store fronts or back rooms in family dwellings. Some families ran multiple businesses under one roof.

For the spiritual requirements of the inhabitants, along with the Congregational church, Payson had a Methodist church, a Bethany Baptist church, and a First Christian church. Church services were regularly attended by almost everyone and lasted most of the day on Sunday. In addition, there were other meetings during the week for religious services, missionary work, and Bible study and prayer, all of which provided a sort of glue to the community.

For more strictly social occasions there were the Masonic lodge, a chapter of the Eastern Star of Illinois, and the Women's Christian Temperance Union. Many other activities were available to fill any other leisure: church-related gatherings; box suppers; quilting parties; socials; singing schools; music concerts; traveling missionaries; lectures of a political nature; corn shucking; barn raising; rag-rug sewing; weddings; patriotic celebrations; and holidays. Everyone in the town knew each other, as well as the major

---

[5] *A History of Payson, Illinois, 1835–1976*, Payson Bicentennial Book Committee, 1976.

and minor events of their lives. It was a busy, bustling, close-knit little community.

Now fear stalked the inhabitants.

In Quincy, hearses were polished, liveries and harnesses shined, music selected, and sermons prepared for the coming funerals. The crowds were expected to be large.

When the farm women washed the clothes of those who had fought the fire they were overcome by the smell of soot and death as the wash water liberated the smoke fumes. Wives were afraid to be alone in the wash houses and detached summer kitchens. The men found keys, locked doors at night, and took to holding the kindling axe in their hand as they made the last check of the barn.

At the burned farmhouse, relic seekers poked through the ashes. One little girl found a clockworks with wire twisted about the hands and gave it to her uncle.

As was customary, it was expected that a large reward would be offered by the surviving family members to anyone who had information to aid the investigation. Since the family was prosperous, it was assumed the sum would reflect their substantial wealth.

The Monday newspapers were eagerly awaited. Their accounts were lengthy and detailed and contained stark pictures of the scene. They speculated that the crime would be solved shortly but seemed divided in assigning guilt to a murderous stranger or to Ray, the only surviving son. One proclaimed, "It is declared that a motive sufficiently strong to have impelled commission of the crime on the part of one harboring a feeling of malice toward the Pfanschmidt family has been discovered."

Another printed, "Farmers are openly declaring that they know the murderer and an arrest is expected before night." That was the *Quincy Journal,* a paper which for that issue seemed to value speed of publication over accuracy. They misnamed Mathilda, calling her "Christine," and identified Emma as "Estelle." They were also the only paper that mentioned rubber buggy tire tracks; the other papers reported tracks from steel wheels in the barn lot.

Then rumors flew about how the murderer may have been seen!

A prominent local Payson resident reportedly saw a man moving about inside the Pfanschmidt farmhouse on the Saturday night before the fire was discovered. It was claimed that John Robertson, the local undertaker, had seen someone moving in the house when he passed by about 10:00 p.m. He also commented on a foul smell in the area. In another story, he supposedly recounted overtaking a stranger in the middle of the road by the Pfanschmidt farm. This stranger appeared to be "in a deep study" and would not yield the road to the approaching wagon. In yet another account, Robertson simply reported seeing movement within the house. Unfortunately, a few days after the tragedy, he was struck down by paralysis and rendered incapable of speech. He died without regaining consciousness.

In the city of Quincy, two men were seen walking westward across the railroad bridge over the Mississippi River toward Missouri at 2:00 a.m. Both were strangers. They were not stopped.

As a sort of patent medicine against the void of news, people's conversations were filled with innuendo, speculation, and downright fabrication. These in turn were often picked up by the newspapers and reported to a wider circulation.

A stranger with a bandaged hand was seen going from farmhouse to farmhouse in the county. The manager of the Payson branch of the State Street Bank had given the man a twenty-five-cent handout and sent him on his way. Mr. McKenzie, a Payson resident, remembered that this same man had made his way through the area a year before. He proclaimed him harmless and "just a vagabond."

As the days passed and the rumors swelled, Ray was not obliging; he neither broke down in public nor called for justice. The family too seemed strangely silent. C. C. Pfanschmidt, patriarch of the family, perhaps due to shock or to his German reticence, said nothing in public.

Behind it all was the unspoken question: "Who did it?" Was it a madman? Was it Ray? It would be terrible to believe a son could do this. Yet it might be better than believing a monster was loose in their neighborhood.... "Better the devil you know ..."

29

# Chapter 7

~

## Cold Trail and Cold Noses

### Monday, September 30, 1912

The hounds arrived on Monday, brought by H. G. Strumpfer, forty-seven, a deputy state fire marshal who owned a kennel of bloodhounds in Springfield, Illinois. They came at grandfather C. C. Pfanschmidt's request and at his personal expense.

Strumpfer and the dogs had boarded a train in Springfield, traveled to the city of Louisiana, Missouri, and then took the CB&Q Railroad to Quincy on Sunday night. The next morning, Sheriff Lipps took them to the crime scene in an automobile belonging to Charles Achelpohl. The dogs rode with their heads hanging out the open windows sampling the air, their ears flapping in the wind.

Along to witness the tracking was a reporter from the *Herald* who rode in a newspaper-owned car that also carried State's Attorney Gilmer and Ray's uncle Henry Geisel. A third car owned by Jack Flynn contained Mr. Knollenberg, along with another of Ray's uncles, and others. A sharp scent of anticipation hung in the cool September air.

At the farm, two hounds departed the first car. Roger Williams was an English dog about seven years old, his coat a tawny color with a black saddle-shaped marking on his back. His canine partner, Nick Carter, was a

30

Russian hound, also about seven years old, but smaller than Roger Williams. Nick Carter was spotted white and tan, appearing almost roan in color.

By now any trail was at least thirty hours old, and it had possibly been more than sixty hours since the crime had been committed. One misshapen horseshoe track waited in the barnyard, covered by a wooden box. Another hoof print was nearby in the dust.

In 1912, there was scant understanding of how bloodhounds did their work. Bloodhounds were thought to naturally follow human scent by tracking an "emanation from the various ducts in the body" (i.e., minute particles that cradled scent and were picked up by the olfactory sensors in the dog's nose). Strumpfer's dogs were said to have been trained to follow either human or animal scent. It was also believed that wind would blow the scent particles off any smooth surface, such as stone, making tracking difficult or impossible.

Strumpfer opined the fall weather conditions that day as good for cold trails. The hounds were put into harnesses with twenty foot leashes attached. Strumpfer and his other handler led each dog to a track, roughly pushed their noses into the track, and commanded, "Pick it up!" One hound bayed as he caught a scent. The sound was loud in the quiet of the farm, startling the chickens.

Straining ahead, one hound pulled Strumpfer past the ruins of the house, out the farm lane, and off to the right, heading toward Quincy. Strumpfer followed for perhaps a quarter mile as the hound led him past the intersection at Pape's Mill Road. By then Strumpfer was out of breath and realized that many miles of road lay between his current position and the town of Quincy, the dog's likely destination. With this in mind, he signaled Sheriff Lipps to bring up the car and loaded himself, his helper, and both dogs inside.

As they approached a side road, one dog and handler would exit the car. The dog was again required to "Pick it up!" and the pair followed the trail past the turnoff, only to repeat the procedure again at the next intersection. It was a hopscotch journey. There were numerous lanes, roads, paths, driveways, and stretches of unfenced woodland and pasture to be checked.

At long last they reached the edge of Quincy. Coming up Twenty-Fourth Street from the south, Strumpfer and his dogs were confronted by crowds of people lining the sidewalks along State Street where they had gathered to watch the spectacle. At this intersection, the unpaved Twenty-Fourth Street crossed the brick pavement of State Street, and as it continued to the north, the surface of Twenty-Fourth Street was oiled. The milling crowds, the noon heat, and the sharp scent of oil confused the dogs. At Mr. Strumpfer's insistence, all were once again loaded into the automobile and taken, this time, to the courthouse for water and a rest.

About two hours later, Strumpfer and Lipps took the dogs to Twenty-Fourth and Broadway—skipping about a mile of assumed trail over oiled streets. The dogs appeared to pick up the scent again and traveled north about a mile, where they crossed some railroad tracks. They then turned west into a grassy pasture through a gate equipped with a lock. They tracked through a little valley near a brook where they were stopped by a wire fence. The dogs cast about and then turned back to the gate, completing a circle of the pasture.

Exiting the pasture, they turned south again on Twenty-Fourth Street, retracing their earlier route. This time they turned west on Locust Street and entered the Soldier's Home. Following a road through the grounds of the home as it turned north, the dogs passed under a trestle elevating the railroad tracks, turned east at a drive entering the Frese property, and passed into Ray's camp. They were, at this point, about one half mile due west of the wire fence encountered in the little pasture detour.

At the camp, they stopped at a buggy and moved on to Ray's tent, where they nosed some clothes, and then moved to the tent where Ray's horses were tied. There, the handler said, they identified the mare of Ray's team. It had taken almost all day and an unexplained three-mile detour into the pasture to arrive at the work camp.

Later, this same pair of dogs was taken to Esther Reeder's home, where they followed a trail through the Reeder orchard to Thirty-Sixth Street and then south to the Pfanschmidt farm via the Pape's Mill Road. Law enforcement officials were quite pleased with the results. Others were more skeptical. After all, Ray had traveled that road to and from the fire and been many places in Quincy in recent days. Could anyone tell which trail a hound was following? If there were multiple trails, wouldn't the newest one be the strongest? Could a dog decide to follow a thirty-hour-old scent rather than a twenty-four-hour-old scent? It was a mystery. But nonetheless, it seemed that Ray had been identified by the hounds.

*Twelfth Street train trestle, and the Frese store and home at the entrance to "the works," where Ray camped*

Stereoscope card by Sanftleben & High

The community was becoming more polarized. The scales of public opinion were tipping against Ray—especially with the weighty "thumbs" of the journalists affecting the balance.

# Chapter 8

~

## Rest without Peace

### Tuesday, October 1, 1912

On Monday, unmindful of the trailing hounds, Ray went to the Quincy Casket Company and selected caskets for the mortal remains of his mother, father, and sister. What his thoughts were can only be imagined. Tuesday, October 1, he attended the funerals with Esther at his side.

It was the custom at the time for burial services to be conducted at the home of the deceased. Services for the Pfanschmidts were held at the family home of Henry Niekamp, 604 S. Sixteenth Street, whose wife, Hanna, was a sister of the slain Charles. The house was insufficient to hold the mourners, family, friends, and the curious, for the crowd had mounted to about thirteen hundred people by the time Rev. Todd began speaking at ten o'clock that morning.

Teams and buggies and wagons lined the grounds near the house and the streets in all directions, which testified to the many miles people had traversed to pay their respects. At the close of these services, a procession of about one hundred closed buggies went to Woodlawn Cemetery where another crowd, described as at least twelve hundred people were waiting.

Rev. Todd, the retired pastor of the Congregational Church in Payson, assisted by the current pastor, Rev. S. Brown, led the services. With their words of comfort and sympathy, and the solos sung by Mrs. George Reeves and Mrs. Lillian Inghram, even stoic farmers were moved.

The pallbearers were many of the same men who had valiantly and uselessly fought the fire. Now instead of relaying buckets of water to the blaze, they were making trip after trip, carrying caskets from hearse to the grave.

Charles was first into the ground, beside his mother; Mathilda was settled on his left, Blanche placed to the right of her grandmother, leaving a space for her still-living grandfather to be laid to rest when C. C.'s time came to depart this life.

No accommodation was made for a future spot for Ray.

Services for Emma Kaempen followed a similar heart-wrenching theme. She had only completed high school the past spring, passed her teacher's exam, and arrived a few weeks before her death to board in the home of the Pfanschmidts. She had been an energetic if not pretty girl, wearing "nose pincher" glasses on her wide face.

At three o'clock that same day, after services at home, the Kaempen family procession left their residence on S. Sixteenth Street, a scant three blocks from the starting point of the earlier Pfanschmidt funeral. When they arrived at Salem Church, the services were held to an overflowing auditorium, people standing in the aisles.

Miss Kaempen had been active in the church all her life, teaching Sunday school in the German language and keeping up regular attendance even while living twelve miles away. Along with her favorite hymns sung in both German and English came many personal tributes to this beloved young woman. Emma's high school class sent American Beauty roses, their class flower.

From Salem Church, mourners headed in procession to Greenmount Cemetery, where graveside services were held. The line of carriages and vehicles was long, and many others without their own conveyances arrived on street cars. After a last vocal, "The Christian's Good Night," Emma was laid in the ground.

Rev. Leemhuis offered these words: "Man is tempted to doubt the mercy and kindness of an omnipotent God when standing aghast facing a crime of these proportions, especially when the victims are God-fearing and faithful servants of the Lord. However, God permitted this, and while we now stand appalled and our hearts are crushed by the awfulness of the deed and the loss of a beloved one, we know that we shall know the answer to our 'why' in the hereafter."[6]

But without answers in the here and now, the living populace would not be at peace. And certainly, most people were not willing to wait for answers in the hereafter.

---

[6] As reported on the Greenmount Cemetery website.

# Chapter 9

## The Inquest

### Wednesday, October 2, 1912

The Coroner's Inquest convened on Wednesday, October 2. Photos printed in the *Herald* show a packed room, with reporters from as far away as the *Chicago Tribune*; three separate stenographers; twenty-five witnesses; and a crowd estimated between five and eight hundred people. Those who couldn't get seats congested the hall or milled about outside the building.

The six-man jury, with City Physician Dr. H. O. Collins serving as foreman and coroner M. H. Haley presiding, met to continue the gruesome work begun on the Sunday afternoon of the fire. Proceedings began shortly after ten o'clock, with Emil Kaempen called as the first witness. He recounted being awakened early Sunday morning by his mother's piteous cries. Mr. Niekamp had come by the house to see if Emma was there and delivered the news that the Pfanschmidt house had burned and that the people were missing. Emil spoke of identifying his sister by her hair at the fire scene and again at autopsy.

His testimony was followed by the Pfanschmidt neighbors Henry Schreck, Ben Lier, Moritz Lier, and John Lier, who told their accounts of finding and fighting the fire and discovering the bodies. C. C. Pfanschmidt testified about the layout of the rooms in the house and the arrangements of windows, doors, and the porch roof that could have provided a means of escape.

Then the parade of doctors took the stand. Dr. Thomas B. Knox reported the condition of the bodies and spared no graphic detail. He was asked, "In your judgment, doctor, were these persons killed, or did they come to death by reason of that of being burned or from extreme violence prior to the burning?"

Dr. Knox replied, "I would have to answer that after an examination of the only head that we had in a condition to be examined, and the finding of what appeared to be blood in the bedding and wearing apparel and pillow. After examination of those things I would say the parties came to their death by violence before they were burned."[7]

The last witness before lunch was Dr. Charles Erickson, who testified about the blood on the clothing samples given to him. "I think it was human blood." After lunch, three more witnesses testified. And at ten minutes before three, the inquest was adjourned until the following Wednesday, "So that new theories could be worked out."[8]

Ray elected not to attend the Coroner's Inquest, although in his lawyers' offices he was but a stone's throw from its location.

Only four days previously, on the same day as the conversation with Mr. Reeder that opened his eyes to his jeopardy, Ray had retained Emery Lancaster, William H. Govert, and his son, George W. Govert, to represent him. They were the same attorneys who customarily handled legal matters for his family. Ray spent this Wednesday, like every other since he had learned he was a suspect, immured in his lawyers' offices. In fact, since Monday, he had left the law offices only for meals and to attend the funerals. His lawyers kept him closely under wraps and safely out of communication. They were a formidable trio of attorneys.

Emery Lancaster was born in 1877, raised on a farm in Adams County, educated at Knox College in Galesburg, Illinois, and the University of

---

[7] Official record, State of Illinois, Adams County Coroner's Inquest, October 2, 1912.
[8] *Quincy Journal,* October 2, 1912.

Michigan. He was admitted to the Illinois Bar in 1902 and joined the law firm of Ivins and Lancaster in 1904. In 1906 the firm became Govert & Lancaster. Mr. Lancaster was a prominent man in the city, as were his partners.

Lancaster was clean-shaven and wore his dark hair parted arrow straight, slightly off center, over his left eyebrow. His flaring ears sat a bit low on his head, over his severely trimmed sideburns. His mouth was wide, with narrow lips and a clearly defined dip in the upper corner. His tightly compressed lips did not indicate the flights of oration for which he was famous. His eyes were large, wide, and clear. His chin was cleft, protruding above a very tall stiff collar, starched to perfection and framing his four-in-hand tie. His was a commanding presence.

William H. Govert was born in 1844, also raised on an Illinois farm, and completed his law degree at the University of Michigan in 1870. In his long career he had served terms as city attorney of Quincy and state's attorney of Adams County; in addition, Mr. Govert Sr. had numerous business connections and maintained a flourishing law practice.

William Govert was a short dynamo of a man. A contemporary picture showed him in a Napoleonic pose, right hand tucked between the buttons of his dark suit coat. He had a high forehead, where the years had pushed back his dark hair and salted it with gray. His full lips seem prone to explosions of righteousness or anger or perhaps a good belly laugh. He was a man clear on his beliefs and quite certain that one must be mistaken if you did not agree with him.

George Wood (G. W.) Govert was born to William H. and Rosa Wood Govert in 1874. He was raised in Quincy, attended Yale and the University of Michigan, received his law degree in 1900, and became a junior member of his father's firm.

G. W. was a thin-faced, intense man. His receding hair was cut short and plastered into place. His ears carried a slight point at their tops, and his cheeks and chin sported dimples. His nose was angular, with nostrils built for flaring, and his lips were thin and mobile and could frame an imposing argument or mutter an aside with equal impunity. His gaze was piercing and designed to befuddle a witness. There was a slight sense of the predator about his otherwise innocuous appearance.

39

PRESENT DAY QUINCY — PROMINENT ATTORNEYS

JOHN E. WALL.
Wilson & Wall.

GEORGE W. GOVERT,
Govert & Lancaster.

W. EMERY LANCASTER.
Govert & Lancaster.

## *George W. Govert & W. Emory Lancaster, Ray's defense attorneys, and John E. Wall, who was later hired to assist the state's attorney*

Courtesy Historical Society of Quincy and Adams County

Wednesday was a very busy day.

That same evening in the village of Payson, another mysterious attack occurred. J. E. Baugher, the janitor at the Congregational Church, raised an alarm and reported a confrontation with an unknown assailant in the church basement. On his nightly rounds, he apparently was struck in the head, and seeing a shadow, threw a chair in its direction. Baugher left the church and ran next door to the parsonage to report to Rev. Mr. Brown, who accompanied him back to investigate. They found broken glass spread over the floor, and Baugher sported cuts and bruises.

Fortuitously, defense attorney Emery Lancaster was in the area interviewing people and looking for witnesses to help Ray's case. Lancaster arranged to put a guard on the scene, and two young men, Robert Chapman and Alec Cooper, were posted all night to keep the evidence clear of onlookers. Baugher told authorities his story: that a man broke into the church basement through a window and assaulted him as he was making his nightly rounds. The man knocked him down and then escaped.

The community was thoroughly frightened and agitated anew. First ghastly murders just up the road, and now the sanctity of a local church had been invaded. The attorneys for Ray sent bloodhounds, these from a handler in Iowa, to the church on the next day. The dogs trailed south about one half mile to a bridge over a small creek before doubling back to the church. The trail led nowhere.

Investigation revealed that all of the windows in the church basement had been closed and locked. The glass fragment patterns seemed to have resulted from a chair that the janitor threw at what was probably his own shadow in a basement window created by the flickering light of a lamp with no chimney.

Janitor Baugher was arrested for malicious mischief after Dr. Collins and Dr. Johnson said that his cuts and scrapes were not made by a fist or a sap[9] but more likely from contact with a support pillar in the church basement. Although the evidence at the scene did not match the tale told by Baugher, authorities were puzzled over a motive for his actions. It would all become clear in a few more anxious days.

Also on Wednesday, Illinois Fire Marshal Bogardus, who wielded power from the state to subpoena witnesses in regard to fire investigations, but who remained frustrated in his attempts to corner and interrogate Ray, hit upon the idea of pulling in Esther Reeder as bait, in hopes she would lead him to his man.

On Thursday, October 3, Esther was summoned. She was taken to room #515 at the Hotel Quincy and questioned by Bogardus and several others. It was an intimidating ordeal for the young woman to go through alone. She must have alerted Ray to her interrogation and arranged to meet him afterward. When she left the hotel, detectives Barden and Dale followed. Their plan worked like a charm.

The two detectives served Ray with a subpoena as he was listening to Esther's tale. He initially refused to accompany them, but they flashed the special deputy badges given them by Sheriff Lipps and Ray reluctantly went with them, all the while requesting the presence of his lawyers.

---

[9] A sap was a short, leather-covered club sometimes called a blackjack.

Bogardus had timed this carefully. Ray's attorneys were out of town. It didn't matter. Ray would manage quite well on his own.

The *Whig* reported that Bogardus kept the boy in his rooms at the Hotel Quincy until seven thirty in the evening, extracting a statement from him that comprised fifteen pages of shorthand notes.[10]

As the *Herald* told it, "It is stated unofficially, but probably accurately, that the deposition obtained from Pfanschmidt is not at all sensational in character. With the same self-possession and reticence which has characterized the boy ever since the murder was discovered, he answered the questions put to him and his answers were always guarded and generally non-committal. He did not incriminate himself, it is understood."[11]

On hearing of this action, Ray's attorneys were enraged. The *Herald* termed them "wrathy." They threatened to have Bogardus himself arrested—a fine piece of theater had they been able to pull it off. But, in the end, no action was taken.

Thursday evening, the remaining Pfanschmidt family gathered at patriarch C. C.'s home to discuss offering a reward. The family could not agree, however, and planned yet another meeting to discuss it. The family was now divided—over Ray.

Also on Thursday evening, authorities were summoned when a disheveled man wandered in from the countryside sporting red stains on his clothing. Deputy Sheriff William Schaeffer arrested the man, who identified himself in broken English as one Bill Butts. When city physician Collins examined the stained clothing, he pronounced the discoloration "of a vegetal nature." This was confirmed when the man explained that he had been working at a tomato canning plant near Urbana, Illinois. It was deemed he was innocent of murder, but nonetheless "not a desirable person to have in the community." He was released but advised to leave the town and the county.[12]

By Friday, October 4, 1912, nearly a week after the fire, Emma's mother, Louise Kaempen, remained in serious physical decline due to

---

[10] *Whig*, October 4, 1912.
[11] *Herald*, October 4, 1912.
[12] Ibid.

shock. Frustrated by the lack of progress in the case, Mr. Kaempen retained noted Quincy attorney John Wall, paying him privately to assist the State with the prosecution and represent the Kaempen family's interests.

Wall's photo shows thick, curly red hair, grudgingly parted above his right eyebrow yet refusing to lay flat and relinquish its curl. His gaze is straightforward, his eyes padded by bags and shadows. Wall's face is long, his chin cleft. His mouth holds the hint of a smile at the corners, as though he could tell a story to bring howls of either laughter or tears, as the occasion and his mood commanded. There was a softness about his face, a fleeting sense of a poet trapped within the attorney; a feeling that he might too readily be identified with tragedy at some hidden personal cost. He had the demeanor of a crusader for justice about him, as well as a shining gift of oratory.

It was on Friday morning that the church janitor, J. E. Baugher, incarcerated in the Quincy jail, suffered an epileptic fit. "He fell to the floor from a bench in the jail, writhing and moaning and frothing at the mouth. When he recovered he was questioned by jailor Monk Frey but remembered nothing of the fit."[13] So the missing piece in the puzzle of the crime at the church was supplied by a medical condition. It became one case solved by the authorities.

But this resolution did little to alleviate the mood of the county. Concern had now reached beyond the local area into neighboring states.

It was also this Friday that Sheriff Loftus arrived from Iowa, sent by the governor of that state, who selected him for his knowledge of criminology as he had written a book on the subject. Loftus came to lend his expertise to the local authorities and detectives in solving this crime.

He joined a multistate cast, a collection of representatives from multiple jurisdictions, each with his own interest to further. Chicago Police Chief Schuetler sent two detectives: Barden and Bates; Governor Carroll of Iowa sent C. W. Tobie of the Burns Detective Agency, Chicago branch. Tobie would fulfill his Iowa contract and stay on for a time. Speculation was that Tobie was also working for the Pfanschmidt family.

---

[13] *Herald*, October 4, 1912.

The *Herald* fed the rumor furor with tales that Ray loved to play cowboy and emulate the ways of the Wild West. He reportedly carried a pistol much of the time and favored broad-brimmed hats cocked over one ear to accentuate his favored western attire. It was reported that neighbors often complained of his fondness for shooting off his revolvers at the slightest pretense. They said Ray loved to make a flashy appearance and sometimes drove his team decked out in long leather fly nets that reached nearly to the ground. He seemed to pay a great deal of attention to the exterior he presented.

But the big news on Friday came when Ray's attorneys issued a demand that State's Attorney Gilmer arrest their client immediately so that they might clear his name. Gilmer declined to be baited. He merely issued a statement saying he was developing facts that would either clear Ray or provide proof of his guilt. He would not be rushed.

The local papers continued to contribute to the unrest in the area. By Sunday, October 6, the *Quincy Herald* questioned in print the lack of a reward offered by the Pfanschmidts.

"The good law-abiding citizens, those who want to see justice done and crime punished are united in endorsement of the *Herald*'s position that a reward should be offered immediately by the county toward the discovery of the Pfanschmidt murder. As one of the detectives from abroad states, it is simply astounding that nothing of this kind has been done."[14]

One upstanding citizen donated ten dollars to begin a reward fund and was of the opinion that many other citizens would also contribute. The Iowa sheriff was "simply astounded" that there was not yet a reward offer by the relatives. He went on to say, according to the *Herald*, "People about Quincy do not seem to appreciate that this is one of the most horrible tragedies in the entire history of criminology in the country."[15]

---

[14] *Herald,* October 5, 1912.
[15] Ibid.

Iowa Sheriff Loftus proclaimed that Sheriff Lipps should have arrested Ray on Monday when the bloodhounds trailed to his camp, and that Ray should have been forced to tell his story before he talked to any lawyer. The *Herald* printed this opinion on its front page.

Where the story continued inside the paper, the *Herald* cited a damaging story from the Illinois State University paper, the *Daily Illini*. Ray had been there to take a "short course" a few years earlier.

> "The record which Pfanschmidt left here was by no means a good one, for he was found guilty of robbing his roommate, Charley Elt, of $35. Elt and Pfanschmidt lived together during the latter's short stay here at 504 E. Daniel Street, Champaign. Elt, with the aid of Dean T. A. Clark and L. C. Kent was able to get back the money."[16]

---

[16] *Herald*, October 5, 1912.

# Chapter 10

~

# Evidence in the Vault

## Monday, October 7, 1912

To construct an outhouse, a hole was dug about three feet long, up to five or six feet wide, and several feet deep. A small wood-frame house was positioned covering this pit. It would have a solid wooden floor with a bench built against the back wall. In the bench was at least one circular opening, upon which a person sat to relieve himself or herself. A "two-holer" had two openings. Various scraps of paper—often old newspapers or catalogues—were supplied for cleanup, and sometimes a bucket of powdered ash or soda was included to sprinkle down the hole to help curtail odors. The characteristic half-moon carved in the door for ventilation became a sign that marked restroom doors for years after the invention of indoor plumbing. When the pit became full, a new pit was dug, and the outhouse was moved to a new location.

In this era, "vault" or "closet" was the common term for an outhouse.

On Monday, October 7, handyman Claude Hubbard finally got around to the next thing on his chores list. He worked for Mr. Frese (for whom Ray also was doing work) and had been told some time ago to construct a new vault and to demolish or move the existing one. What with the furor over Ray and the murders and the comings and goings and searches at the nearby camp, Mr. Hubbard had thankfully relegated this unappetizing chore to a low priority. But things seemed quieter now, and the job had to be done.

The new construction was to be a vault for the sole use of the Frese family, while the workers at Ray's adjoining camp had another option for their use. Hubbard planned to use the old existing building to line the walls of the new pit, and he planned to construct a new topper. Mr. Hubbard said of the existing building that it was "pretty well dilapidated, settled down in the earth considerable. I dug a hole in the ground to size of the old building to put in this vault for a wall, and built a new one on top of it." The old building was a "three-hole"—with two seats 18" off the floor and one only 10" for a child's use.

It came as an unwelcome surprise to Hubbard to see something lying beneath crumpled newspapers, under the floor at the south edge of the little building when he overturned it. He took a stick to lift the item off the top of the night soil on which it rested and saw that it looked like clothing. It looked like khaki clothing, the sort Ray wore. Upon seeing this, Ray's foreman, Ben Holeman, immediately prevailed upon him to stop working and not to move anything.

Hubbard dropped the stick and stayed to guard the spot while Holman went to Frese's home to call authorities. Holman was reluctant to give too much information over the phone, so he simply said to Sheriff Lipps, "Come out here quick. There is some trouble here."[17]

Lipps, along with Detective Young of Young's Detective Agency of Chicago, who had been hired by the Kaempen family about a week previously, hurried to the campsite. One look at the garments was enough for the sheriff to instruct his deputies to find and arrest young Ray.

Deputy sheriffs Schaeffer and Coens began the search. They determined that Ray was at the home of his uncle Henry Niekamp, and they hurriedly jumped on a streetcar to make the arrest. They almost succeeded. When the two deputies were a few blocks from the Niekamp home, Sheriff Lipps himself passed them in a car headed in the opposite direction, with Ray

---

[17] *Herald*, October 7, 1912.

already in custody. The deputies could do nothing but turn back empty handed, robbed of their moment of glory.

As reported in the *Herald*, the dialogue at the door of the Niekamp house went like this:

> Sheriff: "Well, we have found your suit where you threw it away."
> Ray: "Oh you have?"
> Sheriff: "Yes, and we have found the red necktie which you wore on Friday night with the suit."
> Ray: "Oh, yes. I sometimes do wear a red necktie."
> Sheriff: "I guess you will have to come down to the jail with us."
> Ray: "All right."[18]

The *Herald* characterized Ray's delivery as "unconcerned," "careless," and "callous" and reported that he was sitting in the jailer's room, seemingly completely at ease, reading the Sunday comics when John Gilmer, the state's attorney, arrived. The only apparent sign of nervousness on Ray's part was a refusal to meet anyone's gaze directly, except for Mr. Govert, his own attorney. At the jail, Gilmer read the formal warrant arresting Ray for murder. Govert demanded an immediate hearing to clear his client's name, and the hearing was set for one thirty that afternoon.

Ray was taken to a room and strip searched. It was reported there were no blood spots from last week's crime on his underclothing.

---

[18] *Herald*, October 7, 1912.

# Chapter 11

# News and Public Opinion

## Tuesday, October 8, 1912

While Ray sat in jail, his grandfather talked to a reporter from the *Herald*. Charles Christopher Pfanschmidt, known as C. C., was born in Muehlhause, Germany, in 1831. Originally their name was Pfannenschmidt, after the pewter-making trade the family worked in for generations.

The family emigrated from Prussia and settled on land near Quincy when C. C. was three years old. At twenty, he inherited the family farm and married Mary Limb, who was born in England. They made their home in the village of Burton, Illinois, where they produced ten children. At the time of the fire, Mary had been dead seven years, and C. C. had retired to a solid home on South Twelfth Street in the German section of Quincy, sometimes called "Calf Town."

C. C. received the reporter in his two-story red brick home, one of six exact copies built on the block. The no-nonsense houses sat near the street on lots that were narrow and deep, with barns or stables at the back on the alley. The small front porches and clean, swept walks were kept spotless by the proud citizens.

The *Herald* reporter managed to nail down a number of rumors and unearth some interesting news. Old Mr. Pfanschmidt quashed the notion that Ray and Esther had secretly married. He disclosed that Ray was still a minor and could not get a marriage license without consent of a guardian or parent.

C. C. denied that he had banned Ray from his home, saying that his house was full with his daughter and her husband, Walter Herr, visiting from Kansas, and Ray had decided to stay with his Uncle Niekamp. Mr. Pfanschmidt then said he had visited the sheriff the day after the fire and agreed to pay any expense to find the perpetrator. He had paid for the bloodhounds and their handlers: "It cost me quite a good deal, but less than I expected."[19]

Mr. Pfanschmidt detailed the family meetings concerning a reward. Some objected on the grounds that if the detectives were pursuing the line that it was Ray, a reward might induce them to "gather up a lot of things and force the crime upon him." No consensus had been reached before the actual arrest, and afterward a reward seemed irrelevant.

The reporter asked about the bloody clothes found near Ray's work tent. Mr. Pfanschmidt said he was too feeble to go himself and see the evidence so sent Charles Achelpohl as his surrogate, along with other family members. Then Mr. Pfanschmidt was asked if he thought Ray was insane. His emphatic reply: "I think he is in full possession of his faculties. He is as bright and smart as anyone."

Mr. Pfanschmidt expounded his opinion. "If a man is insane enough to commit a murder, he ought to be put where he cannot murder any more. He should be treated like any person. I once knew of a man who killed his lady love with a butcher knife. He was sent to an insane asylum. In a few years he was turned loose from the asylum, and he is now in business in Chicago, just as sane as you or I."[20]

Mr. Pfanschmidt's tone brooked no objections. "No, he is sane, and I do not think a defense of insanity would be right." Furthermore, in case his

---

[19] *Herald,* October 8, 1912.
[20] Ibid.

stance wasn't quite clear, he himself had gone to the offices of Mr. Govert and Mr. Lancaster to tell them that if they found out Ray was guilty, they were to drop the case![21]

Family members present at the interview agreed that things looked bad for Ray. They recollected how Ray was very contained and did not easily show his emotions. A disclosure by Mrs. Herr of finding Ray in tears at the fire did not seem to carry the same weight as Grandfather Pfanschmidt's pronouncements.

At the door, in a final plea to the reporter's kinder sensibilities, Mrs. Herr said, "Be as considerate as you can. We still hope that it is not true, you know. Be as considerate as you can for Father." The *Herald* reporter included that statement "in a spirit of consideration."[22]

One other person who broke his silence this day was E. W. Charles Kaempen, Emma's father. The *Herald* included his interview in the same article. Kaempen pulled no punches. "It distressed me beyond measure to be forced to suspect that this young man was guilty of the terrible crime, and yet in my mind I felt positive from the first that such was the case."

The article ended with this quote from Mr. Kaempen:

"I cannot but feel most deeply that the crime should be fastened on the young man, but I shall use every effort to see that justice is done. I have engaged John Wall to assist the prosecution. I owe it to my dead daughter, to my family, and to this community, which has overwhelmed me with kindness and sympathy, to see that absolute justice is done, and that the punishment be inflicted to the full extent of the law. This I propose to see done, no matter what expense it may involve."

---

[21] *Herald*, October 8, 1912.
[22] Ibid.

# Chapter 12

~

# Ray Indicted

## Wednesday, October 9, 1912

R ay did not attend the second part of the Coroner's Inquest when it reconvened, but he was even closer than before. The meeting was held in the circuit courtroom just upstairs from his cell in the county jail building. Although his circumstances had changed dramatically, to all appearances Ray was oblivious to the proceedings above him. Witnesses said he spent his time reading and talking about anything except his present troubles.

The courtroom, which could hold by contemporary accounts seven- to eight-hundred people on the main floor plus hundreds more in the gallery was completely and quickly filled. Ray's attorneys were in attendance, along with current State's Attorney Gilmer and his assistants. Fred Wolfe, a candidate in the upcoming election for state's attorney was there, along with local detectives, fire marshals, and detectives from out of state, plus the numerous witnesses.

At ten fifteen in the morning, coroner Haley called the role and found all accounted for. He passed most of the morning in recalling witnesses from the previous week, reviewing their testimony and having them agree to it or correct it. By the time the court adjourned for lunch some in the crowd had already left early in an attempt to beat the rush, eat a quick lunch, and return to secure their seats for the afternoon session. Strategy, timing, and drama would play a big part in this case, even among the onlookers.

Court was set to resume at 1:20 p.m., and coroner Haley wanted to begin with Esther Reeder. She, however, did not make her appearance until twenty minutes after the session had begun, so Haley was forced to begin with Deputy William Schaeffer. Schaeffer testified that he had taken the maker's tag off the clothes found in the outhouse near Ray's camp and traced them to the New Hub Store on Hampshire Street where he discovered that a clerk, Charles Ellerbrecht, had sold several khaki suits to Ray.

Miss Reeder finally arrived, attired in fashionable black and white. It was reported that she wore a black skirt and a black silk waist (blouse), a large handsome black and white hat, and black silk gloves. She wore rimless glasses and had long, fluffy brown hair.[23] Clearly reluctant to hurt Ray, under oath she seemed to have trouble remembering things. Esther did speak about the khaki clothes and red tie Ray wore to visit her on the Friday before the fire. She admitted that those clothes looked the same as the ones shown to her in the basement of the courthouse. As soon as her testimony was over, she fled the courtroom.

Esther's father, Daniel Reeder, followed her on the stand. Reeder testified about the team of two small sorrel horses and the buggy Ray drove to his house on that Friday. He also put Ray back on the road by 10:30 p.m. He too confirmed Ray's wardrobe choice for that evening was khaki from head to toe.

Next on the stand was Charles Ellerbrecht, the clothing store clerk. He identified the lot numbers on the clothing tags and said they had been special orders from Chicago, delivered more than a week before the fire. In addition, Ray had purchased the one khaki suit the store had in stock on the day he placed his order for three more. This brought the total of identical khaki shirts and pants to four suits, or eight individual pieces in Ray's possession.

---

[23] *Journal*, October 9, 1912.

Ray was firmly tied to the blood-spotted clothing found in the vault.

In the trail of evidence, the next witness, Walter Dingerson, placed Ray on the road to Payson just before midnight on Friday, the last evening the family was seen alive. Dingerson testified that he was headed home toward Payson around eleven o'clock. South of Quincy, near Mast Corners, the turn to the Reeder farm, he overtook an undercut buggy, pulled by a team of small bay horses. He followed that buggy for a time but it was moving slowly, the team only at a walk. Eventually he pulled around and passed, but the other buggy's side curtains were secured so he could not identify the driver. He did identify the team again later. It was Ray's.

A second piece of damaging testimony came from H. A. Jenkins, owner of a garage and automobile accessories business on South Seventh Street in Quincy. He testified that Ray was in the habit of leaving his team tied across the street from his place of business. Jenkins said that Saturday night, September 28, the night the fire started, he saw someone he thought was Ray unhitch that team and head south, toward Payson, between 11:00 and 11:15 p.m.

After hearing testimony from many witnesses, the coroner's jury signed a statement that said the cause of death for Charles, Mathilda, and Blanche Pfanschmidt and Emma Kaempen was "by being murdered with some form of sharp instrument."

It also stated: "We recommend that Ray Pfanschmidt, son of Charles A. Pfanschmidt be held to the actions of the grand jury without bail." Coroner Haley agreed.[24]

The day after the inquest, the sheriff received a Writ of Mittimus from the coroner, directing him to hold Ray until the next grand jury convened. The grand jury term normally coincided with the dates of the circuit court and so would not begin its next session until the third Monday in January 1913.

The coroner's verdict removed the necessity of holding a preliminary hearing for Ray. He would wait out the chill fall and dreary winter months in county jail while both the authorities and his defense searched for evidence to shore up their cases.

---

[24] Transcript of the Coroner's Inquest.

The day after the inquest, a reporter for the *Herald* cornered Ray's attorney about what angle the defense would take. Govert denied the current rumor that he was planning on having a competency hearing for Ray, or that he would use a defense of insanity. Mr. Govert stated, "The innocence of our client will be his only defense. It is sufficient."[25]

Finally, three long days after his arrest and a day past the coroner's verdict, Ray received a jailhouse visit from his family. His father's brother, Uncle Fred Pfanschmidt, his aunt Mrs. Petrie, and another aunt (probably Mrs. Herr from Kansas, who was not recognized by the sheriff) arrived to see him. They were allowed a cautious visit in the watchful presence of two deputies. It was a stilted and short affair, consisting of inquiries as to his health and little else. Deputies reported there was no conversation of any consequence.

The defense team had hired detective Mr. A. G. Lund of the Burns Detective Agency. According to the intrepid *Herald* reporter, Lund had tracked the mysterious stranger, with his broken English and tomato-stained clothes, through the countryside. He concluded, as had the sheriff, that William McKenzie was an innocent tramp. Lund also admitted that he had uncovered the same evidence against Ray as had Lipps.

Yet there were some other viable possibilities for perpetrators of the crime. The most tantalizing was the "Axe Man Theory." In 1912, the concept of a serial killer had not been considered. Yet there were cases of multiple murders as early as 1885, when a man in Texas killed five women; in 1902, Joseph Briggen's California pig ranch yielded the bones of at least twelve men; and, closer to home, there were a series of unsolved axe murders in at least five states across the Midwest.

As the concept of a serial killer only evolved years later, so too was a model for multistate cooperation of law enforcement officials completely lacking at this time. With little communication or coordination between officials, it was next to impossible to connect crimes or see patterns when such a killer existed and traveled. However, newspapers did carry the happenings from other locales, and some people began to string together the "Axe Man" theory.

---

[25] *Herald*, October 10, 1912.

The string of murders attributed to him went like this: In Colorado Springs in September 1911, Alice May Burnham, her six-year-old daughter, Alice, and three-year-old son, John, were found dead in their cottage. Next door, Henry Wayne, his wife, Blanche, and their two-year-old twin babies were also killed in their sleep with an axe. These bodies went undiscovered for two days. There was no apparent motive.

On October 19, 1911, in Ellsworth, Kansas, William Showman, his wife, and their three children were murdered while sleeping by an assailant with an axe. Their bodies were not found until the following day. Bloodhounds called to the scene took scent from a cloth the murderer used to wipe his hands and tracked him to the Union Pacific Railroad line. The axe was left at the scene of the crime. Suspicion fell on an ex-brother-in-law of Mrs. Showman who had recently been released from prison.

Next, in the spring of 1912, just days before the infamous massacre in Villisca, Iowa, Rollin Hudson and his wife were killed in Paola, Kansas, by an axe-wielding assailant.

Three months prior to the Pfanschmidt murders, in June 1912, Villisca, Iowa, was the scene of a slaughter: J. B. Moore, his wife, their four children, and two young sisters visiting them were all killed with an axe. A total of eight bodies were discovered, with no known motive or suspect. Eventually, a suspect in the Villisca crime would be brought to trial. However, the details of his confession did not match the evidence, and he was acquitted.

Three weeks after the Villisca murders and less than two months before the Adams County slayings, the William Dawson family in Monmouth, Illinois, was killed. When Dawson, caretaker for a church, failed to have the sanctuary ready for Sunday services, the deacons went to his home. There they found the bodies of Dawson, his wife, and child bludgeoned to death with an axe.[26] Monmouth was across the Mississippi river from Iowa and only about a hundred miles north of Quincy. Rail lines connected the cities.

One federal officer, M. W. McClaughry, looked at the number and location of axe crimes committed and wondered about a connection. Agent

---

[26] *Ellsworth Reporter*, October 19, 1911.

McClaughry, whose father was warden at a Kansas penitentiary, thought there was a likely candidate for many of these crimes incarcerated in the penitentiary in Jefferson City, Missouri. There were striking similarities between the crimes committed by Henry Moore and this string of murders. McClaughry interviewed Moore several times. In May 1913, McClaughry claimed to have tied Moore to twenty-three unsolved slayings in the Midwest.[27] Moore was never officially charged, however, and died soon after. The cases were never officially closed and remain listed as unsolved. The concept of a roving madman wielding an axe remained the subject of speculation and fear in the countryside.

Among the populace in Quincy, little thought was spared for the age of an offender, but there existed an attitude of protection toward the women involved. No matter the opinion held of Ray's guilt or innocence, there remained polite and curious sympathy for his lovely fiancée, Esther. In the days after Ray's arrest, the striking young woman appeared to be a unwilling celebrity. By the standards of any day, she was a pretty girl, correct in her behavior and demeanor. Her clothing and deportment were reported in detail at each appearance. She seemed honest and sincere yet reluctant;[28] in short, she was the very picture of a tragic romantic heroine.

The arrest of her fiancé was Esther's third tragedy in as many months. Her beloved mother, Susan, had died at the family home August 6, 1912, after being bedridden for weeks. The official cause of death was listed as "carcinoma of liver,"[29] and she was buried two days later in the little family cemetery on the Reeder farm. Esther's mother had lived on the family farm ever since her marriage in 1874, at the age of nineteen. She had been born only six miles away, and Esther's grandmother, Mary Hadley, was credited with being the first white female baby born in Adams County.[30] A photo

---

[27] Serial killer crime index www.crimezzz.net/serialkillers/M/MOORE_henry _lee.htm.

[28] *Journal*, October 9, 1912 (Headline: Ray Held by Verdict of Coroner's Jury Today).

[29] Death certificate.

[30] Adams County History, p. 1075.

shows Susan Reeder with dark curly hair piled atop her head, wearing lace, a broach at her throat, and small gold earrings. She looks alert and pleasant, a slight smile on her face. There is no record of what she thought of her daughter's engagement to Ray.

Esther also had to cope with the results of a paralytic stroke her father, Daniel, had recently suffered, possibly caused by the stress of watching his wife of thirty-nine years lose her battle with liver cancer. Probably it did nothing to improve his disposition. Esther's father also came from pioneer stock. His father had staked a claim to one thousand acres of Adams County and lived in a log cabin before building the first frame home ever constructed in the area. It was the house that Esther still called home.

Folks wanted to know where this young lady's affections stood after the tragedy and Ray's arrest. Esther's statement was simple: "I shall not break off my engagement with him until it is proven surely that he is guilty. I believe that he is innocent."[31] She would stand true to Ray.

Her father, when asked a similar question had nothing to say about the matter.

The consequences of the murders continued to accrue. On October 26, 1912, the administrator of the estate of Charles Pfanschmidt held a public sale to disperse the remaining unburned property. Fred Pfanschmidt signed the sale order on October 5, less than a week after the tragedy. The livestock and crops in the field could not afford to wait while people grieved. They required care and ownership and husbandry.

The terms of the sale were these: "All sums under $10 cash in hand, all sums over ten dollars, a credit of six months will be given, purchaser giving note with approved bankable security." They also offered a 6 percent cash discount for items costing more than ten dollars paid by cash at the sale.[32]

The bill of sale listed the following property: "1 pair of geldings weighing 1,400 pounds each;[33] 1 10 year-old brood mare; 1 family horse; 2 good 2 year-old colts; 2 fresh milk cows; 1 Jersey (cow) coming fresh; 2

---

[31]  *Herald,* October 11, 1912.
[32]  *Herald,* October 10, 1912.
[33]  Work or draft horses.

milk cows coming fresh in 40 days; 2 cows giving milk; 4 heifers; 1 short horn bull; 10 brood sows; 36 spring pigs; 35 fall pigs; 1 fat hog weighing 325 pounds; 1 gang plow; 1 sulky plow; 1 corn planter; 1 riding cultivator; 1 walking cultivator; 1 hay tedder;[34] 3 plows; 2 harrows; 1 potato digger; 1 disc; 1 mower; 1 hay rake; 1 disc drill; 1 truck wagon; 1 surrey; 1 top buggy; 1 spring wagon; 2 hay frames; 2 sets double harness; 1 set double driving harness; 2 sets single harness; 1,500 bushels oats, 8 tons of hay, 80 acres growing corn in the field; 16 stands of bees; 1 pair of scales; 1 cream separator; 1 1 washing machine; and other articles too numerous to mention."[35]

This was the entire inventory of a prosperous farm of the time.

By January 1913, when the grand jury convened, Ray was in his fourth month of confinement. Conditions in the dark cell had replaced his tanned, healthy look with a paler, waxy complexion, and lack of exercise had added pounds to his frame. The jury, however, had to dispatch other cases before it could take up the matter of Ray.

In the first few days of its term, the jury dealt with a minor who was charged with setting multiple fires and was considered likely to be sentenced to the asylum for the criminally insane rather than the reformatory; a case against Andrew Watts, a "colored man" charged with assault with a straight razor with intent to kill one Florence Perkins; William Carpenter, charged with attempted arson in which he set a fire in his father's house attempting to burn a satchel that was suspected of containing evidence that would implicate him in a murder near Warsaw; Richard Barnett, charged with multiple counts of burglary at a millinery company and a shoe store; and a man charged with taking "indecent liberties" with one Gertrude Perkins. In the last case it was noted, "both colored." The man in question had an additional grand larceny charge involving the theft of clover seed from an establishment in nearby Golden, Illinois.[36]

---

[34] This machine gathers cut hay into windrows.
[35] *Herald*, October 10, 1912.
[36] *Herald*, January 11, 1913.

## *1913 Adams County grand jury members*
Photo courtesy Quincy University

On January 23, when the grand jury convened at last to hear the case against Ray, it was a certainty that they would indict him. To those who watched or followed in the papers, the curiosity was that it still took them eight days to do so.

The *Journal* reported that the delay was not due to a lack of evidence or reluctance on the part of the jurors. In fact, it took precious little time for the empanelled jury members to agree to send Ray to trial. But this jury wanted to know the evidence. Before they were done, they called a veritable parade of witnesses, more than had ever testified before an Adams County grand jury. It took most of an entire newspaper column to list their names.[37]

The town demanded a trial and these men worked to craft indictments that were free of legal loopholes that might offer a savvy lawyer the grounds

---

[37] *Journal*, January 31, 1913.

for a technical escape. They wanted to ensure that the automatic motion to quash by the defense would have no legal standing through an error on their part. The reputation of Ray's legal team was well known, and well respected, if not well liked in all quarters.

The grand jury was careful not to be too explicit. Four indictments were returned against Ray, and each contained six counts but did not specify the type of weapon or the manner of death. They simply named the victims and accused Ray of murder and of arson to hide the evidence.

Illinois law decreed that the accused was to face his jury and be given a copy of his charges. On Friday, January 31, 1913, when all was ready, a bailiff was sent down to the basement of the building to bring young Pfanschmidt from his cell to officially hear the charges against him. Ray seemed completely composed. The only words the prisoner spoke to the bailiff were, "All right."

The *Journal* reported that Ray never faltered, blanched, or changed expression. It called him "sphinx-like" and "sullen."[38] The *Whig*, on the other hand, called him a "pitiful" sight, dressed in the same wrinkled suit he wore upon his arrest. A *Herald* reporter saw him inhale deeply as the indictments were read and "swallow convulsively." This astute watcher also saw Ray's eyes meet those of the Kaempen contingent as he was leaving the courtroom. Their stares made Ray shiver, drop his gaze immediately, and move nearer his escorting deputy.[39]

After the official reading, Ray's lawyers, as expected, filed motions to quash every count on each indictment. The defense team did not expect to prevail. Rather, the motions were designed to test the charges for weaknesses. The next steps in the legal minuet would be these: a hearing on the defense motions to quash the indictments would be held; followed by a preliminary arraignment at which Ray would enter a plea; and then a trial would finally follow. So January ended, and Ray

---

[38] *Journal*, January 31, 1913. In this story the *Journal* also included a reported rumor that Ray was ready to plead guilty in order to save a portion of his estate.
[39] *Herald*, January 31, 1913. The *Herald* also reported that there was plenty of evidence to convict Ray and that the grand jury was ready to indict on the evidence from the Coroner's Inquest alone.

had yet to tell his story. He had not yet spoken his plea of "guilty" or "not guilty."

The frustrated town was eagerly anticipating a spectacle of a trial. They wanted answers. They also sought diversion from worry concerning the reliability of the city water supply and the eighty cases of typhoid currently plaguing the town.

On the day following the grand jury indictment, their caution over wording proved their wisdom. On Saturday, February 1, the coldest day of the winter, in a courtroom packed with a couple hundred onlookers, attorney Lancaster persuaded Judge Albert Akers that the defense team needed more time to examine the language in the fifth count of each indictment. Foreshadowing the manner in which the trial would be contested, Lancaster took exception to the statement that the murder was committed with a sharp weapon, a further description of which the jury "could not give." Ray's attorneys argued that "could not give" was inexact and open to interpretation as to whether or not they had evidence, and they chose not or would not reveal it for some reason.[40] Judge Akers agreed to continue the case until Monday, February 3.

The one notable development of a personal nature was that Ray appeared in the courtroom wearing nose glasses. The *Journal* noted that he once or twice adjusted these rimless glasses as though he was not used to having them upon his face.

The following Monday, the courtroom contest began again. On this day, the defense team prevailed and the fifth count of each indictment was dismissed. It was argued that the phrasing used was not proper, since it was not susceptible to be disputed or proved. The State did not contest this and seemed content to go forward with five counts in each indictment instead of six.

More than five months after the tragedy, attorney Lancaster, speaking for Ray, finally announced a plea of "not guilty." It was anticlimactic, in the extreme, to the packed courtroom of people who had hoped to hear the words fall from the defendant's own lips.

---

[40] *Journal*, February 1, 1913.

With barely a pause, the defense team stated that they would file motions for change of venue and a change of judge. Because Judge Akers had visited the farm on the day of the fire, the defense felt that this might create an unconscious prejudice in the judicial mind. The State quietly entered their motion requesting that the trial start on Monday and announced that they would prosecute Ray for the murder of his sister, Blanche.

Now the town expected a reaction from Ray. If his attorneys would not allow him to tell his story or produce a justification, then the central character in the drama must surely provide some reaction to his situation and his jeopardy. Ray did not oblige.

The *Journal* seemed particularly bent on unraveling the mystery of Ray's composure. On Saturday, February 8, 1913, in an attempt to provide "insight into his real nature," they consulted a phrenologist and published a lengthy front page article that included a character sketch of Ray.

Phrenology traces its roots to Aristotle, but it was Franz Joseph Gall (1758–1828) who is considered the founder of the movement. Gall assigned to the brain specific physical sites for particular mental activities and believed that intellectual and moral characteristics and abilities are inborn. He also believed that the shape of the skull represented the development of various traits and mirrored the size and degree of development of the underlying brain areas. According to Gall, "The brain is composed of as many particular organs as there are propensities, sentiments, and faculties which differ essentially from each other."[41] Therefore, the bumps and indentations on a human skull, when measured, gave accurate information about the character of the individual.

In the early twentieth century, the science of phrenology was revitalized with the growth of interest in evolution and criminal anthropology. It would soon butt heads with practitioners of the new science of psychiatry. In the early 1900s, psychiatrists were called "alienists," and their field would eventually take center stage. However, phrenology would never completely disappear. It would find a new direction with proponent Paul Bouts (1900–1999), who devised a method of combining his discipline with

---

[41]  History of Phrenology, http://www.phrenology.org/intro.html.

typology and graphology to create an approach called psychognomy, which maintained popularity in Europe throughout the twentieth century.

It was to this field of study that the *Journal* turned for information and understanding of the enigmatic man who was either a terrible villain or a victim wrongly accused. The phrenologist reached these conclusions:

Far from being a strong and fearsome villain, Ray was described as a weakling with a thin, slanted jaw (not the lantern jawbone of a determined fellow) and a thin and weak upper lip. He was characterized as a "degenerate," indicated by his misshapen protruding ears, and as having a "stunted intellect." Apparently his "bump of combativeness" was missing and in its place was an indentation, showing him to be "void of fighting spirit"; but his "bump of secrecy" and the one indicating sensual desire were well defined and indicative of "periodic association with dissolute women."

The strange conclusion of this article seemed to be that there was more to learn about Ray. Although he was a "degenerate," secretive man, certainly capable of slaying four people in their sleep, he yet, perhaps, did not constitute a threat to anyone else. It seemed like an assurance to readers of the *Journal* that the authorities had arrested the right man; the threat was over; the accused was completely uncaring and deserved what would surely come to him at trial.

Meanwhile, on Monday, February 3, the battle of affidavits escalated in the courtroom. In an attempt to buttress or refute the request for a change of venue and of judge, both the prosecution and defense were piling up sworn oaths that, depending on their agenda, the signors either would or would not be able to serve on a fair and impartial trial jury. Reams of paper would be consumed before this conflict was resolved.

Govert presented only three affidavits saying that Judge Akers might be prejudiced by being at the fire. One was signed by the defendant himself; one by a man who worked for a collection agency in Quincy; and one with the mark of an illiterate farmer from the Riverside district north of the city.

Judge Akers had driven out to the fire with his wife and others on that fatal Sunday afternoon and found a great crowd of sightseers already there. He had talked for a time with some people he knew and voiced his opinion that the fire was no accident. Even though he had said nothing to indicate a prejudice against the defendant, Akers knew that to deny the petition for a change of judge would give the defense immediate grounds for appeal for any verdict reached. Judge Akers therefore recused himself from the trial on Saturday, February 8, 1913. The subsequent legal events would now fall under the stewardship of Judge Harry Higbee of Pike County, Illinois.

In an unfortunate or perhaps intentional juxtaposition, the *Herald* ran directly beneath Ray's front page story another article with the headline: "Missouri Boy Was Slayer of Father." It told of a twenty-one-year-old man, Lee Hoyt, who bludgeoned his father to death for being "too severe with him."

On Monday, February 10, the full cast assembled to contest the change of venue issue. It was extremely important to both sides, as the outcome of the trial would be influenced mightily by the locale in which it was held.

Ray was taken from his dank cell up one flight of stairs to the sheriff's office, and then up another stairway to the courtroom. Before entering into view of the crowded courtroom, his handcuffs were removed. He was led to a chair facing the judge, flanked on one side by his lawyers and on the other by a deputy sheriff. Once seated, he assumed what would become his standard pose: legs crossed, hands resting in his lap, scarcely moving, and paying no attention to those in the audience.[42]

The prosecution team, who sat in the three opposing chairs, included the newly elected State's Attorney Fred G. Wolfe, attorney Rolland Wagner appointed as his assistant, and John E. Wall, still on retainer from the Kaempen family.

Wolfe came from a pioneer farm family in the nearby village of Liberty, where he was born in 1876. His great-grandfather and grandfather were active members of the Dunkard church, and great-grand sire being the first preacher of the sect west of the Allegheny Mountains. He had graduated from the University of Michigan law department in 1909 and was married to a local woman, Nita Williams.

Wolfe had a teacher-ish look about him. His pince-nez glasses sat in front of wide, slightly startled eyes. His brown hair, longer than the other

---

[42] *Journal,* February 10, 1913.

lawyers' was not pomaded flat to his head, but rose softly above his brow, with some strands escaping, slightly unruly above his ears. His square jaw sported a cleft but seemed ill paired to his narrow, firmly closed mouth. His collar was in the new style—shorter and exposing his neck. His tie was slightly askew. In overall appearance, Wolfe seemed somewhat ill-prepared, or perhaps taken faintly unawares.

## Fred G. Wolfe

*Mississippi Valley Magazine* circa 1913,
Courtesy Historical Society of Quincy and Adams County

Wagner, who attended both Michigan and Northwestern universities, had been admitted to the bar in 1909. He and Fred Wolfe had been friends since childhood. The *Herald* proclaimed Wagner "unquestionably one of the ablest young lawyers in the county," and went on to say there would be "absolute harmony in the state's attorney's office."[43]

Attorney John Wall was a local man who had attended Chaddock College law department and upon passing the bar gone west to Salt Lake City. There he gained trial experience before returning to his home city. At the time of these proceedings he had a flourishing practice in Quincy.

Govert, for the defense, began by pointing out that the law makes no provision for a numerical battle of affidavits. This was not to be a contest between the total of about one hundred that the defense would provide showing prejudice, and the number the prosecution could provide claiming otherwise, which numbered a whopping twenty-four hundred sworn statements! The law only required proof that prejudice was shown, and a change of location was mandated.

The defense further asserted that the county officials themselves, Sheriff Lipps, etc., had issued statements proclaiming Ray's guilt, as had their officers and deputies. Local press coverage was also cited as highly prejudicial against their client. A third prong in their attack was the prominence and social standing of the two families involved, as well as their popularity. Public sentiment had reached such a peak, they added, that their own law firm was suffering from effects of rumors and reports against it because of their involvement in this case.

Wolfe rose and made the counter claim for the prosecution that the majority of potential jurors in Adams County held no ill feeling toward Ray.[44] He also denied any wrongful statements on the part of officials involved.

Wolfe said "the statements made to the press by Adams county officers, had not been colored by the daily papers of the city, but that the papers had simply published detailed accounts of the murder in their columns,

---

[43] *Herald*, November 7, 1912.
[44] Ibid.

not distorting the facts, nor coloring them to satisfy the morbid desire for sensationalism on the part of reporters."[45]

In fact, Wolfe affirmed, there was a feeling that the young man should be given every opportunity to establish his innocence. He asked Judge Higbee to deny the motion to move the trial. Three hours later, after much wrangling and in front of the largest crowd in the courtroom to date, Judge Higbee so ruled. The Pfanschmidt trial would stay in Quincy.

This denial of a change in venue constituted a major setback to the confident defense team. They immediately filed for a continuance as the prosecution asked for a trial date. Judge Higbee set March 3 to hear the next round of motions.

As a parting shot, State's Attorney Wolfe issued a public statement saying that Ray had made it known to him and the sheriff and another attorney that he wanted to plead guilty to the charges against him, and would have, except that his attorneys stopped him. The defense countered, issuing a vehement denial, and a statement that Ray was in danger of going insane if kept any longer in the small, dark, unventilated cell in which he was confined. Govert said Ray was confined for twenty-one out of every twenty-four hours in a five-by-seven-foot cell and then only allowed as far as the corridor for exercise. Ray had no access at all to daylight. Govert said his client was sane now, and "there will be no defense of insanity at the trial … unless the boy is driven insane by his treatment in jail."[46]

The sheriff replied that Ray was in the only cell strong enough to hold an accused murderer.

---

[45] *Journal,* February 11, 1913.
[46] *Herald,* February 11, 1913.

## *Adams County Courthouse, Quincy, Illinois*
Courtesy Historical Society of Quincy and Adams County

# Section II

# The Trial, March 1913

# Chapter 13

# Jury Selection: Good Men Are Hard to Find

## March 1913

On March 4, the defense did an about-face, withdrawing their motion for a continuance and demanding instead an immediate trial. When the trial date was fixed as March 18, a second change of presiding judge had to be made. Judge Highee could not hear the case at that time so the task fell to Judge Guy Williams of Havana, Illinois.

The defense's rush to trial was based on an obscure provision in the Illinois statutes. At that time circuit courts had fixed dates of operation and all cases before them had to be concluded before the term ended. Ray's trial would most certainly take more than three weeks and extend beyond the end date of this court. If his trial had not concluded when the term expired, Ray would be freed on a technicality. Govert & Lancaster were earning their fee.

On March 6, 1913, a *Journal* reporter interviewed Ray in his cell, where he declared he was "feeling fine as milk." In the reporter's opinion, the young man's general demeanor disproved the rumors that incarceration had put him "in danger of losing his mind."

Ray cheerily credited a fellow prisoner who played the violin with helping to pass the time. "That fiddler in the other cell helps out. His music does a whole lot to break the monotony of confinement." He also claimed to have gained thirteen pounds, thanks to the jailer. "See that fat fellow over there?" Ray reportedly pointed to jailer "Monk" Frye. "Well, he's a good feeder, and I guess he must be feeding me pretty good."

On March 8, 1913, the *Quincy Journal*, on its front page ran a photograph of Ray taken about a week before the murders, wearing his trademark khaki outfit, complete with wide-cuffed gloves, a broad brimmed-hat, lace-up boots, and red string tie. The text proclaimed, "Young Pfanschmidt is charged with the complete extermination of his immediate family and a young woman boarder in the family—complete annihilation of his own flesh and blood for pecuniary gain, a crime remarkable for its atrociousness and rarity."[47]

The article underscored the difference between the confident, swaggering Ray in the picture and the completely reserved, rather unkempt Ray wearing nose glasses and sitting quietly while his attorneys argued for his life. That same day Ray celebrated his twenty-first birthday behind bars.

Four days later, the state legislature of Illinois managed to plug the legal loophole that could have set Ray free. In an emergency operation, both houses of the legislature simultaneously heard a bill that bypassed the committee stage to speed into law a provision stating that, once begun, any case before a circuit court could be concluded despite the fact that the term had expired.[48] The bill passed its final vote by a margin of 115 to 0 in the State House and 35 to 0 in the State Senate and become law on the eighteenth of March, during Ray's trial.[49] This was the first but not the last time in which this case would produce lasting legal changes.

The cast was assembling. The Burlington Railroad had delivered the Hon. Guy H. Williams to Quincy to preside over the trial. Judge Williams set up his headquarters at the posh Newcomb Hotel for the duration of the trial.

In a standing-room-only situation, the elaborate Quincy courthouse could pack more than fifteen hundred people into its main courtroom.

---

[47] *Journal*, March 8, 1913.
[48] *Journal*, March 11, 1913.
[49] *Journal*, February 18, 1913.

A press table had been set up in front of the judge's bench for six local reporters and another half dozen from papers outside the city. The official court reporter, James McNutt, had ordered a half gross of new #2 lead pencils to record the proceedings.

Sheriff Joe Lipps called in all available deputies to ensure order. A local paper printed a stern warning to the lawyers involved: "There is no occasion for trickery or sharp practice on either side—nor will it be tolerated by those justice-loving persons who will be watching the trial of the case.... The lawyers in this case are on trial just as truly as Ray Pfanschmidt is; and it will be a good thing for them if they clearly understand this fact. The people are the court of last resort; and that court will not tolerate any polly-foxing or sharp practice on the part of the attorneys." The paper offered this as a "friendly tip."[50] It was a succinct expression among the citizenry of the hunger for conviction.

And so, jury selection began. And court was immediately recessed for an hour because not all prospective jurors had arrived from the country. Justice waited for the eleven o'clock train. When the opening proceedings resumed, the crowd was quiet, orderly, and with assistance by the deputies soon filled the main floor and the balcony to capacity before it spilled into the hallways and onto the courthouse lawn. The throng spanned all ages, occupations, and social classes.

On the first full day of wrangling over jurors, the two sides, by their questions, hinted at their concerns and case structure. Prospects were queried by the state on their feelings concerning the death penalty, about circumstantial evidence, as well as any opinions they might have formed. The defense inquired about a prospect's ability to ignore everything heard outside the courtroom, especially if it was not included as evidence in the trial, and about their ability to hold the defendant innocent unless all other possible theories had been disproven. The defense also tested whether the prospective juror could find Ray innocent if the case proved him guilty of some crime *other* than the one cited in this trial. It was a thought-provoking question.

---

[50] *Journal*, February 18, 1913.

Many admitted to holding strong opinions that would need stronger evidence to overcome. The prevailing opinions were not on the side of Ray's innocence.

It became apparent by the rapid rate of dismissals that a larger pool of men would be needed to fill a jury box.[51] The call went out for deputies to bring in another one hundred prospects. True to form, the defense objected to this Order for a Special Venire. Their objections were overruled and the three deputies sent out. The defense also objected to the jury being put under the charge of the sheriff once it was empanelled. It was agreed that a deputy, Frank McNay, would assume charge of the jurors.

Hopeful rumors flew about town that Ray was thinking of confessing. But still, he said nothing. However, as jury selection began, a change seemed to come over Ray. He stirred from his casual pose and became interested in the proceedings. He engaged in conversation with his attorneys about various prospective jurors and paid attention to the entire process. This was a departure from his careless demeanor and nearly absolute stillness in previous court appearances.

The newspapers interpreted the change as a sign of mental struggle within the defendant. The *Journal* reported "all is not well and one of the most pronounced symptoms of mental ill at ease is an obstreperous lump in his throat. Pfanschmidt frequently tries to swallow this lump and when he does so, his Adam's apple is very conspicuous on account of its clumsy movements."[52]

As the screening of jurors continued, the courtroom, although full, was not as crowded as on the first days. Early attendees wanted a look at Ray but were content now to wait for testimony to begin. When that happened, officials expected the crowds to set records.

By March 28, the third special venire of one hundred men was exhausted, and the jury remained one man short. The blame for this long, drawn-out procedure could not be laid solely at the feet of the defense. The

---

[51] Women were still fighting for the right to be on juries in the middle of the century. Even after gaining the vote in 1920, their right to serve as jurors was restricted or denied. At this time they could not vote.

[52] *Journal*, March 21, 1913.

prosecution excused many men who would not apply the death penalty on strictly circumstantial evidence, or who said that such evidence would have to prove guilt unquestionably.

On Saturday, March 29, 1913, the tally, as printed in the *Journal* stood as follows:

- Four hundred forty-one prospective jurors summoned to appear (in seven different groups or venires)
- Thirty-two excused by the court
- Three hundred forty-six excused by the attorneys
- Eleven accepted as jurors.[53]

Once again, the three deputies were sent into the county to procure fifty more prospects. Only one vacant seat remained. Eventually a twelfth man was agreed upon. The final jury consisted of:

- Frank Greenough, thirty-six, bricklayer and concrete worker from Clayton, Illinois
- William Hunter, fifty-six, machinist, from Lima, Illinois
- William Shackleton, fifty-five, bridge carpenter, from Quincy, Illinois
- C. W. Seifert, twenty-two, insurance man from Quincy, Illinois
- Albert Carter, fifty-five, painter, Camp Point, Illinois
- Frank Stowe, forty-four, livestock buyer, Camp Point, Illinois
- George Schulz, fifty-three, retired farmer, Camp Point, Illinois
- S. G. Sparks, sixty, traveling salesman, Camp Point, Illinois
- Herbert Willer, twenty-two, traction engineer, Quincy, Illinois
- Cecil Yates, thirty-one, laborer, Quincy, Illinois
- Charles L. Aldag, thirty-one, cigar maker, Quincy, Illinois
- T. S. Robbins, twenty-two, stationary engineer, La Prairie, Illinois

---

[53] *Journal*, March 29, 1913.

# Chapter 14

~

# The Trial Begins

## Saturday, March 29, 1913

The transcript listed it as:

"People of the State of Illinois, Plaintiff, vs. Case No. 2055 Ray A. Pfanschmidt."

And it began this way:

"Be it Remembered that on the trial of this cause at the January Term, A.D. 1913 of the Circuit Court of Adams County, Illinois, before the Honorable Guy R. Williams, Judge, and a jury, the Plaintiff, to maintain the issues on their part, gave in evidence on their behalf as follows, that is to say …"[54]

There followed more than two thousand pages of typewritten transcript.

On Saturday, March 29, 1913, the opening statement as made by State's Attorney, Fred Wolfe, laid out the case to the jury as the prosecution intended to prove it. The defense objected during the opening statement, and things heated up from there.

Wolfe spoke for about an hour and a half, telling the tale the State would seek to prove. This was basically the same storyline that the

---

[54] Microfilm roll 30-5263, p. 1122.

newspapers had trumpeted in bits and pieces since the previous autumn, but Wolfe had named six discrete parts: the "corpus delecti" (the crime itself); the motive; the plan; the circumstances; Ray's presence; and Ray's consciousness of guilt.

Their account proclaimed Ray the murderous son, motivated by pressing money problems on several fronts, who wanted the insurance and the family farmland to sell. The case revolved around greed, pride, a beautiful fiancée, a complicated timeline, a botched explosion, Ray's lack of a valid alibi, and the fire that was supposed to hide the evidence. The State promised convincing evidence, bloody clothes, eyewitnesses, and aborted confessions. The audience was riveted.

In the hush of an attentive courtroom, Wolfe concluded with these words: "Gentlemen of this jury, it becomes necessary for the State to demand the life of this young man on the evidence which we will be able to bring before you."

On completion of the State's opening statement, Govert rose and asked the bench to allow postponement of the defense opening statement until after the State presented its evidence. Judge Williams denied this motion, so Govert waived the defense right to deliver an opening statement to the jury. The audience rippled with murmurs of disappointment and surprise, robbed of a preview of Ray's case.

Ray's camp maintained its inscrutable silence.

After adjournment that first evening, Judge Williams refused to grant Ray any time in the courtroom to consult with his attorneys. The prisoner was escorted back to his cell in handcuffs.

Court began again on Monday, March 31, at 8:30 a.m. The courtroom doors were opened, and a crowd of nearly thirteen hundred people poured into every available space. When capacity was reached, the deputies secured the chamber doors, and at 9:00 a.m. the story began to emerge, under oath.

Ray appeared cheered by the hopeful wishes and the presence of relatives. Henry Geisel, Fred Pfanschmidt, his aunt Mrs. Walter Cook, cousins Mrs. Edith Keim and Arthur Pfanschmidt, his wife, and Mabel Pfanschmidt were there seated behind him. But Ray's customary smile faded and he shifted restlessly in his chair as the State's opening remarks laid out in great detail the points scheduled to be proven against him.

His fiancée, Esther Reeder, was also in the courtroom, appearing drawn, nervous, and in dread of her coming testimony. She was not the same rosy-cheeked girl she had been before.

Another part of the divided family, Ray's grandfather C. C. Pfanschmidt sat stolidly on the prosecution's side of the courtroom. The State's table held attorneys Wolfe, Wall, Police Chief Koch, Sheriff Lipps, and another attorney, George Wilson, who was assisting.

The prosecution needed to establish the identities of the victims, so the first witness called was a shopkeeper, Harvey Groce, from the village of Payson, one of the last people to see Ray's family alive.

Some well-known facts were now confirmed by testimony. Mr. and Mrs. Pfanschmidt drove to Payson on Friday night, September 27, 1912, in their surrey,[55] accompanied by Blanche and Emma Kaempen. The ladies planned to attend a rally of the Progressive Party, held in the Bank Hall just north of Groce's Store and Lunch Counter. The Progressive Party was the relatively new political invention and vehicle of Col. Theodore Roosevelt. The Payson Band would play, and it looked to be an entertaining evening of small town socializing and politics. Charles planned to have a shave and a visit in the barbershop of Tom Ruby and then meet up again with the ladies at the meeting hall.

Groce's was one of two stores on the village green that would buy excess produce from farmers and supply a multitude of things their land could not produce. When Charles Pfanschmidt stopped in Groce's Store he was after a smoke and purchased a quarter's worth of cigars. The two young ladies bought candies, and Mathilda treated herself to a hot bowl of oyster soup at the lunch counter.

In one of the many tantalizing pieces of information that would be elicited by the attorneys but not allowed into testimony, Harvey Groce began to describe a conversation he overheard between Mathilda and

---

[55] A surrey is a "two-seated top rig"—a light wagon pulled in this case by two horses, with two bench seats and a flat roof with open sides.

Groce's wife, mother-in-law, and brother-in-law. Both defense attorneys shouted "objection" in unison; the judge ruled the topic immaterial, and it was not recorded.

Testimony moved on to the timeline of events. Groce thought it sometime after 10:00 p.m. but before 11:00 when he saw the Pfanschmidts climb into the surrey for their three and a half or four mile trip home. He presumed this since after the store closed, he arrived at his own home at quarter till midnight.

The next witness was proprietor George Wagner of another Payson store. He spoke of Mathilda Pfanschmidt purchasing gasoline and kerosene from his store at various times. There was a great exchange of objections because the sales tickets Mathilda signed were written by *Mrs.* George Wagner, but she had not been called to testify. Her husband appeared in her stead.

The handwritten store tickets admitted as evidence were a running tally of credits when Mathilda sold her excess butter and eggs, and charges when she procured things, such as a paint brush, soda, coffee, starch, gasoline, sugar, peppers, D (Dutch?) cleanser, tea, peas, macaroni, two soaps, Atlactus,[56] matches, lemons, Mason jar lids, and embroidery needles. She also sometimes purchased tin cans, silk thread, puffed wheat, puffed rice, and chocolate.

Mathilda's last ticket, on the night of September 27, included Red X Lye, ammonia, toothpicks, and more sugar and coffee, which amounted to a total of one dollar and sixty cents. She sold the store two pounds of butter for fifty cents and five dozen eggs worth a dollar ten. It all came out even.

Next on the stand was the barber, Tom Ruby. Charles spent at least two hours in his shop that last night and engaged in lengthy conversations. Ruby was not allowed to speak about the things Charles told him that evening, especially not his plans for the following day.

The State then put on a parade of people testifying to the apparent health of the Pfanschmidts on that night and the fact that they had not been seen since then. Albert Lawrence, a "hack driver," and Roy

---

[56] Silk worms were grown on the area fruit trees, and these were likely for her orchard.

Peter, Payson resident, were the first two called. Mr. Lawrence described Mathilda as a "pert, lively woman" who was in good health that night.[57]

Peter testified to seeing a one-horse buggy sitting in the Pfanschmidt barnyard at 4:00 p.m. on the following day, Saturday, September 28. He also told of seeing four bodies before they were removed from the ruins, and after many objections was allowed to say that he could identify one body as Blanche by her hair.

At one point during cross-examination came this exchange:

Govert asked, "You say the *only thing* by which you could identify Blanche was her hair. Where was her hair when you saw it?"

Peter replied, "Well, it was on her head, braided!" His dry observation pulled a smattering of giggles from the onlookers, of the kind that erupt unexpectedly in the midst of stress or grief.

The judge admonished the onlookers: "I don't want any more laughing in this courtroom!"[58]

It was only slight relief to the solemnity. Wolfe pressed on beyond the topic of hair, and Roy Peter testified about that strange burning odor he smelled on the breeze Saturday, long before the fire was discovered.

Neighbor E. W. Peter came to the stand. After much wrangling between trial lawyers, he admitted that he saw the bodies but did not try very hard to determine identities. He was obviously uncomfortable but finally testified that he heard Ray say, "This body here is Sister. I can tell by her hair." Over many and varied objections, the court refused to strike that answer.

In exasperation at the difficulty of legally establishing identities to the burned bodies and firmly establishing the deaths of the family, Wolfe asked, "Have you seen anything of the Pfanschmidts, either Charles Pfanschmidt, or Mathilda Pfanschmidt, or Blanche Pfanschmidt, or Emma Kaempen, since the morning of that fire, I mean alive?

Peter said, "No, sir."[59]

Another close neighbor, twenty-one-year-old Gustave (Gus) Kaufman, was called. He told of cutting weeds but seeing none of the Pfanschmidts

---

[57] 30-5263, p. 1147.
[58] 30-5263, p. 1154.
[59] 30-5263, p. 1155.

on Saturday. That evening Kaufman left his house about 5:00 p.m. and headed south driving a steel-wheeled, one-horse buggy to visit the Curran family. By the time he returned home at 10:00 p.m., the little shower had settled the dust in the road.

The judge and attorneys then spent a great deal of time trying to get clear on the geography of roads bordering the Pfanschmidt farm. It was here that the road from Payson on its way to Quincy curved from its east/ west path to a more northerly direction. The area had a second road that led directly south from the Pfanschmidt's driveway toward the village called Fall Creek. To further complicate matters, a third road, the alternate route to the city called the Pape's Mill Road, entered the Payson/Quincy road on the north end of this same curve. The Pfanschmidt's nearest neighbors, the Kaufman farm, sat at the southwest corner of the Pape's Mill and Payson/ Quincy roads.

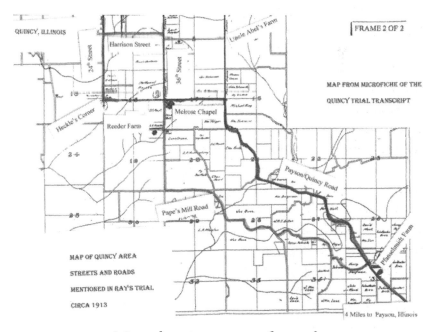

*Map showing routes from the Pfanschmidt farm to Quincy*

The State established that Kaufman left buggy tracks on the Payson/ Quincy road sometime around 11:00 p.m. on Friday night. After, having stabled his horse, Kaufman was in his house and gone to bed by about eleven thirty. He remembered nothing else until his dad awakened him at about 2:00 or 3:00 a.m. with the news that the Pfanschmidt home was burning.

Kaufman, who ran the short distance to the fire on foot, said that by the time of the fire, there were wheel tracks that crossed the ones he made earlier. They came from the direction of Quincy, entered the Pfanschmidt drive, and exited again. This indicated that these tracks were made between his 11:20 bedtime and the fire at 2:20 a.m.

A great debate then began as to what kind of wheel created the tracks in the barnyard and the road: the provocative question was, Did a "steel tire or rubber rim wheel" leave those imprints? Just as there were no DNA tests or dental X-rays to positively identify the bodies, there were no devices to record or analyze the tracks in question. Officials did the best they could.

After the noon recess, Govert zeroed in on the critical question of time. He managed to lead Kaufman to admit that he didn't look at a time piece and so could not be certain about the time of the fire.

To establish the layout of the house, the State then called George Behrensmeyer. He was an architect who had drawn to scale the plot of the house and outbuildings using an old exterior photo and information from the defendant's grandfather, C. C. Pfanschmidt.

William Long was next to sit in the witness chair. He was the postman who faithfully delivered mail six days a week with his horse and buggy on Payson Route #2, which included the Pfanschmidt residence. The Pfanschmidts subscribed to only one Quincy paper, the conservative-minded *Herald*. When he made his rounds that Saturday, the mailbox was empty and waiting and he filled it with the newspaper. On Sunday morning when he visited the tragedy, he noticed that there was still a paper in the box, uncollected.

Long testified that his delivery Saturday included only that single newspaper. Since the family had been in Payson on Friday, he thought it was likely that they had gathered their other letters or circulars directly from the village post office. A letter mailed in Quincy on a Thursday would have reached the Payson office by Friday evening at the latest. That empty mailbox and a missing letter would soon become key to establishing a motive for murder.

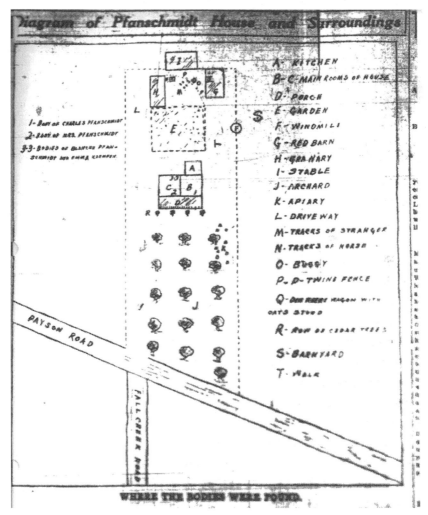

*The Pfanschmidt farm—numbers showing locations of the bodies*

The *Herald*

With a forced disregard for continuity, the State now called to the stand Everett Clutch. Unfortunately, the witness's mother had fallen ill, and he wished to travel to attend at her bedside. So Clutch, owner of a lunch-stand business on the north end of Quincy, came out of sequence to tell his part of the story. Jurors heard that he had served Ray at his lunch stand near Seventeenth and Broadway in Quincy on Wednesday night, September 25, of the fatal week.

The jury was quite familiar with such stands, which usually were a temporary wood frame building equipped with fly screens and both a walk-up window and a counter and stools inside for patrons. Most who came for the 5¢ or 10¢ meals picked them up at the small service window cut in the wall facing the sidewalk.

The term "lunch" was applied to any meal other than breakfast, dinner (served at noon), or supper and could be consumed at almost any hour of the day or night. Often lunch-stand business picked up late at night when country folks were facing the long drive home from the city. Ten to 11:00 p.m. was a prime time for a "lunch," but often it was eaten as late as 1:00 or 2:00 a.m. Generally, Clutch said, he closed before 2:00 a.m.

The State pointedly asked Clutch if anyone else had interviewed him about this timeline. In a preview of things to come, the opposing attorneys engaged in a heated exchange in front of a rapt jury and courtroom audience.

Wall: "State whether or not any inquiry—without stating what it was—had been made of you by anybody to ascertain whether or not Mr. Pfanschmidt had been there on the Friday night before the fire?"

The defense objected. The court asked: "What is the purpose of this question?"

"The purpose is to show that the defense had an interview with this man with reference to Mr. Pfanschmidt's whereabouts," Wall answered, and the defense objected to that statement being made in the presence of the jury.

"The jury will not pay any attention to that statement of counsel."[60] The judge overruled the objection and allowed that line of questioning to

---

[60] 30-5263, p. 1192.

be explored. Clutch testified that Lancaster interviewed him about an hour and a half before the sheriff had come to call.

The jury heard Clutch say that he did not know the defendant until that Wednesday, when Ray introduced himself as *the* "Dynamite Pfanschmidt" who had been written up in the papers. An article in the *Journal* on May 13, 1912, detailed a demonstration Ray held for Payson School students in which he blasted a tree stump to smithereens and scattered wooden bits over a far wider area than strictly necessary. The removal of large tree stumps with their stubborn root systems was long a problem in clearing new land to farm. Dynamite was one way to solve the problem. Ray seemed to have enjoyed the noise and the notoriety as much as the results.

Clutch was adamant that Ray was at his place at nearly 11:00 p.m. on both Tuesday and Wednesday and no other time. The defense suggested that it might have been other dates: Monday and Wednesday perhaps; or Wednesday and Friday. Clutch refused to agree, but his details were scanty. He could not tell the jury what Ray was wearing because, he admitted, the screen obscured his view. He was sure, however, that Ray wore a "stiff hat" on his head.

Clutch reported that they discussed the car parked in front of the Arcade Dance Hall just across the street from the stand, where the "Ellington Boys" were playing. Ray claimed to recognize the car as belonging to his cousin, Roy Pfanschmidt. Finally Clutch was dismissed to travel the twenty-five miles to be with his ailing mother. It would be days before the jury could come to see the pivotal difference made according to which evening Clutch served Ray.

Next to testify was Fred Pfanschmidt, the forty-year-old youngest brother of Charles, who appeared to choose his words very carefully. He and the jury were shown the drawing of the farm and asked about changes since the fire. Fred admitted to being a bit lost in describing where new posts had been set or where others were removed. He said simply, "When I get away from home I am not right on direction."

What the jury got from Fred was noncommittal testimony and body language that demonstrated a wish to be off the witness stand as quickly as possible. He was under the unforgiving glare from the prosecution table of C. C., his father, yet trying to support Ray. It was an extremely uncomfortable position. He managed to say nothing of substance.

Next to appear was neighbor John Lier, who lived about a quarter mile due north through the field as the crow flies. John Lier told of leaving Quincy at midnight on the fire Saturday, with a friend in a one-horse buggy. He traveled east on State Street and detoured as far as Forty-Eighth Street where he deposited his friend, Ernest Sturhahn. Then he turned south on what was called the Angle Road, until it connected back to the Payson Road, and let his horse navigate the familiar ten-mile route home while he dozed.

He was unsure what time it was when he reached his home. He roused himself to do the necessary stabling duties and only then noticed a strange red color in the sky near the Pfanschmidt farm. John Lier rushed through the dark fields and arrived to find his brothers Ben and Moritz already watching the horror, along with another neighbor, Henry Schreck.

When asked what they did there in the smoky darkness with only their bare hands, and the blaze consuming the home, Lier said simply, "We looked at it … and we wondered where the people were."

Shortly they roused themselves and began to take action. John Lier told of going to another neighboring home, the Schnellbeckers, to use the phone while his brothers began to look for a way to put water from the windmill tank onto the blaze.

Lier recounted that he had worked as a hired hand for Charles Pfanschmidt for about a week and a half just before the fire. He knew their horses—three work horses and one to pull the buggy—were all carefully tended. When Lier entered the barnyard, he found three horses in one barn and one in the other. All the hay mangers were bare of feed, and "Dick," the black horse, was so hungry that when Lier rattled the oats bucket he tried to climb over the manger at the front of the stall.[61] Lier said the horses were very excited and anxious to get to water.

He was asked about the milk cows and the necessary sunrise and sunset milking routine. Soon after calving, cows were separated from

---

[61] 30-5263, p. 1203.

their calves and milked by hand, with part of the milk reserved for human consumption. If their udders were not emptied twice a day, it became painful for the animals and they would stop producing milk. The Pfanschmidt cows were not in their accustomed place in the barn lot the morning of the fire. Where were they?

Eventually, the cows were trailed to the north end of the farm, having managed to escape to the literal lure of a greener pasture. Lier, over the objections of the defense, testified that the cows appeared not to have been milked at all on Saturday.

The jury was next diverted by a squabble over how much John Lier knew and would be allowed to say about the family provisions for sleeping space when company was coming. Lier explained that the two bedrooms upstairs were used differently at different times. The usual arrangement was for Charles and Mathilda to sleep together in a double bed in the east bedroom. The west bedroom held two beds and was occupied by Blanche when no one else was there. When a male visitor, usually Ray or C. C. came to visit, Mathilda would move across the hall, leaving Charles and the other man to share the double bed in the east room while the women would occupy the two beds in the west room.

When Lier admitted that the Pfanschmidts told him about the mutable sleeping arrangements and that he had not heard it from Ray himself, the defense objection was sustained and the jury instructed to disregard his statements.

Attorney Wolfe quizzed Lier about the locations of the bodies in the fire. Being a man of few words, his answers were sparse but graphic. He placed one body in the cellar beneath the east room and three bodies in the west room; one alone and two lying together. He told of them being badly burned, and when asked about the body lying alone in the west room, he said, "Why, the head was burned off pretty badly." He identified Blanche as one of the two bodies lying side by side, that were "not burned as bad."[62]

Next, Wolfe led the witness ahead in time to a point after Lier had found the cows and the bodies had been removed from the ruins. Lier

---

[62] 30-5263, p. 1208.

reported various tracks in the barn lot that had been protected by a makeshift fence of twine and boards plus one horseshoe print covered by an upturned wooden box. As he related it, Ray came from up near the burned house and told the former hired hand, "Any time you have a little time you can move that junk. They don't have any use for it." Lier thought that by "they" Ray meant the officers and began removing the barriers. He was, after all, accustomed to following Pfanschmidt orders.

The defense erupted into objections, and the court struck the answer identifying the unnamed "they" as an official or "officer." Undaunted, Wolfe deftly prompted Lier to tell how his fence-dismantling efforts were stopped by an actual police officer, Mr. Scharnhorst, who told Lier to replace the twine fence and leave the protection around the tracks.

This prolific witness, of few words, produced these opinions: the tracks were made by small horses, about the size of Ray's team. The buggy Ray drove was a "short turn, undercut, steel-tired" affair of relatively light weight. The farm had two gas or oil cans, one with a faucet at the bottom and one with a spout at the top. Lier said he saw two cans at the fire scene—one near the house and one somewhere out in the orchard. The one in the orchard was dented.

Wolfe asked innocently, "As if it had been run over by something?

"Yes, sir," was the answer, causing a strident defense objection. That answer was stricken from the record.

The State moved on to a discussion of the tools at the farm. Lier was asked about the sort of work he was hired to do, and related a standard litany of farm chores: he plowed corn, trimmed hedge and "builded [sic] some fence." He described a hand axe with a handle about eighteen inches long and a big blade, saying it was kept in the granary near the house when he worked there. Lier told of helping Scharnhorst hunt for the hand axe at the farm, as it was the only tool that seemed to be missing. And he told of taking a shovel several days later and turning over the ashes, with no result.

Wolfe asked about the axe found just the previous month in the ruins. Lier said he was with his brother, who had discovered it on the east side of the cellar under the ashes and sitting in some kind of jar. The axe handle had been burned away. He also mentioned a "spot" on the blade. By this point, the defense team was objecting to every phrase, seeking to have any mention of this axe removed from the record. The court allowed all the testimony to stand.

Wolfe smoothly progressed to another sort of sharp implement—the corn knife. A corn knife was a long-bladed, wooden-handled machete-type tool useful for a variety of tasks such as chopping weeds out of corn rows or cutting the corn stalks to use for feed or bedding. Lier recalled one such knife the family kept stuck in a butcher block at the chicken house and used to kill chickens. That knife was there at the time of the fire.

Wolfe asked about a conversation at the fire scene, when Ray asked if Lier or his brother had any whiskey with them. Lier said no, but his brother Ben went "down home" and fetched a bottle, which they "lay down" somewhere. Ray was informed of its location and took a drink—apparently only one, as far as Lier knew.

Lier testified that in the fire, bricks from the two chimneys had fallen on top of the tin roof. The tin remained intact, and they had to punch holes through it using a pitchfork, and then thread wire through the holes to pull away the hot metal. Wand supplied the wire, but Lier was not sure where it had come from.

Jurors got the picture that Lier was the helpful sort. He said that when Ray arrived at the fire scene driving his team of small sorrel horses with white markings on their faces, he tied them to a telephone pole out at the road. Lier later led the horses by a circuitous route to water and feed, carefully skirting all the buildings and avoiding the barn lot area where the mystery tracks were protected behind their flimsy barrier.

Prosecution attorney Wall questioned Lier about seeing the defense attorneys remove something from the ruins. Lier told a tale of watching one evening as Ray's lawyers toted off a wheat sack of the standard two bushel size that contained something with a long handle. Lier guessed it might have been an axe. Surprisingly, the defense table remained silent during this exchange about mysterious implements carried away, perhaps attempting to consign it to irrelevance by their lack of attention.

Then the venerable Govert rose to take a turn at the witness. He had Lier describe again the route he took home that Saturday night. They explored how rested the buggy horse was, how the temperature that night was cool—they agreed it was "crispy"—and how he met no one else on the road. Lier also said his usual travel time between the farm and town was about two hours. They explored the timeline for all the feedings and findings of livestock, agreed that Ben Lier finally milked the Pfanschmidt cows on Sunday evening, and agreed that Lier only took a good look at the tracks one evening after the fire when he was asked to examine them by Fred Pfanschmidt and Lancaster.

Lier recollected digging in the ashes on the west side of the house where he found a watch engraved with Mrs. Pfanschmidt's name, which he gave to the sheriff. He was asked, "Did you or your brother find two hammerheads with the handles burnt out that were taken by Mr. Lancaster and myself from the scene of the fire?" Lier: "Why, I don't remember seeing them there."

The defense had presented this answer for the contents of a wheat sack taken from the farm, if the jury could reconcile hammerheads lacking handles with the long shape originally noticed protruding from that sack.

The defense gathered steam. They asked about subsequent searches of the ruins. Lier testified that he and his brothers searched after the fire but could not seem to remember exactly when. One farm day can blend into another, as the routine is very much the same, but Lier seemed completely unattached and was unwilling or unable to assign timeframes to his actions.

Govert grilled him about the number of times detective Young was present and searched the farm, implying that Young had been there daily for almost a month. Yet oddly, nothing was found until March 1913, literally just days before the trial began.

In an incredulous tone of voice, Mr. Govert asked, "You found this ax on March 17th, is that the day?"

The witness replied, "Yes, Sir."

"Not October 17th?"

"No, Sir."

"You found the ax on the 17th of March of this year that is this present month, not last October?"

Lier replied again, "No."

The jury was left to speculate how something so important could have escaped discovery and been left lying in the open ruins for more than six months. Govert quickly moved on to plot the route over which Lier led Ray's team to water at the fire, and Lier admitted that he led the team as close as within seven or eight feet of the fenced-off tracks.

Govert returned to the wheat sack. Lier confessed that he had, for the defense lawyers, unlocked the granary where the tools were kept. In a detailed analysis of the tools stored there, Lier listed single-bitted and double-bitted axe heads. He saw a single red spot on one face of the double-bitted axe. Lier also remembered seeing the hammer heads in question but called one of them an old hatchet and the other a hammer with one flat face and one rounded one.

As a final point, Govert asked if Lier had ever seen Ray take a drink before. The answer came: "No, sir, I never knew of him drinking." Govert took his seat.

By this time Lier must surely have wanted to escape the confines of the stand, but the attorneys were not done with him yet. Wolfe was curious about where Lier found oats to feed to the horses. From the granary there in the barn, came the answer. Were there any other oats around? Mr. Wolfe inquired. Defense attorneys were immediately on their feet to object. This was not redirect examination, they said, but the court overruled them and the witness continued.

Lier recalled seeing some oats in bags, but he was not sure how many sacks were there. Wolfe tried to get the witness to say there was enough for a wagon load, but between objections and Lier's reluctance to commit to a number, the question was never answered. Lier finally admitted that he believed the number of bags would be shy of a full load.

The farmhand was then exhaustively led through questions designed to show that Miller's mule team tethered in the orchard could not and did not come any farther into the lane or approach the covered tracks. Then Lier was asked about finding door locks in the ruins. He admitted to finding the front door mechanism. It was locked, with the key in it, and Lier thought it was given to the sheriff.

Govert stepped up to modify the vision of a flaming house with a locked front door. "Was that front door kept locked from time to time?"

"Sometime it was, yes, sir."

Finally John Lier was allowed to step free of the witness stand.

Ben Lier, who admitted to being John's brother in a family of four boys and a father, was next. Ben agreed that the view of the Pfanschmidt home was obscured from his house, with only the barn and the chimney visible through the trees. He told of discing corn ground and hauling pumpkins on the day before the fire, but not seeing his neighbors.

He then told his story of being awakened by a light in the night, raising the alarm on the phone, and hurrying to the fire. Since no one was around, he assumed the family was not home when the fire broke out. Ben talked of calling Henry Geisel to see if the Pfanschmidts were in Quincy and then returning to form a bucket line to quench the flames. Ben noticed a buggy and a wagon standing in the barn lot, one inside and one outside the barn. That was when he realized the family must be still inside the burning house.

Ben Lier spoke in more graphic detail than his brother, of the bodies revealed in the ruins. The body in the cellar was "just the main part, the breast. The arms, legs, and head were gone." Of the single body in the west room, he said, "The head was burned away. We could just see that it was a head: one hand was burned off and the legs and feet were burned off." And he added that the two bodies lying side by side had some remnants of clothes covering them.

Ben's simple words held the full impact of the horror. In the courtroom heads bobbed when bare-headed gentlemen peered around ladies wearing hats and sent searching glances toward Ray, looking for some reaction.

Wolfe began to ask about other objects found in the ruins. Ben reported that about a week after the fire he searched and found a bank with some coins in it, eyeglass frames (but no lenses) that Mrs. P. wore, and some finger rings in the ashes of the west room. The coins in the bank had melted.

According to Ben, the axe, minus the handle, was found in a pile of broken crockery and jars in the cellar beneath the east room. As far as he knew, it belonged in the granary with the rest of the tools. He had noticed a couple of peculiar spots on the blade that looked like rust.

Then Ben was asked if he talked to Ray at the fire. "Just a very few words."

"What did you talk about?"

"Ray just asked me if I would stay with him. I just said yes." Ben believed Ray was asking if he'd take care of the place for Ray. Ben confirmed the whiskey story, saying he got a bottle, stashed it in the surrey, and told Ray where it was. When he looked for it later Sunday night, it was not there. He'd never known Ray to drink before.

Through this entire line of questioning, the judge offered helpful suggestions to the new state's attorney on how to rephrase a question that had called forth an objection. For example, when Wolfe posed the question, "Did Ray Pfanschmidt carry any water to help put out the fire at that time?" the defense objected, and the judge said, "Ask him what he did." The rewording became: "What did Ray, if anything, with reference to helping put out the fire after he got there?" And Lier answered: "Well, I seen him carry some water."

After another circuitous march through old territory about boards and tracks and other teams being watered, the witness was given to Lancaster for cross examination. The defense immediately questioned the timing of events. Ben agreed that he had been asleep a "good part of the night" before he was awakened and agreed that he never once looked at a timepiece between being awakened and dawn.

Lancaster and Lier discussed the degree of light and the visibility in the barnyard. Lier said he could see tracks but admitted he couldn't distinguish the different kinds.

Smoothly, Lancaster slipped in a statement: "You could not, as a matter of fact, tell whether they were big or little, nor whether they were buggy tracks, whether they were made by steel tires or rubber tires. Did you help to cover the tracks?"

The State let this pass.

Lancaster then tackled the axe in the cellar. Ben Lier said that they were "stirring in the ruins," hoping to find Emma's keys to the schoolhouse when he shoveled into the pile of crockery that once stored provisions, turning the pile upon itself. Lancaster suggested that it was "disarranged" to such an extent that, "You don't know whether the axe was upstairs and had fallen down into the cellar or not …"

"No," was the answer.

Having muddled the axe's original location, Lancaster got Ben to admit again that the axe was not found in the first searches; and if it had been in the ruins all that time, it was exposed to the weather and particularly the cold winter rain and snow.

The defense progressed to the topic of undercut buggies. These were the speedsters of the day, build to corner sharply, lighter than many buggies, with cutouts in the body that allowed the wheels to turn tighter; that made quite a stylish appearance. These buggies were not nearly as numerous as the more traditional styles and were noticeable for their unique silhouette.

Ben said, "I don't know of anybody that has got any that I know; I see quite a few going along the road."

Questions were asked in what seemed to be an entirely random order about the tracks, the weather, the whiskey, the road, the lack of mud. Wolfe, for the State, got another turn with Ben to clarify that brother John had come home from Quincy but had not been to bed before the fire was discovered.

Lancaster took another turn and asked about the uses for a hand axe, suggesting that it might have been in the house to cut up some meat, or to break up ice for the ice cream maker. Ben resisted such ideas. In his mind that old axe belonged in the granary, not the house.

Wolfe then tried asking Lier a question about other tools, but the defense objected. Wolfe offered to recall Lier, and the court said, "You can ask him a question; you don't have to recall him." So they revisited the corn knives. It was established that the granary and the smokehouse were always kept locked and the Liers had the keys. On another turn at cross-examination, Lancaster established that Ray had not been out to the farm since the fire. Finally, having been passed between prosecution and defense numerous times, this witness was excused. There were, however, still two Lier brothers to go.

Moritz Lier was called next. He spoke so quietly that the court was forced to admonish him to speak up. His contribution concerned the coal-oil lamp from the smoke house that was used to light the way to the barn lot to "hunt for tracks and see if anybody was there." He told of watching George and Fred Schnellbecker and John and Ed Wand take the lamp and follow the lane out toward the road.

In the midst of repetitious testimony, Moritz Lier related a short conversation he had with Ray down by the well. "I said to him, 'This was too bad,' and he said, 'Yes, it was too bad.' I asked him when he had seen the folks last, and he said 'Saturday.'"

"This was on Sunday that you had this conversation, was it not, it was on Sunday morning?" Wolfe's voice rose.

"I believe it was Sunday." Moritz seemed unsure.

"What Saturday did he say he saw them last?"

"I thought he meant a week before." Moritz's answer deflated the excitement.

The lawyer and witness then covered all the usual topics—tracks, gas cans, searching the ruins, axes. Moritz remembered Ray holding up a gasoline can and calling it to the attention of the sheriff. The State and the defense got into a shouted exchange about whether or not Moritz could testify about seeing a bucket of spoiled milk sitting next to the cream separator.

Govert climbed to his feet and attempted to establish that no one really knew what time all this happened. Moritz did remember talking to a man named Miller with a mule team who claimed to have been watching the flames ever since eleven o'clock. The State objected to this answer and had the testimony stricken from the record. It did not fit their theory to have the fire burning that early.

Moritz talked about searching the ruins "whenever we had a little time or come by there." By the time of the farm sale, the basement had gone from being almost level—full of debris—down to having only a few feet of bricks and such left in it. "We dug around in it every time we could go down there."

Govert asked politely, "That would be quite often?"

Moritz said, "Yes, sir."

Govert observed that whatever remained in that cellar had lain there "pretty thoroughly exposed" and proceeded to ask a question about the oil cans. Moritz seemed to remember seeing three of them. Shortly thereafter, Moritz was excused.

At this point court was adjourned for the day.[63]

The crowd scuffled into their woolen coats and scarves and headed out into the chill air to discuss what they had heard.

When the trial resumed on Wednesday, April 2, 1913, the *Herald* commented on the change in courtroom demeanor of the taciturn defendant. "Ray ... is assisting his attorneys in a material way, it would appear. He is in whispered consultation with them frequently and apparently makes suggestions as to the line of questioning to be followed out on the cross-examination, which are apparently followed by his attorneys. The boy really is looking better as the trial proceeds. There is more animation in his face, and less of the sullen, impassive, defiant attitude which characterized his conduct and appearance during the early stages of his trial."

The first prosecution witness to sit in the chair this day was Henry A. Gredel, a visitor to the scene on the Tuesday after the fire, who had been accompanied by his young niece. Gredel said that, as children do, she collected odd pieces that appealed to her, and one piece came to her uncle's notice. It was a small burned and warped square clock about six inches on a side, with an odd bit of wire wrapped around the hands. He turned the clock over to the sheriff a few days later.

Then the crowd stilled and straightened and shifted in their seats as the next name was called: Peter B. Lott. When asked to state his business, the fifty-year-old man said, "Police Business," and only after that admitted to the title of chief of police. Lott had ridden to the fire with Detective Scharnhorst in a "machine" driven by a young man named Hiedbreder from the State Street Bank. They parked the automobile at the road and walked into the farm through a large and ever-swelling crowd. Lott was escorted to the barnyard and shown the buggy tracks, which he confidently

---

[63] *Herald,* April 1, 1913.

judged to be fresh and made by steel tires on a short turning rig. He measured the distance between the wheel tracks with a piece of binder twine, held on the other end by Mr. Edwin Buerkin.

Lott saw only one undercut buggy at the fire scene, and it belonged to Ray. Comparing the length of string from the barnyard tracks to the space between the wheels of Ray's buggy, Lott determined they were a match. The defense objected, and a portion of his answer was stricken from the record. Then Lott said he took an additional piece of twine and measured the tracks again at a second point.

Wolfe asked the question again: "How did the string you measured the track with compare with the wheel on the buggy?"

After an overruled defense objection, Lott answered, "They correspond with the measurements of the wheels on the buggy."

With every question from the State, the defense leapt to its feet with objection and exception. Nevertheless, Lott claimed there was only a quarter to half inch difference between the twine cut to the length between the barnyard tracks and the wheels on Ray's buggy. Again, the judge helped the State rephrase questions into an allowable form, prompting, "Could you tell by looking at the wheels ..." Only once did the defense made an objection that was sustained.

Between interruptions, Lott testified that one wheel on Ray's buggy had a flattened spot due to the thinness of his steel rims. After many minutes of objections and rephrasing, Lott stated his belief that this dishing of the wheel would account for the small difference he observed in the measurements.

The sheriff testified that the hoof print in the barn lot was made by a hind foot that wore a horseshoe with a three quarter inch long bar, called an "interference calk," running lengthwise of the hoof. Some horses traveled in such a way that a hind hoof could overreach, striking and injuring a front foot or striking against the opposite leg, potentially laming the animal. A "calk" was an extra piece of iron added to a horseshoe that corrected this problem by limiting the foot's range of motion. Horseshoes often bore distinguishing marks, such as calks, nicks, cuts, or a shape that could, under the best circumstances, identify the track that an animal made.

Sheriff Lott said that after he noticed the misshapen track on the "off" side,[64] he examined Ray's team, which were in the barn, thanks to the attention of John Lier. Lott took the "off horse," cleaned its rear hoof, planted it on a brushed-off portion of the barn floor planking atop a sheet of paper, and traced around the hoof with a lead pencil. It was a match to the barnyard track. Both the twine and the piece of paper bearing the drawing were admitted into evidence for the State.

Lott also inspected a front shoe track from the "near horse" and compared it to fresh tracks from the near horse Ray had brought to the fire. They too were a match. This was damning evidence, for the likelihood that another pair of horses could produce tracks in that exact sequence was nearly impossible.

Lott told of being introduced by William Abel to Ray at the fire, who called Ray "my sister's son." The blunt sheriff asked, "You mean the one that burned?" The reply was affirmative.

Lott reported that Ray had followed him around and talked to him three or four times before they were introduced. The defense objected vehemently but was overruled. The sheriff testified that Ray showed him a "strange oil can" burned by the fire, which he picked up, waving it about at the end of a pitchfork. This particular can had a rather large dent on it.

According to Lott, Ray seemed "concerned," and had the appearance of being "tired." The defense was still interrupting with objections after every utterance, but they were all overruled. Having cast Ray as fatigued, the State now moved on to the condition of his horses. After three tries, Wall managed to get his question into acceptable form, and Lott was allowed to tell the jury that in his opinion, a drive of ten or fifteen miles, even at breakneck speed, could not account for the state in which he observed Ray's horses.

Lott's opinion was, "It hadn't ought to do it, no, sir."

Questions returned to the roundness of the buggy wheels, and this time the defense and the judge exchanged words. The bench got a trifle

---

[64] From the driver's seat, the "near" horse is hitched on the left, the "off" horse on the right.

testy when the defense objected to words spoken by the judge. At one point, Williams said to counsel, "Let my remarks stand. I was only explaining it. If you don't want me to explain myself or my ruling, I won't do it. I only wanted to make my ruling clear on this matter." Incessant interruptions and instructions as to what they might or might not consider was confusing for the jury.

At last, Govert squared his shoulders and addressed the sheriff. The sheriff admitted that the rain that Saturday night was light and not enough to create mud. By ten o'clock on Sunday morning the roads had returned to the same dusty state as before the little rain had created a thin top crust the night before. And there was a great deal of traffic coming and going along the Payson/Quincy road to the fire. The sheriff guessed at least five hundred people were at the scene by 10:00 a.m.

Now came some astounding news. After all the wrangling over the boxes and boards, Lott testified that the track he measured was *beside the box*, not under it. Indeed he never moved that box at all to see if there was another shoeprint beneath it. Nor was he sure what was under all those boards; he had never looked!

Govert pointed out that the pencil tracing Lott made of the horse's hoof seemed to have about four different lines on it that varied from each other by one quarter to half an inch. Lott explained in so many words that he had had to shift around to complete the circle, but all the lines were made that morning. The drawing was then cut from the paper with a pocket knife and laid over the tracks near the box for comparison.

There followed many more questions about locations of prints and tracks, and which ones Lott did or did not measure, which went on for long, dragging minutes. Then came questions about the measuring string. Was the twine stretched tight? And didn't twine have some elasticity inherent in it, with its loosely twisted construction? How was it marked to be cut? Did they hold their thumbnail there and then knot it as closely as possible?

"Yes," said Lott. "That is about the way it was done."

Lott saw the same dented oil can that Ray showed him the day of the fire still lying at the farm when he visited there the following week. He also rather grudgingly admitted that hard drives would affect horse teams differently. Finally Lott was excused.

The next to testify was a man pulled three hundred miles from his new residence in Chicago. He was Frank B. Weaver, a watchmaker who had worked at the O'Dell's Jewelry Store in Quincy during September 1912. O'Dell's was located at 168 North Fifth Street in Quincy and was a source for the beautiful things in life: fine jewelry, watches, sterling and plate silver, small art statues, candelabras, and serving pieces. The mosaic tile floor and high pressed tin ceiling created an atmosphere of hushed service. Clients entering the store drifted slowly down a center aisle flanked by ornate glass showcases containing treasures and topped by small bouquets of fresh flowers.

Weaver told of Ray coming in about eight fifteen on Saturday morning, September 28, 1912, with a broken double-case[65] pocket watch. His man's medium-sized gold pocket watch was missing the ring that attached it to its chain, the case was sprung, and the balance jewel was broken. The back bore the engraving "PHS[66] Ray Pfanschmidt," and a date. Ray told him of running over some wire that caught the watch and pulled from his pocket. Weaver had repaired this watch previously.

Weaver said he teased Ray about looking tired, and the boy answered something about working hard and staying up late. Weaver reported Ray was wearing a new-looking, clean khaki suit, although he was uncertain about the type of tie or hat.

Wall then handed Weaver the burned clock mechanism. Weaver said that arrangement of wires could not have happened accidentally caused the fire. He said those wires had been deliberately wound about the hands of what used to be an eight-day clock.[67] This particular arrangement of wires would have stopped the clock after it had run out about fifteen minutes.

---

[65] A double-cased watch has a covering on both sides—one over the watch face, another over the back, where frequently a picture would be placed.
[66] Payson High School.
[67] Meaning the clock could run for eight days without needing winding. Typically clocks were wound every Sunday.

On cross-examination, Govert pursued issue of Ray's attire. Under questioning, Weaver admitted that all he could say for sure was that Ray had on a khaki jacket. He could not tell the type of pants or shirt or hat or tie or overcoat or raincoat.

But what about that burned clock? Govert ascertained from Weaver that the piece of wire wound about the two clock hands was the wire that would have connected the clock to its alarm. Further, the glass dome that covered the clock face would have been removed before any such wrapping could occur. This twisting of wire, according to Weaver, was made prior to the fire because there was no break in the wire's ash coating that would have happened had it been done after burning. What Weaver could not tell was whether the clock was operating when this was done. That distinction would be a crucial difference. Govert let Weaver off the stand, no doubt disappointed that his testimony denied that the wire-wrapped clock was contrived by the fire.

That evening's *Journal* headline read, "Police Chief Lott Connects Pfanschmidt with Murder of Relatives and School Teacher." Choosing amid all the day's testimony, the paper highlighted the clockworks and wires with the boldface question: "Had Arranged Explosion?"

When Wall called undertaker Hermann Stoermer, the mood in the courtroom deepened again; feet shuffled as bodies shifted. Stoermer told of arriving at the fire while the bodies were still lying in the ashes. He helped remove all four of them to the yard and wrapped them in sheets until Mr. Freiberg arrived with his ambulance and they were loaded for transport. By the time the bodies arrived in Quincy, nearly twelve hours had passed since the fire was discovered.

Stoermer's disturbing contribution was the observation that the pillows and mattress portions under the bodies were "pretty badly soaked with blood." Over defense objections, the court allowed this testimony to stand.

Stoermer seemed extremely reluctant to commit to any other details and even vacillated over the amount of blood on the bedding, debating the meaning of "saturated." "I didn't examine it ... it was more like glancing at it." He sounded oddly uncomfortable on the stand and dodged offering a definitive opinion on whether or not a person would bleed after death. It was his business to bury people, not offend them by his opinions.

The defense, of course, moved to strike all his testimony. The court declined.

Then Lancaster arose for the defense and Stoermer seemed much more willing to answer questions. He agreed with Lancaster that he did not mean to say it was blood on the pillow. In fact, Stoermer admitted that he did not even know how to test for the presence of blood. But when prompted, he offered the opinion that a dead body could bleed steadily and profusely from its veins after death. He also described the bodies' journey to town as "just rolled in a piece of canvas" and jolted and jostled about for the ten miles to Quincy. It seemed a callous statement.

The State called to the stand Dr. Thomas B. Knox, physician of eleven years standing in Quincy. He was the first in a procession of medical witnesses. Dr. Knox had been asked by City Physician, Dr. Collins, to attend the autopsy. He recited the roster of those present: Dr. Center; Dr. Erickson; Dr. Collins; George Koch; Joe Freiburg; John Gilmer; and Emil Kaempen, and his father, Charles.

Knox described the bodies in striking detail, first stating that three were female but the gender of the partial body was impossible to determine. The examiners began with the body of the Pfanschmidt daughter, Blanche. Knox reported that her feet and hands were completely burned off just below the knees and elbows. The top and one side of her head were completely destroyed, but her hair was pretty well preserved on the back of the head, hanging in two large braids. Some portions of her face remained, but her nose and skin were burned off. A large gold filling in her front tooth survived but less than half of her skull remained.

Gasps and soft sighs rose from courtroom listeners as Knox said, "The body was so thoroughly cooked or baked … absolutely nothing … you could not tell anything about it. The moment we started to open it, it was still steaming."[68] The bodies had been left as fragile as eggshell by the fire.

---

[68] 30-5263, p. 1352.

When Wall asked Dr. Knox about a substance found on the two or three pillows from the autopsy, an ensuing defense objection was immediately sustained. Undertaker Stoermer had mentioned a single pillow—not two or three. No prior testimony had tied multiple pillows to the bodies, so for now, Wall moved on to the clothing, where he had better luck. Dr. Knox identified a swatch he cut from the nightgown and undershirt at the autopsy.

The counsels progressed to arguing about the number of mattresses examined. Finally Dr. Knox managed to state on record, "The surface of the ticking was stained with blood, and on opening it, the blood had soaked through to a considerable extent." This opened a crucial topic: Had the victims been killed by the fire or before it?

Wall needed a clear statement and asked, "State to the jury whether a body that has been burned will bleed after death."

Knox said firmly, "It will not!"

Objections flew from Govert and Lancaster. The judge and Wall "conferred together in the absence of the jury," and the court struck that testimony.

Wall regrouped but again encountered an objection. The judge asked Knox directly, "Could you tell from the circumstances indicated at that time whether [the blood] came from these bodies before or after they were burned?"

Dr. Knox answered, "Yes." And the court overruled the defense again.[69] Then, since a discrepancy did remain concerning the bedding, the court struck all this testimony concerning bleeding before death. The courtroom and the jury had now heard a considerable amount of disallowed testimony. As the battle for Ray's life went on spectators were engrossed, but the grisly testimony was interrupted for lunch recess.

When court resumed, Joe Lipps, the sheriff of Adams County strolled to the witness stand. Wall inquired about the number of pillows and mattresses he saw at the autopsy. Sheriff Lipps replied there were two mattresses and one pillow.

---

[69]  30-5263, p. 1358.

"What," asked Wall, "was upon those mattresses and pillow, if anything?"

"Bloodstains," answered Lipps flatly from beneath his bushy moustache.

Thus, Lipps solved the problem and tied two mattresses and one pillow from the fire scene to the autopsy room. The court allowed him to identify the stains as "blood" over strenuous and repeated defense objections. Lipps stated firmly that the mattress holding the two bodies seemed saturated halfway through its depth and across its whole width.

After this damaging testimony, Lipps left the stand without facing any cross-examination. The defense would wait to tackle this witness.

When the State recalled Dr. Thomas Knox, the judge intervened to ask a further question of Lipps about the identification of the mattress; then he asked Dr. Knox if he had an opinion on the subject of blood flowing from the bodies before or after they were burned.

The defense objected, but the court ruled in favor of its own question, and Dr. Knox once again was allowed to say, "The blood flowed from those bodies before they were burned!"

The prosecution probed across case boundaries when Wall asked the doctor this question: "Assuming the body, which had been pointed out to you as the body of the Pfanschmidt girl, had received a wound similar to what was found on the Kaempen girl at that place, state whether or not there was enough of her skull left to have any evidence of that wound."

Outraged defense attorneys voiced objections.

The judge asked: "Is it your position that you can only go into the condition of the one body?"

"Yes, sir," was the unequivocal reply.

Wall fired back. "We claim we can go into all of it for a good many reasons."

The court agreed, "I am inclined to think you can too. The objection will be overruled."

So the courtroom and the jury were allowed to consider the mortal wounds inflicted upon the second body on that bloody mattress, the young school teacher, Emma Kaempen. But Emma's death was not the basis for this trial. Here Ray was facing charges of murdering that other young woman on the mattress—his sister, Blanche.

With the ruling against the defense, testimony was allowed to proceed detailing the wounds on Kaempen. Knox said, "That body had received—there was a fracture of the skull over the left eye, also a fracture of the superior maxillary or upper bone of the mouth; the mouth or teeth were all loose on that side of the mouth; the mouth and throat were full of dried blood."[70]

The defense repeated: "We object to any description of any wound on anybody outside of the person's body for which this suit is brought." But the stating of this objection after each question and each answer was for naught; the court overruled them all.

Knox described one wound on the teacher's skull running from front to back beginning above the left eye, and penetrating the skull for more than an inch. He would not speculate about other wounds as the remainder of the skull was missing. In his opinion, the damage could have been caused by a sharp instrument like a hand axe. This body, as did the other, wore a nightgown and undershirt, and some parts of her stockings also clung to her feet.

At this point the court lost patience with the continuous defense interruptions. The judge requested that the record show that the defense objected, and that the "Court permits this line of examination over the objection and exception of counsel for Defendant."

To which ruling of the court, the defendant by his counsel, then and there excepted.

The thrust and counterthrust of words continued: question, objection, overruled; answer, objection, overruled. It was likely that the jury simply tuned out the attorneys and listened to the witness. Dr. Knox testified about all the pieces of garments collected from the three women. The fourth victim was also mentioned, as one sample of material was obtained from that body. All that remained from it was a sad piece of hickory shirting about the size of a palm.

---

[70] 30-5263, p. 1367.

Finally, Govert got his turn at the witness. He tried various scenarios to get Knox to say that blood might flow from a burned body after death, but with little luck. "Suppose [a body] were cut across the head ten or fifteen minutes after death, would the cut across the head bleed?"

"No, sir," said Dr. Knox.

Govert asked and reasked the same question with slightly altered wording, until an exasperated Dr. Knox answered: "Either I don't understand you, or you don't understand me."

Govert concluded with a final question about the body of Blanche: "Was there any evidence of violence on that body at all?"

"No," came the reluctant answer.

Wall, on redirect and after more verbal maneuverings, ascertained that Dr. Knox believed that the large amount of blood found on the mattress had to have come from wounds prior to death. So the subject of blistering arose: a living body will blister, a dead body will not, according to Knox. There were no blisters on the unburned portions of the body identified as Blanche.

Next the bailiff called to the stand Dr. H. O. Collins, city physician for Quincy, thirty-nine years old. Once again, the listeners revisited the grim autopsy tables, this time paying special attention to the corpse with the wound over one eye. Even the defense was tired by now, and restated, without shouting, their objection to the entire line of questioning concerning a body not the focus of this trial.

Wall, referring to Blanche, asked, "Assuming that the body with the long, light hair and the prominent teeth that you spoke of had received a wound of that same character, state whether or not there was enough of the skull or head of that body left to show that kind of a wound."

Govert, eyes flashing, jumped to his feet in objection. The court in rare agreement, said, "I do not believe you are warranted in that assumption."

"What assumption do you refer to, Your Honor?" asked Wall.

Judge Williams replied curtly, "The assumption that it received identically the same sort of wound as was found on the other body."

"Take the witness." Wall left it for now.

"We do not care to cross-examine him," was Govert's reply.

Following the doctor, Fred Pfanschmidt, administrator of his brother's estate, delivered testimony of a more personal vein. Fred spoke of his brother as "Charley."

Holding their position that the bodies had not been identified, the defense objected when Fred was asked how old his brother was when he died. "We object to the question, if the court please, it not appearing that Mr. Pfanschmidt is dead."

Exasperated, the judge replied, "I think the jury are as much in a position to say whether that was the family as this witness. I presume he came to that conclusion formed by the surrounding circumstances that that was the family. Are not the jurors in a position to draw that same conclusion as much as he is? The objection will be sustained, and the answer will be stricken."

Wall probed about life insurance policies. Charles had two, one for $2,000 another for $3,000; and Ray's mother held one for $1,000. Fred reported that he had made a claim for payment of these policies and that he had acted as guardian for the defendant until Ray reached his majority on his twenty-first birthday.

Fred described the farm as about 133 acres and estimated the cultivated portions could bring $90 an acre. He thought the machinery and livestock were worth about $3,400, and, in addition, the Payson Mutual Insurance held a policy on the home. The grief-stricken Pfanschmidt was then excused from the stand.

Then it was Dr. Charles Erickson's turn to testify. He had practiced eight years in Quincy and was thirty-three years old. After the usual initial questions Erickson was asked how much blood was on the mattress. He replied simply, "Quite a lot of it; profuse."

The defense took exception to the fact that no testimony had been given to show that the two bodies at the undertaker's premises were associated with, and lying on, the *same* mattress upon which they were found. Ray's trio of attorneys was masterful at revealing each technical flaw in the prosecution's case.

Dr. Erickson mentioned additional wounds to the body of the schoolteacher. He reported that two of her teeth were loosened and there appeared to be a wound at the top part of her mouth near the nose. He said this wound to the head, "...extended through the bone, to the table of the skull, through the table of the skull; it was a deep incised fracture of the bone over the eye."

"What did it penetrate, if anything?"

"It penetrated the skin and bone and went through the bone to the membranes of the brain."

In Dr. Erickson's opinion, the wound over the eye was made by a sharp blade and the wound to the mouth, by a blunt instrument. The courtroom murmured at talk of two weapons. The nature of the murder became a degree more horrible; two weapons could mean two assailants. Fear sharpened glances cast toward the defense table.

Dr. Erickson in a calm voice said that a dead body will bleed only until the vein that was severed is emptied or the blood had coagulated. Wall asked if temperature affected coagulating blood. Dr. Erickson replied, "It will coagulate quicker when the temperature is higher."[71]

Govert stood before the doctor and explored the confusion caused from water being thrown over the mattress while fighting the fire. "Now then, after the blood had flowed down under a body and water was thrown on there, could you determine by examination of the mattress afterwards, what kind of blood had been there on that mattress?"

"No, sir."

Govert persevered, "The blood and water would unite and form a solid mat of the feathers in the mattress, so you could not tell just how much was blood and how much was water?"

Dr. Erickson replied, "No, I don't think I could."

The tenacious Govert tried again to get some testimony into the record saying a dead body could still bleed after death, even if some portion was burned. Dr. Erickson granted only some "oozing" but not a hemorrhage. Finally the witness was excused.

The next witness shifted focus from gruesome wounds to fascinating family dynamics when the patriarch of the clan was called. Charles C.

---

[71]  30-5263, p. 1410.

Pfanschmidt, an aging, white-haired man with the hard stare of his uncompromising German heritage and the unshakable conviction that his grandson was guilty, rose and took the stand. Shoulders jostled as the packed courtroom audience leaned forward.

His eighty-two years and recent sorrow had left him bowed, but his will and authority were a force to be reckoned with. "With a resonant voice that could be heard very plainly in all portions of the room, the aged grandparent told in a remarkably clear manner for a man of his age of several things that happened prior to and just after the death of his son ..."[72]

Another paper described the same scene very differently. "Mr. Pfanschmidt came from his sick bed, where he has been confined for several days with winter cholera. He was very weak, and his physicians declare that his condition is serious. The old gentleman, realizing this fact and in view of his age, he might perhaps be unable to rise again from his sick bed during the trial, insisted upon giving whatever evidence he could and so rather out of his turn, he was placed on the stand and testified ..."[73]

In a respectful tone, Wall began with the happy occasion when C. C. stayed with his son to attend the Payson Picnic. The 19th Annual Old Settlers Picnic was held in the village on August 25, 1912. It was billed, and rightly so, as the greatest event of its kind in Adams County. The governor of Illinois, Charles Deneen, spoke in the afternoon, but the festivities had begun at 10:00 a.m. with a parade of decorated automobiles and horse-drawn carriages and wagons. The Fifth Regiment Band from Quincy provided a concert, and an exciting hot-air balloon and parachute leap were other highlights of the day.[74]

C. C. recounted the placement of beds during his stay, agreeing with previous testimony. He added that the stairway ascended from the south, beginning near the front door. Both bedroom doors opened into the rooms from a small landing, which had a window facing south. Because of the stairway, the east bedroom was about three feet smaller than the west

---

[72] *Journal*, April 2, 1912.
[73] *Herald*, April 2, 1912.
[74] *Whig*, August 22, 1912; *Journal*, August 30, 1912.

room. Each bedroom had two windows facing the Payson/Quincy road, opening above the front-porch roof.

Outside, a brick walk circled the house. The front door separated four windows and opened into a little hall that divided the east room from the west room. The east room downstairs had a side window, and a chimney and a doorway to a summer kitchen that sat off to the north. There was a storage closet tucked into the stairway wall. C. C. described a shelf between the front windows that held "a clock on the centre of it and some knickknacks on each side." It was, he added, "just what you would call a farmer's clock ..." C. C. recounted that this east room functioned as a parlor or sitting room, and in the winter was also used for a kitchen where they would eat and cook.

A summer kitchen was built off the north side of the house behind the east room.[75] It had one interior doorway access from the main sitting/dining/kitchen room and one outside door facing east that opened onto a porch running along the entire east-facing length of the farmhouse. This single story summer kitchen had the only north-facing window in the home, plus a second window on its west wall. The room held two stoves, one hooked up to a chimney, the other a gasoline stove. The summer kitchen itself was not above the cellar but sat on a rock foundation. The cellar, which could only be accessed from doors outside the building, extended only under the east room. C. C. also confirmed "Charley" had a little round alarm clock that he kept upstairs in his bedroom, and Blanche had a gold front tooth.

C. C. was asked about Saturday night, September 28, just before the fire. His daughter and son-in-law, Walter Herr, had arrived on the four o'clock train from Wichita, Kansas, and many family members had come to visit, Ray among them. Both C. C. and Uncle Walter were teasing Ray about having on a new suit with a new shirt and tie too. Ray had admitted to purchasing several.

Wall asked, in the crucial details over what Ray was wearing and when, "State whether or not in that conversation in your house, Ray Pfanschmidt

---

[75] A summer kitchen was used for cooking in warm weather to isolate the heat from the house and to help prevent fires. In winter, cooking was done in the main part of the home to capture the additional heat.

at any time said to anybody anything about having missed a suit of clothes that belonged to him."

"No, sir, he did not."

The import of this question would later become apparent to the jury.

C. C. testified that Ray came also on the previous Sunday, September 22, and put his team in the stable off the alley behind his grandfather's home. He left the horses there, and his grandfather fed and watered them twice that day. At some point, C. C. looked into Ray's buggy and saw under a lap robe a revolver belt full of cartridges, but the holster was empty.

When Ray eventually returned to collect the team, his grandfather testified, "I didn't say anything to him at that time at all ... but I looked at him strong in his eye."

C. C. related a conversation from the following evening, Monday, September 23. "'Ray, I understand you are going into the auto business too.' He said, 'Yes, there is lots of money in that.' I said, 'Yes, with you it is always money, money, money.'"

The defense objected energetically at these words. Wall argued that it showed motive, but the court sustained the objection and ordered the statement stricken. The State took exception and circled around to have C. C. testify: "I told Ray there myself that evening—says I, 'Ray,' just this way, 'You are going to the dogs and you are going damn fast.'"

To which the court said, "That may be stricken. This objection will be sustained and that answer will be stricken and the jury will pay no attention whatsoever to that answer. Do you understand me, gentlemen? You will not pay any attention to that statement whatever." The jury indicated that they understood the court's directions, but the grandfather's emotional words lingered in the courtroom.

The State asked C. C. if he mentioned the McNamara's to Ray. To which C. C. proudly stated, "I said, 'You are going exactly where them dynamiters out in California are.'" This statement the court allowed into evidence.

Then, in an apparent reversal, the judge threw out all of the grandfather's testimony, beginning with the finding of the gun belt. He remonstrated with the State that they were not following the line of examination that was originally indicated. Chastened, Wall dutifully returned C. C. to consideration of the drawing of the burned farmhouse. In all of this, the mention of a lap robe in Ray's buggy faded, and its very existence would later be denied by Ray.

Govert, on cross, proceeded to illustrate that the eighty-two-year-old man could not state exactly, in feet and inches, the dimensions of the farmhouse rooms or the exact location of the windows. Otherwise, he made little headway and soon excused the formidable patriarch.

Shortly before five o'clock, Wolfe, for the State, began to examine Dr. Charles D. Center, a Quincy physician of nineteen years' standing, engaged in the practice of medicine and surgery. He took the jury back to the autopsy tables.

Dr. Center negotiated the one-braid, two-braid body identification over the ever-present objections by the defense. His presentation was more technical in tone than the previous physicians'—using vocabulary like "the anterior portion" and the "abdominal wall" and speaking more precisely about the wounds on the teacher's body. "One over the left eye and one on the right side of the head, approximately at the junction of the hairline with the skin of the forehead."[76]

"The wound over the left eye was of force sufficient to have produced a fracture of the skull, but in producing that fracture, it had also sheared off a protruding ridge of bone overhanging the eye. The wound on the right side and top of the head was a clean cut wound through both tables of the skull."

Dr. Center explained that he could not measure the entire length of the wound because the skin was burned away, but the cut in the bone was a "true cut and was probably an inch and a quarter or an inch and a half in length with a fracture extending from the termination of the cut further along the bone."

This wound certainly would have been fatal, according to Dr. Center.

The two sides spent many long minutes debating if the doctor could testify that the wounds were not *self*-inflicted. Eventually Center stated, in

---

[76] 30-5263, p. 1437.

so many words, that he did not believe the woman struck herself in her own head. Naturally, counsel for defense objected strenuously. It was unlikely that anyone in the room believed that Emma had gone mad, killed the others, set the fire, wounded herself with an axe, and laid down to die.

A vociferous verbal brawl ensued next about whether or not the doctor could testify about his opinion on the position of the victim when the wounds were inflicted and if she had been standing, lying, or sitting. The defense was somewhat mollified when the verb employed in the question was changed from "inflicted," to wounds "received." Eventually the doctor stated that Emma could have been struck while in the same position in which she was discovered.

Then the State asked the witness about the position of the assailant as demonstrated by the direction of the blows. Dr. Center said, "The wound in the upper right side of the head was received from the front, in my opinion; the wound over the left eye was received from the front and to the left of the individual receiving it, in my opinion."[77] Murmurs could be heard from the press table in the hushed courtroom. Had this young woman faced her attacker? Could that young man at the defense table have stared her down, axe in hand?

Dr. Center agreed Emma had died before the fire. He saw no blisters on the unburned skin and stated that, in his considered opinion, a body would not blister after being dead at least six hours.

"What becomes of the blood in circulation of the body after death?"

Dr. Center told the prosecutor, "All that can do so leaves the surface of the body and goes to the deeper organs."

Over continuous defense objections, Dr. Center said that the amount of bleeding after death could vary. "The condition of that pillow was of interest to me because I wanted to satisfy my own mind about the quantity of blood that had been spilled on that pillow, and knowing that feathers did not take up liquids well, I went into the pillow to see how deeply the feathers had been saturated."

"How far down in the pillow did you find any blood?"

---

[77] 30-5263, p. 1445.

"I don't think I could give any linear distance; the depth of that saturation is about the only answer I could make to it, I will say one-third of an inch of the feathers were saturated."

Asked if the person resting on that pillow bled from a wound before or after death, he stated simply, "From a wound before death."

A short time later the defense declined to cross-examine the witness. Dr. Center left the stand.

Continuing their disjointed presentation and fractured timeline, the State called Henry Schreck, a farmer who lived "west, but a little bit north" of the Pfanschmidts. He was a neighbor to the Kaufmans and was awakened by the telephone alarm the night of the fire. He presented testimony as someone who had looked at a clock. Schreck said it was "ten minutes after two," and the house was practically down.[78] "The highest part was about, oh, say, half as high as it ought to have been; on the northwest corner, there was one pole as high as that corner of the building ..."

He recounted the list of arrivals, the firefighting efforts, and the buggy tracks. "They came in and turned around ... they went the way a man would drive from the Pfanschmidt home to Quincy, that is if he was going the nearest way." According to Schreck, Fred Schnellbecker and Ed Wand had discovered the tracks. He said the tracks were fresh and left by a steel-tired buggy.

When his turn came, Lancaster attempted to confuse the issue of the size of the horse tracks: "[Is] there not as much difference in the size of the feet of horses of the same size as of people of the same size in the size of their feet, is that not true?" Schreck admitted that might be so but stood firm that the wheel tracks were made by steel tires: "at a guess, a three-quarter-inch tire."

This witness was dismissed, and court was recessed for the day.

---

[78] 30-5263, p. 1455.

# Chapter 15

# Forensic Evidence

## Wednesday, April 2, 1913

Day three of testimony began with fifty-nine-year-old John Wand,[79] described by the *Herald* as an "intelligent German farmer." He began by relating how he and his son, Edward, reached the blaze a bit after 2:00 a.m., finding the northwest corner of the house about six-feet high with some pieces of siding still in place. He told the familiar story of the fire and finding the tracks.

Then things became more complicated. Wand saw several sets of tracks. One set was made by Gus Kaufman, returning after the rain shower; one was Geisel's buggy, and the other was the mystery buggy. "There was one coming south that was the first track, then there was a track coming from the north, what I call from Quincy; of course that track went into the Pfanschmidt yard and that track came out again right in the same wheel marks, of course the track again would come south. Then there was another track made by the mule team that was farther north; then Mr. Geisel, he came and crossed that with a rubber-tired buggy, and he run pretty close to the track coming from Quincy."

---

[79] 30-5263, p. 1467.

Here at last was a witness who had seen the mystery buggy wheel marks next to a track made by a rubber-tired buggy.[80]

The State brought out a map of the barn lot. Wand's finger traced the route. "When it came in it drove in and turned right around ... towards the south. It made a turn over where the granary is here and then went south out to the main road." The farmer observed, "Well, there was one shoe on the horse, which had kind of weight on it and bent out; and the track of the shoe had a mark on it, and I took a box and covered that up."

Wand had also watched Ray. "I seen him go down to the barn lot and look at those tracks, and then he was walking around about the barn looking about whether he could see tracks; he was looking for something."

When the prosecutor inquired: "How did he appear with reference to being emotional, sad or otherwise?" Ray's counsel objected, reminding the jury, "People are not all of the same nature; some people are not emotional." But the neighbor was allowed to answer. "He did not seem to mind anything."

On cross, Lancaster questioned Wand and reminded the jury that water from the firefighting efforts thrown into the areas where the bodies were discovered made the quantity of blood appear more plentiful. Then questions moved on to those tracks in the barnyard.

"Did I understand you that the tracks didn't stop at all from the time it entered the lane at the road and went through the lot, back down the lane, back to the road?"

"It did not stop at all."

"You could see that it stopped on the grass right by the house as far as you could tell by the tracks?" Lancaster pressed the witness.

"They didn't tie unless they tied out away from the hitching post; it might have stopped right beside the house."

"Did it?"

"I said it might."

"What is your best judgment?"

---

[80] While it was obvious to those testifying in 1913, it is worth noting for today's automobile driver that direction was apparent from the orientation of the hoof prints left by the horses pulling the buggy.

"I don't know."

"Is there a post there?"

"Yes, sir."

"Did the horses go to the post at all?"

"No, sir."

"They stayed right in the lane, did they?"

"No, sir, they turned out a little."

"Did they stop there?"

"I could not tell."

Unsatisfied, but forced to leave the issue open, Lancaster turned to questions about Ray helping to preserve evidence. Oddly, the lawyer implied that Wand had previously said that Ray, himself, covered the track, but now under oath, Wand denied it. On the map, Wand pointed out where the shoe marks he covered had been found, on a straight line as the tracks entered the barn lot, and not from where the buggy tracks curved into circles.[81]

After more wrangling, Wand was let off the stand. Reluctantly his son took his place. Edward Wand was thirty-two and lived with his father. As he recounted the well-known litany of helplessly watching the fire, it seemed that what was first heard as powerful tragic testimony was slowly becoming commonplace by virtue of repetition. The horror was leaching away.

Edward spoke of going to the barn when the firefighting finally began and noticing tracks in the early predawn light. He reported his finds to Geisel, and they began to investigate.

Confused by the questions, and not helped at all by the court's attempts to clarify things, Ed testified that there were four vehicles in and out but that only one set of tracks went as far as the barn lot. He agreed about the steel buggy tires and the freshness of the tracks.[82]

Lancaster then took a spin at Ed Wand and got him to admit that he saw nothing odd or unusual in the shape of the tracks. Lancaster also quizzed this witness about changing his testimony, implying that Wand

---

[81]  End of roll 30-5263.
[82]  30-5264, p. 12.

previously said he could not tell the type of tire by looking at its tracks. Ed Wand corrected the attorney, explaining that at that particular time, he simply *refused* to give an answer.

Wall asked a convoluted question to clarify things. "At the time you answered Mr. Lancaster with reference to this conversation on February 13th and you stated down there that you would not say that, did you know at that time that he was representing the Defendant, Ray Pfanschmidt?"

"Yes, sir, I did," Ed Wand firmly replied.

"What did you mean when you said that you would not say that—did you mean that you would not talk to him about the case?"

"I meant that I would not give him any information."[83]

It was clear. Ed Wand would only answer any given question for a single set of lawyers. If he had told one side, he would refuse to answer the same question for the other side.

After he was excused, a ten-minute recess was called. The obstinate witness left, head scratching, shuffles, and amused throat clearing in his wake.

Abandoning the tracks and the fire, the prosecution next called Clark Hubbard, and the story circled back to the bloody clothes. Hubbard worked for Joe Freze, who lived just north of the Quincy city limits, and said he knew Ray and the layout of Ray's camp.

Finally, Hubbard tackled a job he had been putting off for about a month: replacing the outhouse. Frese, being a well-to-do man, had in his outhouse three holes: two of adult height (eighteen inches off the floor) and a shorter one for children (ten inches tall), each one being about twelve inches in diameter. During the demolition process, when Hubbard tipped over the building, he found a suit of clothes pushed up under the floor boards and positioned so they were hidden from view of anyone using the facilities.

Then the trial ventured further into the sometimes garbled but critical record of Ray's attire. In describing the clothes that Ray usually wore, Hubbard said, "Well, it was a yellow suit. Something resembling yellow. Yellow overalls of stuff called khaki suit. A suit and shirt and over jacket,

---

83  30-5264, p. 15.

overalls. That's as near as I can describe it … he always wore a tie, as well as I remember … Well, it was a kind of purple-red. I couldn't describe the color exactly."[84]

His story continued. "When I turned this vault over there was a gentleman working with me, and he took a stick and began to ask questions and punch around the clothes. I told him to let them alone …" Hubbard notified Frese, who called the sheriff. Meanwhile, men from the work site—Ben Holeman, Lee Wiemelt, Willis Seehorn, Gus Hutmacher, and some others—gathered at the discovery.

Who did he think the suit belonged to? "It resembles the suit I saw Ray Pfanschmidt wear all the time that he was there," Hubbard replied. The defense moved to strike this vague statement, and the court sustained the motion.

Wall rephrased this question several ways until it reached a form the court allowed, and Hubbard reiterated, "Well, I said at the time that it was, and I still have the same opinion." Lancaster again objected but the court agreed to strike only the words, "I said at the time that it was." Wall persisted, "What I want is, state whether or not, in your best judgment, that was Ray Pfanschmidt's suit you got out of the vault that morning."

"Yes, sir."

Despite disallowed testimony, the jury had now heard this man say four times that the suit from the vault belonged to Ray.

Paper—part wrapping paper and part newspaper—had been found lying beneath the suit and was caught on a nail and pulled free when he overturned the vault. Hubbard did not know which newspaper was the source, but parts of that paper were given to private detective Young.

How many suits had he seen Ray wear? Govert inquired of the workman.

"I saw him wear one suit at a time," came the phlegmatic reply.

To the probing Govert, Hubbard admitted that he did not know how many suits Ray owned; that he didn't examine Ray's appearance closely before the fire; that he couldn't actually tell one set of identical suits from

---

[84] 30-5264, p. 19.

another; and that he did not notice any badges or buttons or marks on the clothes Ray had worn on Friday. But then Hubbard said he saw Ray on that Saturday afternoon before the fire, wearing a gray overcoat and a stiff hat, which was an oddity for Ray. Hubbard could not say what Ray wore under the coat.

"Were those garments scattered out on the surface?" Govert wanted more details of Hubbard's find.

"They were in a string. They were not in a bundle. They were laid out loose.… I saw three pieces. There may have been more, I don't know … a shirt, a blouse, and overalls. A blouse or jacket. I don't know which you might call it." The clothes were on top of the surface and stained but not wet.

Hubbard described for Wall the layout of Freze's property. The vault in question was about one hundred yards north of the railroad track, about one hundred yards from Ray's tent, and about forty yards from the wagon shed. Govert on his next turn at questioning established that this outhouse was a mere thirty feet from the Freze home and store because it was reserved for the use of the family. Hubbard was excused.

The bearer of the bloodied clothing, Sheriff Joseph Lipps, returned. Sheriff Lipps admitted to Wall that some pieces had been cut from the garments.

"Will you look," asked counsel for the State, "at the coat and show me what portions that you say have been cut out?"

The defense thundered to its feet in protest at the display of these garments to the jury, but the court overruled them. Lipps explained that, prior to this trial, the clothes were taken to Chicago for testing, where about eight pieces were separated by Dr. Hektoen. Others were cut out for analysis in both Urbana and in Springfield, Illinois. Pieces of the bloody mattress and pillow from under the two women's bodies were also removed for testing. The jury listened to a description of clothes soaked in urine and dirtied by some fecal matter. "The pants were turned inside out and the outside of them were not soiled," the sheriff assured the jury.

Wall asked Lipps to identify an axe head found in the ruins, and he complied, noting that the "Lier boys" had marked it with an "X" and that his deputy had filed two additional scratches as identification marks.

This blade was also taken to Chicago, where Dr. Hektoen took some scrapings.

With a flourish and a gleam in his eye, Wall handed Lipps a dollar bill and asked if this blood-spotted bill was also tested for bloodstains. Nodding, Lipps agreed and was then excused. The court recessed for lunch.

The jostling citizenry were a source of distraction and irritation to Judge Williams. "After he rapped for order this afternoon, the Judge called attention to the fact that order must be maintained in the courtroom. He declared that the confusion yesterday afternoon was very annoying to him, and if it was repeated this afternoon he would issue an order preventing any person from standing anywhere in the court room. This would force about 400 persons out of the courtroom. The crowd this afternoon was the largest yet present; every inch of available space in the courtroom was filled. The ventilation of the courtroom was poor and all the windows were thrown wide open."[85]

Ben Lier was recalled, handed the axe head to identify, and recounted its discovery in the ruins nearly six months after the fire. Lier said they were searching yet again because the Kaufman's could not find their spare key to the Hibner schoolhouse where Miss Kaempen had been teacher. It was hoped that Emma's key might still be found in the ashes. Lier said that the debris where the women's bodies lay had been screened but no key found, so they were searching the other side of the house in the cellar. As it turned out they didn't find the key but instead found a coin bank and a couple of rings and an axe head.

The prosecution called its next witness, and Dr. Ludwig Hektoen, prominent physician and pathologist grandly progressed to the stand. He stated impressive bona fides: he was an 1887 graduate of the Chicago College of Physicians and Surgeons, and he studied at the University of Wisconsin, at the University of Berlin, as well as in Prague, one of the universities of Sweden and in Liverpool. At present he was director of the Memorial Institutions for Infectious Diseases in Chicago; a professor of

---

[85] *Herald,* April 2, 1913.

pathology at the university and Rush Medical College. He was, in short, a big-city expert come to town.

In 1913 science had made some amazing leaps. Finally there were tests to determine the presence of human blood. One was the "microscopical test." Hektoen admitted this one was not perfect and could not determine if blood was human or animal. There was a "precipitant test" or "biological test," and when conditions were "proper" the results were accurate. In every instance, on each piece of clothing, Hektoen assured the jury, "The spot was found to be made by human blood."

Between making vigorous objections at the defense table Govert and Lancaster scribbled notes and conferred in whispers as Hektoen discussed the axe. "I found that the material from the top of the axe, as indicated, gave a precipitant test for human blood. And the material scraped off from two other places on this axe, while containing blood, did not give the precipitant reaction for human blood."

Hektoen proclaimed that the material on the pillow, the mattress, and the dollar bill all contained human blood. Lancaster rose to match wits with the doctor, beginning with the microscope test. Hektoen said that the first step was to find a corpuscle and measure it.

"What is a blood corpuscle?"

Hektoen replied, "It is a little, red microscopical body that is present in blood and gives the blood its red color."

Lancaster wanted specifics. "How large is a human blood corpuscle?"

"To state ordinarily, it is one three-thousand two-hundredth of an inch in diameter."

Lancaster was delighted when Hektoen cited such a specific measurement and launched a volley of questions: Could they vary? Would they vary between a child and an adult? Would they vary by disease? Could a person have several sizes at the same time? What shape were they? What does a dry blood corpuscle look like? How many do we have? What size is a rabbit's corpuscle? Or a guinea pig's? Or a dog's?

Hektoen, a veteran of many witness stands, remained calm and concise, answering the questions without defending his science or his procedures. He was learned but seemed possessed neither of humility nor truly effective communication skills. Prompted by Lancaster, he described the serum test. "Well, it depends on this general fact. We will cite a specific instance of that. If a rabbit, we will say, injected directly with a human blood, that would develop in the blood of a rabbit, a substance which, under proper conditions will cause a cloudy condition, cloudiness, a precipitant to form in the human blood; and if this test is made in the proper way, that cloudiness is found only in human blood."

He riveted the courtroom with a description of the complex test procedures. A rabbit would be injected with human blood three different times, one day apart, and twelve days later, blood was removed from the rabbit's ear. This rabbit blood was allowed to clot in a slanting tube, until it released a clear serum. Then the material to be tested was moistened with a precise .85 percent solution of salt and water.

Interrupting the doctor, Lancaster ran through a lengthy litany of possible mistakes, miscalculations, and resulting errors. What if the solution was too much? Too little? No salt at all? Rabbit blood in the serum? Timing off?

Hektoen continued his explanation. The piece was soaked in saltwater for anywhere between thirty minutes and two hours, and then if the salt solution was not "absolutely perfectly clear, we drive out the material that makes it cloudy by submitting it to a rapid centrifugation."[86]

Lancaster interposed a key question. "Now, if this suspected article were to have dye on the clothing or the other substances from which it has been taken, would that make any difference?

"It might, but it didn't in this case." Hektoen defended his results. The doctor seemed perfectly happy to expound, educating the courtroom on the various tests available, but Lancaster, papers rustling, steered him back to the case at hand.

Hektoen supplied more details. "One way is this: that if there is a small quantity of blood in the salt solution, then if you blow through it, froth forms, and it remains for a while. Whereas, if it is a ordinary salt solution, the bubbles disappear at once. Now, by comparing this solution

---

[86] 30-5264, p. 53.

that I had made from this material with the solution of known human blood of known strength, I found froth on the solution from the material, disappeared in about the same way, as it disappeared from the solution of know human blood, and by dilution of one part blood to 1/1000 parts of salt solution."

Lancaster's eyes gleamed at this golden opportunity that presented itself and inquired: Wouldn't it matter how hard you blew the froth? Certainly, the good doctor admitted. Then he was forced to give the answer over and over and over again, that to the best of his ability he blew the same way each time.

The "1/1000" answer next received Lancaster's attention, and a faint smile momentarily curved the corners of his thin lips. "In other words, only one part in a thousand contained any blood … and the other 99% parts were the solution itself?"

Hektoen had become slightly testy. "Yes, sir, I haven't finished my answer." He continued, "In the second method to determine the strength of this solution, is by adding a solution of nitric acid, and if on adding a few drops of 25 percent solution of nitric acid to this solution of suspected blood, and then heating it carefully, one obtains just the faintest opacity. This one may represent a dilution of blood of at least one to one thousand."

Lancaster seemed doubtful. "It *may* represent a solution of blood, *one to one thousand*?"

Hektoen plowed on. "Of course, all this is preliminary tests; they are not tests that determine the presence of blood absolutely. They are just indications."

Lancaster continued to sow doubt for the jury. What happened to the rest of the solution? Was it discarded? Was it used over? What about the acid? Did you test its strength? Did you make it yourself? What is the formula? Does the formula change if you weaken it? If the strength isn't right would you get results? Could anyone see these results?

Eventually, Lancaster lost momentum and Hektoen finally reached the heart of the matter. "Now then, we come to the making of the actual test," said the doctor. "We place a small quantity of the clear solution, and the suspected blood material in the smallest tube, and then we take a small quantity of the serum of the rabbit, which I have been talking about, and then by means of a small, fine glass pipette, we let the rabbit serum rundown to the bottom of this tube, so that it becomes a layer at the bottom, so there is a short junction between the rabbit serum and the solution of the suspected material. Now, if the material contains, actually does contain human blood, there will form, within a short time, at the room temperature, a layer of cloudiness, which is very distinct and sharply defined. And that is a positive result; that is a positive test."[87]

Lancaster had regained his energy and questioned this cutting-edge science. What if the room was too warm or too cold? What if it was rabbit blood or another animal, or some of these tests had not been accurate— what about the result then? If a student did it, would it have the same results? If anything was wrong anywhere, would it throw off results? Did anyone help you? Was anything left where someone else had access to it? How long did it stand? Does the test always work?

The barrage of questions seemed to fall harmlessly about the doctor. Did Hektoen test all the patches in the same way? On the same day? With the same rabbit serum? Wouldn't it have been better to use other rabbits? What about some other animal? Was it checked for other kinds of blood than human?

"I tested it for horse blood, cow blood, hog's blood, cat's blood, dog blood, guinea pig blood, rat's blood, chicken blood," was the comprehensive reply.

Now Lancaster took up the axe head tests. Hektoen admitted that the condition of the iron played a part in the condition of the sample. What about rain? Hektoen admitted that blood could be washed away, or rust might interfere with the sample. For the jury, the doctor pointed to two areas on the axe, one on the edge and one on the blade itself, where the samples could not be identified as human. When Lancaster returned to the defense table, counsel for the State rose to do damage control. About all those possibilities for imperfections and errors, did they happen?

---

[87]  30-5264, p. 58.

"In my experiments in this case, they were made under perfect conditions in every way," Hektoen stated emphatically and on that note was allowed to leave the stand.

Another doctor followed. George Sorgatz, from Springfield, Illinois, was a physician and bacteriologist, and a recent graduate of Northwestern University who examined two samples. One definitely tested positive for human blood, the other results were indefinite.

Lancaster plowed the same ground but in a shorter, more concise manner. He discovered that the piece that had tested positive for human blood was from the trousers while the sample from the coat was inconclusive. He made this witness admit that he had not performed such a test for human blood in more than a year. Sorgatz then escaped from the stand.

Ben Holeman, Ray's employee, resumed the stand. Holeman and his wife lived in one rented room at the home of Mr. and Mrs. Joe Eakins (a.k.a. Aikins) in Quincy. On Sunday night after the fire, Ben was called from his room by Ray who had an errand for him that involved taking a street car to Ray's grandfather's house the following day. Ray was hunting for change for a dollar to provide the car fare. He swapped his bill for coins and left fifty cents on a table for Ben to use.

Holeman was supplanted in short order by Joe Eakins. He was asked about changing the dollar for Ray and whether it was a silver dollar or a paper one. In a curious exchange, the testimony went this way:

"What kind of money, silver or paper?" asked the State.

"Well, I'm inclined to think it was paper."

The judge intervened: "Well, do you remember?"

The witness answered, "Not positively."

The defense's "Motion to strike" was ignored.

"Is that your recollection?" the judge asked again.

"Well, from what I learned later, I had an idea it was a paper dollar," replied the uncertain Eakins.

The prosecutor interjected: "What is your best judgment whether it was paper or silver? Now then, where did you put it?"

No answer came from the witness.

Judge Williams asked again, "That is your recollection at this time?"

Eakins said, "My recollection is it was paper."

The court ruled, "Let it stand."

Eakins said he put the paper dollar into his money sack with some other dollars from the bank. The next morning, he dumped everything out and counted it and found a blood spot on one of the bills.[88] Eakins identified the bill with the blood spot shown him by the prosecution.

Govert wanted to separate Ray from this blood-spattered money. Did Eakins look at the bills given to him by the bank? No. Did he look at the one Ray gave him to see if it was spotted at the time? No. What did he do with the money in the sack? On Monday, he put some of it in the bank, but Eakins said he kept the blood-spotted bill for about ten days before his wife spent it at Anck's Butcher Shop.

Wall recalled the eminent Dr. Hektoen to the stand. A defense objection loudly pointed out that no tie had been established between this particular bill and Ray, but the judge allowed testimony to proceed. Hektoen declared that he had detected human blood on the bill in question and then vacated the witness chair.

Fred Schnellbecker next took the stand, and testimony ricocheted back to the night of the tragedy. Schnellbecker, the neighbor due east of the Pfanschmidt farm, was notified of the fire by John Lier's telephone call. Schnellbecker had started toward the barn lot to see if the family buggy was there when he found the wheel tracks. He swore that he saw fresh, steel-tired buggy tracks and the hoof prints of two small horses that had made a short turn in the barn lot and then headed back out to the road, turning toward Quincy. Lancaster took the farmer through the shower the night before, verified that there was not enough rain to form mud, and established that the only variance in the tracks was about a twelve inch veer away from the hitching post toward the house.

Fred was replaced by his brother, George Schnellbecker, and questioned first by Wolfe. He said, under Wolfe's questioning, that the bricks from the chimney had landed on top of the tin from the roof, and he thought that on Sunday morning Ray's team looked like it had been driven pretty hard.

---

[88] 30-5264, p. 73.

Lancaster took a turn at this Schnellbecker brother. In questioning George about the number, direction, and amount of buggy, horse, mule, and other assorted tracks, Lancaster managed to confuse things to such an extent that the judge was again forced to issue a warning about laughter in the courtroom. Eventually the judge too became confused and posed his own question.[89]

George Schnellbecker had obviously been warned of Lancaster's smooth ability to ask confusing questions. He was so careful and literal in his answers that the dialogue began to resemble a comedy routine.

"I am asking you how many tracks were there; you can tell by the number," said Lancaster.

"Do you mean in the lane?"

"At the place where the lane enters the road," clarified Lancaster.

"You mean where the lane enters into the main road?"

"Yes, sir."

"Why—you want the number of tracks?" Schnellbecker wanted to be sure of the question.

"The number of tracks," reiterated the attorney.

"There were four."

At this confusing and meaningless answer, Lancaster gave up and the careful Schnellbecker was released from the stand.

Enter John V. Harris, who told the courtroom he arrived at the fire at about 8:00 a.m. to see men trying to douse flames on the mattress beneath the two bodies. Wall, believing Ray's behavior was callous, asked Harris, "With reference to tipping his hat and speaking to other people, did you notice anything in regard to that?" Outraged, the defense objected, and the judge this time agreed.

The trial transcript records the defendant's counsel saying, "I suppose he breathed a little too." In the stuffy courtroom, the gallery tittered or scowled according to their individual inclinations.

Wall rephrased the question, and Harris was allowed to say, "I saw him introduce the lady that was told to me to be his sweetheart, to my daughter."

---

[89] 30-5264, p. 96.

"In what manner was that introduction given?" probed Wall.

"In the usual manner," Harris replied.

The defense objected, but the court did not announce a ruling.

Wall continued. "What was his manner of acting at that time?"

"Apparently, to me, as though nothing had ever happened."

Defense counsels bounded to their feet; the court denied their motion to strike. Harris also testified how he heard Ray point out the bodies to his lady. "He remarked, 'This was Mother; this was Blanche; this was Miss Kaempen; and this was Father.'"

Lancaster took the opportunity to make further headway against the amount of blood on the bedding and had Harris testify to water being thrown onto it; he then proceeded to the issue of steel versus rubber tire tracks. Harris admitted that the matter could be open to judgment and mistakes. After five questions, Lancaster was finished with this witness.

Chris Haxell, a farmhand from the Schnellbecker farm, was next. He told the familiar story and then relayed a quote overheard from Geisel. "He said, 'If those four bodies are in the fire there was foul play.'" The strident defense objection was ignored by the court, allowing the witness to continue.

Over repeated objections, Haxell testified that in his opinion, only an undercut buggy could have made that barn lot turn, but he admitted that he had limited exposure to such vehicles. To counter the idea that such buggies were rare, the defense listed ten prominent local residents who drove them, including, amid inadvertent gasps and some giggles, the name of the formidable Edith Robbins of Payson.[90]

Wolfe called John Kaufman, a son of neighbor Henry, and the two waded through stories of tracks and weather and directions, etc. Kaufman contributed that he had asked Ray if he was at the farm on Saturday night, to which Ray replied, "No, sir." Ray in return asked if Kaufman had seen anyone at the house on Saturday. The neighbor answered, "I told him no, sir."

Lancaster focused questions on the conversation in the Kaufman home when Ray came to telephone the Reeders. It was there that Ray denied

---

[90] 30-5264, p. 111.

being at the farm on the previous evening and asked if John had seen anyone about the place on Saturday. Kaufman admitted he first reported seeing someone at the Pfanschmidt kitchen window then, but on further reflection realized it was not Saturday but on the day before.

Kaufman's comment about Ray's behavior at the fire was, "Well, he appeared to me as though nothing had happened." Of the other relatives, Kaufman said, "They appeared to be kind of broken." He was released from the stand.

Now the first woman stepped on the witness stand. Mrs. Caroline Wand was the wife of John Wand and lifelong friend of Mathilda Pfanschmidt. She reported that Mathilda was born to the Abel family, along with brothers William, George, Joe, Jonas, and Henry Abel.

Benches creaked as observers leaned forward when Caroline Wand admitted to being one of eight subscribers on a telephone party line from the Payson central exchange, along with the Schreck's; the Albsmeyers; the Smiths; William Speckhart; William Busch; Ben Sneyder; and the Pfanschmidts. She stated that she could recognize Mathilda's voice over the phone, as well as Ray's.

The State asked Caroline to recount for the jury a conversation she overheard on Wednesday, September 25, between Ray and his mother. Counsel for the defense objected, and the jury was led from the courtroom. After a short conference, the court overruled the defense motion and questioning resumed.

Caroline Wand said that at about 9:00 a.m. that morning she listened to a conversation between Ray and his mother. "He asked his mother whether she could not send some books; he had some books at home he would like to have. She said, 'I am coming up this morning myself, Ray.' He said he had three different sets of books there and to bring some of each set. She says, 'When will you be home?' And he says, 'Saturday night, Mother.' That's all I heard about it."[91]

Her testimony verified rumors circulating the countryside. It also explained the "company-coming" sleeping arrangements, which put the

---

[91]  30-5264, p. 126.

women together in one bedroom. Unlike previous witnesses, Govert could not shake her testimony. Mrs. Wand was dismissed and later endorsed in the newspapers as telling a clear story "that did not seem to be rehearsed."[92]

John Wand was recalled and quizzed by the State about the ability of any buggy other than an undercut buggy to make the turn in the barn lot. He swore it would be impossible. During his cross-exam, Govert became antagonistic. At one point he asked a question and then sputtered "is there, how about it?" Followed by, "You don't know very much about undercut buggies, do you?"

After further prodding, Wand testified that a narrow bed "piano box" buggy could make a turn between four and five feet in diameter. This testimony ruled out an undercut buggy as the only one capable of creating those tracks, and Govert dismissed the witness.

A second woman witness appeared, Mrs. Robert (Rose) Hood, who was at the fire and talked with Ray. Wall asked, "What did he say to you?"

Rose replied, "I spoke to him and then I said to him, I said, 'Well, Ray, these people must have been killed Friday night, because I hear that the mail had not been taken out of the box and that different people tried to get them on the telephone all day Saturday.' He said in reply, 'They were around here yesterday all right, because the stock had been tended to.'"

Rose said Ray appeared natural but a little bit pale. The only other thing he said to her was that he intended to go out to Sam Rice's place to start work the next day, Monday morning. Govert did not detain her for a single question.

Policeman Fred Scharnhorst stepped up to the stand. Scharnhorst related a conversation he had with Ray that illuminated law enforcement suspicions beginning even at the fire: "I met him right at the orchard there, and I says to him, 'It is a pretty sad affair,' and he says, 'Yes; I didn't know anything about it until they called me.' I said, 'Who called you?' He said, 'Mr. Niekamp.'"

Wall: "Is that all he said?"

---

[92] *Journal*, April 3, 1913.

The deputy replied, "No, sir; so I asked him where they had called him, and he said out at the works out on Cedar Street. I asked him if there was anyone there sleeping with him. He said, 'No,' but there had been about eight or ten days ago, he had a fellow staying there, but here lately, nobody slept with him. Then he told me he was following the business of blasting out trees and stumps, and I asked him if that was a pretty good paying job, and he said, yes, that he got ten dollars a day and he could hire anybody for $2.50 and he would have $7.50 left out of it. I said to him then, 'You weren't out here last night?' and he says, 'Do you think I was out here and did this?' and I did not say what I thought, and he left me and walked away."

After these opening remarks, Scharnhorst went on to relate that he heard Ray and Sheriff Lipps discussing an oil can, which Ray was saying was a strange can he had never seen before at the farm.

On cross, Govert spent a long time with Scharnhorst discussing the oil can in question and whether or not there were any markings on it. "It was a pretty good dent, ran across, like a team run across it while it was hot," was the reply from Scharnhorst.

The spectator interest rose again as Daniel Reeder, father of Ray's fiancée, took the stand. He was sixty-three years old and in ill health but uncompromising about it. As Reeder took the stand, his daughter turned her gaze to the floorboards. "A short time after the father began testifying, Miss Reeder commenced to cry. Tears trickled over her cheeks all the time the father was telling of things that had happened previous to the fire and after …"[93]

Reeder was asked about Ray's outfit on Friday night, September 27, when he arrived just before dark to visit Esther. He recalled, "I said, 'You got a new suit, and where did you get those leggings?' I said they would be dandy to shuck corn in and he said yes. He said you can get them, I think he said at Koch's Harness Shop."

Reeder said Ray's suit that night was clean and without spots, but he could not recall a necktie or hat or raincoat. Ray had declined to eat even though everyone else was sitting down to the supper table. After the meal

---

[93] *Journal,* April 3, 1913.

was over, Ray and Esther went into the other room, where Ray, dressed in his shiny new clothes was laughing and joking with his sweetheart. Mr. Reeder in his farm clothes remained in the next room with his son, Hugh, and Hugh's wife, Blanche, who were spending the night. At about half past nine, Mr. Reeder retired to bed. A sleepless Mr. Reeder heard Ray leave the house at around ten thirty. He listened to the buggy leave the farm about fifteen minutes after that, which was longer than it usually took Ray to untie his horses and take their blankets off.

Mr. Reeder recalled how Esther and Ray first met about a year earlier, on the last Friday of August in 1911 at the Payson Old Settlers Celebration. Afterward, Ray wrote, asking Mr. Reeder's permission to come to see Esther and "he called from that time on."

Wall wanted the jury to hear of a conversation Mr. Reeder had with Ray concerning his financial state at the time he asked to marry Esther. The defense objected, claiming the question was "incompetent, irrelevant, immaterial, and too remote." The date, which turned out to be the winter or spring of 1912, was close enough for Judge Williams. Objection overruled. Whichever day it was, Reeder said Ray claimed he had $3,000 in the bank, which he would inherit at age twenty-one; and further, he intended to farm land that he and his father were going to buy across the road from the farm. Over multiple objections, Reeder testified that the land in question was the Kaufman farm. Ray confidently bragged to Mr. Reeder that he had already "banked his first thousand" after what he called the Pike County Job.

When, Wall wanted to know, were the Reeders notified of the tragedy? Mr. Reeder thought it was about 4:00 a.m. when they received a call from Henry Geisel, but held by chores they couldn't leave home until about eight o'clock. After feeding and milking, they were driven to the farm by their neighbor Caspar Mast, where Ray met them.

Wall seemed to doubt Reeder's story and asked, "to refresh your recollection," if Ray and his Aunt Petrie had stopped by the house on his way to the farm. Reeder said no. Wall asked him three times in three different ways, but Reeder denied it each time.[94]

---

[94] 30-5264, p. 154.

As he was climbing out of Mast's automobile at the fire, Mr. Reeder said he fired a question to Ray. "I said, 'Is it as bad as we feared?'"

"What did he reply?"

"He said yes."

"How did he act when he made that assertion?" The lawyer wanted details.

"Well, about as natural as usual. I didn't see anything ... he was somewhat nervous, we could see that," was the old man's reply.

Reeder told of walking about with Ray and Esther, looking at the horseshoe prints under a box, and hearing which body was which. He contradicted another witness, saying that Ray had reported that the horses were hungry and probably hadn't been fed all day and that the cows weren't milked. He recalled Ray making a point of showing off the oil can and remarking something about oil being used here. Later, Ray strolled Esther over to some ladies, introduced her, and then left her in their company. All during this time, Reeder said, Ray's demeanor seemed normal.

There were more than a thousand people on site when the Reeder party arrived and even more when they asked Ray to come to dinner and left around noon. Ray reached their house just as they were sitting down to the table, at about one o'clock. Conversation was stilted. No one could think who might want to hurt Charles Pfanschmidt or his family.

Reeder, a troubled father, reported the strained conversation when Ray asked permission for Esther to accompany him to town. "I said, 'Ray, I don't like much to have her go.' And he says, 'Why not?' I said, 'Don't you know that you are strongly suspicioned?' He said, 'Me, under suspicion of killing my father?' 'Yes,' I said, 'I could tell from the actions of the people there.' I said, 'Maybe you did not notice it on account of your excitement, and they have nobody to suspicion, and who's the gainer but you?'"[95]

Ray's own words, as relayed through the lips of his prospective father-in-law, stilled the courtroom audience.

"What did he say in reply?"

---

[95] 30-5264, p. 160.

"He said, 'My goodness a life,' or something like that. I said, 'Ray, do you know where you were after you left here Friday night; can you give any account of yourself every minute?' He says, 'I can.' I says, 'When you left my house Friday night, where did you go?' He said, 'I went to a restaurant.' I have forgotten whether he said Seventeenth and Broadway or Eighteenth and Broadway. He says, 'I got a lunch, and I stayed there a half an hour or three quarters of an hour, and I went from there directly home and went to bed.'"

Wall probed further. Did Ray say anything else about Saturday?

Reeder gazed at the attorney and replied, "Yes, I asked him where he was. He said he was at the garage pretty near all day, then in the evening he left there at half past ten or eleven somewhere along there and went up and played pool or went in a pool room. I think he said he played a couple of games of pool and went right home from there. I said, 'When you were at the restaurant, was there people there to prove that by?' He said, 'Yes, I can prove my whereabouts all the while.'"[96]

The garage Ray named was at Seventh and Maine—Chadwick's by name. Ray had informed Mr. Reeder of his plans to get into the automobile business and explained that he had a demonstrator auto ordered, but the farmer could not remember the brand. Reeder shrugged, saying simply, "I am not posted in autos." When Wall prompted, he agreed that Rambler sounded like the right one. Reeder was, however, very familiar with one of the horses in Ray's team, as it had come from his farm. His son, Hugh Reeder, had sold it to Ray. Reeder's testimony aided the defense, supplying a contradiction to claims that Ray had no alibi or explanation for his movements on critical nights.

But then Mr. Reeder reported an exchange on the night Ray asked for Esther's hand in marriage. Reeder replied, saying, "I knew your mother all her life; I knew you when you were small. I never knew anything bad of you." Ray reportedly answered, "There is one thing only; I had a little trouble while up at school, but that didn't amount to anything." Defense attorneys bounded to their feet, and the statement about "other trouble"

---

[96] 30-5264, p. 161.

was stricken from the record. Esther's father had unraveled the defense and piqued courtroom curiosity with this tidbit.

On cross-exam, Mr. Reeder acknowledged that Ray did seem affected that evening, both by the deaths of his family and by the revelation that he was suspected. And the widower spoke of Ray's emotional makeup. "I have seen him in several instances. He was at my house during my wife's illness a good deal, and at her funeral I saw him, and he is not a man who is easily excited or anything that way, I do not think."[97]

Govert's questions succeeded in clarifying that the "Pike County job" Ray mentioned was work done for Judge Grote and had paid him $1,100. Further, Esther's father cast doubt on the matching of the track, saying it was an oval depression and that Ray's buggy was a very light flat-wheeled vehicle. Then he damaged the defense's case with the troubling admission that Ray never denied that his rig had made those tracks.

The stalwart Mr. Reeder admitted to trouble sleeping ever since he'd had a stroke, and troubled, he stared at the dark all the long Sunday night after the fire. One paper would print that Monday morning, "the State informed a representative of the *Whig* that Mr. Reeder told Ray Pfanschmidt to leave his farm and never return."[98]

Mr. Reeder's final testimonial benefit to the prosecution detailed his trip to the sheriff's basement to view the soiled clothes. Reeder believed the spots were blood and that the clothing was similar to what Ray wore that previous Friday night.

His testimony set the stage for his daughter, Esther, the eighteen-year-old, sweet-faced fiancée of the accused. But before she could testify, a ten-minute recess was called. Hearing this, Esther's composure crumbled. "The girl, accompanied by two girlfriends, left the courtroom. They went into an anteroom where the Reeder girl burst into tears and the other girls had to support her. She all but collapsed but soon regained her composure, and when the recess was up she returned to the courtroom."[99]

---

[97] 30-5264, p. 171.
[98] *Whig,* April 3, 1913.
[99] *Journal,* April 3, 1913.

When it was time to question Esther, State's attorney, Wolfe, was absent from the courtroom, so Wall was forced to proceed. Wall claimed to be a little in the dark about her testimony, so the accommodating judge said he would allow this witness to be recalled if anything was missed.

The press printed details of her demeanor and appearance. "The girl was attired in a neat suit of tan and wore a veil. Her tan hat was also on as she stepped upon the witness stand shortly before eleven thirty to answer the questions propounded by attorney Wall. She was nervous during the whole of her testimony and many times her breathing was noticeable as she continually rubbed her hands. Despite this her answers were quick and her testimony of more advantage to the defense than any introduced so far."[100]

As another newsman described it, "Her manner on the stand was calm and composed, and only in her rapid breathing and in the nervous clasping of her hands did she show this terrible nervous strain under which she was laboring. On the third finger of her left hand gleamed the diamond engagement ring that was given to her by Ray Pfanschmidt. And several times during her testimony she turned this ring around on her finger as if to gain confidence from the thought of her bondage. In strong contrast to her evident emotion and genuine sorrow was the nonchalant demeanor of the defendant. He maintained his air of studied indifference during Miss Reeder's examination, although it was noticeable that he did not let his eyes rest on the witness as is his custom but kept then cast down during the most of her testimony."[101]

Esther was precise and careful on the stand, stating to the quarter hour when Ray arrived and left her home. She painted a warm picture of Ray on Friday night, waiting while the Reeders and their hired hand ate dinner, and then spending two hours with Esther in the parlor while the others remained in the dining room. Esther limited her replies to as few words as possible. When Wall asked if she was still engaged to Ray, she replied firmly but without glancing toward her father, "I am."

---

[100] *Whig,* April 3, 1913.
[101] *Herald,* April 3, 1913.

Ray called Esther twice on Saturday, once in the afternoon and once about 8:00 p.m. The Reeders subscribed to two local phone exchanges, with phones from both the Home Phone Company that Ray used for the afternoon call and the Bell Phone that relayed his evening call.

Esther confirmed what her "Papa" said but was unable to remember any exact conversations about anything of import. She noticed that Ray looked "queer" upon his return to the buggy after the conversation with her father, but she claimed not to remember what she said to him at that time. Esther related a variety of places they stopped on the way to Ray's works: Grandfather C. C.'s home, Chadwick's garage, where Ray entered with his own key, and the houses of some of his workers. She was vague on details and could not remember exactly where Eakins lived, but only that they went there.

By the Thursday noon recess and before the prosecution released her, this bright young lady had answered "No" or "No, sir" twenty-five times, some version of "don't remember" or "don't know" thirty times, and "yes, sir" about fifteen times. When court resumed after lunch, the standing-room-only crowd left an estimated five hundred disappointed people in the corridor without hope of entrance. [102]

A soft-voiced Lancaster was gentle with Ray's fiancée, asking her to explain why they went to the camp (to get a horse blanket to use as a lap robe, at Esther's suggestion) and clarifying that they stopped by Ray's grandfather's house twice: once on the way from and once returning to Esther's home. The missing lap robe went unexplained, although the jury might have remembered C. C. had mentioned peering under one a few days before in Ray's buggy. She was soon excused.

Charles Kaempen, father of the slain teacher, came to the stand. He had owned a construction business in Quincy since 1888 and lived in a substantial three-story brick home with his wife, four sons, and four daughters. Kaempen made the heartbreaking admission to Wall that he had been unable to recognize his daughter's body lying in the ruins. Then, after using the phone at the Kaufman house to call his wife with

---

[102] 30-5264, p. 194.

the dreadful news, he met Ray, who was headed to the same phone to call Esther. To the grief-stricken father Ray seemed "indifferent."

Kaempen did not linger at the fire but journeyed home to mourn with his family. Hours later, he attended the autopsy at Stoermer's, where he did identify his daughter's body.

Govert was now facing someone of his own social standing, rather than a country farmer. He posed only four questions, designed to show how little experience Kaempen had with Ray. The defense hoped to imply that Emma's father could not accurately gauge Ray's reactions.

Now the State was ready to anchor the strands ensnaring Ray in their tangle of evidence. Wall called Marguerite Spindler to the stand. She was a nineteen-year-old teacher from Washington School, another one-room country schoolhouse situated four miles south of the Reeder home on the Pape's Mill Road. Miss Spindler boarded nearby with the William Loos family, but she, like Emma, was in the habit of returning to the city on Friday nights after the school week.

That Friday night, somewhere around at half past ten or close to eleven o'clock, Miss Spindler and Mr. Smith were headed to town, driving his one-horse buggy. They turned west at Melrose Chapel toward Twenty-Fourth Street. Just after they rounded the corner, a two-horse team pulling a high buggy passed them quickly on their right side, the north side of the road. It was headed east, away from Quincy, with its side curtains up and the occupant covered by a lap robe. The driver was leaning away from the Spindler buggy and seemed to be tucking the lap robe into place. Marguerite did not recognize the buggy or the driver.[103]

When Wall called Archie Pape to the stand, the defense objected, claiming they had no notice about this witness, further reminding the court of a ruling that the State was to furnish their list of witnesses by March 10. This name had not been included, so Pape was temporarily dismissed.

To counter this setback, Wolfe himself took the stand to swear that he only learned of Archie Pape's evidence on that Tuesday and provided

---

[103] 30-5264, p. 207.

notice to the court and the defense soon thereafter. The judge granted an opportunity for the defense to examine Pape before he took the stand, and for about five minutes Govert, Lancaster, and Pape retired to the judge's chambers. On their return, the court overruled the defense objection and allowed Pape to testify.

Archie Pape, son of the owner of Pape & Loos Milling Company, said that he knew Ray and his horses. While under a doctor's care, Esther Reeder had spent a few days at the Pape home at 501 N. Thirteenth Street. Ray came to fetch her home, driving that buggy on Wednesday, September 25.

Just two nights later, after midnight Friday, September 27, Pape swore he saw Ray Pfanschmidt's buggy speeding north on Twelfth Street. It was actually about half past two Saturday morning that he saw the team "going faster than a fast trot" and illuminated by a streetlight. Pape remembered, "The curtains were all on and there was kind of a rubber cloth up in front or a cloth, I could not tell which. It was pinned clear up and they were driving through a partition through the center."

The implications of this sighting flew between the spectators. At the press tables, pencils scratched furiously.

Govert addressed the younger man: "Where had you been, Mr. Pape?"

Pape turned evasive. "I had been downtown, been out."

"Where?" Relentless, Govert wanted details.

"Different places ... not exactly any place not particular."[104] Pape, like many young men, did not like being grilled. In clipped answers, he told of leaving work and going to Cushman's Saloon. He could not remember what he drank there, except it was, "Nothing that would hurt anybody." Along his route he visited a couple of "nicolettes"[105] on the south side of Hampshire Street and then went to Cunnane's, a restaurant with a saloon up front. There he dined on fried oysters and about eleven or eleven thirty went to visit a "lady friend" at Eleventh and Broadway. He stayed until a quarter after two in the morning. Govert forced him to reveal the name of his "lady friend" as Rachel Smith.

---

[104] 30-5264, p. 214.
[105] Nicolettes showed short, often hand-cranked, moving pictures and other forms of coin-operated entertainment.

Govert, attempting to rattle witnesses, asked ten questions ascertaining the number of nights between Wednesday when Ray's buggy was at Pape's house and Friday when Archie saw it hurrying up the center of Twelfth Street. The defense attorney crafted another two dozen questions concerning the side curtains and storm curtain,[106] but Pape allowed that he wasn't paying attention to those sorts of details. Govert then meandered through Pape's job, his itinerary before the sighting, and the fact that he was alone when he saw the buggy.

Just as Pape was exhaling a sigh of relief, the court said to Govert, "In view of the fact that you did not have notice of this witness, you may further cross-examine him on next Monday at nine o'clock if you desire to do so. The witness may return next Monday morning at nine o'clock."

Wall called Chester Smith to replace Pape. Smith was an unemployed twenty-one-year-old living with his parents at Eighteenth and Hampshire streets. He contributed little, except to confirm that he was with Marguerite Spindler and that he "had to hurry the horses" a little to give the other buggy room at Melrose corner. The State, having corroborated Miss Spindler's account, moved on.

Willis Seehorn one of Ray's employees, had occupied the tent with Ray at the works. On the stand, Seehorn said he slept there every night in September and that on the Friday before the fire he retired about nine and woke up alone. How did he know the time when he awoke? Seehorn replied, "I looked at my watch." Mr. Wall wanted the jury to know how he accomplished that.

"Have I right to illustrate it?" Seehorn asked if the lawyer wanted an actual pantomime.

"Yes," said Wall.

The literal-minded Seehorn coordinated words to actions: "I took the watch from under my head and I took a match [witness here illustrated by striking a match, etc.] and lighted it this way and saw it was one thirty."

---

[106] The "storm curtain" was a front curtain hung up in very bad weather to protect the driver from precipitation blown into the vehicle.

Watching this pantomime of striking the match on the sole of his foot, a straight-faced Wall continued. "When you saw it was one thirty o'clock, what did you do?"[107]

"I went to sleep." Seehorn guessed that he slept about another hour or hour and a half when he was disturbed by Ray asking, "Kid, are you asleep?"

Seehorn didn't make a reply.

When he next woke at about half past five, he saw Ray asleep on the west cot with his shoes on the ground and the pistol and some change lying on a little stool. According to Seehorn, Ray sometimes slept in his clothes or sometimes removed his shirt and pants and laid them on the floor next to the cot. On that Saturday morning, there were no clothes next to the sleeping Ray.

Seehorn rose, completed his morning chores, and then returned to see if Ray wanted to come to breakfast. When Ray declined, Willis walked two blocks north to the Eakins's home, where he boarded. Ray was up when Seehorn returned and dressed in a blue suit with a gray raincoat, a "dice-box hat, and a pair of low slippers." Willis, who had never seen Ray turned out like that, thought it odd. Ray left the camp about eight thirty still wearing that blue suit. The jury also learned that Ray was usually alone on Saturday nights, it being Seehorn's habit to spend that night at his home in Fall Creek.

Lancaster began to tear apart this story, using words from a statement Seehorn made on October 1, 1912, at Govert's offices. The defense also noted other witnesses to this testimonial, including Silba Lawrence, Fred Pfanschmidt, and "other parties." In a reasonable tone the attorney began by seeking to move Seehorn's bedtime back to eight thirty from the nine o'clock hour mentioned.

Speaking in a firm tone, Lancaster then said, "I will ask you whether or not in October at our office at the time and place heretofore mentioned [you did] say this: 'I heard Ray come in about midnight'? Did you or did you not say what I have asked you? 'I heard Ray come in about midnight'?"

Seehorn flatly replied, "I did not say it."

---

[107] 30-5264, p. 226.

The defense persisted, "I will ask you whether or not at the time and place aforesaid in the presence of the persons mentioned, you said this or this is substance, 'He came in about the time he usually does,' referring to Ray Pfanschmidt?"

The witness denied it again. "I don't know whether that is the answer I gave you there or not.... I don't think I said it."

Lancaster firmly asserted that Seehorn's statement mentioned a passenger train passing about the time Ray arrived, which would be the "Eli" arriving near midnight. Seehorn denied the train in this round of questions. Lancaster relentlessly returned and repeated queries, until finally Seehorn said, "There was so much said about the train, I don't know as I mentioned the name of it," followed by, "I don't know as I said exactly." He moved on to, "I might have said that; I do not know whether I did or not." Finally he ended up stating, "I probably said it." Then Seehorn capitulated entirely and agreed that his memory back then was probably fresher than now.

However, Seehorn wasn't entirely cowed. He regrouped and retaliated, telling Lancaster that he didn't realize the woman in the office was a stenographer taking notes, and he didn't know that he had come the offices in the Blackstone building to give a statement. Seehorn's confusion was confounding, even to Lancaster. He wasn't sure how he got to the building, how many people were there, or what he was there for.

Lancaster, his patience at an end, said, "I will ask you whether or not this matter in typewriting was not presented to you in the horse lot at Joe Maine's place one or two days hereafter by myself and Mr. Geisel and by you read over and signed in our presence?"

Seehorn grudgingly answered, "I never read any article over, it was read to me."

The State objected, and the court ruled that in fairness to the witness, Lancaster should show him the paper he signed. Inspecting the document, Seehorn reluctantly admitted that it was his handwriting.

Having gotten this far, Lancaster forced Seehorn to admit that he had the attorney change some words in the statement after they read it to him, and before he signed it. Lancaster cited six specific things that were changed, showing the typewritten words struck through and new ones penciled in. In each case, Seehorn reluctantly answered, "I might have," but stood firm that he never read the statement himself.

Lancaster moved Seehorn on to talk about Ray's clothes. The witness repeated that Ray left camp on Saturday morning wearing a blue suit and returned dressed in a new khaki suit and yellow leggings at about ten thirty that morning. Seehorn also said Ray's horses Sunday morning were "about as usual."

On redirect, Wall spent some time establishing that Ray could have changed into a khaki suit before leaving that morning without Seehorn seeing; and then moved on to the statement Seehorn made to the defense. "After you made that statement, what if anything, did Mr. Lancaster say to you?" Wall asked.

Seehorn still sounded confused. "On that morning?"

"Yes."

"He told us to get out of town."

Seehorn said that Lancaster read the statement to him, but he never checked to see if it had been read correctly. Seehorn signed it on the back end of a buggy in front of the Eakins house where he boarded.

Wall wanted to completely erase the idea Seehorn had given a voluntary account. "I understand you never made a statement—you simply answered the questions put to you by Mr. Lancaster?"

Seehorn agreed, "I think I did."[108]

Wall asked about finding the clothes in the vault, and this time Seehorn's memory was quite specific. Wall wanted to know, "When was the last time that you saw that red necktie on Ray Pfanschmidt?"

"I saw it on Ray Pfanschmidt on the 27th day of September 1912," said the witness.

Seehorn reported that Ray left the job site on that Thursday, wearing a new khaki suit, pants, and shirt with low shoes and leggings. On the Saturday night Seehorn went home as usual to Fall Creek, returning on Sunday evening, when he saw Ray and Esther at the Eakins house. Ray had

---

[108]  30-5264, p. 243.

come looking for Ben Holeman, who wasn't there. So Ray sent Seehorn in Ray's own buggy to fetch Ben, where he was visiting his brother-in-law. Afterward Seehorn went to the tent about nine o'clock that Sunday night and slept there alone.

Lancaster, holding the signed statement, asked if Seehorn's answers were true when he gave them. Seehorn thought so. Lancaster asked if the answers remained true after they were read. Seehorn thought so.

Seehorn first told the jury that Lancaster was by himself when he brought the statement to have it signed, so there were no witnesses. Further, Seehorn testified that Lancaster was alone when he advised Seehorn to leave town.

Seehorn, becoming more and more muddled, requested a glass of water, which was supplied to him on the stand. To the prosecution's dismay, the witness then proceeded to contradict his prior testimony, saying that Lancaster told him to get out of town before he signed the document, and in the presence of Ben Holeman. It was a statement that made no sense at all.

Out of patience, Lancaster plowed on. Over objections by the State, he asked about the number of times Seehorn had conferred with Sheriff Lipps or Detective Young or State Fire Marshal Bogardus. Seehorn remembered speaking to each of them several times, at several different places but could not be specific. The confused and adaptable Seehorn was finally excused, his inconsistencies unresolved.

Gustav Hutmacher, another of Ray's employees, was next to testify. He agreed with Seehorn's account of Ray's wardrobe: raincoat, suit, stiff hat in the early morning; new khaki suit and floppy hat by eleven o'clock on Saturday when he reappeared, coming up the Q tracks from town. Hutmacher claimed he could tell, by the color, a new khaki suit from one that has been laundered. The suit Ray wore on Friday had been laundered to a much lighter color. Whether or not the khaki suit worn on Saturday was laundered or new, he was unsure.

Wall called Henry Niekamp, of 604 S. Sixteenth Street, Ray's uncle through marriage. Niekamp heard of the "catastrophe" at about 4:00 a.m. on Sunday and carried the news to Ray. He stopped first at Eakins, and

Ben Holeman led him to the tent where he woke Ray saying his folk's house had burned and he guessed they were all burned up.

Ray said, "Uncle, I will be out just as soon as I get my shoes on." Ray told Holeman to hook up his team and drive it to Charlie Achelpohl's drug store at Twelfth and State Street. Then he climbed into Niekamp's buggy and they hurried to his grandfather C. C.'s house. Along the way, Ray reportedly mentioned concerns about a faulty chimney that needed fixing and that perhaps the coroner should be notified. Other than those few words, the ride was completed in silence broken only by the horses' hurried hoof beats through the predawn city streets.

After prompting by Govert, Niekamp remembered advising Ray to dismiss the idea of the coroner and get to the farm. Niekamp also thought it was too early to find an automobile and advised Ray to take his own team, which is what Ray did. After leaving Ray at C. C.'s house, Niekamp returned home. Witness excused.

The State's attorney called H. A. Jenkins to the stand. Jenkins had an automobile accessories business at 120 S. Seventh Street and lived in quarters above it. Directly across, on the east side of that street, was Chadwick's Machine Shop.

Jenkins supplied the jury with a lesson in Quincy geography. He explained that Seventh Street ran due north to the edge of the Soldier's Home, where entrances were handily reached by turning east. It was also easy to leave the city by heading south on Seventh Street then jogging east to the Payson or Pape's Mill Roads. Jenkins was used to seeing Ray's team at Chadwick's, usually hitched to an undercut buggy. On occasion he would see the horses pulling a spring wagon with a DuPont Powder sign on it. He watched Ray's team on Saturday night before the fire, taken from their north-facing position at the hitching post near Chadwick's, turned sharply left, and headed away to the south at about eleven or a quarter past.

Govert, with a mind toward explaining Ray's actions that night, questioned Jenkins. The attorney noted that roadwork undertaken for street car tracks had the north side of Maine Street torn up between Seventh and Ninth streets, which would have necessitated a detour. Jenkins could not remember exactly if that was so. Jenkins did acknowledge that the team was tied in the middle of the block right near the alley and that Ray might have simply gone south to avoid the construction, and then traveled up Eighth or Twelfth to his tent at the works.

Walter Dingerson was next to be questioned by Wolfe. He was returning home on the Saturday night, leaving Quincy about eleven o'clock on a route that took him south, down past Reeders and then east to the Angle Road on his way to the farm where he worked. Between Heckle's Corner[109] and the Melrose Chapel,[110] he passed an undercut buggy with its side curtains up and an egg-shaped back window about eight inches long. That buggy, pulled by two horses with white markings down their faces, was also headed east toward Payson at a slow walk. Dingerson slowed his mare and followed it for a time before he pulled around to pass. He later identified this team and buggy for Sheriff Lipps as it stood tied near the courthouse. It was Ray's team that Dingerson pointed out. Govert and Lancaster had offices across from that same courthouse.

Govert quizzed Dingerson, who verified there was only one person in the buggy but could add nothing more than that. After he passed, Dingerson slowed his horse again and looked through his back window but still could not see the driver. Then he didn't pay any more attention to it at all. Govert, in attempting to impeach this witness with his own prior statements came up against the same stone wall as with the farmhand who would not answer him.

Govert, speaking about the coroner's inquest, asked, "Did you not tell me that you could not tell, at that time and place, that you could not tell [it was Ray's buggy]?"

Dingerson explained, "No, sir, I just told you that I *would* not tell you." He stuck to that story. Witness dismissed.[111]

At about five thirty in the evening, the State attempted to call Clarence Crubaugh, and the defense again complained they had no notice of any witness by that name. The State replied tartly that this was because the

---

[109] Twenty-Fourth Street and the Payson Road on today's maps.
[110] Thirty-Sixth Street and the Payson Road on today's maps.
[111] 30-5264, p. 276.

defense had refused to accept the notice when it was given. The defense answered that they had been busy, and in addition, the date for witness listings had passed.

As it happened, the State had about thirty witnesses that it "discovered" after the listing date passed. The court decided to allow them to testify, but only after allowing the defense time to speak with them out of the presence of the jury. Court was adjourned for the day at 5:40 p.m.

Govert filed an affidavit protesting the irregular nature of these new witnesses and the lack of time for the defense to prepare. It also stated that one witness was identified as "Crawbaugh," but no one by that name could be found. In another place he was called "Crubaugh." The defense would let no technicality pass unrecognized or unchallenged.

Testimony placing Ray on the street at late hours just before the fire was terribly hard on the sympathetic relatives in Ray's camp. His strongest supporters were the Geisel, Cook, Niekamp, and Petrie families. There was now a slight crack in the foundation of compassionate family members. On Friday, Uncle Henry Geisel issued the following statement to the *Herald*:

"I was much downcast after yesterday's testimony. The evidence of Archie Pape seemed so strong against Ray that I admit I left the courtroom that night distressed. I even told friends that if those things were true, then Ray Pfanschmidt should throw himself on the mercy of the court. All of the relatives have repeatedly urged Ray that, if he is guilty, he should confess. Since last night I have learned several things which clear matters somewhat and everything doesn't look so dark to me as it did last night. I can't tell you just what these things are which I found out but you will know in time. We have not noticed any difference in Ray's manner since the taking of the State's evidence has begun. We still believe Ray is innocent, though of course we do not know positively and beyond doubt. We still will stand by Ray until we are convinced at the boy's guilt."[112]

---

[112] *Herald,* April 4, 1913.

# Chapter 16

# Bloodhounds

## Friday, April 4, 1913

Court resumed at nine o'clock. The disputed witness, Clarence Crubaugh, came to the stand and announced good-humoredly that he spelled his name "any way it is written on a check—including Crawbaugh and Crawlbaugh." He was a single man making his home in Quincy for the past three years, working at the Home Telephone Company.

He testified that he and his lady friend, Miss Lewis, were near Cook Avenue and Twelfth Street at about midnight on the Saturday night of the fire. He left Miss Lewis's home on foot just after 1:00 a.m. and was walking slowly the mile south to the Cedar Creek Bridge near Ray's camp. Crubaugh said he could usually walk it in about twenty minutes, but he was in no hurry that night. He had crossed the creek and headed up the hill toward the gate at Soldier's Home when he heard a buggy coming, headed north. It was a high buggy, pulled by two small horses, and the side curtains were up. He paid no attention to where it went after it passed him but judged the time was sometime between one thirty and 2:00 a.m.

In a seemingly unrelated question, the State asked Crubaugh if he had ever worked on the Payson phone exchange, and if it was possible by cutting off a fuse to isolate the Payson phones from Quincy connections. Crubaugh said yes. The defense objected but was overruled.

Govert next tried to obfuscate the time and the distance of Crubaugh's midnight stroll but made little headway. The witness was bounced back and forth between direct and cross-examinations until finally the court asked Govert if he would want Crubaugh again next Monday, and Govert replied, "We can't tell." Crubaugh was ordered to report again on Monday.

This was the third witness to dispute Ray's whereabouts late at night.

The State brought Ben Holeman back the stand. Holeman had known Ray for fifteen years and was well acquainted with his team. There was a horse and a mare which was always hitched on the right-hand side.

He recalled Ray on Saturday morning as wearing a light rubber raincoat and stiff hat. He thought Ray had on khakis under the coat as he left camp. He testified that Ray's trademark ties were "kind of stringy on the ends … where he chewed the ends of it," and said Ray was wearing a khaki suit and red necktie on Saturday night.

Ben had examined the suit found in the outhouse and identified it as belonging to Ray. The State confidently took him through the litany of items found, and Holeman positively identified each piece as belonging to his employer. Ben also swore that he saw blood spots on the pants near the hip pocket. This testimony was allowed to stand despite vigorous defense objections.

Holeman described the east sleeping tent, and the west tent where clothes and supplies such as dynamite caps were stored. He said there were three new khaki suits in the west tent on the Thursday before the fire, when Ray loaned him one to wear to a picture show downtown. With a smile, Holeman recalled that lighthearted moment when the young boss dressed his friend and helper in a new suit identical to his own. Holeman's wife enhanced their resemblance by teasing Ben into wearing a red tie to match Ray's. It gave the jury a glimpse of perhaps the last happy evening for them all.[113]

Holeman then related being awakened when Niekamp arrived with the news of the fire. Only a short time later Ben had Ray's rig at the drugstore near grandfather C. C.'s house. Ray soon whistled him up from down the

---

[113]  30-5264, p. 295.

block and took over the team. Contrary to orders, Holeman had not taken the time to either feed the ponies or grease the buggy before hitching them. Holeman later told Lancaster that Ray's team that morning "looked to me as though they never had been drove at all."

A somber Holeman related the story of Ray changing a bill for carfare coins and how later he called back with different plans. Ben was to pick up the team at C. C.'s house on Monday morning, instead of Sunday night. When horseshoes were removed from Ray's team, Holeman was there and verified that the mare's shoe was taken from her right-hind foot.

Wall wanted to explore the dynamite work Ben and Ray had done on Thursday afternoon, September 26. Holeman was left working alone for about four hours while Ray went to another uncle, Geisel's, to dynamite some stumps. Wall was quite curious about how dynamite was ignited. Holeman explained that it was done not with a time fuse but with electricity. There was some of the timing fuse in the storage tent, but for the stumps they used a flexible little wire that bent easily and set the charges off with electricity. Wall did not ask his opinion of the clock hands wrapped in wire.

Spectators murmured on hearing that Ray and Holeman had traveled four miles back to camp in only forty-five minutes that day, even though the speedy little team was pulling the heavier work wagon filled with the DuPont tools and supplies. Holeman told Wall that he checked his own watch, which was how he knew the exact time. He did not see Ray's watch at all that day, but remembered, "The only fob I ever saw Ray wear was a little strap with a round leather button which had the letter R on it."

Ray's wardrobe resumed center stage when Lancaster asked if the tag numbers on the suit that Holeman borrowed on Thursday night matched the tags on the other new suits. Ben hadn't noticed, but he had kept that suit,[114] and it still had the ticket on the coat. The number was T-83150, size 40, and "role" was marked there. The coat at present was still at home in Ben's closet.

Holeman also identified the shoes removed from Ray's team. He had the horseshoer weld a piece of baling wire through holes in the shoes so

---

[114] The "suit" seems to refer sometimes only to the jacket rather than an entire three-piece ensemble of jacket, shirt, and pants that is normally covered by the term today.

they would be inseparable. He also marked one dot on the gelding's shoe and two on the mare's. On the stand, Holeman said to the attorney, "You told me to do it."

The police guard at the Soldier's Home depot, Henry Love, came to the stand. He recalled a conversation that occurred around the middle of September 1912, when Ray wanted to know about coming through the gates late at night. Love said he thought Ray was asking about walking through the Soldier's Home, not driving, and said the gate had never been found open from a late-night drive through. Since the gates were fastened with a chain but not locked, his testimony added little.

Ben Holeman's wife, Opal, was called to testify. She took the stand, baby in her arms. Opal verified that Ray did indeed chew on the ends of his red neckties, leaving them as frayed as the one found in the vault. Ray had jokingly pulled his tie out of his shirt and showed her its ends only a few days before the fire.

The next witness, H. G. Strumpfer, stirred a buzz of excitement. He was the forty-seven-year-old owner and handler of the bloodhounds from Springfield, Illinois, and also a deputy state fire marshal.

Pureblood hounds, he announced from the stand, are "human trailers."[115] Strumpfer got so far as to say that the names of the dogs he'd brought were Roger Williams, an English dog, and Nick Carter, an imported Russian dog, when the defense counsel made strident objection to the entire subject line of questioning.

The judge excused the jury while he determined the nature of the defense's objections to any and all testimony about bloodhounds. The lawyers lobbed legal precedents back and forth. Wall cited Illinois cases in support of his argument for admitting this testimony. Govert and Lancaster volleyed precedents from Indiana, Ohio, and Nebraska but cited no cases in Illinois where such evidence was excluded. Judge Williams said he would need time to consider, since the precedents named were for trails much fresher than this one, which was at least sixty hours old. When Wall, who needed this testimony, offered to cite a case where the trail was also

---

[115] 30-5364, p. 316.

sixty hours old, Williams decided to allow testimony to go forward, with the provision that it could still be stricken later. The trial resumed and the jury was allowed to return and hear Strumpfer's tale.[116] Judge Williams would eventually rule that the evidence on a trail sixty hours old was admissible, at which point the defense formally notified the court of its objections and was overruled.

In the afternoon session, Strumpfer regaled the audience with accounts of how he trained his dogs over a twelve-month period to follow humans, but also to trail horses. According to Strumpfer, dogs were started on fresh trails, fewer than twenty minutes old, and every day of the training cycle the trail offered to them was increasingly older and colder. Of the pair, Nick Carter, the Russian dog, was better at the work and by the end of his training, followed a trail that was seventy-four-hours old. Weather conditions, which included some moisture in the air rather than a hot, baking sun, were near perfect at that time.

In open court before the jury, the lawyers argued whether the dogs' previous criminal cases could be cited to prove competency. Wall stated twice that the dog had trailed sixty-three humans. Under oath, Strumpfer said that his best estimate of the number of trails the English dog, Roger Williams, had followed since his training was somewhere in the neighborhood of six to seven hundred. And he swore they were accurate in the results.

Wall mentioned a criminal case in Waterloo, Iowa, from November 1912, and defense objections flew. Strumpfer was not allowed to talk about one other time he brought Nick Carter to Quincy to find a lost man, but he managed to tell the jury that this Russian dog had followed probably thousands of trails. Strumpfer said proudly, "Yes, sir, we have caught them with the goods on as evidence, and we have had many convictions."

The defense again objected and asked that the remark be stricken. The court ruled, "The jury will not take into consideration the last statement of this witness; he should not have made it and it should not be considered by you."[117]

---

[116] *Herald,* April 4, 1913.
[117] 30-5264, p. 327.

Wall returned to the subject of following scent trails older than sixty hours. Strumpfer bragged, "This Russian dog trained quicker than the English dog; he learned rapidly; he came rapidly on a cold trail and quicker than the English dog; it was about six months of his time that he took the sixty-hour trail under favorable weather conditions." The handler went on proudly, "They were trained upon a horse's trail as old and as cold as the human trail; but usually we hardly ever find a horse's trail, that is not so frequently as we would a human trail of that age."

After more defense objections were overruled, Wall edged closer to the crux of the matter. He asked Strumpfer if the conditions in Quincy when he arrived were good enough to track a cold trail. "Yes, sir, it was favorable for trailing a trail sixty hours old," came the unequivocal reply.

Bouncing to his feet, Govert repeated his request to have all this material removed from the record, but the request was denied, so he turned his attention to the witness. Govert delved into a dog's natural proclivity to follow either a human or animal scent. Strumpfer advised that bloodhounds all have natural aptitude in a "measure" but grudgingly admitted that training was important.

Govert wanted to know what exactly the dog follows.

"It is the substance that comes from the sweat glands or other ducts that falls on the earth or anything …"[118] Strumpfer explained.

"He takes some object or emanation falling from a body in the way of minute particles and that creates a scent?" Govert wanted specifics.

"Yes, sir."

"And that scent will adhere naturally, would it, to the ground for a time, or to objects?"

"Yes, sir, it will adhere except to stone or something it cannot get into … on any polished surface the wind blows it off," Strumpfer explained.

The two managed to agree that the atmosphere is never completely still and that substances cannot be fixed in the air. On the subject of scent on the soil, there was a difference of opinion.

---

[118] 30-5264, p. 333.

Govert maintained that "any scent that fixes itself to the soil would require contact of the body with the soil."

Strumpfer disagreed: "Not necessarily so, for this reason. The substances that fall from the body—a man may be riding a bicycle or riding in a buggy and some people throw out stronger scents than others, and these substances fall from the body in the buggy and go to the earth without them touching the ground."

An incredulous Govert asked, "Do you think there is a bloodhound in existence that can follow a man in a buggy, the man not touching the ground, simply follow the man's scent?"

"I know it, I have had that experience," claimed Strumpfer.

"Could they trail a man in an automobile?" Govert wondered.

"That will depend on the conditions ... for two reasons: the automobile travels much faster than horses, and there is a terrible suction of the machine. Especially if the road is dusty and it covers up the trail or wipes it out. If you drive through vegetation of some kind, such as weeds, you might do it," Strumpfer said.

Govert probed, trying to show the jury that without an impression or scent object to begin from, Strumpfer's dogs could not pick up the trail of a man riding in a buggy. "When have you had any other experience of trailing a man without any imprint upon the ground and without that man having reached the ground at any time; or touched the vegetation?"

Strumpfer puffed out his chest. "Well, there is several of them, some of them go back quite a ways."

Govert inquired about following a scent after automobiles had stirred up the dust on the road, and asked if it mattered how high off the ground the man sat in the buggy.

"Yes, sir," he said, it mattered.

Did it matter if the trail went over oiled streets?

Strumpfer considered. "I think the oiled surface or any scent arising from it, I think it would be confusing; I say it might; I have not had experience enough along that line to testify intelligently."

Govert was confident that the jury would recall Ray's buggy was a high one, and that literally hundreds of buggies and many cars had stirred up the dry road between Quincy and the fire scene before the hounds arrived.

Govert turned his focus to one particular case, that of Jack Shaw in Virden, Illinois, in December 1912, where bloodhound Nick Carter had apparently failed in a rather spectacular manner. Strumpfer, stretching his suddenly tight collar, seemed unable to remember this specific case or that exact time in Virden or even if this individual dog was there. That far distant case from three months ago, more or less, seemed to have entirely slipped his mind.

Govert reminded him how Nick Carter trailed two miles out of the city, with no luck. Shortly after, the wanted man was found within twenty feet of the starting point of the trail, dead by his own hand.

Strumpfer stood his ground. "That might have been the case; I don't remember."

"You have no recollection at all?" Govert's eyebrows rose in surprise.

"Indeed, I have not," was the shrugged reply.

Govert turned to a case from last month, a much closer timeframe. Strumpfer also denied any recollection of the case in question, when brass had been stolen from a tractor engine and his dogs came to track the thief. Strumpfer could not remember. He listed his excuses: he would have to check his records; he didn't bring his records; no one told him to bring his records.

Govert, by now extremely frustrated, faced a man who could only remember his successes. Changing focus, the attorney asked how a layperson could tell if dogs were actually on a trail. "I mean the average layman, who knows nothing about bloodhounds, would have to depend upon whether a trail was an accurate trail or not, would have to depend upon the truth and veracity of the man handling the dog?"

Strumpfer agreed, "As far as anybody else's knowledge would be concerned."

The onlookers stirred, caught in the rising level of exasperation. Govert probed to determine whether training or breeding or instinct fueled the dog's tracking ability. "Is it not the bloodhound's scent, its ability to detect the scents from other animals as they pass only a more highly developed sense of smell?"

"Only by breeding, they have been bred for hundreds of years for that distinct work," Strumpfer said, defending the hounds.

"It is just a supernatural power?"

"No, sir,"

"I will ask you if it is not a developed sense of smell."

"I told you it was."

"Then it is not instinct, is it?" Govert's tone conveyed his irritation.

"It is just a natural instinct it has gotten by breeding." Strumpfer combined the concepts.

"Do you distinguish between instinct and the senses?"

"I don't know what you call it; I call it a developed instinct," Strumpfer answered, unconcerned with petty distinctions.

At this point, Judge Williams was forced yet again to admonish a laughing audience.

Strumpfer carried on. "The dog's natural instinct is to take the human scent; his accuracy and reliability depends upon his development, and his development depends upon the effluvia that is formed in the nose of the dog by the scent."

Govert wanted the handler to agree that training influenced a dog's ability to trail. Strumpfer denied that a dog's tracking ability increased with training, but only the dog's ability to know how to use that ability grew. The spectators were grinning again. Strumpfer, enjoying the attention, spoke directly to the attorney about his inability to comprehend the ways of bloodhounds: "Well, you are not a dog man; it will take us all afternoon."

Govert retorted, "Well, you are here to teach us something on that." Then he posed questions designed to point out that the handler was reading and interpreting the dogs' signals, while no one else had any real way to know if the handler was correct. All results, according to the defense, depended on the ability and truthfulness of the dog's handler.

Moving on, Govert found that Strumpfer had absolutely no recollection of July 1910, when the dog Nick had been unable to follow a track after a man got into a rig at the end of a cornfield and ended the trail. Govert listed other times and crimes and trails for which Strumpfer's memory was entirely blank. Strumpfer could offer no explanation as to why his recollection was empty on these cases, while older ones cited by Wall were crystal clear in his mind.

But Govert had his suspicions: "You would not remember the occasion of which either one of these dogs failed."

Strumpfer replied, "No, sir."

"That would not make an impression upon your mind?"

"No more so than if I made a catch."

Govert pressed the point. "It would not be so unusual a matter that it would impress itself upon you?"

"Well, we don't catch everybody we go after; it is just as liable to be one way as the other."

Judge Williams had a few questions of his own, and Strumpfer immediately became clarity itself. He explained to the judge that trailing a human came naturally; trailing another animal still depended upon the dog's sense of smell but also its education, for instance, on how to distinguish a human's scent from a horse's.

Seeking another avenue to discredit the dogs, Govert inquired about their breeding. He established that Strumpfer hadn't bred them himself but relied upon the dog's registration papers rather than firsthand knowledge. Roger Williams, a tawny hound with a dark saddle on his back, had been bred in Kentucky by a man named Williams. Nick Carter, a more compact dog, had been imported from Russia, and was roan colored, spotted white and tan.

Govert again insisted that the judge strike all testimony concerning the dogs and their performance, for among other reasons, the attempt to prove their capacity through their pedigrees had not been sufficient. To refute this claim, Wall marched Strumpfer through his own expertise and on to testify that regardless of registration papers, Strumpfer would swear that the dogs were pure bloodhounds; that they were registered by the American Kennel Club; and that AKC registration meant they were pureblood, and so were their dams[119] and sires.

---

[119]  The female parent of the animal.

Govert objected to this reasoning as "unsubstantiated, hearsay, irrelevant, incompetent, immaterial, and all references to accuracy as ungrounded." Again the court allowed the testimony to proceed, and finally the witness could begin to tell his story of the trail from the fire scene.

Strumpfer's memory recovered as Wall resumed questioning. He recounted that it was the twenty-ninth or thirtieth of September when they arrived fairly early in the morning, on the Q (the Chicago Burlington & Quincy, or CB&Q Railroad), from Springfield, Illinois, by way of Louisiana, Missouri.

Strumpfer told of being met by Sheriff Lipps and two other men at the depot and taken to the crime scene, where the dogs were put into a working harness. Strumpfer explained, "The harness is made with a breast collar like the harness for a horse, which goes over the head and a shoulder strap back behind and has a girth underneath the belly there with a buckle to keep on the breast collar. Then there is a strap running back over the back with a ring on it, and this ring works freely over the back of the dog. In that ring we have a twenty-foot leash, and I worked back at the end of the twenty-foot leash."

He described uncovering the tracks protected by the boards and boxes and starting the dog from a horse track. Strumpfer said the hound bayed to signal it had taken a scent and trotted down the lane toward the road towing his handler. "We followed that right along I think practically until we got to I believe Twenty-Fourth and some street." There the trail came to a brick street (State Street), where crowds were thick and hampered the dogs. Strumpfer let the dog work all the corners until "he finally lined out Twenty-Fourth Street going north to where they had been oiling the streets." At that point, Strumpfer remembered that they loaded everyone back into the auto and drove to the courthouse.

About three quarters of an hour later the dogs and handlers were delivered by auto to Twenty-Fourth and Broadway where Nick Carter picked up the scent again, and "I finally got the English dog interested too and got him hold of it, and he and the spotted dog both took the trail and went north."

Strumpfer detailed the trail through the pasture where the dogs wandered for a time until they were stopped by a wire fence. Here, said Strumpfer, they found the track of a buggy and horses that had made a circle, and they followed it back out and south on Twenty-Fourth Street. At Locust Street, the dogs turned west, went along a gravel road through the Soldier's Home, and reemerged on Twelfth Street.

They trailed north to a store (Frese's establishment) and turned in to a camp or grading grounds. Strumpfer told the jury that the dogs had gone "trailing on up to a tent and they went into the tent; then came back from this tent to a buggy and worked over the buggy the neck yoke, the tongue, single-trees and the double-trees and from there they went to a shed to where there was a team hitched in a stall. The spotted dog went to the one I think which was furthest and scented him and passed that up and came to the one furthest west and sat down and in his way indicated that this was the horse he was trailing …"

As a clinching detail, Strumpfer added that the dog had trailed on the right-hand side of the road all this time, and the indicated horse (the "off" horse of the team) had a hind foot bearing a shoe with the same marks as those presented in the barn lot.[120] Wall, with a flourish, then offered the shoe taken from Ray's horse, which Strumpfer identified.

Wall asked if Strumpfer could tell by the way the dogs acted if the trail was an old or a comparatively new one. Strumpfer admitted he could. Wall asked, How did the dog act upon that trail; how did they work?

"Strong, I had no trouble whatever in following it," was the proud reply.

The defense, having objected to this entire line of questioning, at this point was uncharacteristically silent.

Wall had a second trail, which he then attempted to introduce, when that same day the dogs had followed another scent beginning from the Reeder farm. But this time the court sustained defense objections, and that trail, wherever it led, was not allowed into evidence. Judge Williams posed

---

[120] 30-5364, p. 364. Strumpfer had given a detailed description of the shoe track under the box, which the dog scented.

a direct question, asking if taking the dogs off the trail had any affect on them being able to resume tracking. Strumpfer said "No," and testimony was allowed to continue.

Lancaster addressed the witness, beginning quietly, "Which dog picked up the trail first after dinner at Twenty-Fourth and Broadway?"

Wall objected on the grounds that the question assumed "dinner."

Lancaster obligingly rephrased, "Well, after a little amount of intermission or vacation?"

Strumpfer found his memory failing once again. He did not remember if the English dog picked it up again, or when, or who was handling the other dog, or how and when he got the scent.

Lancaster, noting a discrepancy with earlier testimony, asked, "Are you not testifying about two dogs?"

"I am talking only of Roger now." Under Lancaster's steady gaze and rapid questioning, Strumpfer backtracked, vacillated, and seemed to contradict pieces of his previous testimony. He testified that both dogs got the scent, but he was not sure where; the scent came from the track under the box; or maybe from some of the other tracks nearby; he was not sure if Roger Williams was put into the auto because he and Nick were ahead; he trailed all the way to Twenty-Fourth Street; well, maybe they got in the auto to rest and then got out at the crossroads; maybe they went a mile or two and then sat down to rest; maybe they got into the machine.

Strumpfer finally recalled, "No, sir, I think I rode some in the automobile, and then got out, maybe at one or two crossroads."

"Didn't you ride all the way, except to get out at some of the crossroads?" prodded Lancaster.

"No, sir … I think I got out at all the roads, the crossroads, and lanes." Strumpfer stuck to this assertion.

Near the intersection by Melrose Chapel, Strumpfer remembered the dogs turning off and going down a byroad a ways, but they turned back. How often did this happen? Lancaster wanted to know. He also pointed out that Strumpfer had said "dogs," but there was only one trailing at that time. Strumpfer wasn't sure but thought that both dogs were together.

Then Strumpfer's answers became more confusing. He denied that when the dogs left the main road the other handler was in the car and said he hadn't been up to that time. Next Strumpfer claimed that he had been running on foot all the way.

"How far can you run without stopping?" Lancaster snapped.

Strumpfer said he didn't know; he never measured. The jury had already learned that Melrose Chapel was five or six miles from the Pfanschmidt farm. Then Strumpfer's memory conveniently failed again. He no longer knew where or when or how long either or both dogs got into the auto; how far they trailed off the main road; how many crossroads there were; which direction they went; or how many times he himself got out of the auto.

Eventually, testimony deteriorated to this exchange:

Lancaster was tired of the equivocating. "If you did pass it, and if there is a lane leading from the road, where you passed, did you test that to see whether your dog went up there?"

"Maybe I did and maybe I didn't," was Strumpfer's reply.

Since Ray had traveled these roads in several different directions, Lancaster thought "back trails" an important concept. He wondered if a bloodhound trailed only in the direction the scent was laid, in order to follow a trail.

Strumpfer agreed. "That's it; if the trail was coming out of town the dog would turn and follow it out of course, but he would not follow it in town when it was coming out." Lancaster thought that a well-trained dog was also taught to "back trail," but Strumpfer denied it vigorously.

The attorney inquired if there was any place the dogs had gotten confused, and Strumpfer admitted there were several such places. He noted that one was west of the Pfanschmidt farm where a buggy had left the road and turned in to some bushes. When Lancaster pointed out that there was a ditch along that piece of road, and it would not be possible for a buggy to even reach those bushes, Strumpfer did not answer.[121]

Do trailing dogs hold their noses pointed up or down? was Lancaster's next inquiry. That "depends" on the nose of the dog, and his experience,

---

[121] 30-5263, p. 375.

Strumpfer said, adding that Nick Carter trailed with his head between eight and fourteen inches above the ground. An experienced dog would have learned he can find the scent higher.

"In getting it higher, it is not so good, is it?" Lancaster asked.

"I suppose it is not." Strumpfer seemed uncertain.

"It diminishes as you go up?"

"The dog does not seem to think so."

"Well, I am asking you."

"I am not a dog. I don't know."

"Do you know which is the easier for the dogs?"

"I told you I did not personally, I never took a scent."

Lancaster turned the witness's words against him. "Would you not have to take a scent before you would know anything about these things you were talking about?"

"No, because you become educated with the dog in his work." Strumpfer stood his ground. Strumpfer finally decided that he believed a dog scented as high as it could hold its head, and it could take a horse scent higher than a human one. Nick, he offered, was considered a "cold nosed" dog and worked with his head held higher than most.

Lancaster again offered the opinion that a person "could see him trotting down the road, would not know he was trailing at all, would they?"

Strumpfer did not know the answer to that. Then Strumpfer created a messy situation for the prosecution. Lancaster asked if experts on bloodhounds don't sometimes turn them loose to trail. Strumpfer replied blandly, "I don't know of any experts in this country."

Lancaster asked, in all innocence, "Are you?"

Strumpfer answered, "I don't profess to be an expert."

"Are you testifying as an expert?"

"Not that I know of," said the dog handler.

The dismay evident at the state attorney's table eventually reached Strumpfer, who noticed that he was in trouble. Finally he admitted to having "knowledge," but said, "I don't consider myself an expert because I learn something new every day."

"As you understand it, experts are not capable of learning anything more?" The defense attorney delved deeper.

Then the judge weighed in. "That is your idea of it?"

The witness said, "That is my idea; because you will learn something new in the business every day."

The court addressed the prosecution table. "Does he think he can't be an expert if he's learning new things?"

"Yes," was the answer.

The defense could not let this rest. "Do you call yourself an expert?"

Strumpfer was stuck with his own words and forced to answer, "No, sir."[122]

Pleased, Lancaster returned to the topic of the dog harness in tracking. He specifically wanted to know if a hound could be trained to respond to it in the same way that a horse responds to reins—in other words, to receive cues from his handler. Strumpfer first claimed not to know anything about that and then later reluctantly admitted that it might be possible; and that if such were the case, the trail might not be an honest one. Then with some faint instinct for self-preservation, Strumpfer backed away from this, saying that he still believed a dog would take the scent regardless of the handler's knowledge.

Lancaster asked, "Did you not on this trip make or jerk the leash on this dog and say pick it up, pick it up, pick it up?"

Strumpfer replied, "I may have done that unconsciously."

"Didn't you do it for quite a while on this trip?"

"I say I don't remember; a man might do it unconsciously."

Lawyer and witness then argued about how far the trail went into the empty pasture and how much of Twenty-Fourth Street was missed when the dogs returned after their "vacation" at the courthouse. There were actually nine intersections involved along the part of the street the dogs skipped, but again, Strumpfer's failed memory and lack of knowledge of the city left him unable to answer.

Finally, Lancaster reached the heart of the matter. Supposing, he said, dogs were taken off a trail, and the same team and rig traveled the same

---

[122] 30-5263, p. 378.

streets in the same direction, only now the scent was two hours old instead of twelve hours old. Which scent would the dog follow?

Strumpfer said the dog would follow the scent it had been given anywhere, any time he could get it.

How then could a handler tell it was a newer scent? The dogs would work it stronger, was the reply. And, by Strumpfer's own testimony, Nick Carter had worked stronger from Broadway onward. The defense attorney wondered if that didn't mean it was a newer scent. Strumpfer dodged: it might have been the condition of the ground instead.

"Then from the way the dog worked on a trail, you can't say whether it is the same trail, but you can tell it is a trail made by the same animal? You can't tell whether it is the same trail that you had been formerly following." Lancaster hoped the jury was taking note.

"No, sir." Strumpfer agreed.[123]

Both dogs had also been confused at the intersection of Twelfth and Locust and again near the entrance to the Soldier's Home. Lancaster posed multiple scenarios in which the same team of horses traveled back and forth over those streets in the time since the trail from the farm had been laid down. How would the handler know if the dogs had switched trails?

Wall, sensing danger, objected, but the judge thought this point was important to settle and overruled the prosecution. Lancaster posed the question again. Strumpfer almost wiggled his way out by saying that since his dog was trailing one horse in the team, specifically the one on the right, the handler could determine the direction the trail was heading by the side of the road the dog chose after a turn. His answer wasn't clear or convincing.

"If these trails came in together say for one or two miles, you could not tell which one it was, could you?" Lancaster asked.

"Yes, sir, if there was any great time elapsed between the two trails; he would work much more stiffer on a hot trail than on a cold trail."

Lancaster pressed on. "You told me that when the dogs worked more vigorously out on Broadway that it was not a newer trail; didn't you tell

---

[123]  30-5263, p. 383.

me that?" Lancaster was unrelenting, repeating Strumpfer's past answers. Finally he concluded, "The way he works does not signify whether it is an older or a fresher trail?"

Strumpfer was forced to answer, "Not always."

As the questioning progressed to the dogs' behavior at the Frese property, the jury must have wondered what, if anything, about their behavior could be construed to have any meaning at all.

In an effort to reestablish credibility, Strumpfer then claimed that his dogs went onto the property, past the buggy, and picked up a *human* scent, which they followed for a ways before returning to the buggy. He reported that one dog went to one horse, left it, and then went to the mare, where he signaled by sitting down, that this was the horse he was trailing.

Lancaster was incredulous! "What do you mean that they passed near that buggy and picked up a human scent?" Did Strumpfer know how many humans had been in that buggy? Lancaster proposed instead that Strumpfer left the dogs in the tent and fed them some bread as a reward.

The handler had absolutely no recollection of this, but the idea of a trail of breadcrumbs caused a new round of giggles in the courtroom. Judge Williams, however, was not amused and rapped his gavel sharply for silence.

Strumpfer repeated that his dogs went past the buggy; switched to a human scent; went into the tent; out and around a bit; went back to the buggy; and then to the horse that pulled it.

Lancaster's level of disbelief was soaring. Questioning why the dog switched scents, he cried, "How did he know this was the buggy? He did not trail the *buggy*, did he?"

State's counsel objected but was overruled.

Lancaster demanded clarification. "I will ask you whether or not he trailed the buggy at all?"

"No, not the buggy."

"Then when he came to that buggy, why did he drop the horse's trail or scent and pick up the human scent?"

Strumpfer once again changed his story, adding new details to bolster his tale. He now said the dog sniffed the buggy between the wheels and about the wheels before he headed to the tent. He elaborated that the dog trailed to the tent, east out of the tent, and then between the tents and maybe even into the other tent—he was not quite sure.

Lancaster inquired which human being who had been in that buggy would the dog choose to trail? Strumpfer could only reply that it was someone who had been in it within the past sixty hours. By now, the jury had heard of several humans who had ridden in that buggy within that timeframe.

When the dog started from the farm, did he have both a human and a horse scent to trail?

Strumpfer said, "No."

"How," wondered Lancaster, "would you command the dog to drop the human scent and go back and find the horse?"

"The dog does it himself," Strumpfer said, denying any responsibility.

By now it was apparent that no one could establish for certain which trail, be it horse or human, the dog was following. It was confusing, contradictory testimony.

Lancaster then asked if the dog could have trailed the man who had unhitched the team.

Strumpfer halfheartedly agreed. "The chances are it would be the scent of the man that unhitched the team, but not necessarily so."[124] Perhaps they were following two scents, mused Strumpfer.

How far could they do that? Lancaster wanted to know.

Strumpfer felt they could go thirty feet for sure (that being the distance from the buggy to the tent) or maybe sixty feet, but they couldn't do it very long before losing one scent or the other.

Lancaster switched topics. How many times had Strumpfer come to Quincy for this case? Two—well, actually, three times. What was he paid? Strumpfer finally arrived at a figure of $52.00 in expenses, plus a fee to boot, for testifying. When Lancaster now relinquished cross-examination, he had asked Strumpfer more than three hundred-fifty questions.

---

[124] 30-5264, p. 395.

Wall, regaining his feet, again attempted to show by this witness that the hounds followed another trail, starting from the Reeders' house, going directly east until it hit the Payson Road, and from there to the Pfanschmidt farm. The defense objection was sustained and blocked this testimony. In a parting psychological thrust at the defense, Wall asked Strumpfer who had paid his fee the first time. "Mr. Ray Pfanschmidt's grandfather," came the reply.

Witness dismissed. Strumpfer had occupied the stand from 11:00 a.m. until after four thirty in the afternoon.

Just before five o'clock in the afternoon, Ray's employer, Joseph L. Frese (a.k.a. Freese or Freze), thirty-year-old storekeeper and supplier, was called to give his testimony. Frese had contracted with Ray in August 1912 to grade out places for a railroad track spur, coal bin, and wagon road.

Wall inquired if Ray made any money on that deal, and Frese replied, over defense objections, "Why he lost." Frese had seen Ray the Friday night before the fire at about eight o'clock in the evening when Ray had come to ask for an advance on his payment, which Frese provided.

Wall asked about gasoline and cans. Frese remembered once Ray asked to borrow some gasoline, and Frese took him to the shed where it was secured. There, in Ray's view, he retrieved the key, unlocked the padlock on the door, and then returned the key to its hidey hole about ten feet away.

Frese also remembered that among the gasoline cans on his premises, there was one five-gallon can that had been deeply dented by a delivery wagon hitting it nearly dead center. That can went missing just about the time of the Pfanschmidt fire. Frese offered further, "It is what is commonly called an alcohol can.... It was a long-shaped can, with a pointed top, with no spout, just a hole in it."[125]

On Saturday morning, September 28, Frese met Ray downtown, in the presence of Frese's lawyer, Mr. Gilmer,[126] and they talked about the work contract. According to Frese, Ray claimed he would fulfill his contract as promised and not give it up. Gilmer, who had initiated this conversation,

---

[125] 30-5264, p. 404.
[126] Frese's attorney, Gilmer, was also the state's attorney at the time of Ray's arrest.

offered the opinion that from the rate the teams were working, it would cost nearly double what Ray was getting.

So far Frese's testimony was mainly secondhand reports or speculation, and the judge interrupted to ask if somewhere there was a comment made by Ray, and was the State going to show it? Wall said to Frese, "Tell what Mr. Gilmer said to Ray Pfanschmidt."

The defense, of course, objected and included a direct poke at the State's attorney in their wording. The record reads: "Counsel for Defendant objected to the question on the ground that it was incompetent, immaterial, and irrelevant, and the statement of an attorney who is not anxious for a settlement of a satisfactory nature." The court overruled this objection.[127]

After further wrangling, Frese reported, "Mr. Gilmer told him he had better stay out there and attend to his business; that he was losing money every hour, and [Ray] said it was impossible for him to stay out there all the time, beings he had other business to attend to."

Govert deliberately rose and faced this man, who had just testified that on Friday night Ray needed money, yet on Saturday morning gave his promise with apparent unconcern to continue in a money-losing contract.

He began with the gas can. Frese said it used to have a wooden jacket around it with his name painted on it, but, "It was about mashed off when I last saw it." And when exactly was that? Frese wasn't sure. The can was used by his delivery boy to carry oil and gasoline to customers, but because Frese owned eight or ten cans, he only missed this one when he had too many orders and not enough cans. Also, there was no particular spot where cans were stored: sometimes they were kept inside, sometimes outside, maybe on the porch, maybe in the wagon. It was only after the fire that he noticed the can was gone.

Now, concerning the money, Govert extracted an important clarification that, rather than an advance, Ray had only asked for payment for work done to date. Their contract specified total price but not detailed payment terms. Frese had expected to pay it all at the end when the work was finished.

---

[127] 305264, p. 406.

By that Saturday, the defense figured that Frese, at the contracted price, actually owed Ray about $1,000 for excavations already completed. Frese was astounded at that assertion. Govert further calculated that by the time of the fire, Frese still owed Ray $600 or $700. Frese flatly denied this.

The disagreement spread to the dispersal location for the excavated dirt. Frese was testy about where Ray put it. Govert asked if, under the terms of that contract, Ray had the right to dispose of the dirt in any way he pleased.

Frese was irritated. "He took that privilege."

Govert was reasonable. "Didn't the contract give him the privilege of disposing of it wherever he wished?"

"He had no business to put it on other people's premises; it had to be removed, as I or the railroad officials desired."

"And was it not provided that the dirt taken from the excavation was to be dumped wherever it was the most convenient on your premises?"

"He did it, didn't he?"

Govert repeated the question until Frese finally and grudgingly admitted: "The contract said so, yes, sir."

Having proved Ray was within the terms of his contract and ignoring the obvious bad blood between the two, Govert tackled the critical matter of Ray's clothing. Frese admitted to being in Ray's tent on Monday after the fire when he saw two khaki suits that looked like they had been "laundried," folded up one on top of the other. Other than that, Frese maintained he was completely unaware of the clothes Ray wore on the days near the fire. He could not recall shirt, hat, shoes, tie, or leggings.

Wall wanted to ask about Ray's profit margin, but the defense objected, pointing out that it was not redirect examination. To remedy this, Frese was dismissed and then immediately recalled for further direct questioning. Wall inquired about a twenty-dollar lawsuit filed against Frese by Ray's former employee, Mr. Hutmacher, for money Hutmacher said Ray owed him. The suit asked Frese to pay out of the money still owed to Ray. Eventually all this matter was stricken from the record, but the jury added it to the list of Ray's money troubles.

Lawyers and witness debated the profit or loss Ray would realize on the job itself; about Lancaster coming to Frese to demand payment of the full $1,000; and the fact that no settlement had as yet been reached with Ray's guardian. Since the witness was testifying without producing the contract in question, it could not be determined if it was a losing proposition. Witness dismissed. It had been an electrifying few minutes, with all attorneys on their feet and decibel levels high.

Casper Mast was next to occupy the witness box. He lived near Melrose Chapel, worked for Daniel Reeder, and was the one who drove the Reeders to the fire. When they arrived, the lane into the farm had been roped off, so Mast left his auto on the road and the group walked through the orchard. There they met Ray, who, Mast said, put his arm around Esther and kissed her. Miss Reeder, who was paying close attention to this testimony, buried her face in her handkerchief and began to cry as Mast told of the kissing.[128]

While at the fire, Mast looked into the sheds and saw two vessels near the cream separator, one holding cream and one containing "what I call clabbered milk … when I touched the can, tilted the can to one side, the milk parted from the can." Milk had been allowed to sour—a waste the thrifty Pfanschmidts would never have permitted to happen, had they been alive.

Before Wolfe could ask Mast to explain the general working of a cream separator, the jury was excused so the judge and the State could confer. When the jury was recalled, Mast was asked if he could tell just by looking how old that milk was. Amid strenuous defense objections, Mast said, "Why, in my judgment it was at least a day and a half to two days old."[129]

Wolfe next called Iris Spencer, of Payson. Immediately, the defense objected that this was another witness not on the first list supplied by the prosecution.

Brooking no nonsense, the judge said, "I want to know now; did you have an opportunity of examining this witness last night?"

---

[128] *Journal*, April 5, 1913.
[129] 30-5264, p. 423.

Govert admitted, "I saw her last night …" Upon hearing this answer, the court overruled the defense's objection.

Iris was an operator at the telephone station that serviced the Pfanschmidt party line. She had tried several times on that Saturday afternoon to raise someone at the house for a party calling from Quincy, but she never got a response. The defense did not bother to question her.

Wolfe then called another "late addition" witness to the stand and the usual objections and overruling occurred. When he could begin, Wolfe posed Mr. Keasel a number of questions about what he saw Ray doing at the fire, but the witness continually answered in the negative. Keasel didn't see Ray uncover any tracks or move any boards or show anyone anything at all. Wolfe was so nonplussed at the responses that the judge inquired, "Are you taken by surprise at the testimony of this witness?"

Wolfe answered, "Yes, sir, I am."

Judge: "I will allow you to refresh his recollections by proper questioning; I do not consider the question last asked as a proper one." When the flummoxed Wolfe still made no headway, the witness was dismissed. Court adjourned at 5:55 p.m.

When court convened on Saturday, April 5, E. M. Miller, age thirty-four, of New Canton, Illinois, came to the witness chair to add his layer of contradictions to the trial. On the night of the fire, Miller, a farmer, started toward Quincy from about four and a half miles south of New Canton in Pike County, Illinois. He traveled in a steel-tired buggy pulled by a "little span" of mules and arrived at the fire early on, when there were only four or five men there. Miller said he pulled into the orchard, stopped about a hundred feet south of the burning house, and never took his mule team any farther into the farm.

On cross, Miller testified that he left the fire about two thirty after spending an hour or an hour and a half there. How did he know the time? "By a man's watch."

Wall objected strenuously to defense questions that broached the subject of time, saying that it wasn't proper cross-examination since the State had not asked Miller about time. The judge overruled the State's objection.

Miller, delighting the defense, swore that he first saw the fire from about a mile north of Plainville at about half past 11:00 p.m., when he was five or six miles distant from the flames amid hilly, wooded country. Most importantly, his testimony set the ignition time about three hours earlier than any other testimony and at a time when Ray was accounted for in Quincy.

Miller added that on this dark and chilly night, he saw bodies still in the fire. At one point, he saw a flaming face about twelve inches below the tin that had formed the roof—and maybe another near it. A horrified courtroom heard details:

"What did you notice about the flesh on the head or on this face that you saw burning?"

"Just as I discovered it, the flesh fell off."

"About what part of the face did you notice that?"

"The eyes fell out and the blaze come up through the eye-holes."[130]

That picture could give even the stolid farmers on the jury nightmares and likely for weeks after ruined many dreams.

On redirect, Miller was again taken through his timeline and quizzed on distances: twelve or thirteen miles from New Canton where he started, to Kinderhook where he got a shave; eleven more miles to Plainville; another nine or ten miles from Plainville to the fire. Miller drove "at a pretty good rate" (meaning somewhere between four and six miles per hour) but slower after he left the fire. All told, he would have traveled, about forty-five miles since leaving home. Miller firmly denied snoozing at the reins for any of that time. Despite the State's best efforts, they could not shake Miller's account, and the fact remained that his times did not fit their chronology.

Ray's Uncle Henry Geisel, age fifty-two, came next and corroborated these times. He testified to meeting Miller around 4:15 a.m. near his home close to Melrose Chapel. Geisel arrived at the fire about forty-five minutes later and said he had been driving "right along."

The prosecution brought Casper Mast back to say that his family accompanied him to the fire in his automobile, along with Mr. Reeder,

---

[130] 30-5264, p. 434.

Esther, and Mr. Reeder's grandchildren. Over defense objections, Mast told of his wife reprimanding some noisy children running about and playing near the ruins. She said, "Be a little more quiet around there." And Ray, who was watching, replied, "Let them alone, let them have their play."[131]

Was this evidence of Ray's uncaring attitude or his wistfulness at the thought that he would never again be that carefree?

Mast remarked to Ray that it did not appear to be Saturday's cream that had spoiled in the separator and asked how many cows Mr. Pfanschmidt milked. Ray answered, "Dad milked three." To Mast, Ray displayed no evidence of emotion at all.

Then the State brought Albert Plank to the stand to begin the tale of the investigation following the fire. Plank was at the scene on Monday, September 30, accompanied by Gustav Hutmacher, and his folks, who waited in the car for the half hour they were there. Plank noted the others there. "George Koch, the sheriff, the fire marshal, deputy fire marshal, and Mr. Buerkin and Mr. Fogal; quite a number were there."[132]

He examined the markings under the box and observed Fogal inspect the track and measure it with "his scale and calipers or dividers, different instruments for measuring." Plank told of noticing the irregular shape of the track and checking to see that it matched the shoe he had removed from Ray's horse at Twelfth and Cedar in the presence of the sheriff and other officials. His next actions seem inconceivable to any protocol of evidence-gathering procedure.

"State whether or not at any time any shoe was fitted into that impression."

Plank replied, "It was…. I fitted it as carefully as a man could do it into the imprint in the ground to see whether it was perfect or not."

The State asked if Plank had been careful in removing that shoe from the horse's hoof. Plank, who was not a blacksmith, affirmed that, "It was carefully taken off without bending in any manner, shape, or form."

---

[131]  30-5264, p. 443.
[132]  30-5263, p. 447.

Moving along quickly, Wall instructed the witness, "After this shoe was fitted into that track, tell the jury whether anything else was done with the track."

"There was an impression made of it with paraffine [sic]."

The prosecution realized this odd reversal in the sensible order of events, for Wall spent additional time and questions reaffirming that the track had not been altered before the impression was made.

Even the judge chimed in: "Do you mean it was the same before and after the shoe was fitted in it?"

"Yes, sir," came the answer.

The defense loudly objected to "any impression of that shoe after the shoe had been fitted into this track three days after the alleged impression was made." The court overruled the objection, noting that the testimony "goes to the weight rather than to the competency."

But as testimony went on, the courtroom heard of still more incompetent procedures which had been performed to create a "paraffine cast" from the print beneath the box.

Wall plowed ahead. "Now then, before any paraffine impression was made into that track, tell the jury what the condition of the imprint was with reference to being clear or otherwise."

Plank said blandly, "Why, the one I saw under the box looked as though someone had taken their foot and scraped over it and filled it up."

Wall stayed calm. "How was that dust removed?"

Plank explained, "I went to the machine and got the automobile pump and blew it out."[133]

Voice raised in anger, the defense said, "We object to any appearance of the track after a man has pumped over it with any kind of a pump three days after an impression was made." They asked to have all this testimony stricken from the record. The court overruled the objection.

Wall did his best to tidy things up. "After you had blown the dust off, as you call it, with the pump, what was the condition of the imprint then?"

[133] 30-5264, p. 451.

Plank replied, "It showed up very plainly." Astonishingly, Plank went on to say that the other print, the one not protected by the box, was actually clearer than the hidden one, so they made an impression of that one too. After it hardened, they took up the casting, washed off the dirt that had stuck to the "paraffine," and handed the casts over to the sheriff.

Govert went on the attack. He attributed the missing barrier of twine and planks to when the box was kicked aside for the dogs to find a scent Monday. His questions showed that the outlines of the track by Tuesday or even by Monday evening were "so irregular that it could not be told whether it was a horse track or a sheep's track."[134] Not to mention there had been people walking all over, and chickens running free, scratching about in the barnyard.

Govert asked Plank if he tried to blow the dust out with his breath before he used the pump. Plank admitted that another man had lay down on the ground and tried to blow the dirt out of the track, but that hadn't worked. After two of them had both tried to no avail, they resorted to the air pump.

Plank pleased the defense when he said that the track had been made in mud that had dried and hardened. Previous testimony had established that there wasn't enough rain on that Saturday night to form mud. He also admitted they found the second imprint only by guessing where the horse's hoof would likely have landed and using the pump to clear that area. Nothing remained on the surface to show a print existed there at all as the wagon tracks were obliterated by this time. Witness dismissed.

Deputy Fire Marshal A. H. Bogardus, thirty-eight, of Springfield, Illinois, eagerly took the stand. He had arrived in Quincy on Tuesday, October 1, reported to Sheriff Lipps, and gone to the Pfanschmidt farm in a car belonging to Tony Gilmer, the state's attorney.

Bogardus told the same story of clearing the track and leaving it unharmed and clear with its impression of a lug on the outside of the shoe and a slightly longer heel. He authorized sending a deputy to remove the suspicious shoe from Ray's team, a project he said took only about an

---

[134] 30-5264, p. 453.

hour. This timeframe seemed unlikely given the distances involved and the necessity to find tools or a blacksmith.

Bogardus was not allowed to state that it was his opinion the fire was begun by arson, although his work entailed investigating all suspicious fires to determine if they were arson and who started them.

Wall directed him to talk about his conversation with Ray at the Quincy Hotel on the late afternoon of October 3. Wall asked how that had come about. Bogardus related that he had been searching for Ray with no success. Then he hit upon a simple but ingenious strategy involving the use of an unsuspecting Esther Reeder as bait. She was subpoenaed to appear before Deputy Fire Marshal Bogardus at the hotel. After her interrogation, deputies trailed her, and in fewer than fifteen minutes she met up with Ray. Deputies caught Ray by surprise as he listened to her tale and hustled him back to the fire marshal, where Mr. McNutt, the court reporter, used shorthand to take down Ray's statement.

The defense offered vehement objections. They claimed that as Bogardus was a state official, any statement made to him by the defendant, by definition, could not be a voluntary statement. The court overruled them, and Bogardus obligingly handed the statement to Wall.

Bogardus said he informed Ray that he could refuse to testify but that unless he talked, he would be subject to a hefty fine. Ray immediately requested his attorneys, but Bogardus replied that the Illinois Fire Marshal Act gave him power to exclude everybody from the room. And, due to careful planning by the marshal, Ray's attorneys were away from the city.

Ray was facing, in hotel room #525, an eager and hostile audience consisting of the fire marshal, the two officers who had brought him in, Deputy Fire Marshal Sloan, Sheriff Koch, and the court reporter.

Bogardus reported that he said to Ray, "Don't you think your folks were murdered?—and he said, 'Yes'!" The courtroom buzzed with excitement. At once, the judge said that statement would be stricken from the record and had the jury removed after instructing them to "pay no attention whatsoever to that answer." But the idea that Ray acknowledged that murder had been done was explosive news.

With the jury removed, attorney George Govert put his father, William H. Govert, also part of the defense team, on the stand to relate what was said after Ray's forced talk with Bogardus. The elder Govert spun a long rambling story, saying Ray had been told that if he didn't make a statement he would be arrested.[135] And further, if Ray refused to testify, it would signify guilt. The defense contended that the young man felt he had no other option than to submit to questioning.

Wall began the cross-examination of the senior Govert, and tempers heated. Their versions of the occurrence were radically different. To Wall, the investigation was completely legal, and Govert was merely concerned because he thought Ray might have incriminated himself. Wall further claimed that the elder Govert threatened the marshals and tried to nullify the statement in case it showed Ray's guilt. Govert countered that he was outraged over the apparent abuse of the power of the State of Illinois and that Bogardus was exceeding that authority.

It seemed a draw as the senior Govert vacated the stand.

Wall then brought Sheriff George Koch to relate his version of the events and heard a much nicer story. Ray was offered a chair and given repeated warnings of his rights and the assurance that Bogardus wasn't interested in the murders, only the fire. But he also confirmed the implied threat by reporting that Bogardus warned if Ray didn't talk he would go to court.

Bogardus came back to the stand and said in his defense, "Before any statement was taken, I said to him; 'Mr. Pfanschmidt, if you mean to stand on your constitutional rights and say to me, that anything you may give here, at this hearing would incriminate you, then you do not have to testify; but if you do not stand on your constitutional rights, and the evidence don't incriminate you, then you must testify under the Fire Marshal Act.'"

At that point, court was adjourned for the weekend.

---

[135] 30-5264, p. 467. The story begins here and continues for several pages.

# Chapter 17

# The Prosecution Builds Its Case

## Monday, April 7, 1913

When the trial resumed on Monday morning, the defense managed to win a round. In a long address, the judge painstakingly attempted to explain, out of the presence of the jury, the differences under law between "admissions" and "confessions" and said the following about the statement Ray made to Bogardus:

"The statement as contained in this offer had not arrived to the dignity of a confession. But there are many statements in that offer which would tend to show an admission or which would show or admit the existence of certain facts which the State was interested in showing in this proceeding, the same facts which they have already shown and other facts which are incorporated in the statement of the State's Attorney to the jury."[136]

The judge, after more wandering legal verbiage, arrived at a conclusion. Whether Ray's statement was called a "confession" or an "admission," it had to be voluntary to be admitted in court. By his own words, Bogardus had excluded its admissibility. "If it had not been for this one statement

---

[136] 40-5264, p. 476.

of the examiner, why then, of necessity the holding would have been different," said Judge Williams.

When the jury returned, the court simply said that it had determined that the statement Ray gave to Bogardus was not admissible and all things that occurred in the presence of the defendant at the Quincy Hotel were stricken from the record. The jurymen were to pay them no attention.

In a flanking maneuver, Wall questioned Bogardus about the next time he visited with Ray, which happened at the jail. The defense objected, insisting that anything said by Ray to Bogardus was not a voluntary statement. The court told Wall, "In the event that the conditions at a former examination were, as I have indicated, that you must show the non-presence of those conditions at a future examination as the presumption would obtain that the duress, as at first existing would continue to exist."[137]

Trying to prove the "non-presence" of coercion, Wall persevered.

The defense objected to any testimony pertaining to the previous conversation, and the jury was again excused. The court ruled that it was up to Bogardus to relieve Ray of any perception of duress or obligation before anything Ray said could be considered as voluntary. The judge therefore banned any further testimony about conversations when Bogardus was present. After another two hours of legal wrangling, Bogardus was dismissed. The defense had successfully prevented Ray's statement from being admitted.

Sheriff Lipps returned to the stand, and prosecutor Wall questioned him about how often Ray's attorneys visited him. Lipps replied, "Well, I would have to take that from the jailor; I told him to keep track of the days; the days they missed, not the days they came there because I figured they would be there every day. I told him to keep track of the days that the lawyers didn't come down to the jail."

Having demonstrated that Ray was not denied access to his lawyers, Wall recalled Bogardus to talk about another of the occasions when he spoke to Ray. The defense objected and the court said it could not rule until later, after researching admissibility of such testimony. Frustrated, Bogardus left the stand.

---

[137] 40-5264, p. 480.

The prosecution moved on to Ray's friend, Harvey Scott, age eighteen, an employee of the Cottrell Hardware Company. Harvey remembered Ray coming into the store on the Saturday night of the fire between half past seven and eight o'clock and staying until the store was locked up at nine thirty. Then he, Ray, and Miller went next door to the Mission Pool Room and played pool until ten thirty or a bit later. Afterward Scott and Ray walked a block and a half to the Parthenon Candy Kitchen on the south side of Maine Street between Fifth and Sixth streets, where they enjoyed some ice cream. Ray headed east at the corner of Sixth Street and Maine, while Scott turned south toward his home. When Scott got home after walking two blocks it was 11:05. To him, Ray had seemed perfectly normal all evening. The defense had no questions.

Wall then had another thought and recalled Scott to find out if Ray had asked about mail or any letters sent to him in care of the store. Scott did not remember Ray doing that; nor did he know if Ray had used either the Home or the Bell telephone at the store, which subscribed to both services.

George Koch, at that time a private detective, was recalled to the stand. He stated that he had been hired by C. C. Pfanschmidt and sent to the farm on Sunday. Koch said, "I of course looked at the ruins and talked to several of the gentlemen who seemed to have charge, and I went to the wagon yard and got busy investigating the best I knew how."[138]

By the time he arrived, Koch could drive into the lane up as far as the granary but not into the barnyard; Ray had left for the Reeders', and the bodies were gone. Koch agreed with the prosecution that the buggy tracks were fresh, steel tired, and had a very short turning radius, but he was unable to follow them any distance because they had been obliterated by vehicles such as his own automobile.

With not much else to see at the farm, Koch went back to Quincy and visited Sheriff Lipps. He and the sheriff returned to the farm, arriving at dusk, about 6:30 p.m. A crowd remained but was smaller than before. Wall led him through his description of the odd shape of the horseshoe,

---

[138] 30-5264, p. 492.

and Koch agreed that the tracks he found had been made in mud, although the ground was dry by his visit.

About 7:30 or 8:00 p.m. that same evening, Koch and the sheriff went to Ray's camp and conducted a search. "We made a search in both camps; there was one camp in which there were two cots; we searched the bed clothing and everything in that tent. The floor I did in particular; I got down to see if I could find anything on the ground. We found a belt, which had cartridges around it, and a scabbard and a .32 caliber revolver hanging from the center pole of the tent."[139]

Near the head of the cot on the east side of the tent, Koch found a gold ring that would attach the top of a watch to a watch fob. On the stand, he casually pulled this piece of evidence out of his pocket and offered it to the attorney.

In the other tent, Koch reported "quite a good lot of clothing, dynamite caps, fuses, batteries and such." He described finding khaki clothes, some underwear, linens, and shoes. In particular, he found a pair of low-cut shoes with stubby toes, a pair of what seemed to be brand new leggings, russet leather leggings, some soiled linens, and a khaki suit that seemed to have been "worn some." There were also some new khaki clothes. The one thing the searchers did not find was a buggy robe or lap robe.

On Monday morning, September 30, Koch was back at the farm. This time he noticed the gas can with the funnel-shaped top and the dent in its side. Finding nothing else of note, he trekked back to Ray's camp for another search. The courtroom heard yet another description of the outhouse, including the report that Koch had peered into the holes that day without seeing anything unusual. He returned to the camp Monday evening and found Lancaster, Geisel, and Fred Pfanschmidt there as well. The bloodhounds had also arrived at the camp before Koch. He saw them both sitting near the buggy—or maybe he saw one in the car and one near the buggy. He seemed unsure.

On Tuesday afternoon he returned to the farm and this time came upon a group of investigators. Koch brought Plank with him and later

---

[139] 30-5264, p. 497.

accompanied him to remove a shoe from one of Ray's horses. On that trip "we stopped there at the last blacksmith shop on Twelfth Street and borrowed a pair of pinchers—one of those arrangements for unclinching a horseshoe nail," to remove the shoe without bending it or pulling it out of shape. The two men successfully removed the right hind shoe from the mare, which was then taken back to the barnyard and fitted into the print before the paraffin impression was made.

According to Koch, there was dust in the impression, but his automobile air pump was out of commission so could not have been used to blow dust from the tracks. The loose dirt was blown out by Fogal, on his hands and knees huffing and puffing. The paraffin was heated there in the yard, poured into the track, and then allowed to sit until it cooled. He thought the ground was a kind of light-colored clay.

He described for Wall additional details of Ray's camp. Entering the Frese property from Twelfth Street, it was about sixty yards to the water closet and another sixty-five or seventy-five yards to the tents Ray occupied and the construction area. The land sloped uphill from Twelfth Street, and the entire property was bounded on the east and south by the curve of the high-banked railroad track, which then passed above Twelfth Street on an elevated crossing.

If you followed the railroads tracks due east from the camp for a bit more than a mile, you would reach the very pasture the bloodhounds investigated before arriving at the works. Koch testified that he walked through this pasture, crossed the live flowing stream, Cedar Creek, and was headed directly west to Ray's camp when he unexpectedly ran into a new three-strand barbed-wire fence. "It looked like it had been set up there to block that road off; it was in a good condition, perhaps better than the other fence that had been set across there, since the road was made." At the point where the fence obstructed the road, he was only about five blocks from Ray's camp.

On cross-examination, Govert probed into Koch's investigation of the camp and especially the bed clothes and pillows. "Did you find any blood on them?"

"No, sir."

The jury listened as Govert politely asked Koch about his experience with firearms, and Koch replied that he had quite a little experience with them. Had he examined the revolver to see if it had been fired within the past day? Well, yes, he had. And had it been fired? No. How could he determine that, Govert wondered.

Koch answered, "Well, there was lint in the end of the revolver. I was looking to see if it had been fired and that is the reason I broke it and looked in it, and I was satisfied it had not been and I put it back."

Once again clothing became the topic. Govert led Koch to explain to the jury that by "soiled" he meant worn, not bloodied. Koch found, on his afternoon search, one khaki suit, lying on the tent floor with galluses, or suspenders, attached and faded from the laundry but obviously having been worn. There was also a box that he thought held two new, never-worn khaki suits. When he returned to the tent that evening, there was a pair of new heavy leather russet leggings, also without blood spots, and the revolver was gone.

Koch thoroughly searched the camp, the works, Frese's barns and lofts and hay mangers. He said he was helped at one time or another by Mr. Young, Mr. Bogardus, Mr. Sloan, Mr. Schaeffer, Mr. Lipps, and Mr. Buerkin. They found nothing of import.

It was clear to him that on Monday morning, September 30, there were no bloody clothes to be found in the vault, although it was almost full of "matter." There were no openings in the outside walls, and, in fact, the vault was set tight in the ground all around the edges. The only way a suit could have gotten into the place where it was found was through one of the holes. Inside the floor was solid, the seats firmly attached. There was an argument as to whether it might have been possible to see the clothes in the position where they were found, but then the court struck all testimony about this issue.

Wall asked Koch if, in all his searches, he had found a red string necktie. "I did not."

But then to Govert's repeated questions, he admitted there may have been ties there but not red ones. Koch said he saw no holes of any kind in the clothes taken from the vault. Govert repeated questions about holes in the clothing; perhaps he wished to imply that doing the violent crime Ray was accused of would likely have resulted in some damage.

The long and dramatic trial took a physical toll on the venue as well as its participants. "Long before the court had convened this afternoon, deputy sheriffs were kept busy turning spectators away after the courtroom had been filled. The gallery has been condemned, and consequently the crowd was crowded into the lower floor."[140] The weight of the overflow crowds had damaged the structural integrity of the beautiful old Quincy courthouse, and space became even more precious.

When court resumed, Wall recalled Dr. Center to the stand. He handed him the axe blade found in the ruins and asked if this weapon could have caused the wounds to Miss Kaempen. Over strident objections, the court allowed him to answer, "It could have been."

What about that partial body—could it have had portions cut off? Dr. Center replied, "In my opinion, it had been." Over strenuous defense objections, he continued, "From the appearance of the remains, I should judge that all of the body, not appearing, had been cut off." This confirmation elicited horrified gasps from the spectators.

What exactly was left of that body? Wall wanted details.

Dr. Center replied, "A portion of one thigh, and the hip on the corresponding side, the hip or portion of the hip on the opposite side and the lower part of the trunk."[141]

Ignoring the murmurs in the courtroom, Wall explored the nature of Miss Kaempen's wounds, asking about the significance of the large blood clot in her mouth, which was "sufficient to fill the cavity of the mouth." He closed in on the central issue. "State to the jury whether or not in your opinion that blood got into that position before the body was burned."

Dr. Center answered confidently, "The mouth was filled with blood before death."

The defense was adamant that this evidence was "not proper under the issues in this case" and should not be allowed. The judge overruled them

---

[140] *Journal,* April 7, 1913.
[141] 30-5264, p. 530.

each time they protested and testimony concerning the other bodies was soon detailed for the consideration of the jury.

The doctor said by his estimation the amount of blood in the human body was about one twelfth or one fourteenth of the weight of that body. Wall fished for an evaluation of how much Emma's head wound bled, considering the body's position upon a pillow. What could the doctor tell the jury about that quantity?

"A sufficient quantity to cause death," was the flat reply.

The defense was incensed, but the judge refused to strike the answer. Wall went on, seeking more details: "I mean with reference to pounds or ounces, in that respect, could you tell?"

"I would say at least two thirds of the blood in that body could escape thru those wounds."

How did Dr. Center think this life was ended? "… death came by violence other than by fire."

In defense of his client, Lancaster rose for cross-examination. He had the doctor stand in the witness box and illustrate the extent of damage, demonstrating on his own body which parts were left on the lump of flesh found in the basement. He made little progress, however, and Center was dismissed.

The next witness in the procession of physicians was Dr. Thomas Knox.

The judge heard the latest objection by the defense and said, "Your objection may go to all of this line of examination. The record may show that counsel for defendant objected to all examination of this witness concerning the appearance and other testimony relative to the condition of the bodies at the time of the autopsy, or otherwise, and relative to the opinion of the witness as to the cause of death of these bodies other than that named in the indictment No. 2055. The objection is overruled."[142]

Dr. Knox said of the partial body: "It had the appearance of being cut down through the center; not quite the center but in an angle just below the hip coming up about thru the center taking a course a little

---

[142]  30-5264, p. 538.

above the hip just cutting the lower quarter." According to Dr. Knox, this disassembly had definitely been accomplished before the body burned.

On cross-examination, the testimony took an even more macabre turn. "How long would it take to cut up a body like that?" Lancaster wondered. "Wouldn't it would take many blows, a long time, and a lot of effort?"

Dr. Knox contradicted this saying that "a saw would do it, and pretty easily; after all, there was only one bone there in the thigh. The cut to the hip bone was smooth and most likely done with a saw. The other cuts were most likely made with a sharp knife because the edges were even."[143] The witness was dismissed, and the courtroom drew a collective breath.

In order for their theory about Ray's movements to work, the State needed to prove a later start time for the fire than the eleven o'clock or so, provided by Miller's testimony. Wall called Claude Peter to support their timeline. Peter said he left the village of Payson at about midnight traveling to his home near the Pfanschmidt farm. In those thirty or forty-five minutes, he saw no evidence of fire or flame.

Peter agreed about the fresh tracks made by small horses and an undercut buggy, but this time Lancaster drew from Peter, who also owned an undercut buggy, the opinion that these buggies were fairly common. In fact, there was nothing about this style buggy to attract attention. The court drew the line when Lancaster characterized them as a "young man's buggy," sustaining the prosecution's objection that this was not a proper question.

In another whipsaw change of pace and topic, one of Ray's employees, forty-five-year-old Silba Lawrence was called to testify. He told of Ray giving him a ride home from the works to his Chestnut Street lodging on Friday about six o'clock in the evening. He saw Ray again about 7:00 a.m. on Saturday morning at work, dressed in a stiff hat and a light-colored raincoat. On Saturday night, when Ray gave him another ride home, he wore a white collar and a blue-colored coat "if I remember right." Lawrence admitted that he did not know what Ray wore beneath the raincoat which was called at the time, a "cravenette."[144] He thought that later that same

---

[143] 30-5264, p. 541.

[144] "Cravenette" was a system of waterproofing woolen fabrics and was used in the manufacturing of raincoats.

Saturday morning when Ray came back to the works about ten or so, he was wearing his khaki suit.

Saturday evening, while taking Lawrence home, Ray made a stop at the headquarters building of the Soldier's Home. In the buggy, they traveled the same trail the dogs would later take, entering through the Twelfth Street gate and leaving by the one near Eighth and Locust streets.

Lawrence saw Ray on Sunday evening, September 29, when Ray stopped by with Esther in the buggy to give over his time book and ask Lawrence to keep the men at work until he heard from him again. There was nothing unusual about the team or the buggy or Ray that attracted Silba's attention. Lawrence, who had had known Ray since his childhood, would have noticed any odd behavior had it been there.

Wall had more questions. Was it raining on the Saturday morning when Ray wore that raincoat? Yes, drizzling. And, yes, Lawrence had seen the raincoat at least once before.

Lawrence described in detail the exact location of the clothing found in the vault. He said the pieces were laying "right back" against the north edge of the vault strung out from east to west. Lancaster pointed out that was the arrangement after the house had been overturned, intimating that the very tipping over of the wooden structure might have changed their location.

Next came publisher William Robinson of the Liberty, Illinois paper. Robinson, a former teacher, had for five years served as the principal of the Payson School and as a teacher in the high school. Ray had been his pupil for three of those years and graduated in 1909. The class motto that year, identifying their ambition to always seek to be better, was, "We stand for plus." Robinson was handed the pin found on the bloody clothes and identified it as the class pin of 1909. The defense let him leave quietly, asking him no questions.

Interest in the courtroom rose as the schoolteacher Emma's brother, Emil Kaempen, took the stand. He told of last seeing his sister alive on Friday night a week before the fire and, sadly, of identifying her body lying next to Blanche at the undertaker's establishment. He then related a troubling exchange with Ray, whom he had never met until the fire.

"I walked up to Mr. Pfanschmidt while he was standing south of the house in the orchard, and shook hands with him; I asked, 'Is this Ray Pfanschmidt?' He says, 'Yes.' I says, 'I am Emma's brother.' Then I says, 'This is a terrible thing; you have my sympathy.'"

What was his reply? There was none.

Ray had said nothing.

Emil continued: "I asked him how four people could smother in a house of that kind. He said he did not know." That was the end of the exchange.[145] The defense did not ask a single question. It seemed unacceptable that Ray made no return exchange or expression of sorrow and condolence to Emil Kaempen.

Wall called A. D. Kaylor to the stand. He ran a stable, worked with horses, and purchased feed for them as part of his business. The defense began raising its litany of objections, which by now signaled to the courtroom that something interesting or potentially damaging was coming.

Kaylor remembered buying oats from Charles Pfanschmidt in 1912, paying him eighteen dollars and fifty cents. Wall wanted to know how long before the fire he purchased that load of oats, but the defense sprang to its feet with an objection that was sustained. Kaylor left the stand without resolving details of that load of oats. The defense then succeeded in having his entire testimony stricken from the record, objecting with the usual "immaterial, incompetent, improper, and irrelevant."

Testimony returned to the hoof print with Wall's next witness, who also had a spelling error in his name, being John Fogal—not Fogel. This occasioned a ten-minute recess to allow the defense to examine the witness. Fogal was a Quincy businessman, manufacturing elevators, automatic gates, and fire doors at Seventh and Maine Street for the past sixteen years. He had driven Dr. Knox to the fire scene in his automobile on Tuesday, when the paraffin impressions were made.

Fogal's testimony at first seemed to benefit the defense. He saw buggy tracks almost completely defaced by the chicken scratches, and the horse

---

[145] 30-5264, p. 567.

track was very indistinct. Then the tone of his testimony began to shift. The soil was clay and "intermingled with cinders or ashes, but very little," and blew away when he got on his knees and puffed at it. He calculated the general area where that same horse hoof would have landed and puffed away at the dust until he uncovered another perfect track. Unfortunately, the shoe with the distinctive calk "had come in contact with a cinder or a pebble and that would not permit the shoe to go down in the clay to make a deep enough impression."[146] So one track had a calk imprint but the next one didn't.

Fogal agreed that the horseshoe was fitted into the track before the wax impression was taken. He found a third track, fitted the same shoe into it, and then created the second wax mold. The mold-making process sounded like a Boy Scout project. "Some made the fire to heat the wax; we took a spirit stove out with us and it proved to be inadequate, and the boys gathered up wood, built a fire, and I believe all contributed a little in the general preparation." Fogal said he made the cast and took his time being very careful with it.

When Wall asked about the automobile pump, Fogal replied, "After the work was done on the tracks, Mr. Plank brought an automobile pump, a pump for inflating the tire, and suggested that he had something there, and he put it down in the ground and began blowing in some tracks, but not the tracks we were working with."

Thus, yet another version of the dirt-removing auto pump entered into testimony.

Govert rose with further issues. For example, wasn't this the very first paraffin impression Fogal had ever made of a horseshoe? Didn't it require some experimentation to prepare the ground? Govert moved to the search for tracks and evoked images of Fogal on hands and knees, huffing and puffing away at the dust for several feet before finding a second track, only to discover it was too shallow to be of use.

Govert's questions reminded the jury that the shoe was fitted into each track before any wax impression was created. "Not [from] any one [track]

---

[146] 30-5264, p. 573.

did you take a paraffin impression before the shoe had been fitted into the tracks, did you?"

"No, sir." Witness dismissed.

Wall recalled John Lier to elicit a chilling detail. Over defense objections, Lier's testimony began this way:

"State whether or not Mr. C. A. Pfanschmidt, during his lifetime, kept about his premises a meat saw of any kind."

"Yes, sir, as I remember ... a small meat saw."

"Now state whether or not you have seen that meat saw since the fire about the premises any time?"

"Not that I can remember."

Govert approached to clarify things. When was the very last time Lier noticed the saw? He thought it was a year ago last winter, when the Pfanschmidts butchered. Did he mean one year before the fire? Yes. Witness dismissed.

Charles Ellerbrecht, fifty-eight, was called to the stand. He had been a clerk for two years at the Hub Clothing Company at 523 Hampshire Street and had known Ray since he was a small boy. Ellerbrecht attested to selling Ray some khaki clothes—one set in August on the twenty-ninth, and then more on September 19, which had to be special ordered for Ray. He confirmed that the Hub store was the only place in Quincy you where could purchase the Rosenwald & Weil brand, manufactured in Chicago.

Govert carefully elicited the information that the three suits were identical and matched the one Ray purchased the previous month. The three new suits (coat size 40, pants size 32-33) were put into a single box and handed over to Ray. Although the garments might be sold elsewhere in Illinois, the manufacturer was a wholesale outlet only and did not sell directly to the public.

Payson telephone operator Laverda Whitcomb reached the stand, and testimony took a different turn. Telephone operators at the time knew *everything*, since they were able, and not averse, to listening in on all conversations. Operators were essential as they manually moved wires on the switchboards, which plugged in to complete the circuits between the calling parties. Laverda worked at the Payson telephone central office located in Dr. Gabriel's office building in the village.

In 1912 it was considered long distance to place a call from Payson to the nearby cities such as Quincy, Illinois, or Hannibal, Missouri. Wall asked Laverda if, on the night of the fire, any long distance calls came for the Charles Pfanschmidt family. Over defense objections, the woman answered in the affirmative.

Miss Whitcomb was not allowed to say that the other operator told her the call was from Mrs. Kaempen, as that was ruled hearsay. Although not allowed to mention that the caller was female, she did testify that the calls came over the Quincy Bell network and there were six or seven of them beginning at about seven o'clock in the evening on Saturday.

The prosecution returned to Ray's Saturday evening whereabouts and brought forth Frank H. Kathman. Ray had introduced himself to Kathman a few days before the fire, when they met by chance in front of Chadwick's Machine Company. Kathman worked at the Stern's & Sons clothing company at Fifth and Hampshire, where, on Saturday, Ray had purchased a flannel shirt, a pair of hose, and possibly a necktie. "I have a faint recollection of a necktie, but I can't recall it positively," said Kathman. Afterward, Ray vanished through Stern's front door sometime between five and seven in the evening.

Govert questioned the apparel salesman about what Ray was wearing that night, but Kathman could not say. The clerk adamantly refused to name any piece of wardrobe Ray wore, not having noticed his shirt, hat, collar, or if he was carrying a parcel or a suitcase. Surprisingly, Kathman was observant enough to correct Govert's description as to the color of Ray's new flannel shirt. Govert termed it "gray," but Kathman disagreed. It was a "dead grass color.... You may term that a tannish green." The clerk acknowledged that Ray paid for the clothes at that time but couldn't say where he went afterward. Witness dismissed.

In an attempt to reestablish the credibility of his witness, Wall recalled the bloodhound man, Strumpfer, who had since examined his records in an aid to clarify his spotty memory. Perhaps the specter of a perjury charge loomed, for he returned to admit under oath that he wished to correct his testimony in some instances, although it remained "substantially the same."[147] He stated that the dogs *were* at three of the places that Govert had mentioned, working on the trails of fugitives.

Govert returned to question him, with a certain degree of relish. Govert bombarded him with questions about his previous denials and his inability to remember an event from only three months ago. The defense uncovered nothing new but perhaps cast seeds of doubt on the veracity of the witness. Or perhaps not—the men of the jury thought their own thoughts.

The superintendent of the Soldier's Home, Col. James O. Anderson, was called and questioned about roads through the facility. He listed three gates on roads passing through the grounds: one was located at Fifth Street, one at Twelfth Street, and one on Locust Street near Eighth Street. Each of these entrances had a guard house, which meant that even after the official 8:30 p.m. closing time there remained a presence at each gate. The main gate was on Fifth Street and had two men lodged there; the new gate at Twelfth Street housed one in a guard house set a distance back from the road. Anderson said there was a streetcar track near the Locust gate, but thick shrubbery would prevent anyone from bypassing the closed gate. Ray traveled these roads almost daily.

Charles H. Achelpohl was called. He was manager of the Quincy Home Telephone Company but at the time of the fire had been in the drugstore business. Ray came into his store about seven or eight o'clock Sunday night after the fire and used the phone to tell "Ben" not to come fetch his team. Ray's uncle William Abel was also there, and in the course of conversation was asked to accompany Ray to visit the lawyers the following morning. Achelpohl's testimony contradicted Ray's account of when he first talked to his lawyers.

Wall next called Frank Schupp, who had worked at the Cottrell Hardware Company for sixteen years. He sold Ray supplies such as "dynamite, fuse and caps, and such, like engineer's tools and other items," beginning about May of 1912. Schupp came armed with a paper, which

---

[147] 30-5263, p. 593.

he consulted to say that last September, Ray owed Cottrell's the sum of $530.18. To date, nothing had been paid toward that balance.

Govert stood up to neutralize this testimony. Ray had had his account there for a long time, correct? Yes.

"That account ran up and had been paid from time to time?"

"Yes, sir." Schupp testified that Ray had previously had balances as high as $800 and paid them on time.

And, pressed Govert, "his credit has been very satisfactory to you?"

"Yes, sir."

Wall asked more questions, this time concerned with fuses. Did Schupp ever sell Ray a timer fuse? "We have sold him fuses, but never termed them time fuses; that is not the term they are called by the manufacturers ..., we call them a single and a double tape fuse."

Wall pursued his agenda, asking how long it took a "single tape fuse" to burn a foot.

Schupp answered, "It takes possibly a half or three quarters of a minute." That was the type of fuse Ray bought.

On cross, Govert reasonably inquired if this sort of fuse and dynamite were commonly used for grading on farms and blowing out ditches and stumps.[148] It was indeed right for that work, Schupp agreed. In short, there was nothing special at all about the items Ray purchased.

Wall had one more query. "What happens when a burning fuse reaches its end, if there is nothing there?"

"It spits out a blaze about three quarters of an inch long," Schupp replied.

Wall wanted the jury to figure that about seven feet of fuse would provide the five minutes needed to exit a house and drive away in a buggy before the little "blaze" at the end of the fuse reached waiting gasoline or coal oil or rags.

The topic changed to automobiles, when Wall called Charles Chadwick, owner of Chadwick's Machine Shop, to take his turn in the box. His store

---

[148] In this time, when horsepower was literally four-legged, the use of explosives to loosen quantities of dirt and to break large heavy objects such as boulders and tree stumps into manageable pieces was common practice.

was located at 115 S Seventh Street on the west side between Maine and Jersey, bordering the alley to the south.

Chadwick recalled meeting Ray about the first of September, after corresponding with him about an automobile. Ray was in the market for a used auto, but Chadwick didn't know of an available secondhand car at that time. Later when he wrote to Ray about a used vehicle, he received the answer that Ray no longer wanted such a car. By then Ray had decided only a new car would do.

So Chadwick obliged by mentioning the Rambler brand automobile. Ray wrote to the factory and asked to speak to a company representative, who duly appeared in Quincy and ensconced himself in the plush Newcomb Hotel. Chadwick attended a meeting there with Ray and the Rambler representative but the deal was not concluded. Chadwick later heard from the representative that a contract had been closed for two cars. "One was a five-passenger touring car; the other was a Roadster. The five-passenger touring car at wholesale price was $1,485."[149] The Roadster, which was to be a demonstrator car, would cost Ray $1,435. The five-passenger car was for Ray's personal use.

Over strenuous objections from the defense, Wall inquired "if there was any contract made for any other cars?"

"Yes, sir ... twenty cars."

Wall asked Chadwick what he heard pass between Ray and the Rambler representative. "I could not answer that question because I do not remember any of the conversation whatever, no more than a man selling an automobile to anybody else; I could not stand off and tell word for word what he said."

Finally, between objections, Chadwick said there was a 20 percent profit margin in the sale of these cars. At this, the court allowed the part of the answer about profit to be stricken from the record. When asked about his partnership with Ray, Chadwick said it was there "in a way; they[sic] were to furnish garage room to Ray." The defense objected and the court concurred; the answer was stricken. Then the prosecutors admitted, feeling

---

[149]  30-5264, p. 507.

slightly foolish, that they did not realize there had been a written contract. Chadwick said he could produce the written contract, although he had neglected to bring it with him to court.

Answering Wall's questions, Chadwick said Ray was in and out of the store several times on the Saturday the Pfanschmidt home burned. He last saw Ray's team tied on Seventh Street facing north, about 8:00 p.m. He was not sure if Ray used the garage phone but was certain Ray was again in the store sometime after the two o'clock mail delivery on Saturday. Ray appeared to be behaving as usual.

Edwin Buerkin, contractor with the firm of Buerkin and Kaempen, came next to the stand. Buerkin said he learned of the fire shortly after six on Sunday morning and rushed to the farm in his automobile, arriving shortly after seven o'clock. It was there Buerkin first met Ray, through an introduction by his business partner, Charles Kaempen.

Over the course of his time at the fire, Buerkin watched Ray closely. After a trip to take Emma's father back to the city to confirm the tragic news, Buerkin was back at the fire scene by about 10:00 a.m. This time Sheriff Lott was there, and Ray's relatives had also arrived. Buerkin helped the sheriff take a length of binder twine, which they found in the machine shed, and measure the distance between Ray's buggy's back wheels to compare it to the barn lot tracks. They matched. "Exactly; they were very close," said Buerkin.

When they confirmed the similarity, Buerkin and the chief of police went to Ray's team and took a tracing around the left front hoof of the horse hitched on the left,[150] and they then sawed this tracing from the paper with a pocketknife. Buerkin carried this tracing to "the print out in the yard and laid this form that I had cut out over the print."[151] Ray's was the only team and buggy they checked.

Buerkin reported that even after the fire, "Why, I was out there almost every day for a month or five weeks." He was there for the creation of the cast of the hoof print but not there to watch the hounds leave from the

---

[150] The "near" horse in the team; the horse hitched on the right is the "off" horse.
[151] 30-5264, p. 622.

farm. Instead, he watched the hounds when they started from the Reeder home, a trail that was never allowed into testimony.

Buerkin was at Ray's camp, in his tent, and in the field directly east of the camp. In the tents, he said, "There were about two dozen sticks of dynamite, a lot of fuses and caps." What kind of fuse? "Why, it looked like time fuse." The defense objected, saying this witness had no knowledge of fuses, and that there was no such thing as a "time fuse." Overruled.

Govert faced off with Buerkin. He was curious how they marked the piece of twine used to measure the width between the wheels and tracks. Buerkin related that he held one end and the sheriff tied a knot in the other. He also cut a second piece of twine to measure the two tracks in the second spot in the dirt. Buerkin remembered there was about a three quarter inch difference between the two strings.

Govert wondered where they measured the buggy. At the top of the wheels, Buerkin reported. Not at the axle? Or in the middle? "No, sir." Buerkin said they measured the wheels at the top and again at the ground, and the difference was that the distance at the top of the wheels was one half to three quarters of an inch wider. Govert thought that there was normally a two-inch difference in the spread at the top of the wheels.

"It is on a new buggy," Buerkin replied. Ray's was not a new buggy.

Did Buerkin know how long that twine was in feet and inches? "No, sir."

"Your only measurement is a piece of twine?" Govert was skeptical.

"Yes, sir, that was stretched tight."

The twine had been left with the sheriff, but there was no way to tell if the string had shrunk or stretched or changed since that time. Govert wondered if perhaps the hoof print had been crossed by the buggy wheel track, implying that this could have caused its odd shape. Buerkin flatly denied that. After making few inroads, Govert concluded and Buerkin was dismissed.

From buggies, testimony returned to automobiles, and Chadwick was recalled to the stand with evidence to back up his statements from the previous day. The contract for the Rambler deal was admitted into evidence and marked State's Exhibit V;[152] Wolfe read it to the jury.

> "The Rambler Motor Sales company, Quincy, Illinois, consisting of Charles Chadwick and Ray A. Pfanschmidt as equal partners agree to do all business in the selling of Rambler cars and any secondhanded cars and accessories on the following terms:
>
> Said Charles Chadwick is to furnish all necessary garage room for storing of motor cars and accessories free from cost and keep the two demonstrating cars in good driving condition without any other cost that the dealers price of necessary repairs and accessories; also to furnish a suitable office for the business of said Company.
>
> Ray A. Pfanschmidt is to furnish all necessary capital for the transaction of the business of said Company.
>
> Both Charles Chadwick and Ray A. Pfanschmidt are to have equal freedom in use of cars and garage in the transaction of business for the company.
>
> All profits derived from any sales or trades under the company are to be equally divided between Charles Chadwick and Ray A. Pfanschmidt."

This contract was good until July 31, 1913, and then going onward until the parties decided to change it. It was signed on September 21, 1912, just over a week before the tragedy. The State was providing testimony that fueled questions about how Ray planned to acquire all the "capital" he had promised to furnish.

Chadwick went on to say that one car, the "demonstrator," was shipped about ten days after the fire; the second one was never shipped. The one

---

[152] 30-5264, p. 636.

that did arrive was sent on to another dealer in Galesburg. The second car was not shipped because Chadwick had no authority to re-place the order for the car, and Ray did not do it.

Once again Wolfe was surprised by the answers of his witness: "This is not what I expected."

The next witness was Mr. Richard W. Farley of Chicago, an employee of Young's Detective Agency for about three and a half years. Before that he had been a detective for twelve or fourteen years. "Mr. Farley is an alert young man, wearing glasses and looking very much like a school teacher. He bears a noticeable resemblance to the published pictures of President Woodrow Wilson."[153]

The Kaempen family had retained Young's agency to help investigate their daughter's death, and Farley was sent to Quincy to be locked up in the jail in an attempt to secure Ray's confession. He was put into the cell block about October 16 or 17 and stayed almost forty-six hours. Interest in the courtroom rose even as the defense was objecting to admissibility of anything Ray said to Farley, claiming their client was under duress while in jail. The court politely asked Govert if he wanted to offer any proof to show that the defendant was under duress. Govert declined. Objection overruled.

Ray claimed to Farley that the authorities had nothing on him, and he had a witness to swear that his team had no harness marks and had refused to drink before starting to the Pfanschmidt farm and that would be an alibi. He blamed a Payson man named Short for staging the clothes in the vault to throw suspicion his way. According to this tale, Ray had on "several occasions cut him out of a girl, and Short out of revenge … had stolen the clothing and placed it in the vault to throw suspicion on Mr. Pfanschmidt."

Farley parroted, "He also said that he had always been anxious to get in with a good crook," and went on to talk about the two banks in Payson that did not have vaults, so kept money amounting to ten thousand dollars in a safe that could be easily broken into. Ray reportedly mentioned that

---

[153] *Herald*, April 8, 1913.

he could pull the fuses on the telephone boxes situated on the outside of the buildings and get safely away. Then Farley swore that Ray offered him $10,000 to bust him out of jail and recommended the jail's north windows, which were unscreened, for their escape route.

It was hard to know if these stories sprang from boredom and the prison bravado of a bright, young, excitement-loving Ray or were a serious request from a boy in fear of the outcome of his trial. A third possibility remained that they were an exaggeration or complete fabrication by the detective/informant Farley.

Govert took over the witness and led Farley through events leading up to his arrest and planting in the jail. Farley said he had been in town, holed up in his room on the fourth floor of the Hotel Newcomb for two days beforehand. He spoke little to Ray that first night when he reached the jail about eight or eight thirty, booked on suspicion "of being a crook." Govert wondered if there was an empty cell between the two of them, but Farley didn't think so. Govert contended that Ray was transferred from the cell he had occupied for the past six months to be next to the pretend crook. The following day Farley talked to Ray until Govert came to call on his client.

Whether Farley heard Ray ask for his attorneys or not, he was nonetheless carefully out of sight in the sheriff's office when Govert arrived. And Ray was back in his usual cell. After Govert's visit, the sheriff staged an "altercation" in which Farley loudly protested being put back into this cell. Later Farley offered Ray some of his special breakfast, which had been ordered from an outside restaurant. Ray declined and said he was used to jail food.

Govert then asked this odd question about Ray: "Didn't he say that it was a great deal better food than he had at home?"

Farley denied it. "No, he did not."

"But he told you that he had always been accustomed to coarse food, that was right?" the lawyer probed again.

"He did not say that exactly; he said he had always been used to coarse food, therefore did not mind the jail fare. He did not say that was what he always got at home,"[154] was Farley's answer.

---

[154] 30-5263, p. 650.

Govert asked several times if Farley knew what Ray and his attorney discussed concerning the jail's newest inmate. Farley shrugged it off, replying that he had no way to know.

Govert inquired about the source for the idea of pulling a bank job or busting out of jail. "Did *you* not suggest first when you were taken down there, did you not sort of suggest that there was an easy way to get out of jail?"

"I may have," Farley admitted.

Under further questioning, Farley stated that he could not tell what time the lawyer returned as he had no watch and couldn't very well see the outside conditions, neither the sun nor daylight. Ray was locked in his cell the rest of the time Farley was there, but Farley was privileged to have the chair jailer Monk provided and sit in the "bull pen"[155] in front of Ray's cell to talk to him. Prior to this there was only an uncomfortable bench available for prisoners.

"You did not think that raised a suspicious circumstance in Ray's mind as to why you were there?"

"No, sir."

"You were there on suspicion with a stab in your back, and they furnished you some accommodations down there, some luxuries, and a good wooden chair, and instead of giving you bread and molasses and sour hamburger, they gave you a good meal?"

At this point the State objected and their objection was sustained.

On the second day of his sham incarceration, officials again moved Farley into the jailer's office, out of sight while Ray's attorneys were visiting. Govert first came alone and then returned a bit later with Lancaster.

Farley, remembering the lawyer's demeanor, observed with a twitch of a smile, "You were very much exited when you came out of there."

"I looked very much excited, did I?" Govert had detected the undercover Farley and was infuriated.

"Yes, you were hardly able to talk." Fraley's grin was a bit larger.

---

[155] This was the area within the locked part of the jail, into which the cells opened. It was a privilege sometimes granted by the sheriff, allowing inmates to mingle there.

The courtroom erupted in gales of laughter. The transcript noted, "There being a slight confusion in the courtroom at this time, the court, 'I hope we won't have any more laughing: I had occasion to make this announcement last week, it will not be permitted.'"[156]

"I was quite beside myself that morning ... did I talk?" Govert had his own sense of humor.

Farley, grinning now, said, "It may have been talk."

"You do not know what it was?" the lawyer persisted.

"No," admitted Farley.

This brought another round of giggles and guffaws from the audience, but Govert didn't seem to mind. Govert, through his questions to Farley, conveyed a showdown with Sheriff Lipps, when Govert told the sheriff it was no use keeping Farley down there any longer. Govert said, "I told him it was just as well to put Mr. Young down there as you?"

Farley: "The exact language."

Sheriff Lipps had denied any knowledge of the "operation," but Farley was released a few hours later and any and all charges against him were dropped.

Govert probed for the truth. "[Lipps] did know, however, what you were down there for?"

"Yes, sir," answered Farley, confirming that the sheriff had lied to Govert.

Then Govert charged that even an article in the paper about Farley's arrest was a plant. Farley said he didn't know anything about it until Mr. Viehmeyer read it to him while he was in jail.

"Didn't I tell you at that time when I came out of there frothing at the mouth that you had been in town before your arrest too long not to be known?" There was an echo of anger in the attorney's tone.

"Not that I recollect."

"Then you went back and told Ray Pfanschmidt that we accused you of being a sleuth?"

"Yes, sir."

---

[156] 30-5264, p. 653.

"How long did you remain after that?"

"Probably half an hour."

Ray had been firmly warned by his lawyers not to talk to Farley or anyone else. Govert was attempting to convince the jury that Ray had always known that Farley was a plant and was passing the time by feeding him a line of goods. Govert asked if Ray said anything about breaking any banks.

"No," the detective reported, "only that he'd gotten arrested once for stealing in Champaign and shooting a schoolmate in the nose, I believe it was."

Govert alleged Farley had asked Ray if he was interested in hypnotism and if he would be a good subject, but Farley denied saying that. The courtroom was left to wonder if Farley had the ability to hypnotize people, or if such a session had been contemplated by the sheriff.

In response to further questions, testimony revealed that the cover story for holding Farley was that the sheriff was telegraphing Chicago, Kansas City, and St. Louis to see if he was wanted elsewhere. But Govert discovered that the officers hadn't gone so deeply into their subterfuge as to concoct actual telegrams to complete their story.[157] Farley told Govert that on the occasion of his arrest he pretended to be drunk and carried a wad of cash that appeared to be hundred-dollar bills. He asked a saloon keeper to exchange two of them. Farley claimed the bills were genuine and supplied by his employer H. F. Young. Since his release from his bogus imprisonment (during which he was paid thirty-five dollars per week while he was working), he had returned to Quincy twice more to continue his investigations.

Wall returned to be sure that the jury understood that Farley's salary was not dependent on any specific testimony. "It would not militate against you telling the truth in any respect," said Wall. On that note, a very entertaining witness was dismissed.

One newspaper wrote: "Despite determined efforts on the part of the defense to tear down the testimony offered by Richard Farley, a

---

[157] 30-5264, p. 656.

Chicago detective, the State managed to get some weird statements of Ray Pfanschmidt before the jury this morning, and although there was nothing said by Pfanschmidt to Farley that would incriminate the youth with the murder, his conversation with the detective, it is thought by the State, will have an effect on the jury."[158]

In an unusual display of continuity, Wall followed Farley with his boss, Herbert F. Young of the Young Secret Service company of Chicago, Illinois. Young, who would turn thirty-nine on the eleventh of the month, was hired by Charles Kaempen Sr. and Emil Kaempen.

Young said, "The purpose of my visit to Quincy and employment by Mr. Kaempen was to make an investigation to see if his daughter had been murdered and to find the person responsible for the murder, if a murder had been committed."

Young reported he was paid at the rate of twenty-five dollars per day plus expenses, which was his normal rate. He began his investigation at the fire scene on October 3,1912, and found that "strange oil can" was still lying at the site. The next time Young was there, he found "a good many things." He discovered three axes, a saw, a small hatchet, and a shoemaker's hammer. The hatchet and shoemaker's hammer were lying on top of the foundation wall close to the cistern at the northeast corner of the building. One axe was in a wagon shed on the north side of the granary; another was in the granary, and the third in the barn was in back of a barrel.

Young saw two flat-topped five gallon oil cans, and a smaller "Daisy Oil" can, which was glass lined with a tin jacket with cutouts so you could see the glass. It was sitting near the cistern at the northeast corner of the house.

Young's search was comprehensive: "I searched through the smokehouse; I looked in the vault; I searched through the barn; and I searched through a part of the granary. The granary was filled with oats. There was a good deal of oats in the barn, and I searched through what they call the cow shed and the chicken house, an outhouse that was along the road north of the house and [east] of the barn lot, sort of an extra barn that had some

---

[158] *Journal,* April 8, 1913.

things stored there. I walked all around the hog pen and crossed through them and searched around the straw pile on top of them and around the sides, and I walked all over the property." The search took him all day, except for a break for lunch in Payson.

On another day, Young and the sheriff shoveled through the ashes in the west part of the ruins but not the cellar. They emptied the cisterns and the vault, finding part of what looked like a man's undershirt and some portions of a woman's skirt.

In the barn, they found something else. Young said simply, "I found a piece of corn stalk with blood on it.... It was about four or five inches long and about three quarters of an inch wide."

Among the audience, eyes widened and some shoulders unconsciously stiffened at hearing mention of blood found in the barn. Without pausing, Young continued in his clear and concise manner detailing the efforts to solve the mystery.

"I went up into the hayloft and first by observation satisfied myself that the hay had not been recently changed. Then I came back again, and as I was unsatisfied and I forked the hay over, I looked down as far as I could go without digging it all out. I went downstairs on the main floor of the barn where the buggies were standing, and I raked the hay off the floor and looked to see if I could find any blood spots on the floor, underneath where I found the cornstalk. I also looked in the mangers and under the mangers, and in the stall where the horses were kept, back of the stall, around in the cleats on the side of the barn, underneath the floor of the barn, in the oat bin, thru the salt box and feed boxes, thru the barrels and everything that was closed up. I looked thru a box of clothing that was hanging in the corn crib, I looked thru everything I could find in the barn and thru the buggies. I made the same search again in the granary except where the oats were. They were too thick, and I could not look thru them at that time.

"We also climbed on top of the different buildings; that is to say on those I could not see upon; I looked around in the rafters in the barn and the outhouse that I spoke of before, and I climbed up and looked into that. Mr. Buerkin also was with me that day. I also searched in the cornfield, which was west of the house, and another field, which was east of the house, and northeast of the house there was a meadow that had a sort of ravine, where they apparently had used it as a catch-all; there was a lot of cans and rubbish they had discarded, and I searched that. Then I searched along the road from the Pfanschmidt home to Quincy; each time I went by there, some search was made and it was becoming more thorough every time we went by. I walked along the fences and the hedges and thru the edges of the fields, in the woods, and along the creeks and the edge of the bridges we passed, and these little creeks between there and Quincy, and we looked into, well, I don't know the names of these particular places because I am not acquainted with them, but there was a well near a bridge that we looked thru. I think in a general way that covered the search."

Wall asked if he found anything else. Two corn knives were added to the list.[159]

Then Wall asked about the field in Quincy north of the railroad crossing which the bloodhounds had visited on their trail from the farm. What did he find there?

Young reported, "Well, I observed at the place where the wire of this bob-wire fence crossed the creek, a stone that was sitting near the edge of a pool of water, and from this stone, it ran in a, it would be a westerly direction, some oil that had trickled from the stone into that water."

Perhaps the prosecution imagined Ray appropriating Frese's funnel-topped oil can, setting it over the fence behind the works into the empty pasture where he could retrieve it later in his little buggy, which had no storage area large enough to conceal such a container from view. Young could report only the oil spot on a rock in a small puddle in the middle of a pasture.

When Wall asked about his investigations at the work camp, Young, who was articulate and thorough, answered "in fact, I talked to every man, woman, and child I found around there, except the little babies, and they were quite too young." He also accompanied Lipps when the clothes were found and watched them and a piece of newspaper removed from the vault. What about the spots on the clothing?

---

[159] A corn knife is similar to a machete but weighs a bit more, and the fifteen-to-eighteen-inch blade widens toward the end. It has only one cutting edge.

"There were spots sprinkled all over the suit practically, all up and down the front, beginning about here [indicating], I should judge. There were spots all over the trousers when I saw them. All over, when I say all over, I mean they were probably a few inches apart, and on the front of the coat there were spots on the sleeves and shoulders clear up around the collar, around as far as about the centre where I have my hand [indicating] on the back. There was some spots on the trousers right here [indicating], of three tips looked like a man's fingers had been put right there, right over the hip pocket …"[160]

Wall asked, "What were those spots?"

The defense angrily objected, but was overruled.

Young answered, "I would say by looking at them, they were blood spots. I am not an expert, however." The court allowed his answer to stand.

Young next told of bringing the clothes to the sheriff's office and putting them downstairs in the furnace room to dry, along with the pieces of paper. It was to this hot, dark basement room that Esther Reeder and her father were then called to identify the clothing. And it was on this same day that Young finally met Ray Pfanschmidt, when he accompanied the sheriff to make the arrest at the home of Ray's Uncle Niekamp.

Young described what happened at the front door: "The sheriff said, 'Ray, I want you to come to the courthouse; I have got some things I want to talk to you about.' Mr. Pfanschmidt answered, 'All right.' And the three of us walked into the room. He walked into what I believe was the kitchen and from there into another room, which was a sort of sitting room. This lady, who I think was his aunt got his coat, got his hat, and Ray Pfanschmidt brushed his hair, put on his necktie, and I helped him on with his coat. In the meantime, the Sheriff and I both searched him for concealed weapons and we went out, got in the automobile, and Mr. Pfanschmidt sat with Sheriff Lipps coming straight to the courthouse and I stood on the running board of the car."[161]

At the courthouse, Ray was taken to the jailer's room where Lipps told him, "Ray, you are under arrest, charged with murder, and you have the

---

[160]  30-5264, p. 671.
[161]  30-5264, p. 673.

right to stand on your constitutional privilege and anything you might say may be used against you."

The prosecution asked detective Young how Ray answered. The defense, on their feet, objected strenuously to the admission of any words spoken by Ray in the jail, claiming they were said under duress. Objection overruled. Wall led Young through a recital of denials: there were no promises made, no threats made, no force exerted. Young remembered he said something like this to Ray: "You are in a pretty bad fix, my boy." Ray did not answer.

The defense objected again, loudly contending that since Ray did not reply, it was not a conversation and therefore not admissible. The court said, in essence, that might be true in some states, but not in this one! And he overruled the objection. To accommodate the defense and help the trial move along, the judge then instructed the court reporter to show this same objection as being made after each question on this matter.

Young, continuing his testimony, told of holding Ray's watch, examining it, and noting the numbers and the inscription before Govert blustered into the sheriff's office. The defense next objected to any testimony about what the attorneys said to their client, but this too was overruled.

Young reported that Govert "walked as close to Mr. Pfanschmidt as he could and told him not to talk to anybody. He says, 'You are under arrest, charged with a serious crime, and as your attorney, I tell you not to talk.'"

Then Govert, according to Young, addressed Sheriff Lipps. "He was close to him, he says, 'You have no right to question him, no officer has a right to question a man while under arrest, charged with a serious crime.'"

Young was not about to stand still for this. When no one else spoke up, "I answered and told him what he said was absurd, that an officer certainly had the right to ask questions of a man under arrest, that we were intelligent, and that we understood what he wanted his client to know, and he could save the rest of his argument if he was going to make a speech."

The enthralled listeners could picture the effect this retort from the big city detective had on Govert. Young recounted that Govert shook his finger at Ray, admonishing him to be silent. Then Sheriff Lipps chimed in, saying that if Ray was innocent, he should want to talk, and he "followed with the remark that maybe that was the reason that Govert didn't want his client to talk, because he might say something that would be used against him." The defense objected. The court overruled the objection.

There was no conversation in the jail after that, Young reported, and Ray was led off to a cell.

Young mentioned another conversation about a week later, with Ray in the jailer's room and others present: the jailer, the sheriff, and Dr. O'Neil. Wall led Young through the standard litany that nothing was promised to or coerced from Ray at this time. Young said he introduced Ray to Dr. O'Neil of Chicago. Again the defense objected at every question, but the objections were universally overruled.

Young said that Dr. O'Neil "spoke kindly" to Ray at great length, and finally, after pressuring Ray a good deal, got him to mention some names of people who might be responsible for the crime. A few of these names had already been heard in the courtroom: Frank Short; John Lier, a Mr. Beilstein, and neighbor Kaufman.

Young asked why Short was named, and Ray explained he and Frank Short had been friends but that Short was a "brutally revengeful sort of fellow who tried to get back at him some way." Ray told a story of following Short and watching him crawl in the window of a lady friend, after removing his shoes and hat. Ray took the shoes, tied the laces together, threw them over a tree limb, and carried the hat into town, where he gave it to some boys along with the story. In return, according to Ray, Short told things to Miss Reeder about Ray that were not true.

Mr. Beilstein and Charles Pfanschmidt had some trouble over the shooting of a cow, but Young didn't remember the details of that story. Ray had no explanation for mentioning John Lier but said his father and Kaufman had had trouble over land. Later Young reported to Ray that he had investigated the four people mentioned and found the stories of their involvement to be untrue.[162]

Ray apparently made no reply.

In yet another jail conversation, Young recounted how he and Deputy Schaeffer laid out the case against Ray, in generalities. They asked no

---

[162]  30-5264, p. 689.

questions, but Young explained that "hard things" had been discovered that Ray was unaware of, which would only come out in court. He told Ray that he was a young man who would never rest until he had unburdened himself of this "load"; that he was causing his people and the community a load of time and trouble and expense and that "nobody would be satisfied until all the facts in this case had come out." Young strongly recommended that Ray tell his story and "throw himself on the mercy of the court and ask for clemency and say he was terribly sorry."

Young testified that Deputy Schaeffer, on another tack, inquired if Ray had ever given any thoughts to the "Hereafter," if he had any religion, and then Schaeffer asked if Ray realized "that sometime he would have to face his Maker?" Ray replied that he didn't have any particular religion, but he did think of that. A short time later, he was returned to his cell for the night.[163]

On the following night, they again pulled Ray from his cell, and Schaeffer took the lead. Ray admitted that he had thought over their last conversation, and the talk turned to the fire and in particular, the oil cans found there. Ray, for the most part confined his answers to "yes" or "no," although he did explain how the family sleeping arrangements changed when a guest was expected.

Schaeffer drew a diagram of the house and had Ray indicate where the odd can was found. Ray said it was back of the door in the hall and pointed to a place behind the front door. Young said that Ray put dots on the drawing to show where the can was usually kept.[164]

They pressed Ray to talk, this time suggesting that Ray could tell his Uncle Fred Pfanschmidt the story, or at least talk over with him the idea of telling his tale. Ray agreed that this would be helpful but said there was no real hurry and it would probably be easier for Fred to come on Monday than on Sunday. Young, Schaeffer, and Lipps, scenting a break in the case, hurried out to locate Fred Pfanschmidt.

Fred was not home, so they brought a different uncle, William Abel, to the jail. Since Ray was afraid to believe what Young was telling him,

---

[163]  30-5264, p. 693.
[164]  30-5264, p. 695.

the detective asked Uncle Abel to listen while Young repeated this advice to Ray: "If you, instead of appearing unconcerned about this matter and showing no emotion, would say that you are very and sincerely sorry, that you realize that you have made a mistake, that you want to rectify that mistake and take whatever medicine is due you as a man and the sooner you start to take that medicine, the sooner you will be cured and that much sooner you will be at ease; besides, you have certain people of whom you think a good deal and some of your relatives and sweetheart, Miss Reeder, if you spend all your money and then are convicted, you will not be able to do anything for them. If you want to do anything for them you can save your money and save your peace of mind by telling all about this. Now I will leave you to talk it over with your uncle."[165]

Young left Ray and his uncle in private to discuss the best thing to do. Fifteen or twenty minutes later, Abel called the officers and said that Ray would tell all he knew the next night, if he could first see Esther; talk to his Uncle Fred to get his financial matters straightened out; and also speak to his lawyers. Young, unwilling to delay, sent Abel back to try and get him to speak at once. Ray stood firm on telling it all the next night, Monday.

Young admitted telling Ray that the attitude of his lawyers was making him "appear more guilty." Ray had no reply. However, an eruption from the defense table did occur, and that single piece of testimony was stricken from the record.

In the afternoon session, a prickly Govert rose to face Young on the stand. He began by asking about the substantial sum of money Young earned during his two months of work on the case and questioned him about his employee, Farley, of the jail plant/bank job notoriety. Govert asked questions about the axes, tools, and corn knife Young found at the farm, and why they were not put into custody at that time. The corn knife was later sold at the auction in which personal property from the Pfanschmidt estate had been dispersed. Young thought that since it had been found in plain sight, stuck in a chopping block, the logical conclusion was that it had been used for killing chickens, not dismembering the family.

---

[165] 30-5264, p. 698.

Govert tested Young's memory on what day which search yielded a given piece of evidence. Young was unflappable. Govert moved on to the clothes and especially the "matter or filth" left on them from the vault. Young said there was some, but not much. "[the] coat was doubled up and somewhat wrinkled; my judgment is that it would not appear confined to one spot, but sort of sticking to the coat.... I think there was not on the trousers; there might have been a little, but I do not recall it."[166]

Then Govert asked who was awaiting Ray's arrival after his arrest, and Young enumerated the officials present in the jailer's room. Govert, himself, was kept upstairs separated from his client for some considerable time after Ray was in custody. The attorney was fuming about it still.

Young spoke of the confusion that occurred when the lawyers were finally allowed access to the prisoner. "My recollection is that you came into the room first; there were several people standing outside looking thru the bars.... I think Mr. Coens admitted you; I think Mr. Scharnhorst and Bumster, the gentlemen representing the *Herald*, and the gentleman who now represents the *Whig*—I believe he was working on some other paper at that time ... , and the jailer, Mr. Frye, he was there all the time. There were a number of other people but I did not know them, but they all came in; that is, I suppose they did—who could get in, except Schaeffer, Buerkin, the jailer, and myself, they all came in when the door was opened to admit you."[167]

Govert, satisfied with establishing that he had been kept from his client, leapt into the matter of all those jail conversations to which he had already loudly objected. Young stated that he brought Dr. O'Neil down from Chicago to examine Ray and assess his mental state. For this service, O'Neil was paid one hundred dollars.

Govert asked if those conversations took place through the bars of Ray's cell; Young responded they were held in the jailer's room, with Ray seated comfortably in a chair. Young firmly rejected the idea that the jailers required Ray to do anything or that he had been allowed free access to the prisoner. Returning to the topic of Dr. O'Neil's visit, Govert wanted to know how

---

[166] 30-5264, p. 708.
[167] 30-5264, p. 710.

long that conversation lasted. Young believed it was two or three hours one evening, after which the doctor returned to Chicago. The sheriff, the deputy, and the jailer, as well as the detective were present while the doctor examined Ray. Apparently oblivious to the lack of privacy, the officials sacrificed any sense of intimacy in favor of having witnesses. Govert accused Young of making suggestions and pointing out suspicious circumstances to Dr. O'Neil as he was talking to Ray. The private detective denied it.

Attention next focused on Young's attempt to trap Ray by planting his operative, Farley, into the cell block. Farley was already in town when the doctor examined Ray but not yet in place under, as Govert called it, the "plans of your devising." Young rejected that, saying he had gone back to Chicago the same day that Farley was placed into the jail and only returned to Quincy three days later.

Govert asked when the conversations with Ray occurred and Young answered that it was always in the evening or at night. The "talks" lasted for periods as long as six hours and would stretch as late as one o'clock in the morning or once until 2:00 a.m. When Govert honed in on the time Schaeffer asked Ray about his religious beliefs, there was an entertaining foray into the reasons why Young kept memoranda of the dates of his activities. Govert ascertained that it surely was not to aid their client. Young allowed that he kept track to fix the dates in his own mind, and not for any other reason. He then added, "If he had taken my advice it would not have been necessary to use them at all."

Govert asked if Ray had "requested the privilege of these meetings." Young said not so far as he knew, nor did Ray object to the meetings. Govert pounced. "Whether Sheriff Lipps went after him, and upon his refusal to come out, he was compelled to come out by Sheriff Lipps, you do not know?"

The State objected and was overruled.

Young calmly replied, "Except on one or two occasions I was always in a position where I could hear if he made any objections; he never made any objections."[168]

---

[168] 30-5264, p. 718.

Govert inquired about the other times and further speculated that all Young had to do was suggest to the sheriff that he wanted to see Ray, for him to appear.

Young said, "Not exactly."

Govert asked somewhat acidly, "To be real exact, what did you do?"

"Well, to be real exact, my position was one in which I could not pressure to tell the sheriff what to do.... To be real exact I could not pressure to tell the sheriff to do anything of that kind; I only suggested that, and he did it. You asked me how he came to be brought out."[169]

This baiting and bickering between them went on for some time, until eventually they arrived at the bone of contention. The attorney said, "You never consulted his attorneys about the conversations with this young man, did you?"

"I never tried to consult them but once."

"You never suggested that they attend any of the meetings that you had at the jail with reference to this young man, did you?"

"Not after the first time I tried to talk to them; they would never stand still so I could talk to them; I am referring to you."

Before an amused audience, Govert, referring to the time of Ray's arrest, asked, "That was on an occasion when you were putting questions to this young man down in the jailer's office and while I was being detained upstairs?"

Young denied keeping the defendant from his counsel. "I don't know of any time when I put questions to anybody while you were detained."

Govert hammered the point that Ray had been instructed by his attorneys not to talk, and that Ray had said so to Young several times during those sessions. Young swore, in return, that any time Ray said he wouldn't talk about a subject, it was changed.

When Govert then accused Young of thinking he knew more of what was best for Ray than his own attorneys did, Young politely agreed. Govert suggested that since the detective was in another's pay at the time, this was hypocrisy at best, and possibly something far worse. Young denied it,

---

[169] 30-5264, p. 718.

saying that Ray knew he was in the employ of Mr. Kaempen. Young also said he told Ray nothing more than what was in the newspapers, which was a matter of public record.

"Did you tell him the attorneys were simply in it for what there was in it for them?"

"I did."

"And that they could get all of his property?"

"Yes, sir." Young was unrepentant.

Govert inquired if Young knew whether Ray's attorneys were being paid more or less than he himself was making, or if their fee was contingent upon the outcome of the trial. Young professed complete disinterest in the payment arrangements for the defense lawyers.

The questioning turned to Ray's cell, which consisted of round iron vertical bars set into flat crossbars. Did Young know that Ray was locked in there for twenty or twenty-one hours each day? The State objected, and the objection was sustained as not being proper cross-examination.

Govert inquired if Young ever told Ray that there were people lined up to pull the hangman's trap when he was found guilty. Young denied that absolutely. Young also denied that he or anyone else promised a light sentence for Ray; or that he would work for Ray's pardon; or that he heard what Miss Reeder and Fred Pfanschmidt said in their conversations with the prisoner. By this time, Young was declining to agree with anything Govert said. There the flavor of mutual dislike was apparent to the onlookers. At last Young was dismissed, perhaps having gained a small taste of how Ray felt during those "conversations."[170]

Sheriff Lipps then reappeared on the witness stand, and this time Wall was interested in the whereabouts of the mysterious oil can. Lipps said he first saw it sitting in the defendant's buggy. He then told of clothing he found that Sunday at Ray's camp: two new khaki suits, plus an old coat "kinda covered with mud," and a pair of trousers, both of which had been "laundried." He also listed soiled collars and shirts and underwear and socks, plus a pair of new leggings of a "kind of tan" colored leather.

---

[170]  30-5264, p. 727.

"Were conditions the same when you returned later for another inspection?" Wall asked.

Lipps replied, "Oh no.... In the west tent they were about the same, but in the east tent they were not.... When we went to the east tent there was a scabbard, a cartridge belt, a revolver with a clasp on it closed, and as Mr. Koch was looking around under the clock, I took this down and took the revolver out of there, and as I did there was a leather watch fob fell out of there with the initial R on it." The watch fob was covered with mud and "looked as though someone had stepped on it. The gun was very hard to break;[171] it took me quite a while to break it; it was loaded."

By the third time the sheriff visited Ray's camp that same Sunday, the cartridge belt was still hanging there, but the revolver had gone missing. Between the sheriff's visits, Ray and Esther had been to the camp, perhaps the parties only missed each other by scant minutes.

But Wall was specifically looking for evidence of a lap robe—did Lipps ever see one? No.

Wall next trailed back to the dogs' activities on Monday. Lipps told the tale from his own perspective. Upon reaching the farm, the dogs were taken out of the automobile and back to the barn lot. Strumpfer started his dog, Nick, on the track under the box; Achelpohl and the chauffeur handled the other dog. Lipps told of following the dogs in the auto, loading them up, and unloading them to trail past each crossroad.

When the dogs reached Twenty-Fourth and State streets, the fresh oil confused them. They were loaded up and taken to the courthouse for a rest. About forty-five minutes later, the dogs were returned to Twenty-Fourth and Broadway where "finally they got headed north and started to running." They went north beyond the railroad track where they trailed into a field headed west and a bit south toward Frese's camp but were stopped by a barbwire fence.

Wall: "Now, after getting to the fence, which direction did the dogs go?"

Lipps replied, "It looked like there was a circle there, or a buggy that had turned around there and came back the way they came in, coming out

---

[171] That is, it was hard to open the breach and examine the barrel.

to Twenty-Fourth Street at the gate there at that pasture. Then they went south on Twenty-Fourth to Locust, then west a mile to the Twelfth Street entrance at Soldier's Home where they paused and circled again before going on to the Eighth Street gate and entering the Home's grounds on the angling road to the Headquarters Building , and then on to Frese's place."

Lipps watched as the dog Nick Carter walked around the horses tied in the shed and then sat down next to one. Afterward, the dogs were taken back to the courthouse until about 4:00 p.m. when they were put onto that second trail from the Reeder's house, which was not allowed into evidence.

The topic jumped to Tuesday, October 1, when the paraffin cast was made. That project entailed another trip to Quincy to find Ray's horses, which were by then in a pasture at Joe Eaken's house north of the Frese property, remove a horseshoe, and take it back to the farm. Lipps was quite careful to say that the shoe fit exactly into the barn lot imprint. He had kept the wax impressions ever since.

Lipps told about being notified about the clothes on Monday morning a week later. It was about eight thirty when word came to go out to the camp. Lipps spoke of seeing the clothes lying in the vault, removing them, and placing them in the "engine room" of the jail to dry. Then he, Young, and Buerkin got into his automobile to arrest Ray.

The court called a recess after Lipps told of taking Ray into the jailer's room. The crowd stayed, reluctant to leave their seats for fear of missing a single minute of what might come next.

After the recess, and over defense objections, Lipps was allowed to say that he told Ray "he was under arrest, charged with murder. I asked him if he had anything to say. He said, 'No,'—he would not talk as his attorneys told him not to talk." Lipps agreed that Ray didn't have to talk if he didn't want to.

Lipps was asked what was said in the jail between Govert and Ray, and the defense immediately objected on grounds of client confidentiality. The court replied that it couldn't have been confidential in view of the others present. Govert said wryly, "It is as confidential as it could be under the circumstance." Objection overruled.[172]

---

[172] 30-5264, p. 755.

The courtroom again heard a description of Govert in a towering tirade. Lipps said, "Mr. Govert, when he came in, he was very excited, and he told Ray, he says, 'Don't you talk to any of them; don't you open your mouth; don't talk to any of them.' Then he says to me, 'You have no right to question this fellow, you have no right to talk to him at all.' I says, 'Well, now I have, I will talk to him whenever I feel like it; he is in my charge.'" Lipps illustrated the fact that Govert had few friends or supporters among the law enforcement officials who had come to the stand.

The defense then launched a barrage of objections regarding all testimony concerning things said to Ray when Ray would not reply. The defense contended that if their client did not answer, it was not a "conversation" and should not be in the record. A frustrated Govert said, "If he answers it is admissible, or refuses it is admissible, and if he remains silent it is admissible. If he is not put on the stand, the fact that he is not put on the stand could not be taken as evidence against him and his refusal to answer could not."

The judge replied, "I am inclined to think it is a proper line for cross-examination; it is for the jury to determine; it all goes to the weight." Defense objections overruled.

Wall had some trouble with the sheriff's testimony because he tended to supply labels like "advised" or "counseled" to conversations. Wall repeatedly told Lipps to simply state what was said and let the jury decide the rest. Lipps, obviously not well practiced at testifying, struggled along until they came to the day of the coroner's verdict.

Lipps had talked to Ray. "I asked him if he had heard what the Coroner's Jury did. He said 'yes.' Well, I says, 'You see, they have held you without bond, and we haven't given all of our evidence; that we will have enough under cover to give you the rope.'"

According to Lipps, Ray's only response was to grit his teeth.

Finally, the defense prevailed with an objection and the teeth gritting comment was stricken from the record. Additionally, the court sternly reminded the jurors that it was their duty when something was removed from the record to "make up his mind right then and there not to consider such statement."[173] When asked if they could do this, all the jurors answered in the affirmative.

Wall and Lipps struggled to find an acceptable way to enter into the record the conversation in which Ray asked to talk to his uncle. Eventually the story was told that Lipps brought Abel to see Ray and allowed them a private conversation. Afterward, Lipps came back into the room and Abel said, "Ray said he was going to tell me all about it tomorrow night."

The sheriff agreed to let Ray telephone Esther to come. This was done early Monday morning, between seven and 9:00 a.m. Esther readily agreed to come but didn't arrive until Monday evening between 5:00 and 6:00 p.m. In fact, everyone gathered on November 17, including the attorneys, the sweetheart, and the faithful uncle. But no explanation came after all. Lipps did not get a confession. But Ray had managed to see Esther alone for the first time since his arrest.

In the courtroom, "The raindrops could be heard beating against the window panes, but still Ray Pfanschmidt was unmoved. A stream of light flooded the spaces behind the railing late yesterday afternoon just as Sheriff Lipps told of the promise to make a complete statement of the crime. The light gave the spectators and others a better chance to study the features of the young defendant, but all were doomed to disappointment. His mouth did not quiver. He swallowed with the same ease and his eyes wandered about the room after he had frequently consulted his attorney. Esther Reeder was seated in her usual place on the second row of seats in the east part of the courtroom. Many times her glances met those of the prisoner, and smiles between the two were numerous. Ray Pfanschmidt came into the courtroom ... with his clothes pressed, a clean shave, and his light hair neatly combed."[174]

Lancaster faced Lipps for cross. The sheriff was vague on the details of Ray's incarceration, and the defense called him to task about his inability to be precise. "Are you just as sure about that as you are the conversations you have been telling about here? ... Is it more difficult to remember

---

[173] 30-5264, p. 764.
[174] *Journal*, April 9, 1913.

whether a man has been confined in a cell one week or two weeks than to remember the details of a dozen conversations such as you have detailed to the jury here?"

The State objected.

Lipps said that after about a week in jail, Ray was moved to the "Bull Pen," in the north part of the jail. It was a big enclosure where there was room to walk around but never any daylight. "It does not get sunlight; we don't get any sunlight in any part of the jail," Lipps said.

Ray was put in cell number 3. This was a seven foot by five foot box with the top, bottom, and sides all made of boiler iron and steel, except for the door, which was the only opening. The jail had no light fixtures in any of the cells, each of which contained nothing but two bunks and a "toilet" consisting of an open sewer trough running along the back wall. Ray spent up to twenty-one hours a day in this dark, smelly vault. And he was kept there until two or three weeks before the trial, for all the months since his arrest last October.

Lancaster, decrying both Ray's living conditions and those lengthy grilling sessions, asked the sheriff if Ray had ever been threatened. He evoked Lipps's statement about having "enough to hang him," and thereby introduced previously stricken statements back into testimony.

The court said, "Did I not strike that out?"

People's counsel answered, "Yes, sir."

Undaunted, Lancaster carried on, asking if the sheriff didn't also tell Ray that he had been offered money for the privilege of pulling the gallows trap. Lipps stoutly denied it all. Lancaster accused Lipps of consenting to Ray's visit with his uncle only in hope of gaining information, since before that, the sheriff had not allowed Ray to make calls or send out messages. All incoming messages were opened and inspected by jail officials. Lipps simply denied that he was able to hear any part of the uncle's conversation.

Lancaster led the sheriff to spell out arrangements for Ray's attorneys to visit, especially the certain marked place where the lawyers had to stand, and a position to face so the deputy at the other end of the corridor could observe. All conversations with Ray were conducted through the cell bars under eyes of the watchful deputies. After the first couple of visits the attorneys were never allowed to speak with Ray in private.

Lancaster forced Lipps to admit that there was one time Ray did not want to come out and be questioned.

Lipps recounted, "He said he would not come out."

"What did you do?" asked the attorney.

"I walked in and said, 'You will come out.'"

"You took him out, did you?"

Lipps shook his head. "No, I never touched him. I says, 'You will come out; whenever I come in here to get you out, why, you will come; you don't have to talk but you will come out, you will obey my rules.'"[175]

The sheriff could not recall exactly at which interview this occurred but thought it was one of the later ones. Often, Ray was in bed when they roused him. Even at those times, he was made to get up and speak to the officers. Lipps claimed that was because Ray would sometimes go to bed as early as seven o'clock. Lancaster explained to the jury that there was no place for Ray to sit except on the bed.

Lancaster asked if the sheriff gave the others locked up in there the same sort of treatment, and Lipps answered, "They have not been charged as he has."

The sheriff did admit that he gave the informer, Farley, a chair but claimed it was because he had a bad back. Otherwise, no one was furnished a chair. Of course, he went on, the jail had never kept someone as long as they held Ray.

Questions went back to the fire and the traffic and the oil can— seemingly, the queries rambled about bodies, mattresses, dogs, and intersections along the road to Quincy. Then Lancaster zeroed in on the bloodhounds and their handler. "As a matter of fact, the old dog was the only one that made that trail or was used?" Lipps agreed with the attorney's assessment.

Did Strumpfer really walk or run with his dog halfway to Quincy? Lipps reported that the handler ran—just to the first lane or maybe a bit

---

[175] 30-5264, p. 787.

beyond. That first lane was Kaufman's, and it was less than a block from the Pfanschmidt driveway.

Lancaster got on a roll and into a rhythm: Did he go five miles? No. Did he go four miles? No. Did he go three miles? No. Did he go two miles? No. Did he go one mile? No. Did he go three quarters of a mile? Maybe.

Lancaster shortened the distance in his next question, asking if this "half mile" that Strumpfer went, was in the center of the road.

The sheriff admitted it was; then the attorney asked if this was the same road that all those rigs came along to and from the fire. The sheriff again agreed.

What happened at all those twelve or fifteen crossroads along the route? And what happened at Geisel's driveway?

Lipps was unsure but thought the dogs checked that lane, went in a ways, and came back out. Lancaster asserted instead that the auto passed by the Geisel lane at a rate of "several miles an hour and never stopped there at all." Lipps denied that.

By the time the group reached the camp, according to Lipps, the young dog was left outside and only Nick was trailing. He personally did not see the dog and handler go to the tent, then to the buggy, and finally come back to the team.

Lancaster now asked if the dog trailed over to the vault? It was a vital question.

Not that Lipps saw.

They talked about the revolver. Lipps said that it had not been fired within the past twenty-four hours, so he left it there in the tent. Then they revisited the clothing and agreed that none of it had any suspicious blood spots on it, nor did the blankets or bedding.

Lancaster's questions turned to the farm and the track casting. The jury was treated to descriptions of the dust and the chickens and the suggestion that someone had stepped on the track before the cast was made. Lancaster pointed out that it would have been far fairer to make an impression before the shoe removed from Ray's mare was placed into the imprint, asking Lipps to agree. The State objected.

Lancaster reiterated, "In laying the shoe in the impression as it was, you get an impression of what the impression was after the shoe was laid in, and not as it was before, did you not?"

"I suppose you would." It was hard for Lipps to concur with the defense.

Wall rose to mend the image of the sheriff and his dreadful treatment of Ray. "Did you have any other prisoner in the county jail incarcerated on the charge of murder?"

"I did not."

"What was the reason to put him in [that] particular cell?"

"For safe keeping."

"What diet did he get compared with the other prisoners?"

"He got the same diet."

"And didn't [Ray] say he was glad to get out and talk?"

"He did."

And, in fact, had the sheriff said he had received information that made him concerned for Ray's safety? Wall asked how many times, and the sheriff answered, "Yes indeed, as many as four times and perhaps six.[176]" Lipps also declared that Ray never had complained about his treatment. The lighting and sanitary conditions were the same in each cell in the jail. Lipps ended by saying, "I always treated him the best I knew how under the circumstances."

On this note, court was adjourned.

---

[176] 30-5264, p. 808.

# Chapter 18

# Jailhouse Informant

## Tuesday, April 8, 1913

Court resumed with Lipps still occupying the stand. Through redirect testimony he told of the drawing Deputy Schaeffer made showing the front of the house and the gas can's location. Then Wall moved Lipps to a jail conversation in January 1913, with Deputy Shafer and another prisoner, Viehmeyer, who had also been used to try to obtain incriminating information from Ray. Deputy Schaeffer again recited the list of caveats: no promises and no threats involved or implied by anyone present.

Spectators listened closely as Lipps related parts of the conversations Viehmeyer reportedly held with Ray. Schaeffer asked Ray if he told Viehmeyer that he wasn't worried about fingerprints because he had worn gloves. Ray declined to comment, saying only, "I will talk when the time comes." When Schaeffer asked Viehmeyer if Ray had said it, the other prisoner agreed, "That is what he said."

The story continued. Ray, according to Viehmeyer, admitted that he met Dingerson on the road that Friday night. But in the conversation before the sheriff, Ray refused to speak, much less confirm anything he supposedly said through the bars to a fellow prisoner.

The defense was emphatically objecting at each and every question but was repeatedly overruled. Speaking between voluble interruptions, the sheriff related Viehmeyer's story of Ray saying his family was accustomed to having a "lunch" upon returning home and that he had helped his father with the surrey that fateful Friday night. Unfortunately, this tantalizing conversation consisted entirely of "he said that; he said that ..."

Wall abandoned the hearsay tale to discuss the class pin found on the left lapel of the suit of clothes in the vault. Dr. Erickson removed the pin, and the sheriff washed it free of filth and marked it with a "cross" on the back. Lipps had had it ever since.

Testimony traveled to that field the bloodhounds had visited. Lipps noticed buggy tracks there, but either the ground was very hard or the footing was loose, and shoeprints were not preserved. Lipps was sure the wheels were steel rimmed; however, he could not tie that track to Ray's team without clear prints.

On cross examination, Lipps admitted that he did not know if the gate to the pasture was chained and locked at night. He knew that Viehmeyer had been kept in jail after his wife got her divorce, on what Lipps called "contempt of court." Lancaster suggested that Viehmeyer had a special arrangement as a paid informer and accused Lipps of putting Viehmeyer into the "bull pen" in front of Ray's cell to gather information.

Lancaster succeeded in getting the sheriff to own up to the fact that he often talked to Viehmeyer in the evenings when the others were locked up. At the time of the four-way conversation previously testified to, the sheriff was already in possession of a written statement from Viehmeyer. The defense, however, had never been allowed to read this statement.

Lancaster pointed, "Is that the same statement that John Wall has here from which he acquired in questioning you?"

Wall addressed the judge, "I want to say that I never examined him from a solitary statement I had here."

Lancaster was undeterred. "I want the printed one."

Wall was equally adamant. "I have not used it, and when I use it you can get it."

227

The judge stepped in. "Mr. Wall says it was not used, and I did not observe it being used."[177]

Thwarted, Lancaster returned to questioning Lipps. He learned that the contested document came from several meetings with Viehmeyer, beginning as far back as Ray's first or second week in jail. Lipps took notes and gave them to Schaeffer, who had them turned into a typewritten statement.

"Is it a typewritten statement similar to the one Mr. Wall has lying on his desk, the one underneath?" Lancaster wanted that report.

Lipps shrugged. "It is something like that, yes, sir."

Lancaster conjured up the jailhouse interrogation. With the statement of the informer neatly typed and in the hands of the deputy, the sheriff brought Ray into the room; then Viehmeyer appeared. It had been an ambush.

But Ray had remained as tantalizingly out of reach as that statement buried under the papers on Wall's table. "I will wait until the time comes before I will reply," was Ray's stock answer. Or, "Get my attorneys." But Lipps did not call Ray's lawyers.

It was confirmed that this confrontation had been held in the ladies inmate section of the prison away from everyone. Lipps offered the feeble excuse that he did not want Ray to find out what was in the evidence vault in the jailer's room.

Lancaster turned sarcastic. Was it that the sheriff was afraid Ray would work the combination of the big iron vault door in the presence of the two lawmen? Of course not, the sheriff admitted. The vault wasn't even locked. Lancaster offered the opinion that an unlocked safe could be easily remedied, but the sheriff shrugged it off.

Logic turned this excuse from flimsy to transparent, and eventually even the sheriff realized it, finally admitting he took Ray to the other end of the courthouse to hide him. "I took him where no people could get to us."[178] It also conveniently moved Ray out of earshot of the other six or eight men then occupying cells and far from any visiting attorneys.

[177]  30-5264, p. 827.
[178]  30-5264, p. 832.

On redirect, Wall extracted testimony that Lipps had "got wise to" Ray's thought of escaping back in October or November of 1912. Finally the lawyers finished with their questions, and Lipps was surely happy to be dismissed.

Wall called Deputy Schaeffer, first saying pointedly to the court, "Before examining Mr. Schaeffer, I want to show you that I am not going to use any memoranda."

Lancaster was not amused. "I know, but it is there."

"But I am not going to use it and have not used it." Wall's words sounded smug.

It was reminiscent of two children quarrelling over a toy.

On the stand, Schaeffer, who had been a deputy in Adams County for twenty-two years, had to be instructed by the State's attorney to say only what he did and saw and to leave out all his conclusions. This was very difficult for him.

"I can't tell this without coming to some conclusion," said the intrepid deputy.

In stilted, careful language, Schaeffer told of seeing a surrey in the barn at the fire scene and finding inside it a package of what he believed was about fifty cents worth of sugar. He also produced a little card with a drawing on it, dated on the back October 16, 1912. This rough sketch had an F to indicate where Ray's father slept and dots for the location of the mystery oil can.

Then the questions turned to a jail conversation from February, during which Ray faced Lipps, Bogardus, and Schaeffer, which triggered a defense objection and a long discussion about the part Bogardus played in the conversation. Eventually the court sustained that objection and ruled that any testimony about conversations when Bogardus was present was not admissible. This was a boon for the defense and created a corresponding problem for the prosecution, tainting all the information the fire marshal had gathered.

Wall progressed to the matter of the broken watch. Schaeffer said Ray told him that his watch fob got caught in barbed wire, which pulled the watch out and broke it. Another time the watch was mentioned Bogardus had been in attendance, so that story could not be discussed. Recess was called, and stirring and stretching rustled throughout the room.

When court resumed, Wall asked if Schaeffer had been present for the conversation between Abel, Young, Lipps, and Ray. Again the litany of "no coercion" was recited: no threats, no inducements, no promises, and nothing that could be construed as any of the above.

Schaeffer was not a practiced witness, so Wall had a difficult time keeping the deputy on point. There were so many conversations referenced that even Judge Williams got confused and tried to clarify things about who said what and when. After a verbal struggle, Wall tugged from Schaeffer an account of one conversation in November 1912, when Ray said he had no money and no one had left him any. Ray also told Schaeffer that he had never been all the way through that pasture east of the works.

In its cross examination, the defense flatly asked Schaeffer if advising Ray that he did not have to answer was a ploy so that Schaeffer could later testify that Ray refused to talk. Govert then accused Schaeffer of telling Mr. Reeder that if Ray confessed, the deputy and the sheriff would try and get Ray a ten- or twelve-year sentence. Schaeffer denied he ever said anything like that. The defense persisted, asking if there hadn't been a conversation when Mr. Reeder told Schaeffer that the deputy didn't have the power to keep a promise like that.

"No such conversation took place that I remember of."[179] The expression on Schaeffer's earnest face caused some in the courtroom to break into laughter and forced the judge to admonish them.

Wall called the indefatigable sheriff back to the stand to ask if Govert was truly excited when he entered the jail and saw that Farley was there.

Govert objected.

Wall said, "It is to corroborate Mr. Farley on what took place ..."

Govert objected further. "It may have been enough to excite anybody, but I do not think it material."

"The conversation was made to appear to be a laughing matter and inferred to the jury that there was nothing in Mr. Farley's statement. You

---

[179]  30-5264, p. 867.

can cross examine a witness in such a way that would infer that what the witness is telling is mere chaff." It was a somewhat backhanded compliment from Wall, but this time the court agreed with Govert. The objection was sustained.[180] Lipps vacated the stand.

Charles Achelpohl came back to the stand, and testimony returned to the bloodhounds. Achelpohl, a staunch friend of Ray's grandfather C. C. Pfanschmidt confirmed that each and every crossroad was checked for fifty to one hundred yards before and after the intersection. And he confirmed the route of the dogs as Strumpfer had previously testified.

One new detail emerged when Achelpohl claimed that he saw in that pasture north of the railroad track an imprint of a horseshoe that looked like the one under the box in the barn lot. He called it to Strumpfer's attention. He also watched as the dog Nick Carter found the buggy and then the horses and came to rest by one of the horses.

Govert took his turn to question him, and the courtroom heard a confusing list of roads and directions and springs and bridges between Quincy and the Pfanschmidt farm, including the lane about a block south of Harrison Street that led to Uncle Abel's farm. Achelpohl did admit that the dogs were not taken from the car at the entrance to Henry Geisel's farm. His story presented a vivid picture of the bloodhounds' confusion on the edge of Quincy when Nick Carter first went west on State for about a half-block and then returned and circled the intersection four or five times before heading north down the center of Twenty-Fourth Street. At about Kentucky Street, the dog circled back toward State Street again and then turned back north. At that point, Strumpfer brought the dog back into the automobile.

Govert called out a list of all the streets that had not been checked along Twenty-Fourth Street: Jersey, York, Grove, Maine, Hampshire, Vermont, and a little narrow road on the east side between Maine and Vermont. When the dogs returned, they resumed trailing about six blocks north at Twenty-Fourth and Broadway, skipping that entire section of street. Achelpohl defended that decision because the street had been oiled. A skeptical Govert

---

[180] 30-5264, p. 869.

thought the city was unlikely to oil an empty road and there were no residences at that time between Kentucky and Jersey streets.

This brought the court to the noon recess on Wednesday, April 9.

After lunch, Wall's first witness addressed the money motive. Henry C. Sprick had been a cashier at the State Street Bank for the past five years and had known Ray for the past six or seven months. In May 1912 Ray opened a commercial account at the bank, which allowed checks to be drawn upon it.

Sprick came equipped with his "memoranda book" and could note that he'd had a conversation on the fifteenth of September with Ray regarding an overdraft. The bank had sent out a notice, and Ray responded promptly. Nonetheless, Sprick admonished the young man. "I told him I did not like to encourage overdrafts there, and he must try to provide for it beforehand if possible; also went into detail about his contract. He said that he would get his money at the conclusion of the work out there. He wanted to know what to do about arranging for the overdraft, stating that his father was not present, but he suggested another party, which was suitable to us, and he closed up the account that day."

Sprick said that the amount of the overdraft was $111.00 and that there was a second, which had occurred on September 28 for a bit more than $300.00. In addition, Ray was indebted to the bank for three promissory notes in the amount of $150.00, $500.00, and $300.00. These notes were given "partly to cover the overdraft and partly to check against."[181]

Wolfe then produced a copy of the letter written to Charles A. Pfanschmidt from the State Street Bank on the twenty-eighth of September 1912.

Govert took over the witness. Sprick said he went to the fire on Sunday and saw Ray placing a box over a horse track in the barn lot. He testified that the $111 overdraft had been covered by the $300 note and further that the $500 and the $150 notes were guaranteed secure by Charles Pfanschmidt, father of the defendant. According to Govert, all Ray's financial concerns had been dispensed with.

---

[181]  30-5264, p. 891.

Wolfe returned and questioned Sprick further. On that $500 note, signed by C. A. Pfanschmidt, some $196 was to cover an overdraft. Of the $300 note, created about twelve days later, Ray's Uncle Knollenberg was security, as his father, Charles, was in Missouri and unavailable to sign. Mr. Sprick had the notes in his possession. The last note had been repaid, but Wolfe was not allowed to show who satisfied it. Sprick was excused, leaving behind the impression that although Ray played on the edge, he did have all his obligations covered.

Ray's grandfather C. C. Pfanschmidt returned to the stand. According to a reporter, "Mr. Pfanschmidt was unable to walk to the witness stand alone and was assisted by the sheriff. He has been very ill, and his physicians advised against his coming up. Mr. Pfanschmidt's voice was plainly audible although it trembled more than on his previous testimony on the stand."[182]

C. C. testified that on Monday morning after the fire, he had a conversation in which he warned Ray he'd best hire attorneys, and Ray informed the old man that he already had them in place. Additionally, Pfanschmidt testified that he was the one who called in and paid for the bloodhounds. Wall wanted to erase any lingering impression that Ray supported calling in the hounds, but it took a lawyers' bench conference with the jury removed before that was accomplished.

By the time the old grandfather vacated the stand, he had cast doubt on Ray's account of when his lawyers were first hired. Onlookers witnessing the fortitude necessary for this infirm gentleman to appear and testify a second time saw it as a demonstration of C. C.'s utter conviction of Ray's guilt. It was a view the sorrowing man would hold until his death.

The next witness called was George B. Vasen, who owned a store that stocked electrical supplies and equipment and did electrical work. Vasen narrated his conversation with Ray about a relatively new invention, the pocket flashlight.[183] In fact, this item was so unusual that Wall had Vasen explain to the jury just what these contraptions were. "They are a small

---

[182] *Herald*, April 9, 1913.
[183] A portable electric lamp was patented on April 25, 1898. The first EverReady Flashlight was patented on January 10, 1899.

lamp encased, lighted by a small battery that can be carried in the pocket for illuminating."

Ray had been having a hard time deciding which style to purchase. Vasen thought to help Ray make his choice by asking what the light would be used for. Ray had nothing to say about its intended use but finally chose a nickel-plated "search light" and returned to purchase it about four days before the fire. The flashlight Ray purchased was very small: it was 1-7/8 x ¾ x 2-7/8 inches long.[184]

Vasen related another conversation, this one involving batteries. Ray was looking for fuses, which the store did not stock. As an alternative, Vasen advised Ray "that an ordinary thin iron wire or a thin German silver wire could be heated hot enough with batteries to ignite powder."

Wall wanted more details for the jury, and Vasen obliged. "The charge of powder could ordinarily be set off by a small piece of wire by simply passing the current from two dry cells."

"What do you mean by 'dry cells'?"

"Ordinary dry batteries such as used for igniting gasoline engines or used on telephones."[185]

"How would you do that with a fuse?"

The witness responded, "Ordinary fuse has got powder of some kind in it and by simply putting this wire through the fuse would ignite the fuse, this thin German silver or platinum wire, whatever you want to use for igniting it."

"Do you know, Mr. Vasen, whether or not this fuse or this battery could be so arranged that a clock could set it off?"

"Very easily in several different ways," replied the helpful Vasen.

Govert tried to demolish this dangerous testimony and show that a flashlight was a common thing. But Vasen proudly held to his guns, maintaining that there were few places in Quincy where one could purchase such a tool; the five-and-dime stores didn't carry flashlights, nor did Geise's bicycle shop, although Tenks' Hardware store was considering putting

---

[184]  30-5264, p. 909.
[185]  30-5264, p. 908.

them in. Govert had to content himself with mentioning their usefulness and growing popularity with farmers, to which Vasen helpfully added that they were a favorite of policemen too.

Leaving this fascinating subject, Wolfe questioned Chris Freiburg, the foreman of the grand jury that had indicted Ray, about the reason the cause of death was listed as an "unknown instrument." After much arguing, the point was made that the grand jury did not know what kind of instrument had caused the death of Blanche Pfanschmidt.

The next person called to the witness stand was Frank Short, whom Ray had named as a possible culprit in the crime. Short said he went to the fire with a friend, Otis Scott, arriving about eleven thirty after Sunday school. By that time the bodies were lying covered with canvas on the lawn, and the tracks were behind string and covered by boards and boxes. Without preamble, Wolfe asked, "Did you ever have anything to do with putting a suit of khaki clothes out in Frese's vault?"

This caused a strong reaction from the defense. "We have not accused this young man of doing that!"

The judge, however, ruled that the question was "'proper," and the witness firmly said, "No, sir." With that he was dismissed.

The prosecution returned to consideration of money and motive when Harry J. Heidbreder, partner in the State Street Bank, came to testify. Wolfe asked about the other partners in the bank, and when Heidbreder named Govert, it called forth a defense objection. This objection was sustained.

Wolfe wanted more details about the mailing of a letter to Charles Pfanschmidt on September 26, 1912, concerning Ray's overdrafts. Heidbreder testified he personally took the properly sealed and addressed letter to the post office at Eighth and Hampshire streets between two and three o'clock in the afternoon. Heidbreder expected that Mr. Pfanschmidt would receive the letter the following morning, Friday, September 27. Mail at that time was carried by train from Quincy to Fall Creek Station, and then by wagon to Payson for delivery by the route carriers.

Wolfe asked the witness if a similar letter had been sent directly to Ray at the same time. A strident defense objection was sustained, and

Heidbreder was not allowed to answer. This duplicate letter was the reason for the numerous prosecution questions seeking to determine if Ray received mail at Chadwick's shop on that Friday. The prosecution hoped to show that this letter had triggered the whole chain of events.

The State dismissed the banker and announced it was nearly finished presenting its case, requesting a short recess. When court resumed, Freiburg was recalled and quizzed about the wording of the grand jury indictment, including whether or not there was evidence to show a sharp-edged instrument was involved in Blanche's death. There was much verbal wrangling, repetition, rereading, and rephrasing of complicated questions. Freiburg wanted to testify that Blanche's head was not attached to her body, so it was hard to tell what happened. Neither the State nor the defense wanted to allow that into the record. The witness was dismissed with no ground gained by either side.

Wall then cleaned up some other housekeeping details. Sheriff Lipps was recalled to identify the exhibits and say that they were the same as when they had been found. "There was a craning of necks when the various exhibits were offered as evidence to the jury. The courtroom was crowded, but everybody tried to get a 'squint' at the bloody clothes, the bloody pillows and mattress found in the Pfanschmidt place, and other interesting things.

"As the various exhibits were shown, Ray Pfanschmidt peered over the shoulders of his attorneys to look curiously, as curiously as anyone in the big audience at the clothes, etc. He gazed with a sort of sneering smile, as if to say 'even with that you can't convict me,' seemed to play about his face."[186]

The prosecution offered into evidence a plan of the house; the burned clock; the horseshoe; a piece of nightgown; part of a bloody mattress; a piece of bloodstained pillow; exhibits marked "Q" and "T" not described in the transcript; a one-dollar bill; an axe blade; a class pin; trousers; a coat (by now they were at letter designations of A-1, having been through the alphabet once already); part of the paper found in the vault with the

---

[186] *Whig,* April 10, 1913.

clothes; a duplicate of the letter written to C. A. Pfanschmidt by Mr. Sprick; the watch fob; a tag taken from the vault; the drawing by Deputy Schaeffer on which Ray marked the can location; the watch ring found by Mr. Koch; a string necktie; and the shirt from the vault. Despite numerous defense objections it was all admitted into evidence.

Judge Williams addressed the courtroom. "Gentlemen, the State has rested; we will not proceed to take evidence on behalf of the defendant this evening. These gentlemen have been at the trial table for three and one-half weeks, and they say to me that they have been so engaged here that they haven't had the opportunity to arrange their line of evidence. They wish an adjournment over until Friday. We are all anxious to get through this case as quickly as possible. I agree we will be making time by giving them tomorrow in order that they may arrange their line of evidence. It is quite difficult for them to so arrange it until they heard the State's case. I am going to do that; I wanted to explain to you why I am doing so. We are going to take an adjournment today over until Friday morning."

Whereupon court was adjourned.[187] It was Wednesday, April 9, 1913. In the courtroom and throughout the countryside, speculation ran rampant about what would happen next.

---

[187] 30-5264, p. 941.

# Chapter 19

~

# Defending Ray

### Friday, April 11, 1913

On Friday morning, court opened before a crowded room. Among the spectators, Ray had five aunts and three uncles present to support him. Much to the surprise of those in attendance, the defense did not ask to make their long delayed opening statement. Instead they simply called their first witness, Henry C. Sprick, who had previously testified for the State. They began by trying to counter the idea that Ray was without funds and thus negate the money motive.

Sprick testified that the bank had received more than $1,000 from Ray in June 1912. This coincided nicely with the time Ray told Mr. Reeder he had "banked his first thousand." Now roles had switched, and for this portion of the trial, the State was providing the ongoing objection counterpoint. Finally, Wall got to ask Sprick how long Ray's money had remained in the bank. The banker replied that it was there for only six days before being withdrawn.

Wall established that from that time forward, Ray had frequently overdrawn his account, and the bank had contacted both Ray and his parents concerning this problem. There was much confusion about when a check had been presented and when it was credited or paid, but the

State was hammering home their position that Ray was not financially responsible.

In reply, the defense launched an intense attack on the testimony from Strumpfer and the handling of his hounds, as well as their competency and accuracy. It began with a witness called to provide a visual reference for the jury. C. A. E. Cantert was an office assistant and draftsman in the city engineer's office, who drew defense Exhibit #2, a map of Quincy and the surrounding area, including the various routes to the farm. Govert proceeded to quiz him about distances.

At this time, in 1912–13, he identified the city limits of Quincy as Locust on the north, Twenty-Fourth Street and part way Thirtieth Street on the east, and Harrison on the south. The Mississippi River formed the western boundary. This drawing was done on a scale of four inches to the mile.

Wall, on cross-examination, took Cantert through an extensive series of questions illustrating that his knowledge came not from firsthand measurements but from older maps. In fact, Cantert had not been on some of those roads for years. The landowners' names on the farms adjoining the roads came from old maps corrected "as much as possible" from tax records. Cantert had been instructed to color various roads in various colors at the behest of Mr. Govert.

Govert then asked Cantert to testify about a map of the Frese property, which he had surveyed just before the trial. This drawing was done to a scale of thirty feet to one inch. The various existing buildings were marked on this plot, as well as the locations of Ray's tents—which Cantert took from stakes remaining in the ground.

Wall then again quizzed him and ascertained that Govert told him how much of the property to include in the drawing. His drawing stopped about 850 feet east of Twelfth Street and did not include the new "bob" wire fence to the east of the camp.

Wall made sure that the jury knew that the railroad tracks shown on the drawing were elevated, and the trestle, where it crossed over Twelfth Street was high in the air, providing no access from the railroad track to the camp for a team and buggy.

Govert called Henry A. Geisel to testify. Geisel was, among other things, commissioner of highways for Melrose Township, and reiterated that the map of the roads was accurate as drawn by Cantert. Geisel identified the Payson/Quincy road as the one in pink or red on the map, and the Pape's Mill Road in green. The road in purple was Forty-Eighth Street. He also stated that the property owners shown on the map were correct. Wall tried to challenge the accuracy of the map, but Geisel remained firm. There might be a few turns that varied slightly, but overall the map was accurate.

A steely-eyed Lancaster brought Henry W. Konemoeller, chief deputy sheriff of McCoupin County in Carlinville, Illinois, to the stand to demolish Strumpfer's credibility by examining a crime that had occurred in Virden, Illinois. The actual events, as compared to Strumpfer's prior testimony, did not match.[188] The State objected vehemently, but the judge allowed the questioning to proceed in a general way in order to set the stage.

Konemoeller told of Strumpfer arriving at the scene with his dogs about six hours after the body of policeman Jack Shaw was found shot to death in a house a mile and a half west of Virden. The dogs were given the scent from a window ledge and left the yard, crossing a field and investigating a railroad car and a railroad coaling shed before apparently losing the trail and circling back.

Two days later, the shooter was found under the summer kitchen behind the house, dead by suicide. Konemoeller told how he, himself, had heard one shot when he first arrived at the crime scene, before the dogs arrived. On cross, Wall extracted further information that there were eyewitnesses to the actual shooting who saw the gunman jump from a window of the home and run away.

The shooting had taken place on the tenth of December 1912. It was the twelfth when the murderer's body was found under the summer kitchen. The killer had returned to the scene of the crime and ended his own life but was not found by the dog, Nick Carter.

Wall said simply, "So he had plenty of time to go all the distance where the hounds went first and get back to the house?"

---

[188]   30-5264, p. 964.

"Yes, sir," answered the deputy.[189]

Wall pushed on. He got Konemoeller to admit he was not at the scene when the body was found. He never saw the body with the gun to its ear; he didn't know if the blood was fresh or not; he only examined the pistol twenty miles away in Carlinville at the police station and had no idea what might have happened to it between the occurrence of the crime and the time he saw it. It had been all told to him. Everything was secondhand knowledge, other than hearing the single gunshot.

The State firmly objected, and the court struck from the record all testimony except what he saw, and the shot that he heard. Witness dismissed. Still, damage had been done to Strumpfer's credibility.

Lancaster called a second Carlinville deputy, S. D. Holmes, to the stand. This deputy also heard a shot at the crime scene before the dogs came, but he too could testify no further, as he had not been there when the body of the presumed murderer was found. Wall painted the vivid picture of the deputies guarding the house holding the victim's body, hearing the shot, yet not one going to investigate.

Lancaster marched still another Virden, Illinois, native to the stand. Virgil Wood, twenty, arrived at the scene in time to view the victim's body still lying a pool of blood and followed the hounds for the two-and-a-half mile tracking. He also saw the gunman's body two days later when it was taken to town from where it had lain under the summer kitchen, frozen by the winter weather.

Wood was dismissed, having played his part as the defense created inroads into the credibility and reliability of Strumpfer's bloodhounds. Wood was replaced by William Ashby, the flagman at the Twenty-Fourth Street crossing of the CB&Q Railway. Ashby resided in the little house on the railroad right-of-way about one block south of that farm pasture visited by Strumpfer's hounds.

Ashby testified that there were two gates into that pasture. The south one, which the dogs had entered, was a board gate secured with a chain and lock kept in the flagman's house. Ashby was not responsible for locking

---

[189] 30-5264, p. 972.

that gate, only for holding the key overnight until the wagons returned in the morning to haul sand and water from the spring there.

This witness explained that the meadow was a popular picnic spot and buggies regularly went to visit Cedar Creek spring. It had been a busy place last fall with wagons hauling sand and water on a daily basis out from the spring, which was about two blocks into the field and out of view of the crossing house. The witness said, "I was never down as far as Cedar Creek," and he did not check to see if the gate was actually locked at night.[190]

Govert next called Sheriff Lipps as a witness for the defense and delved into the blood-spotted dollar bill. This bill was first pulled from a stack of one-dollar bills at the Illinois State Bank on October 31, 1912. Lipps plucked it from the stack himself, more than a month after the fire and twenty-four days after Ray's arrest.

Wall asked the sheriff if he took the blood-stained bill back to the Eakins to be identified, but the defense objected to labeling it "blood," and Lipps was not allowed to answer. Then Wall wanted to know if the blood spot on the bill was now in the same condition as when it was found. Once again the defense objections prevented an answer.

Wall asked how big the stack of money was that included the bill, and Lipps said about four inches high. Govert was puzzled about how the sheriff was able to recognize the specific bill. "Did you have the number of the bill at the time you were looking for it?"

"I did not," said the sheriff.

"Did you have the name of the bank issuing the bill?"

"I did not."

"Did you know what kinda bill it was, as to being a National Bank bill or a silver certificate?"

"I did not."

"Did you know the date on which it was issued?"

"No, sir, I did not look at the date, I took the number of it."

"You mean you took the date of it at that time?"

"Yes, sir."

---

[190]  30-5264, p. 992.

"Did you have the number of it before that time?"

"No, sir."[191]

Witness dismissed.

Lancaster brought up William Rupp Jr., cashier of the Illinois State Bank, located at the corner of Sixth and Hampshire Street in Quincy. He recalled what happened when Lipps, accompanied by Detective Young, came to the bank.

"They called and wanted to know if we had a dollar bill with a blood spot on it, and that we had gotten from Anck Bros., and our teller looked thru the one-dollar bills. That was early in the morning as I remember, before the bank opened, but I would not state positively what hour of the day. The teller looked thru the money hastily, and then he gave it over as I remember to Mr. Lipps. Mr. Lipps and Mr. Young looked thru it and found this bill in the bunch of bills that was given him. He picked out this one and gave us another dollar instead of this one."[192]

But neither Rupp nor the teller could state where this particular bill had actually come from. It was taken from the teller's drawer in a pile of fifty or seventy five one-dollar bills. There was no way to say positively that it came from the butcher, Anck. There was no record of the number or denomination of bills that Anck deposited, or even if any bills had been included in his deposit.

Wall simply asked if Lipps and Young had any trouble spotting the bill. The cashier said, "No."

Lancaster, in turn, wanted to know if Rupp had looked at the bill and easily seen the same spot. And just how large was this bloody spot?

"I would say about as large, as well about half the size of a dime, I would say; it was rather a small spot; that is as I remember it."[193]

Lancaster next called teller H. J. Butskueben. He readily admitted that he could not find the bill in question when he looked through his drawer, which containing forty or fifty ones deposited by various customers.

---

[191]  30-5263, p. 994.

[192]  30-5264, p. 995.

[193]  30-5264, p. 997.

The defense called William Anck, proprietor of a grocery store and butcher shop. Anck remembered Lipps and Young coming to inspect his one-dollar bills but could not be more helpful than that. He did not know Mrs. Eakins, much less whether or not she spent a dollar in his store.[194]

Having demonstrated that no one really knew where this particular bill came from, Govert then fixed his attention on James O. Anderson, who had testified previously as a prosecution witness. Anderson, superintendent of the Soldier's Home remembered meeting with Ray on Saturday the twenty-eighth of September to receive a contract to dynamite and remove the large number of dead tree stumps from the grounds. Anderson made some changes to the contract presented by Ray. As he remembered, Ray had seemed completely as usual, "Apparently unconcerned."

Wall asked only four questions, designed to hammer home the impression that Ray was entirely unconcerned on that morning. From the prosecution's point of view, Ray should have been concerned after dispatching his parents, his sister, and Emma Kempton less than twenty-four hours before.

Govert ushered Runah I. Miller to the stand. He was eighteen and employed at Morris's Five & Ten Cent Store, but during the past September he worked at the Cottrell Hardware Company. He remembered Ray being in the hardware store and staying until closing time, which was about nine thirty that Saturday night. Miller confirmed that he, Ray, and Harvey Scott went next door and played pool. His story agreed with previous testimony about their evening.[195] Ray had seemed "just as normal."

Then Govert returned to the question of attire. "Do you know what sort of clothes he was wearing that evening?"

Miller was unsure. "I could not state the color of the suit; but I know he had on a suit different from what he usually wore—his working clothes."

"Did he, that evening, when you saw him at eight o'clock or after, wear any khaki suit?"

"No, sir."

---

[194]  30-5264, p. 1000.
[195]  30-5264, p. 1004.

"Do you know whether he had an overcoat that evening?"

"He did."

"What kind of an overcoat?"

"Why it looked to be a kind of cravenette; a sort of cravenette."

"What sort of a hat was he wearing?"

"A derby or dice box."

Govert resumed his seat. If Ray wasn't dressed in the khaki clothes that evening, and if the family was killed on Saturday, the State's case did not make sense. However, if the jury believed the family died on Friday, it was nothing but a bit of obfuscation, and it mattered not at all what Ray's wardrobe was that evening.

The prosecution tested Miller to see if he had spoken to Ray since the fire but got nowhere. Miller had seen Ray in the hardware store once afterward but did not speak to him. Wall sat down unsatisfied and unable to provide the jury with another instance of Ray's callous normalcy after the tragedy.

Lancaster next called A. J. Meyer of Fall Creek. Meyer passed the Pfanschmidt house twice on Saturday. On the first pass, about seven in the morning, he noticed nothing unusual at all. When he came by again about twelve hours later at nearly eight that evening, he smelled something burning. Lancaster queried him repeatedly if it could have been the odor of burning flesh, but Meyer was reluctant to name it so. He did admit that the smell was strong enough for him to stop at the end of the drive and that it seemed to be coming from the home.

The judge asked for more details. "I would like for this witness to give some description of that odor, so the jury can have some method of determining. If you can give us any idea as to what it is like, I will let you do that."

The witness said, "It was offensive."[196]

Wall took over the questioning but had no better luck. In particular, he hoped the witness would say that in the morning the wind was blowing from south to north, so no odors would be apparent from the fire, which

---

[196] 30-5264, p. 1009.

in the State's scenario had been unsuccessfully started late on Friday night. Meyer could not provide the wind direction and was dismissed.

Lancaster presented Roy A. Peter of Melrose Township to the jury. Peter also passed the house twice on Saturday and smelled an odor both times, but it was a bit stronger on the evening trip. Peter had no qualms about naming the smell. "It was the odor of flesh, of powder, of burning hog."

"What did you, in your best judgment at that time, think it was?"

"I supposed maybe he was burning hogs."

Wall could do nothing to change Peter's story.

Lancaster brought Florence, Mrs. Roy Peter, to the stand. She and her sister, Opal Seward, had gone to Quincy in their buggy on Saturday, passing the Pfanschmidt residence sometime between six and seven in the morning. They noticed nothing at that time. But on their return about six or seven in the evening, an offensive odor was apparently coming from the Pfanschmidt home.

Lancaster asked, "Was that odor strong or weak?"

"It was strong," said the witness.

"Was it strong enough to attract the attention of you and your sister?"

"Yes, sir."

"Was it pleasant or otherwise?"

"It was otherwise." Mrs. Peter said she was reminded of burning flesh of some kind.[197]

The only thing Wall could add by cross-examination was that no smoke was seen in the area of the farm—from a chimney or elsewhere. Opal Seward proceeded to the stand and corroborated her sister's story. Opal couldn't say what it smelled like either—nor did she notice wind direction. This witness was dismissed, and the Friday noon recess was called.

During recess a reporter from the *Herald* managed to corner the defense attorneys and asked about the rumor that Mrs. Della Mangold would testify that Ray was at her "place" on Friday night. The lawyers said emphatically it was absolutely untrue. There would "be no repulsive

---

[197] 30-524, p. 1014.

evidence such as women or children cannot hear, presented in this case." At the time, Mangold was known as the proprietress of a brothel at 326½ Maine Street—the heart of the "red-light district."

A crowd had congregated in the corridor outside the courtroom, seeking to secure a place for the afternoon session. The judge had deputies clear the hallways, but many people remained nearby, waiting until the doors were unlocked again at one o'clock. Most of the waiting spectators were female.

At the start of the afternoon session, Wesley A. Hinckle was examined by Lancaster. He lived in Payson, and ran a "teaming business." On the Saturday in question Hinckle passed the Pfanschmidt place four times on his two round trips to haul timber cut on Lier's neighboring farm. He passed the Pfanschmidt's at about seven and eleven in the morning on one trip and again about two and seven on the second trip to Payson. Hinckle reported that the odor was faint at 7:00 a.m., strong at 11:00, not noticeable at 2:00 p.m., and very strong at 5:00 p.m. The odor of burning flesh was the same each time, but its intensity varied. He remembered that the wind changed directions several times that day.

Wall interrogated Hinckle extensively, finally asking, "How do you happen to remember now pretty nearly six months after it happened what way the wind was that morning; have you rehearsed this over with the attorneys in some way?"

"No, sir."

"You never told them anything what way the wind was before you got on the witness stand?"

"No, sir."

Eventually Hinckle admitted speaking to the defense attorneys, but only once—and that was just before noon that very day. Hinckle stood firm that he and the lawyers never mentioned the wind direction. He, like the others, "supposed they were losing hogs by cholera."[198]

Hinckle saw no smoke, and as far as he could tell the house looked perfectly natural. Wall's parting question was, "The only thing that you

---

[198]  30-5264, p. 102.

observed unnatural was that you did not see any life about the house, was it not?"

"Yes, sir."

Govert called Carl Mollenhauer, a twenty-year-old who lived near Paloma, a small village northeast of Quincy. On that Saturday night Mollenhauer had been to the Empire Theater with Miss Lisa May Meyer, who lived about three miles due north of the Pfanschmidt farm. The pair had watched a play called "The Rosary" and then gone to the drugstore at the corner of Eighth and Maine streets. From there they walked to Tenth and State streets, where Mollenhauer's team waited in a livery barn. He hitched his two small bay horses to his buggy and headed to Payson.

Govert had him trace his route through the city and on to the Payson Road, across the bridge over Mill Creek, and up to the top of a hill within two miles of the Pfanschmidt farm. There he turned north again onto a lane that ran north and east for the two or three miles to Miss Meyer's home. Mollenhauer was about half a mile from Miss Meyer's home when he noticed a fire off to the south. His team had driven at a walk for most of the trip from town, at least as near as he remembered, and had met no other vehicles on that journey. After leaving the Meyers' home, Mollenhauer continued another four or five miles to spend what was left of the night at his sister's home in Burton, Illinois, a small town almost due north of Payson. It was "in the neighborhood of three o'clock; I don't know if it was before three or after," when he entered his sister's home after unhitching his team.

Wall wanted to pin down the timeframe, but Mollenhauer wasn't sure if the play started on time, or if it was comprised of three acts or four. He did think it was over at about a quarter before eleven. Wall was adding up the minutes: fifteen minutes in the drugstore; ten or fifteen minutes to walk to the barn. His team was housed in the wagon shed behind the saloon at Tenth and State, and Wall wondered if it was still open. Mollenhauer wasn't sure.

A generous Wall added fifteen minutes to the time for harnessing the team and also pointed out that while Mollenhauer turned east on Harrison, there were alternate routes to reach Melrose Chapel. The State hoped to remind the jury that there was a long stretch of road that could have contained traffic (Ray's buggy, for example) that would have been unseen by Mollenhauer traveling a more easterly route.

How fast did Mollenhauer drive from the Meyer farm to his sister's home? His answer was, "I do not remember; I remember sleeping part of the way." But he did know that the road was quite rough, and he'd had to drive slowly and carefully. He was sure that it took more than half an hour to reach his sister's home, but it might have been more.[199]

Govert's questions let the jury hear that the road was over rolling hills with quite a bit of timber growing along the lane. Next Govert brought Mollenhauer's companion, Miss Mae Meyer, to testify. Miss Meyer reported that she looked at her watch just before the curtain fell for the last time, and it was twenty-five minutes to eleven. She agreed with her companion on all points of his testimony.

Wall ascertained that the pair was seated on the main floor of the theater, rather than in the balcony, in a good-sized crowd. Miss Meyer thought that it did not take longer than five minutes to leave the building at the end of the performance, but she did not remember stopping at the drugstore. Wall quizzed her extensively on their route and distances and how slowly they were driving. Miss Meyer said she was not particularly concerned about the fire and did not tell anyone about it. She thought it was a burning haystack.

She did remember that it was not a very dark night, that the top on their buggy was down, and at no time was it raised. Wall wanted the jury to be clear that it was not possible for someone to mistake this buggy for another buggy pulled by small bay horses, with its top up and side and rain curtains down!

Govert called Floyd W. Munroe, an attorney and the secretary of the Quincy Park and Boulevard Association. Munroe brought with him the official record book, on page 32 of which were the minutes of the meeting held on Tuesday night, September 24, 1912. Mr. Munroe, however, was not in attendance at that meeting, so another man had recorded the minutes. Witness dismissed.

---

[199] 30-5264, p. 1033.

Then the defense called Lawrence E. Edmons Jr., another practicing attorney, who had acted as secretary for the meeting in question. It was agreed that the minutes were truthful, and that the Mr. Pfanschmidt referred to several times in those minutes was the defendant, Ray. Wall uncovered the fact that Edmons was not sure whether Ray was there for the entire meeting or if he had left after his business with the association was completed. Witness dismissed.

Then, with precious little fanfare and no advance warning, at two forty-five in the afternoon, Ray walked calmly and quietly to the stand in answer to his name.[200]

---

[200]   30-5264, p. 1047.

# Chapter 20

# Ray Testifies

## Friday, April 11, 1913

"The boldest move possible was made by the defense in the sensational murder trial this afternoon. The move, which will make or break their case, the move which will convict or acquit Ray Pfanschmidt, the move which, perhaps, will save a life or cost still another was that which the attorneys for the defense made at 2:45 this afternoon when the defendant himself was put upon the stand as a witness.... He walked to the stand boldly and gave his answers with directness and without hesitation."[201]

Govert began simply, saying, "You may state your name."

The answer came in a clear voice: "Ray Pfanschmidt."

Ray was gently led through the basics. He had turned twenty-one this past March 8; had lived with his parents and sister until a few weeks before the fire; was working on a job for J. L. Frese; at the time of the fire was staying at the "works" campsite there. They then moved on to more pertinent matters.

When was Ray last at the farm before the fire? On the weekend before, arriving late Saturday night after midnight, leaving on Sunday

---

[201] *Herald,* April 11, 1913.

morning between eight and nine. Had he been there between that time and the fire?

"I was not."

What was the barn lot like when he was there? It was very muddy. And Ray was driving the only team and buggy he had, the small bay team hitched to the Velie buggy with the standard wheel and the five-feet, two-inch wheel spread.

Govert took him through his activities on the days preceding the fire. On Monday Ray picked Esther up at the Pape residence at Thirteenth and Spring Street and took her home to her father, brother, and sister-in-law. On Tuesday he was at the chamber of commerce building above the Owl Drug Store on Maine Street to attend a Park & Boulevard meeting and present a proposal to clear the city parks of their dead trees using dynamite. Ray took a streetcar to the meeting and afterward walked back to the works from Fifth and Maine. On Wednesday, Ray was again visiting at Miss Reeder's home.

Ray did make a stop on the way home from Esther's on both Monday and Wednesday to get a lunch at Seventeenth and Broadway, although he did not know the name of the lunch wagon proprietor. He was not there, according to his testimony, on Tuesday evening at all.

On Thursday night he was "downtown," with Ben Holeman and his wife, Mr. Eakins and his wife, and Willis Seehorn. During the day he had worked at Uncle William Abel's and Uncle Henry Geisel's.

Now questions about Ray's wardrobe entered testimony.

"When you dressed that morning, what clothes did you put upon yourself, that Thursday morning?"

"A blue serge suit, a light shirt, a stiff collar, a light raincoat, a stiff hat or derby hat."

"When had you last worn those garments?"

"Wednesday evening."

"The Wednesday evening preceding?"

"Yes, sir."

Ray testified that he got up and donned the same clothes he had worn to visit Esther the preceding night; ate breakfast; took his team and wagon to the Cottrell Hardware Store accompanied by Holeman. Holeman was sent on an errand to a "powder house" to pick up some dynamite, while Ray went to his desk at Chadwick's.

From Chadwick's, Ray went to visit Grandfather C. C. on South Twelfth Street, where he changed out of his blue serge suit, leaving it in a closet off the second-floor hall. The raincoat remained there too, along with the derby hat. Ray was not sure what became of the shirt and collar he had been wearing.

At his grandfather's house Ray donned work clothes stored there since the preceding Sunday, which consisted of a khaki suit and a pair of high-laced boots. He then picked up Ben and the dynamite at Twelfth and State streets and drove out to Uncle William Abel's farm, near Thirty-Sixth and Harrison. Ray had promised to blow out a "seap," or swamp, for Uncle Abel, and needed to finish the project.

Govert asked, "In blowing out a seap, it requires what work?"

"It requires boring deep enough to get below the hard pan, and discharging charges of dynamite therein."[202]

At Abel's farm, it required boring down more than thirty feet and involved the labor of both Ben and himself. At noon the two went to Uncle Henry Geisel's for a meal before Ben returned to Abel's and Ray stayed at Geisel's. Just to be sure the jury knew that Ray was no slacker when it came to physical labor, Govert asked, "What order of work was to be done on the Abel farm?"

Ray said, "To bore the holes deeper than we had bored in the morning."

"Was it necessary for more than one man to work on that?"

"I did not have extension enough for us both to work at it."

"What do you mean by that?"

"Connections to make my auger longer."

"Would it have been possible with the equipment you had for both of you to have kept at work on that boring that afternoon?"

Ray answered, "No, sir."[203]

---

[202] 3-5264, p. 1053.
[203] 30-5264, p. 1054.

So he remained with Uncle Geisel to blow some stumps from the meadow, by means of his "blasting machine." Govert asked Ray to describe this contraption, but the State objected. The judge saw no merit in the objection and it was overruled. Ray was allowed to continue.

"It is a large box about 2' high; about 10" square and 18" deep…. It contains a magneto, a high-tensioned magneto. In order to get a charge from this magneto, a lever is raised and pressed down, and the charge coming from the magneto is carried to the caps and fuse. First there is a coil of wire known as the lead wire. The wire consists of a coil of copper wires. There are two wires together, and are insulated and about the size of a person's little finger." Ray explained that this lead wire was in a large coil placed on the ground.

Govert next led Ray through the story of the watch presented to him on May 11, 1909, upon his graduation from high school. He recounted past problems with the ring that the "R" fob was buckled to, and said that there he had no watch chain. Ray had also sprung the back of the watch slightly when he tried to paste a picture in it, but he had not had it in for repairs for about the past year.

What happened to damage the watch that day? Ray said, "As I was firing the last blast, my wire was attached to a tree that I was working upon to keep it from touching the ground, and in firing the blast it threw the coil and it caught my watch fob and jerked it from my pocket and threw it to the ground."

"What effect had it upon the ring?"

"It pulled it out … I pressed it back in, the best I could with the means I had."[204]

Then finding himself in his fiancée's neighborhood, Ray drove the half mile or so south to visit Esther before returning to his Uncle Abel's to retrieve Holeman. When he arrived at Abel's he found the drilling work finished, so Ray "commenced to do the loading." Loading consisted of shoving a stick of dynamite into the hole, tamping it down, and filling the hole with dirt.

---

[204] 30-5264, p. 1056.

Govert asked if the work was muddy and Ray replied that in the morning it was very dirty. "My trousers were practically all mud." At the end of the day, they got back to Holeman's about five o'clock, ate supper, and then Ray returned to his tent to change out of his dirty work clothes. Ray stated that his coat was not muddy, but no further explanation was given to the jury.

Govert carefully pointed out that the muddy shirt and pants, which Ray had owned for about a month and had put on that morning at his grandfather's house, were now left lying on the tent floor. This muddy suit had been the first of Ray's purchases from the Hub store, being a sort of sample. He later ordered three more identical suits, which were delivered before the fire, along with some dark cambric shirts.

Govert asked, "Had this first suit that you had purchased about a month before at any time been washed or laundried since you bought it?"

"No, sir," came the reply.

These four suits were the only new ones Ray had. He told the jury that he had other khaki suits that had been "laundried" several times and were faded and torn, but no specific number was ever given.

When Ray went into the supply tent to change on Thursday evening, the three new suits "were lying folded up in a box in the west tent." Both Ray and Ben put on one full suit. Ray said that he understood that Holeman had later returned the shirt and trousers.[205]

Leaving the wardrobe, Govert asked about sleeping arrangements at the works. He was told that Ray's employee, Willis Seehorn, had for the past three weeks or so occupied the second canvas cot in Ray's sleeping tent. The bedding on those cots consisted of "old blankets and comforts; horse-blankets … from home …"

Ray explained that at night, it was his custom to remove only his shoes and sometimes his coat before sleep. That Thursday night, he left his watch and fob and bow ring in his pocket as he slept. On Friday morning, Ray awakened wearing the new suit he had put on for the downtown excursion the previous night.

---

[205]  30-5264, p. 1059.

Govert was attempting to explain to the jury that prior testimony saying Ray was wearing a blue serge suit on Saturday morning was simple confusion. Ray confirmed that he wore the blue serge suit on Wednesday, slept in it, and then went to the works wearing this odd suit on Thursday morning before going to his grandfather's and then to his uncle's. To be certain that he was understood, Govert asked Ray, "After you had removed the blue serge suit and coat, and the light raincoat and derby hat at your grandfather's Thursday morning, did you take those garments and hat back to the works at any time?"

Ray said emphatically, "I did not."

"Where were they all that time?" Govert wanted a specific answer.

Ray replied, "At my grandfather's."

Ray recounted his Friday activities. He spent time at the works and then went to Chadwick's to check for mail, get his books, and breakfast. He was accustomed to receiving mail at both Chadwick's and Cottrell's shops and was looking for correspondence about other jobs. He spent Friday afternoon in town and returned to the works about five o'clock, after eating dinner and without making "any change of garments in the meantime." Ray had ridden a streetcar back to Soldier's Home.

Back at the works, he met Silba Lawrence, who helped him hitch up his team. Govert used this occasion to point out that the sleeping tents were about fifty yards from the wagon shed where the horses were kept, with the sleeping tent and the supply tent "practically as near together as they could be put." There were no other buildings near them and nothing to block the view of anyone entering the tent.

While Silba was hitching the horses, Ray swapped his coat, this time donning the one with a Bull Moose pin on the lapel. By this point almost everyone in the courtroom was confused. Even the judge had to ask, "Which coat?"

Govert explained, "The coat that he put on Friday evening."

The Court inquired, "After he had changed?"

Govert agreed, "After he had changed."

Govert asked Ray, "Did you on that occasion put upon your coat a class pin?"

Ray answered, "I did not."

Govert asked, "What sort of shirt were you wearing the rest of that evening?"

"A sateen shirt." And Ray went on to note that it was a much lighter color than the three shirts he had purchased at the Hub store, and of a much softer texture. He did also add his traditional red string tie.

When Ray left the camp about half past five on Friday night to take Lawrence home, the only things in the buggy were two halters for his team. Govert asked if there was a pass-through between the front and the rear of Ray's buggy under the seat and Ray said no. Was it possible to conceal anything in that vehicle in the space in front of the seat? No. There was only one small uncovered space behind the seat. Ray's buggy was not built to carry cargo.[206]

He got his supper on Hampshire Street and went out to Miss Reeder's. The young man added here that he forgot to mention that he put on some new yellow leggings "like the army leggings," which he had purchased from the Koch Harness Shop in Quincy. Ray arrived at the Reeder home between seven and eight o'clock and tied the team, as usual, west of the house. When he arrived the family was eating, but Ray and Esther went to an adjoining parlor after about ten or fifteen minutes, leaving her father, brother, and sister-in-law at the table. No one joined the young couple, but they did pass back and forth in front of the door and through the room.

Ray said he left the farm at half past ten and told the courtroom that he and Miss Reeder had spent "a few minutes" together on the porch before he left. He took a few extra minutes to check the harness because, "Early in the evening in coming out, the anti-rattler came loose, and I looked over that to see if it would hold until I got back home.... I had to unfasten a spring, pull a bolt, and replace the bolt."

Ray clearly and succinctly recited, for Govert, his exact route home. "I drove east on the lane to 36th Street, north on 36th Street to Harrison Street, west on Harrison to Twenty-Fourth, north on Twenty-Fourth to State Street, west on State Street to Eighteenth, north on Eighteenth to

---

[206] 30-5264, p. 1065.

Broadway, west on Broadway to Twelfth, north on Twelfth to the camp." He dozed over the reins part of the way.

According to Ray, he fell asleep almost immediately after leaving the Reeders, so when his team, on their own accord, turned west into the Geisel driveway, they got through the open gate before he woke and got hold of the lines. He promptly turned the rig around then fell back asleep almost immediately. He was awakened again at Thirty-Sixth and Harrison, when the team turned east at the familiar crossroad and headed toward Uncle Abel's property. He reversed them again, going back the four roads to Harrison Street. He went back to sleep a third time and later woke on State Street somewhere between Twenty-Second and Eighteenth streets. Ray assumed the team had taken its customary route.

From that point on he remembered staying awake, stopping again at the lunch wagon at Seventeenth and Broadway for food. He recalled seeing and recognizing Mr. Clutch, as he had stopped at his stand twice already that week. This time he purchased "several sandwiches" before driving back to the camp.

At the works, he unhitched and went to his tent about midnight or shortly after. Willis Seehorn was there, and although Ray made a remark to him about the keg of beer Frese had promised the men the following night, Seehorn only rolled over and grunted. Ray wasn't sure if he was awake or not. Govert asked if he heard anything outside the tent before he drifted off to sleep.

Ray reported, "I did … several rigs going over the bridge and a train going by."

"In what direction was the train going that you heard?"

"West." Ray explained that he could tell the difference between a passenger train and a freight train in several different ways, including the length of the train, the speed, and the amount of noise it made. He could count the number of cars by their echo as they went over the railway bridge and claimed he could see the light of the train passing the works. "It was a passenger train," said Ray, "the Eli," which regularly passed his camp between midnight and one o'clock.[207]

---

[207] 30-5264, p. 1072.

Before settling to sleep, he reported that he removed only his shoes, keeping on his khaki shirt, shoes, and coat. He did take from his pockets "some money, some books, and a revolver," which he put upon his stool near the head of his bed. Then he slept until Seehorn called him early the next morning. Ray ignored him and did not rise until the men arrived at the works about seven o'clock.

It was not Ray's usual custom to take breakfast at the works unless he was leaving there to go to another job. Otherwise he would breakfast later. This Saturday morning he got up without changing his clothes, which he had worn "yesterday" and slept in.

Govert inquired about the weather that morning and was told it was slightly cloudy. "Did you at any time put on any outer garment over that suit?"

"I slipped on the raincoat I had worn the night before." Then Ray walked the two hundred yards south and east to the job site where he stayed until about eight o'clock. Ray had changed the men's assignments from working on excavating the railroad cut to digging out the coal bin, but his employer, Frese, thought he should finish the railroad cut first.

Unaware that Frese was headed into town to visit his attorney, Ray went back to his tent and changed clothes, putting on one of his new unworn suits. He left the suit he had just removed lying in the box. Then, according to Ray, he trekked back to the job site and then down the railroad tracks to Soldiers Home, where he caught a streetcar to visit his own attorney, Mr. Lancaster, in regard to his dispute with Frese over work and payments.

Finding no one in his lawyer's office, Ray went on to O'Dell's jewelry store to have his watch repaired and cleaned. Ray verified the details of Weaver's earlier testimony and then told of going to the Hub Clothing Store where he purchased a new sweater jacket. Afterward he returned to Lancaster's still vacant office and then continued a few doors south to the Collins Plow Company in hopes of finding Govert there. He was still looking for his attorney when he was cornered at Collins by Frese and Gilmer, who wanted to talk over the dispute.

Govert asked, "What was the dispute, Mr. Pfanschmidt, between you and Frese about the works?"

"I said that when I finished one part of the work for Mr. Frese, I expected my money, and he said the money was not due until it was all done. I held to my agreement and would not finish any part of it; so he could have the benefit of it, unless I got my money for the part I had finished."

Govert asked how much work had been completed, and Ray said he had moved between ten and eleven thousand cubic yards of dirt. The contract covered digging out the railroad cut, a coal bin, a driveway, and making a roadway, with the original drawing calling for moving about forty-five hundred cubic yards of dirt. Additional elements had later been added to the job.

Ray said he was to be paid eleven cents a yard, of which he had received only $200 at the time of the dispute. After the discussion with Gilmer, Ray accompanied Frese back to the works. He stayed at the worksite until just before noon, when he went back to Soldiers Home to see Colonel Anderson, and then on to Chadwick's and Cottrell's, where he checked for "applications for work" as well as mail.

At this point the judge called the afternoon recess, and reporters scurried off to file stories about the star witness for the evening editions.

The *Journal* of April 12 reported that, "News that Ray Pfanschmidt was on the stand spread rapidly, first to the crowd in the lower corridors of the courthouse and then out onto the street. Within half an hour after the boy had been placed on the stand, standing room on the lower corridor of the building was at a premium, and deputy sheriffs fought with the crowds to keep them downstairs until a recess should be taken. A few left the courtroom when a short rest was given by the court at four o'clock, and these were hurried downstairs while a surging mass, piling over one another, came up the other stairs and rushed into the courtroom. Efforts on the part of deputies to keep the people from crowding were unheeded, and women screamed as they were squeezed against the wall or almost pushed down by the onrush from the rear."

When court resumed, Ray related that he got back to the works on Friday just in time to pay the men about half past four. He then hitched his team to take Lawrence home still wearing, Govert was careful to elicit, the new khaki suit he had put on that morning. Ray was also careful to specify once again that the only things he had in the buggy were horse halters.

Ray made one stop looking for Mr. Bunting, the engineer at Soldiers Home, but didn't find him. So he took Lawrence home and then drove to the Stern Building where he tied his team up while he went to a nearby barbershop for a shave. Ray next visited Smith's Tailor Shop to pick up a suit he had left on Monday to be cleaned. He retrieved his dark brown suit contained in an old suitcase, deposited the suitcase in his buggy, and went on to Thompson's Dairy Lunch for supper.

Full from supper, Ray went to Stern's Clothing Store and bought another new shirt, necktie, and a pair of hose. This shirt was "brown flannel." Ray said, "Some wear them for summer, but I generally wear them in the winter."[208]

Even Govert wondered aloud how many shirts Ray had at that time. "Of different kinds, I don't believe I can tell you." Ray seemed to have lost track but knew that the number was greater than three or four, plus numerous pairs of hose and ties.

After these latest purchases Ray stopped by Chadwick's before driving to his grandfather's house where relatives were congregating. Along with C. C. Pfanschmidt, Ray saw his aunt Mrs. Petrie, her son, Howard, and his aunt and uncle, Mr. and Mrs. Herr, in town from Wichita, Kansas. Also visiting at the house were Mrs. Petrie's daughter, Mrs. Keim, and another uncle and aunt, Mr. and Mrs. Niekamp, and their daughter, Elsie.

Once again, Ray decided to change clothes. He carried his suitcase upstairs, accompanied by Howard, to the room where Howard slept. There Ray removed his new khaki suit. He put on the newly cleaned dark brown suit, and the new flannel shirt, new hose, and a new necktie. Ray placed the khaki suit he had just taken off into the suitcase retrieved from the cleaners, and Howard put it under the bed. Ray also picked up his raincoat and stiff hat from the hall closet where he had previously left them.

Ray invited Howard to spend the night out at the camp with him, sweetening the deal with the offer that this time Howard could have one

---

[208] 30-5264, p. 1081.

of the cots and would not need to sleep on the ground. Then Ray, all dressed up in his clean suit, took Howard to Keim's Store at Eighteenth and State streets. The Keim who owned this store was Howard's brother-in-law. During this thirty-minute visit, Ray repeatedly asked Howard to come out to the camp with him, but Howard held firm, saying it was not possible since his uncle and aunt had arrived and his presence would be required at home.

As far as Ray knew, Howard did not bother to ask his mother's permission, assuming that it would not be granted. So Ray dropped Howard back at the corner of Twelfth and State and returned to Chadwick's store, where the team was accustomed to standing tied. Ray left them waiting and went to Cottrell's, still looking for a letter from his mother.

Ray had last spoken with his mother on the phone early Wednesday morning. Mathilda brought Blanche to Quincy every Wednesday for the young lady's piano lesson, and Ray called to request them to bring along some of his papers, dynamiting books, and blank contracts. Mathilda had them when they met later that day. They also discussed if Ray would be coming home on Saturday evening.

"Did you see your mother and kiss her on the Wednesday before the fire?"

"I did," Ray answered in stark syllables.

Ray saw "Tilde" and Blanche first at Chadwick's Machine Shop and then later at Fifth and Hampshire and a last time at Sixth and Maine Streets. At their last meeting, his mother asked again if Ray was coming home that weekend, and they made tentative arrangements.

Ray was uncertain of his plans. "I told her I could not state definitely as to that yet, and she said if they did not come to Quincy she would write and inquired if I received such a letter, would I be out."

Govert wanted the jury to be clear. "In case you did not receive such a letter from home, what was the arrangement with reference to whether she would be in Quincy, or the family would be in Quincy Sunday?"

"If I did not receive any letter, I was expecting them."

"What was your purpose in bringing your team down town Saturday afternoon?

"If I received a letter, I intended to go home that evening."[209]

Ray checked repeatedly at his mail drops but did not find a letter from his mother, so he expected his family to arrive in Quincy on Sunday. After a last check at Cottrell's, he found his friends Scott, Miller, Schupp, and Baker. From that point his account of activities again agreed with the previous witnesses: the Mission Pool Hall, ice cream with Harvey Scott at the Parthenon Candy Kitchen, and then back to his rig and to camp alone from about midnight until half past four or so the next morning.[210]

The next thing Ray remembered was his Uncle Niekamp rousing him, crying that the house was burned and all the horses there, and they feared the people were burned. He told Ray to hurry and get up.

Ray "slipped on my shoes and coat, came outside, and got in Niekamp's buggy," telling Holeman to grease the buggy and hitch the team. Both Ray and Holeman agreed that he included this rather odd request to grease the buggy in his instructions at that time.

When they arrived at Grandfather's house they found that Aunt Lizzie Petrie very much wanted to accompany Ray to the farm. As soon as Holeman arrived with Ray's "very fresh" team, Ray and Lizzie drove four blocks over to Niekamp's on S. Sixteenth Street, but the Niekamps decided to take their own vehicle and did not accompany them.

Ray drove "as rapidly as I could" to the farm. "I whipped and drove them as hard as they could go,"[211] using the Pape's Mill Road, which was his accustomed route. "Well, it is downhill until you get about a mile and a half from home, all good graveled road with the exception of the last mile and a half ... it is not as hilly."[212] Ray thought that when he arrived there were about fifty people there.

Govert next investigated the matter of the gasoline cans. Ray said he found a gas can "immediately back of what would have been the front door." So Govert asked if Ray looked for the other cans to see if they were

---

[209] 30-5264, p. 1088.
[210] 30-5264, p. 1091.
[211] 30-5264, p. 1094.
[212] 30-5264, p. 1095.

in their regular places, and Ray admitted he did look but could not find any.

"You may state whether or not the gasoline can that you found at this part of the ruins was or was not the gasoline can that had been previously to that time been on your father's premises."

"I think it was," replied Ray.

"What marks, if any, did that can have upon it?"

"It was painted red and had a piece of paper certain colored design on it." Ray further described that under the paint, which had mostly blistered off, the can was galvanized metal and still retained part of its label. Ray remembered calling the can to some peoples' attention but not exactly who he told.

Then Ray's version directly contradicted that of both the chief of police and his deputy.

Govert asked a key question. "Did you at any time on that morning state to Chief Lott that this was a strange can?"

Ray answered firmly, "I did not."

"What did you say?"

"I said this can was in a strange place, or the wrong place, or something to that extent."

"Did you not state to Mr. Scharnhorst that you had not seen this can on the place before?"

"No, sir."

"What, if anything, did you state to him, if you remember?"

Ray replied, "I did not know Mr. Scharnhorst."

Govert asked, "Did you make a statement of that character to anybody that this can had not been on the place before?"

"I did not," answered Ray.

He noticed that the can was dented, but Ray explained this by saying a beam must have fallen on it. State's Attorney Gilmer had told him that the can should be kept, so Ray set it in his buggy to secure it. When Ray was ready to leave, the officials had already gone and not taken the can. When Ray left, he removed it from his buggy and laid it in the orchard.

What about those tracks, did Ray see them?

"Yes sir, I did.... Mr. Sprick and I put the box over them."[213] Ray acknowledged calling Tony Gilmer from Kaufman's house because he was the only officer Ray knew. And Ray further stated his own opinion about calling in bloodhounds was "if it would do any good, to get them."[214] The reason he later told John Lier to remove boards protecting the tracks was that Uncle Fred had said he'd been told that the officers couldn't use them.

Govert asked if Ray was in the smokehouse that morning, and the defendant admitted that he had been, along with his Aunt Petrie. He had gone in there to cry, but his aunt told him to "brace up." That was when he went out and asked John Lier for some whiskey. Ray said it was supplied and he did drink some.

Govert inquired, "Are you accustomed to drink?"

"I am not."[215]

Govert followed the day through lunch and on into Sunday afternoon. Ray reported he and Esther went to Grandfather Pfanschmidt's home for supper, then to Chadwick Machine shop, then to Silha Lawrence's home, and then to the Frese place where they pulled in just far enough to turn the buggy around and head on to Joe Eakins's house looking for foreman, Ben Holeman. It was about six o'clock when they arrived at Eakins's.

Esther and Ray had to wait about an hour and a half for Eakins to find Holeman and return with him. They finally left sometime after eight. Before going, Ray did indeed ask to change a bill for coins to leave for streetcar fare. Ray had had the money he changed for some time, "part of it for several weeks; all of it for weeks, except what I had received in change."

"Did you, at any time, hand him any dollar bill with a bloodstain on it, as far as you know?"

"I do not think I did." But Ray admitted he did not inspect the bill beforehand.

---

[213] 30-5264, p. 1098.
[214] 30-5264, p. 1099.
[215] 30-5264, p. 1101.

He and Esther left the Eakins, stopping back at the camp to retrieve a horse blanket for a lap robe and Ray's revolver. Esther never left the buggy, and Ray carefully reported that he did not remove anything else or leave anything in the tent. He had planned on taking Esther home and returning to his grandfather's house for the night, but plans changed. At Mrs. Petrie's suggestion, Ray called Ben and canceled the planned retrieval of his team, took Esther home, and stayed the night at the Reeders.

Govert worked to discredit the story that Ray hired lawyers on Monday. Ray said he did not contact any attorney or ask anyone else to do so until the Wednesday following the fire, when he made arrangements with Govert and Lancaster.

Having cleared up that matter for the jury, Govert moved on to the dates on that check the prosecution claimed was from April.

"Mr. Pfanschmidt, in writing dates with numbers expressive of the day and month, what has been your habit and custom with reference to stating the day first or month first?"

"The day first," answered Ray.

"Look at the check marked 'Defendant's exhibit 1' and state what was meant by you in the figures following Quincy, Illinois, 4-9-1912?"

Ray explained clearly, "The fourth day of September 1912."[216] Not the ninth of April, as the State had alluded to in their assessment of his reckless financial doings.

Govert explored other territory, some of which did not cast Ray in a favorable light. Ray had only recently reached his twenty-first birthday. Prior to reaching his majority in 1913, Govert asked if Ray had "any knowledge or information as to your rights as a minor with reference to any contracts into which you might enter?"

"I had," said Ray.

"Did you know," Govert probed, "that any contracts entered into by you as a minor could be voided with no legal liability?"

The State flew up in objection, but the court overruled them.

---

[216] 30-5264, p. 1107.

"I did," said Ray, admitting he knew that legally he could get out of any contract. Where had he learned this? "In my school work, studying civics and political economy, and by dealing with Paul Grote, the county judge of Pike County."[217]

Over multiple State objections, Ray managed to testify that he had had business dealings with Judge Grote and had deposited the payments from him. In fact, the final payment was the $1,000 deposited in the State Street Bank in the early part of July.

At five o'clock on Friday, Govert said, "That's all" and surrendered Ray to the eager prosecuting attorney.

---

[217] 30-5264, p. 1108.

# Chapter 21

# Cross Examination

### Friday, April 11, 1913

The *Journal* wrote, "There was a sigh of relief to be heard over the courtroom as Attorney Wall began to speak, for everybody believed that it would be only a matter of a few minutes until the defendant would be so confused that he would by trying to answer the questions, establish his own guilt beyond all reasonable doubt. Yet Pfanschmidt, with the same coolness which has characterized all his actions since he was arrested … kept his composure and made his answers in a quiet, deliberate way…. He spoke in a high pitched yet plainly audible voice, and on only one or two occasions did he show the least confusion, and this he covered up in the next few words."

With relish, Wall rose to dismantle Ray's story, starting by examining Ray's movements on Saturday evening.[218] Ray, misunderstanding, began by denying that he was looking for a letter from his Mother on Saturday. Counsel for the defense rose to clarify the day under discussion, and Ray collected himself and got back on track. It might have been nerves or a simple fear of agreeing with anything the State said, but eventually, the

---

[218]  30-5264, cross-exam begins on p. 1109.

rhythm of the questioning established itself. Ray's answers were clear but careful.

Wall quizzed Ray, seeking to show that his story of asking Howard Petrie to spend the night at Ray's camp was a later reconstruction to establish an alibi. "Then why did you ask Howard Petrie to come and stay at the camp before coming down to Cottrell's?"

"Because I did not expect to receive a letter from mother anymore." According to Ray's thoughts, he would have received the letter asking him to come home by this time, and if by chance it came later, he could either leave Howard in town and go to the farm or take his cousin along with him.

Wall moved on to the telephone. Ray was in the habit of using the one at Chadwick's, wasn't he? Yes. Well, why didn't he call his mother when no letter arrived? Because of the previous agreement, Ray said.

"You weren't that anxious, you did not care to telephone on account of the previous agreement?"

"I supposed Mother would do as she said she would."[219]

From Saturday, Wall circled back to events on Friday evening, asking if Ray frequently went to sleep on his way home. A wary Ray wanted to know what he meant by "home." Wall responded by inquiring which place Ray considered home.

"Sometimes I generally called out where my parents lived as home and my tent as a camp or the works," was Ray's reply.

Ray admitted that if he was asleep, he would not know if he met anybody. Ray said simply, "I don't remember of meeting anyone."

Wall followed Ray's route past the lunch stand, where Ray denied getting anything to drink, and then straight to camp. Wall was very particular about details. Was the door of the tent open? Ray, still guarded, said there was no door, only a flap. Which direction did that flap face? South. When you got inside and closed the flap, was it very dark? Ray hedged, "It was fairly dark." Ray reported he removed only his shoes before getting into the cot and under the covers.

---

[219] 30-5264, p. 1111.

Wall was curious how such a sleepy Ray, lying in his dark tent under the covers, could lie awake for ten or fifteen or twenty minutes before the train came by, and whether he was awake enough to count the number of cars.

Ray said he did not count the number of cars, rather, "I noticed to see whether there was a few or a whole lot of them."

"What were there?"

"I know there was a few."

"You didn't sleep much while you were in your tent?"

"I had my nap out." Ray could not remember if it was a clear moonlight night or not. "I don't exactly remember."

They agreed it was a chilly night, and Wall inquired if Ray had the buggy's side curtain up on the ride home.

"I did not," said the defendant. What about his lap robe? "I had no robe with me.... None at all."

Wall investigated Ray's experience at Clutch's lunch stand. Was it ready to close? Who else was there? Did he see anyone? It was on a busy road that was traveled a great deal, wasn't it?

Ray's answers were careful and guarded. "I am sure I could not say," or, "I don't remember of seeing any."[220]

Wall took Ray further back to the previous Wednesday night visit at the lunch stand, inquiring about the automobiles there that night. Ray didn't remember meeting any, but there were some standing in front of the Arcade Hall.

About his route home, Wall asked: "[Eighteenth and State] is a thoroughfare that is traveled considerable at that time of night by people going out State Street?"

Ray couldn't agree. "I can't say as to that; I travel it quite frequently, and I don't remember of meeting anyone that I knew at that time of night.... I don't know just exactly what time it was. If I met anyone I did not know, I would not pay any attention to them."

Wall's questions swerved back to Ray's Friday night journey from the Reeders' to the camp, and the details were minutely examined. Asked

---

[220] 30-5264, p. 1114.

about his tentmate Seehorn, Ray said with precision, "He was sleeping on the west cot in the east tent."

Before climbing into the cot, Ray took off the raincoat but could not remember if he left it in the buggy or in the tent. He only slept in his "body coat" and lay down with his head to the north.

"You didn't get up when you heard the train go by, did you?"

"Certainly not," replied Ray.

Then Wall led Ray into a difficult position concerning his testimony about the visibility of the lights on the train. "You knew that by the light, by the lights of the train and by the speed of the train, is that right?"

Ray answered, "Yes, sir."

"Where did you see the light of that train from?"

"I can see it from the head and tail; the distance from the head light to the tail light as it went by."

"How could you see it if you were in your tent and had the flap closed?"

"By the reflection on the canvas."

"Could you tell by the reflection on a moonlight night?"

"Where I was lying I could see them."[221] Ray explained that he was interested in trains, having not been around them much. When he first came to the works they disturbed his sleep, and he would watch and listen to them. He still did—when he heard them.

Wall moved on to the topic of dynamite. "Where did you learn that?"

"From the DuPont people."

"They taught you that, did they?"

"Yes, sir, by means of correspondence."

"You took a correspondence course, did you?"

"No, sir."

"What do you mean by correspondence?"

"Catalogue books."[222]

---

[221] 30-5264, p. 1118.
[222] 30-5264, p. 1119.

After that revelation, Ray went on to say that he only knew of two ways to set off a blast: "By an electrical fuse and a powder fuse."

Wall inquired pointedly if an explosion could be set off by a clock, but Ray didn't know about that. He had never tried it. Eventually, he grudgingly acknowledged that he had heard of the method but could not remember if he heard before or after the fire. Then Ray said that he had an old magazine that mentioned it, but he could not name the magazine or the issue, and finally decided it was something he had read while in jail. "I had a magazine since I have been arrested that had that outlined in it to a certain extent."[223]

Wall wanted to know if Ray had followed in the papers the case of the McNamaras, who were using dynamite in the campaign to unionize labor over the country. Ray denied following the case. He was unable to remember any conversation with his grandfather that mentioned the McNamaras, nor had he followed their story.

Wall gave up this line of inquiry and turned his attention to the Thursday night trip to the movies with the Holemans and the Eakins. Wall wanted to know how many suits were left in the box after he and Ben had dressed in new khakis. Ray said, "One."

Wall was unable to rattle Ray's remembrance of days and clothes. Ray said confidently that when he and Holeman went out with the others, there was one clean, unworn, new khaki suit left along with the muddy one from stump blasting, which had the Bull Moose pin on the lapel. Both had been left in the supply tent. When did Ray last see that suit with the Bull Moose pin? He last saw it when he took it off on Thursday night.

Wall probed, "Which suit had the class pin in it?"

"The suit I had worn Monday."

"What had become of that suit?"

"It was there in the tent ... that was the one I put on Thursday night."

"When did you put your class pin on that suit?"

"Monday night before I came uptown."

---

[223] 30-5264, p. 1120.

Ray said he slept in this suit and wore it all day Friday until he changed his coat before taking Silba Lawrence home. He left the coat with the class pin on it, in the utility tent. Ray thought, to the "best of my knowledge" the coat stayed there, in among the other clothes. He said he did not throw it on the floor, but "to a certain extent" folded it and put it on top of the suit box from Mr. Ellerbrecht with other clothes.

Wall had Ray state three times that the coat had no blood spots on it and then asked him, "What did you put it off for?"

Ray replied, "It had a little grease or tar around the sleeves.... Well, it was some I got on it down at Chadwick's shop on Friday ... it was practically oil and dust mixed; it was not what you would call grease."

"Did you get any grease on the trousers of that suit?"

"No, sir."[224]

Wall chided him for putting a greasy coat in with the new ones, but Ray said it was only a little grease. There were also other suits there, of khaki and a gray one. Wall wanted to know if Ray had a dark blue suit, dark blue trousers, or a derby hat. "No" was Ray's answer to all three.

Ray repeated that on Saturday morning at the works he had on leggings and his old black raincoat but no derby hat. The morning was slightly cool and misty, but not really raining. Ray said he put in "most of the afternoon" at Chadwick's.

Wall quizzed his postal habits and discovered that when Ray first came to town, he received most of his mail at Cottrell's. But then he changed to Chadwick's and didn't get many letters at Cottrell's. Mail was delivered to Chadwick's three times a day, and Wall sounded incredulous that Ray did not know there was no mail delivered to Chadwick's after 3:00 p.m.

Tuesday night was next to catch Wall's attention. Ray said he stopped at the Chadwick residence that evening, on Vine, near Sixth Street. Then he walked back to the camp. Wall then scattered questions about Ray's timetable for the week from Wednesday night at Reeders to Monday night at Pape's. He again attacked Ray's supposed sleepiness on Friday night and inquired each night about the time Ray retired, the time he arose, and how

---

[224] 30-5264, p. 1124.

well he slept. Ray always agreed that he slept well, although he was hazy on his rising times; usually somewhere between five and seven o'clock in the morning.

Wall wanted to know how hard Ray worked during the day, and if he was doing anything unusual or hard. Ray began to catch on. Wall asked how many holes were bored on Thursday in soft earth. Ray replied that the boring was done "in hard red clay." Wall pointed out that Ray had been doing this work since June, and Ray retorted that he hadn't been doing any boring.

"Two days of the week you did this boring and that is what fatigues you, that is what made you look so tired Friday morning, was it?"

"No, not in particular."[225]

Wall asked about the incident in which Ray said his watch was broken, and they sparred back and forth about the last time Ray had it worked on (a year ago) and if Ray had ever taken it to another jeweler. "When I took it anyplace I took it to O'Dell's." Had the ring been replaced before? Ray said once when he first got it, but not for more than a year.

Wall focused on the watch fob. Was it on the cot the next morning? Yes. What did Ray do with it, did he put it in the cartridge belt? "No, sir."

Wall wanted to know, "Who put it there?"

Ray named his employee, "Ben Holeman."

Wall wanted to know if Ray ever told Weaver at O'Dell's that he broke the watch crawling over or through a barbed-wire fence. Ray rejected this. "I did not tell Mr. Weaver that." He repeated the plausible story that it was a "wire" that broke it but not barbed wire.

Now the prosecuting attorney moved on to Ray's team of horses and their condition and stamina. "They were well during the week of September 27 and 29, were they?"

Ray replied, "They were not." He said they could stand driving but not as much as when they were well. What was the matter with them? "Distemper." Wall asked about the type of treatment and where he got the "distemper food."

---

[225] 30-5264, p. 1130.

Ray backed down. "I would not call it distemper food."

"What was it?"

"It was brown sugar."[226]

Wall, satisfied that he had shown the horses were not sick enough to require veterinary medicine, progressed to the buggy itself. Ray guessed that his "buggy box," or the space behind the seat, was five or six inches tall by about twenty-two inches wide. Wall wanted to know who cared for the team, and Ray answered that both Willis Seehorn and Ben Holeman tended the horses and sometimes drove them, but they were no one's specifically assigned duty. Ray had owned one horse for about two years and the other since last spring. The mare was the right-hand horse in the hitch, and it was the only way they were ever hitched.

Ray's stock answer now became, "Not that I know of," as Wall pressed him to say if anyone else could have driven the team Saturday night before the fire. When they were parked in front of Chadwick's? Or on Friday night? Had anyone ever borrowed them without Ray's knowledge?

"Not that I know of."

Wall was incredulous that Ray did not remember seeing anyone during his drive home from Chadwick's store on Saturday night. Ray remained noncommittal. "I presume I did, I don't remember any identical one, of seeing it." The jury was treated to the prosecution's almost block-by-block recitation of Ray's route, with the "and you didn't see anyone" litany by Mr. Wall, always answered by a response of, "No, sir."

In addition, they argued a bit about the composition of the streets Ray traveled over—dirt versus gravel, and gravel versus macadam. Wall asked

---

[226] Some distemper remedies from this time before antibiotics included among other things:

| | |
|---|---|
| Common black gunpowder | 1 Tablespoonful |
| Lard | 1 Tablespoonful |
| Soapsuds (stiff) | 1 Tablespoonful |
| Pine tar | 2 Tablespoonful |
| Gum myrrh | 2 Tablespoonful |

(The instructions were to mix these ingredients together and put one teaspoonful of the mixture on horse's tongue twice a day.)

twenty-one questions about street surfaces, but Ray remained consistent: "I cannot tell that for I do not remember."

Wall went back to the time of the fire, with a crucial foray into the wardrobe question. "I forget, did you change clothes that night at your grandfather's Saturday night?" Unflappable, Ray once again recited the story of the brown suit from the cleaners and the new shirt and hose, maintaining that he did not wear khaki after he left his grandfather's that night.

Wall queried Ray about whether Niekamp told him his people were in the flames, and if not, why would Ray want to call the coroner? And did Ray really say that a bad flue might have caused it? And which flue would that be?

Ray declared it was his "recollection" that Niekamp said they were dead, but he was not positive. And the flue in question was the east one, not the west one. Ray laid the whole coroner idea in the lap of Uncle Niekamp, despite Wall's implication that Ray already knew a coroner would be needed.[227] Ray believed that the trip to the farm with his Aunt Petrie took about an hour and a quarter. And even though his path went right past the Reeder homestead, he did not spare time to stop.

Then Wall scored a point by getting Ray to testify that the tracks in the barn lot were plain to see at the time of the fire. Ray was of the opinion that either an undercut buggy or a piano-box buggy could have made that turn but did not follow the tracks because someone told him where they went, even before the bodies were found in the flames.

When Wall asked if Ray met Mr. Scharnhorst, Ray's memory evaporated completely. "If I had a conversation with him, I did not know it." Nor did Ray remember saying that no one had been sleeping in the tent with him for the past ten days, or being quizzed concerning his whereabouts. "I remember a man asking me where I was, but it was not Mr. Scharnhorst."[228]

Ray denied telling anyone about a "strange" oil can. "To the best of my knowledge," he said only that it was in a "strange place." He likewise did not remember his conversation with Mr. Kaempen at the fire. "I don't remember saying anything to Mr. Kaempen about the can."

Wall probed, "What made you think that can had something to do with the fire?"

"We never kept our can in the hall; I did not think the can would be in the house; it was in the basement of what would be the house."

Wall asked if Ray had been counseled by Govert about how to tell his story concerning the can, after hearing Schaeffer's testimony. Ray denied it. Deputy Schaeffer had previously testified that Ray indicated on the drawing that the can usually stayed behind the front door.

Ray's mark was in a small entryway situated between the two downstairs front rooms, at the foot of the only stairway up to the bedrooms. There were no heaters upstairs, or in the west downstairs room, and the can would carry the petroleum tang of gas and oil. Possibly, Ray first told that story in jail, to Schaeffer, to provide a possible explanation for the finding of the can. He did not go further than putting a dot on the paper and did not sign the drawing.

Wall, frustration mounting at Ray's faulty memory, asked, "Can you tell the name of a solitary person that you showed the can and said it was right back of the door?"

"I can."

"Who?"

Ray named, "Elmer Geisel." And later he added Henry Geisel and Fred Pfanschmidt to that list. Ray claimed not to know Mr. Lott at the time of the fire.

Then Wall asked of the can, "It was in front of what would have been the cellar way, was it?"

"Yes, sir."

"It was where anybody going upstairs, in order to get upstairs, would be obliged to go through the blazing gasoline?"

"That is my judgment," answered the defendant.

Wall was now on a roll. He had successfully introduced the idea that a "fire curtain" at the foot of the stairs had been set to prevent any would-be rescuer from reaching the second story and discovering the bodies before the fire had time to do its evidence-destroying work.

Wall asked if Ray hadn't stuck a pitchfork into the can and held it up, proclaiming, "Here's the gasoline can."

Ray answered, "I might have said something like that."

"What did you mean by that expression?"

"Exactly what I said."

Wall wondered how Ray could recognize that can, as it looked so much like any other can, and had Ray seen any cans at the Frese place?

Ray replied, "I never paid any especial attention to gasoline cans."

The day's session came to an end, with many questions still unanswered. Ray remained poised and calm.

# Chapter 22

# A Strong Defense

## Saturday, April 12, 1913

When court resumed,[229] the courtroom was crowded to suffocation. Sheriff Lipps estimated that morning there were perhaps a thousand people in a room designed to hold four hundred, with hundreds of others denied access.[230]

Testimony resumed, and for a time, over-politeness masked the antagonism and mutual annoyance between defendant and prosecuting attorney. Ray, however, soon returned to his habitual two- or three-word replies.

"Mr. Pfanschmidt, you put this can in your buggy, did you not?"

"Which can are you speaking of, Mr. Wall?"

"The can that you picked up on your pitchfork and showed to Moritz Lier as being 'the can.'"

"I did."

"What part of the buggy did you put that can in?"

"In front."

"You left if there how long?"

"Until I left."

---

[229] 30-5264, p. 1147.
[230] *Herald,* April 12, 1913.

Wall inquired how far the gasoline can was from the mantelpiece where the clock with the wire-wrapped hands belonged. Ray judged it was about twelve feet or so. Wall circled again to the can and who Ray had told about it. Ray's memory remained faulty. Throughout the trial, Ray never claimed that shock or the trauma of the tragedy had affected his memory; he simply continued to maintain his unruffled demeanor.

Wall asked Ray again if his horses were slower than usual on the drive to the fire, but Ray refused to be drawn in. His team "traveled good." He "made the trip in about an hour, I should judge…. They were as fresh as usual." He also said, "They were a little warm…. I believe I drove them faster that morning than I ever did."

Wall returned to the khaki suits and tried to trap Ray into a contradiction. "The dirty suit you left in your tent had your class pin on it, is that right?"

"The dirty suit?"

"Yes."

"No, sir." Ray did not lose his place in the order of the clothes chronology.

Wall asked again how the suit got dirty and why only the pants. Ray responded that he had taken the coat off and left it in the spring wagon when boring holes at Abel's, so only the pants were muddy. Wall moved on to the watch fob, and was it muddy, and had Ray ever "tramped" on it. Ray did not remember and had not noticed anything of the sort.

"As far as you know, with reference to the fob, the surface of the fob was perfectly smooth?"

"Until I saw it the other day it was perfectly smooth."

"The other day it was not perfectly smooth?"

"It was dented a little on one side."

They discussed the lack of "tack marks" on the fob. And Wall wondered if there were tack marks on everything that anybody tramps on.[231]

---

[231] Workingmen often made treads on boots by literally pounding tacks or hob nails into the soles, hence "hobnailed boots."

Ray replied, "Most of them, most all heavy shoes have tacks in them." Ray had tacks in the bottoms of his work shoes.[232]

Ray patiently explained once more the sequence of coats he wore. The coat that did not get muddy on Thursday was left "lying around there with the rest of my clothes the same way as usual" in the west tent. It was not the same coat that was folded up and put in the box with the grease on the sleeves and the class pin on the lapel. The coat from Thursday that didn't get muddy had the Bull Moose pin on its lapel.

"What became of the Bull Moose button?"

"I could not say ... it was on the coat the last time I saw it."

Wall wanted the jury to hear from Ray's own lips the chronicle of the class-pin coat. The cross-examination went like this:[233]

"What coat did you have your class pin in?"

"The one I had worn Monday morning, put on Monday morning."

"When had you taken that off the last time?"

"The coat I had the class pin in?"

"Yes."

"I think Monday morning was the first time I put it on."

"How long did you wear it before you took it off?"

"I took it off Monday evening when I changed clothes."

"Where did you have it, in the box folded up or on the floor?"

"In the box."

"And you had never taken it out from that time on?"

"I had."

"When did you take it out again?"

"When I put it on Thursday evening."

"Is that the suit you put on to go to the picture shows?"

"Yes, sir."

"You wore it on Thursday evening?"

"Yes, sir."

"You took that off when you went to the camp?"

---

232  30-5264, p. 1150.
233  30-5264, beginning p. 1151.

"I did not."

"You wore it to bed with you?"

"I did."

"Got up in the morning, still had them on?"

"I did."

"How long did you wear them Friday before you took them off?"

"Until Friday evening when I changed clothes."

"You were wearing that class pin until you got ready to go to see Miss Reeder?"

"Yes, sir."

"You had it on all day long?"

"Yes, sir."

Ray said he did not look especially, but the last he remembered seeing that coat with the pin was on Saturday morning when he changed before going uptown.

Wall wanted to know if there was a clear view from the railroad track to the utility tent. Ray said it was not as clear as to the flap of the sleeping tent since there was a large tree near the tracks that blocked the view a bit. Wall was attempting to point out that no one could have entered that tent unseen and stolen Ray's jacket while the men were at work. Ray countered that the men, while laboring in the "cuts" or excavated portions of the job site would not have been able to see the tents.

Wall did force Ray to admit that the suit found in the vault was his. "Would you have any doubt as to whether this is your suit?"

"Very little."[234]

Wall then did the same with the tie, the shirt, the coat, and the pants. Ray testified that he did not know who had a reason to put the clothes in the vault. Then Wall held out the class pin and asked if it was his. Ray agreed that it looked to be so. Wall inquired if he often wore it, and Ray answered, "I usually wore it on my good clothes."

Wall pushed, wanting Ray to say he had never let anyone else wear that pin, but Ray's answer jarred the rhythm. "I have, but not recently." Ray

---

[234] 30-5264, p. 1154.

was reluctant to name names, though Wall challenged him. "You could not state because you never did it, is not that true?"

"That is not true ... some of my classmates have worn it."

Wall pushed harder, trying to pin Ray into a lie, however small, asking for specific names. "Are they where they could be subpoenaed?"

"Yes," answered a reluctant Ray. Finally, Ray named Amy Short and Esther Reeder as people who had worn his pin.

Surprised by that answer, Wall demanded, "Did you ever give it to any man to wear?"

"Not that I remember," said Ray with a shrug.

Wall moved on to Ray's movements after the fire. In particular, he wanted to know the arrangements Ray had with his men. "How many bosses did you have out there when you weren't present?"

"I generally left Mr. Lawrence to take care of the dump team men, and Ben did the blasting."

Wall asked if he told Holeman on Sunday evening that he could have all the clothes left in Ray's tent, but Ray denied it hotly. "I did not; I never told him at any time that he could have the clothes in that tent."[235] It would certainly not be in character for flashy Ray to be giving away his specially ordered trademark wardrobe.

Wall hounded Ray about not visiting the police station or the sheriff's office on Sunday afternoon. Ray replied that he contented himself with allowing his relatives to deal with the officers and later declined to speak with any officer on advice from his attorneys.

Wall wondered why, if Ray knew he was innocent, he refused those investigating the crime. He was incredulous when Ray maintained he had no knowledge of the defense's investigation or of a detective named Lund, whom the family had hired.

Ray answered, "I had no personal report." This answer he repeated to subsequent questions. Ray denied knowledge of Lunt; he denied knowledge that "a man here from St. Louis" or "a woman from St. Louis ... went out to relatives of Ben Holeman and lived there for some time."

---

[235] 30-5264, p. 1158.

Ray maintained, "I didn't know that."

At last Ray did own up to knowing something but justified his previous answers by saying, "Not personally, I understand that question was not proper to answer for the reason that if I told you what my attorneys told me, it would be hearsay." Ray never met the detectives, but when asked if he knew they were in town, admitted, "I was so informed."

Wall pressed, asking Ray if the plan was to shoulder the blame onto Holeman. "Can you tell what possible object your attorneys had for having this woman out to Holeman's relatives' house?" The defense objected on the grounds that it asked for hearsay evidence, but the court failed to rule. Ray had no idea why a detective would be at Cook's home, although Mrs. Cook was sister to Mrs. Holeman.

Wall sounded almost smug: "You had no reason to suspect anybody, did you?"

"No one that I knew."

"There was nobody that you knew of on top of the earth that you suspected of committing that crime?"

"No one of my personal acquaintances that I knew or that I knew by sight."

"Did you suspect anybody of the commission of that crime?"

"I did." But Ray could not name a name.[236]

When Wall quizzed Ray about the Wednesday evening before the fire, Ray repeatedly said that he was not at the Pape home; he did not see the Pape family but was out at Reeders' house. Ray also maintained that he and Esther did not go buggy riding that night.

"There is no doubt about that?"

"There is no doubt about it."

Was Ray certain he didn't hire attorneys until Wednesday? He was sure. Wall seized upon the Sunday evening phone call from Achelpohl's drug store, when Uncle Abel was also present. Didn't Ray ask Abel to come with him to his attorney's office the next morning?

Ray replied, "Not that I remember of."

---

[236] 30-5264, p. 1162.

Wall quipped, "Is your memory on that subject as good as it is about the trains going over the viaduct?"

Ray backtracked, "I may have suggested it to him, but I don't remember of it."

"You don't remember of it because your uncle testified about it. Haven't you been instructed that when you were contradicted by anybody to say that you do not remember?"

"No, sir."

"Didn't you have a conversation with your grandfather and didn't you tell him that you had already retained attorneys?"

"Not to my knowledge; no."

"You have forgotten that if you said that?"

"I have forgotten that if I said it."

"And if you said it, it was not true, was it?"

"It was not true if I said it."

"What you tell now is true, and what you told your grandfather was false, is that right?"

"I don't think I told my grandfather anything like that."

Wall turned the subject to Ray's drive home on Friday night from the Reeders and wanted to know if Ray typically met automobiles on that stretch of road. Wasn't it a great place for a moonlight ride? Ray answered that he could not "say what would be a popular driveway for the people in Quincy."

What woke Ray up when the horses turned in to Abel's place? Was it the noise of wooden planks on the bridge in his lane?

"No," said Ray, "there was no bridge." The wagon jolted when a rear wheel ran off the culvert and woke him up, but he was still sleepy. Ray said the reins were tied on the "buggy bow ... the support of the top." He didn't remember exactly where along the route he went back to sleep. "I usually go to sleep when riding at night," Ray said simply.

Back to the train lights: How high above the tent is the railroad?

"About twenty feet."

"If you drew a straight line from the railroad track, it would go over your tent and strike Mr. Eakins's property?"

"Yes, sir, on a level."

They argued about the direction of the railroad track. Ray thought it ran exactly east to west, but Wall pushed for an east to southwest direction, which would nicely turn the train headlight away from the tents sitting north of the track. Wall asked about the big cut the tracks ran through just east of Ray's works. "Any light cast from that train, it would be right straight west, would it not?"

"Yes, sir."

"That would not allow it at all to reflect north or south?"

"Not when it went thru the cut."

Ray said his tent was about one hundred yards, or a block north of the tracks, but he saw the taillight on the train and the headlight and the side light. The side light was a green light.

Wall was incredulous. "You saw it plainly: from where you were lying in bed with the flap closed?"

"I saw it through the tent … I did."

They argued about visibility, about Ray's tiredness and sleepiness, about his general habit of paying attention to trains, and which way Ray slept. Ray said he would have to be lying on his right side to see the train; that usually trains have two taillights, but he only saw one that night; and he was under his covers.

Wall wanted to know exactly what Ray said to Willis Seehorn on that Friday night when he got back to the tent. Ray thought it was something about the beer Frese was to supply to the men the next day, but he was not sure of the exact words. Ray remembered he was surprised that Seehorn didn't comment on the subject and decided he was asleep.

They continued to play word games about this. Wall wanted Ray to admit that when he spoke to Seehorn it was to see if he was awake and knew how late Ray was arriving. Their repeated words created a rhythmic chorus.

Ray responded, "I do not think I said, 'Willis, are you awake?'"

"Did you say, 'Willis, are you asleep?'"

"I don't think I said, 'Willis, are you asleep?'"

"You won't say that you did not say that, will you?"

"I won't say I did not say that, I don't know."

"You may have said that and do not remember it?"

286

"I may have and do not remember it."

They disputed about whether Ray saw a newspaper at the Reeders; if he had a conversation with Clutch at the lunch stand; and what nights he was there.

Eventually Ray got confused, saying, "I don't understand you."

Wall chided Ray for bragging to Clutch about being in the papers for dynamiting, and Ray said it was mentioned because Clutch knew his cousin Roy Pfanschmidt.

Then Wall switched to Sunday night at the tent and his revolver. Ray admitted he had carried a revolver for a long while but had had this gun only a short time. Wall accused him of recently buying two pistols from Gunther's store, but Ray countered that it was "several years back." He did admit to buying and trading guns frequently and said he carried them for "various reasons … it was more for shooting dogs for bothering the team."[237]

Ray could not cite a specific instance but allowed that he had shot the odd dog. Wall asked if Ray was "a pretty good shot," and the defense immediately objected to the question as immaterial. The court sustained this objection. Ray said that he took the gun from the camp that Sunday night simply because it was his custom to carry it. He later left it with his uncle Henry Geisel, and Ray hadn't seen it since.

Wall now jumped to Ray's contract with Frese, and his bragging to Sprick at the bank about making 40 percent on the deal. Ray didn't remember. Well, 40 percent wouldn't be true, would it? Ray replied unflappably that he could not say, since he had not settled that contract yet.

Then it was back to questions concerning the fire and the bodies on the lawn. This time Ray changed his story a bit and said that he thought at first that the two bodies lying together on the big mattress were his mother and sister.[238] Next Wall questioned where the hand axe was kept and when Ray had seen it last.

Wall offered the axe head to Ray, who took it and examined it carefully with no apparent reaction. He said that compared to the one he

[237] 30-5264, p. 1175.
[238] 30-5264, p. 1177.

remembered, "It was similar to that. The last time I saw our hand ax at home, it was beaten down more on top than that is."

Wall ventured, "It was very handy to use at short range—it was a very handy ax to use at a short range to strike?"

Objection!

Court: "It is not proper cross examination, in my judgment, the jury can determine for themselves; the objection is sustained." But the audience was mesmerized. Chairs and benches creaked as necks craned for a view of Ray holding in his hands that burned blade.

Wall asked Ray if he noticed the wound on Miss Kaempen. Ray replied, "I saw no wound."

Did he look closely? Was he interested to know how they had been killed?

"I was, yes … I looked at the request of the undertaker to identify them because they didn't think I had been right before." This is the first time this piece of the story had been heard. The undertaker and coroner never mentioned Ray misidentifying the bodies and being asked to take a second look. Ray now remembered identifying them by his mother's false teeth and his sister's hair.

Wall elicited the information that the bodies in the two bedrooms were only separated by the width of the hall and the walls, which left them seven or eight feet apart. At night, the bedroom doors were generally left standing open, but Ray could not remember if they had been open the prior weekend when he had been there.

Then the buggy tracks were discussed, followed by Scharnhorst and his suspicions and conversations with Ray, which he did not remember. On to Mr. Reeder saying Ray was under suspicion and asking for an account of his actions. Ray did remember this but could not recall his exact reply.

Wall investigated Ray's source for knowledge of contracts, and Ray cited a textbook. Wall condescendingly called it "the old chimney corner law."[239] Ray had not heard of this term, but knew "it tells the rights of citizens more than anything else."

---

[239] Meaning commonly held ideas about the law which lacked any formal authority.

Did it mention that Ray would inherit everything only if all the family was dead? Ray didn't "remember reading anything like that.... I don't know as I ever considered anything of that kind; I don't know as I ever thought of it."[240]

Wall neatly tied the idea of inheritance to Mr. Reeder's phrase that Ray "would be the gainer for it." He questioned Ray's movements, which the defendant could recall even though he could not remember his words. Ray said that he told Mr. Reeder that he would take Esther and bring her right back, but he admitted that wasn't what actually happened.

"When you started away from there you did what you pleased about the matter?"

"Not exactly, no." Ray could not remember a single detail of his conversation with Esther in the buggy after leaving her father. He remembered neither what he said to her nor she to him. Throughout the trial, they remained extremely protective of each other.

When they arrived at his grandfather's, Wall wanted to know if Ray told C. C. what Mr. Reeder had said to him.

"I don't think I did." This became Ray's stock answer for questions about the hour spent at his grandfather's house. It varied only slightly to "I don't think he did," when asked if he had been accused by C. C.

Wall wanted to know why Ray wasn't "indignant" about being accused by Reeder and why Ray never "told a soul" about the accusation. Ray did not remember. Wall swerved back to verify that Ray had not driven his buggy into the barn lot the morning of the fire and so established that the hoof print could not have been made then. Ray agreed.

The manner of Ray's phone call to Gilmer was Wall's next issue. Wall observed that Ray "talked to him in a loud tone of voice so everybody present could hear that, did you not?"

Ray wasn't sure whether he did or not, but there were people standing near the phone. What number did he call? Ray simply cranked the handle to summon the operator in Payson and asked Miss Spencer to connect him

---

[240] 30-5264, p. 1183.

to Gilmer in Quincy. Then he went back to the fire and only later placed a call to Esther.

Ray and Wall argued about calling in the bloodhounds, Wall insisting they came despite Ray, not because of him. They disagreed about whether Ray said "get the hounds" before or after Uncle Fred reported that the tracks were no good and to remove the protection from them. They discussed the fact that the hounds would need tracks to scent, but Ray maintained he had no experience with hounds. They rambled on to debate the effect of chickens loose in the yard, and the curiosity seekers, and the fact that the boards were not in anyone's way, and even that the curiosity seekers had no reason to go to the barn lot anyway. By actual count, Wall had at this point asked the young man 1,123 questions, and he neither showed signs of stopping nor had managed to confound Ray.

Onward, Wall meandered to the topic of the cream separator, which was normally kept in the same smokehouse where Ray had retreated to cry. Wall inquired how long he was in there before he began to cry. "I do not know." Nor did Ray know if there was anyone else "out on this entire premises that saw you manifesting any grief on that session." Wall professed having a hard time understanding how Ray could remember his aunt's speech about "bracing up" but not Mast's conversation about the milk in the separator being old. Ray replied that Mr. Reeder was down at the smokehouse and was the one who told Ray about the milk in the separator. Wall asked about beehives, and about Ray kissing Esther and introducing her to people. Ray said it was only a few people. "Not numerous people, no; I may have introduced her to four or five."

Other than that, Ray could not remember any conversation with Esther. He was sure he did not tell her that the people had died one night and the house burned the next, but he did hear things from others. "There were conflicting statements from the people there." He could not remember if he explained his Friday night whereabouts to his fiancée, nor could he remember talking about Saturday or any of his ideas about the fire, or what might happen in the future. While the men of the jury might sympathize with his protective feelings, Ray's faulty memory began to weigh against his credibility.

Wall moved to a conversation with Uncle Abel while they were casket shopping. Didn't Ray say he and Esther would live on the farm? Ray could not remember anything like that, but he knew that he did not think about owning the farm until Uncle Abel asked him about his future.

Wall asked where Ray called Esther from and if he had called anyone else. He began to recite a litany of questions: Did Ray call his folks from Cottrell's or the Parthenon Candy Kitchen or Chadwick's? Ray's answers were always some form of "No."[241]

Did Ray know Frank Dang, clerk at the Mission Pool Room? Did Ray call anyone from there? Ray did not think so. Then Wall asked a question that seemed counterintuitive to the State's case, "Is it not a fact that on Saturday evening just before you left the Mission Pool Room you called up and tried to get your folks at Payson?"

Ray: "I don't think so."

Wall passed on to the clock. Ray said it was an eight-day clock that stood about two feet high, but there was also another clock in the house and the gears of the State's exhibit could have come from that one. That second clock didn't run all the time.

Wall asked about the Navajo rug that Ray and Eakins spoke of on Sunday, which Eakins had offered to sell. Ray did not think he consulted with Esther about which one to choose, but he might have. Wall asked about the price of the rug—was it forty dollars? Ten dollars? Ray did not think they arrived at a price. About his conversation with Holeman about fetching the team, no one else could have heard because the door to that room had been closed.

Back to the tent. There were a lot of horse blankets there, weren't there? "There was one." Ray did not remember any on the other cot. And he did have a lap robe "a year ago this winter." He "may have seen it last summer." Ray usually took his cot blankets to use as a lap robe on cool evenings, which he might have done on Friday night, and then simply put the blanket back on the cot. This information did not help Wall, as no blood spots were found on the bedding.

---

[241] 30-5264, p. 1195.

Over to the horse that did have a peculiar shoe on the right hind foot, but Ray insisted that the track he saw at the farm did not have any mark like that. They argued about whether the track was a clear print; if Sprick, who showed it to him, called it "distinct"; and where it rained Saturday night. Ray answered that he knew it rained in town but didn't know if it rained in the country or not.

Wall then ran down a list of people who had testified to seeing Ray on the road late that weekend. "You didn't see Carl Mollenhauer that night?"

"I did not."

"You did not see Walter Dingerson Saturday night?"

"I did not."

"You did not see Clarence Crubaugh Saturday night?"

"I did not."

Then it was back to Ray's refrain: he didn't see anybody he knew, and no one he *didn't* know that he remembered. He didn't remember seeing any rigs or meeting anyone much of anywhere.

Wall asked, "You don't know whether your horses started to turn west toward Heckle's Corner that night or not, do you?"

"I don't think my horses would have done that."

"For all you know, they might have done that?"

"I do not know … if they had turned west I would have very likely woke up … the change in motion."

"It would have to be a right sudden turn, would it not?"

"Whenever they turned when I was asleep, they always turned pretty sudden."

Wall, however, reminded him that the turns at Thirty-Sixth and Harrison or the turn at Twenty-Fourth and Harrison or the turn at Twenty-Fourth and State did not wake him.

Ray said, "I don't know."

Perhaps the jury believed that Ray was piecing and rearranging actual events to construct his testimony. If so, the false turn toward Heckle's Corner where Dingerson said he spotted him might translate into the story of a turn into Uncle Abel's lane. If the jurors believed Ray had been preoccupied or undecided about what he was going to do after leaving

Reeders on Friday night, they might believe he traveled a short distance in a wrong direction to give himself time to think.

Wall asked Ray if he had been paying attention to the testimony in this case, and if he had "recognized evidence in this case that appeared in your mind to be against him." Ray had.

"And you remember everything very distinctly that is in your favor?"

"I can't say as I do," replied Ray.

"And you do not remember anything at all that is against you?"

Ray answered, "I do."

Wall wanted the jury to hear how often Ray met with his lawyers. The defendant could not remember, so Wall prompted, saying it was as many as three times each day.

Ray said, "Sometimes once a day, sometimes twice, and occasionally three times; but not every day."

After 1,310 questions, Wall took his seat.[242]

But Ray was not yet free to leave the witness chair. Govert resumed the questioning, giving Ray the reassurance of a friendly face.

What was the average time Ray spent with his attorneys? "Ten or fifteen minutes."

Under what conditions? "At times they were brought in front of the cell where I was locked up and sometimes in the corridor, where I was allowed to talk to them thru the bars." The lawyers always had to stand in a certain designated spot and remain there the entire time.

Govert asked about the stoves at the farmhouse. Ray answered, "There was a cook stove, and a gasoline stove in the kitchen, a coal oil stove down in the cellar." The cook stove was a "four-hole stove."[243]

Then to tie up some loose ends, Govert led Ray through a series of denials. Did he tell Viehmeyer that he wasn't worried about fingerprints because he wore gloves? "I did not."

Did he tell Viehmeyer that he had met Dingerson but wasn't recognized? "I did not."

---

[242] 30-5264, p. 1204.
[243] Four openings where cooking pots could be set.

"Mr. Pfanschmidt, did you kill your sister, Blanche?"

"I did not."

"Did you set fire to your father's home?"

"I did not."

"Did you kill your mother, Mathilda Pfanschmidt?"

"I did not."

"Did you kill your father, Charles Pfanschmidt?"

"I did not."

Was Ray at the farm on Saturday?

"I was not."

Was he out there on Friday?

"I was not."

Did he have any bloodstained clothes?

"I did not."

Wall asked for further cross on one matter, the remains of the body of Charles Pfanschmidt. Wall wanted Ray to remember if it was, while in the ruins, lying on top of the rubbish, or if the rubbish was on top of it? Ray was not certain but saw there was rubbish on top of it.

Wall pursued the question. "The body of your father was very likely lying upon the ground floor, was it not?"

"I could not say."

Seeking further information about the cellar, Wall established that the stove down there was a three-holer, setting on the north wall, farther west than east. The cellar floor was cement and there were some vinegar barrels, vegetables, potatoes, wash tubs, and other things stored there.

Then Wall led Ray through the denials again, the "Did you kill—" with "I did not" as the repeated response.

Wall ended with apparent sarcasm, asking, "If you had, you would have taken the witness stand and told it, would you not?"

Ray calmly replied, "I would."

So concluded Ray's time on the stand.[244]

---

[244]  30-5264, p. 1208.

The defense team called other witnesses to clear up some details, the first of which was Ben Holeman. Holeman, in a dramatic gesture, surrendered the coat that Ray had loaned him for that long ago happy evening at the movies. Ben said he returned the pants to the box, and if he had borrowed a shirt, it was also returned shortly after he wore it.

On cross-examination, Holeman specified that he returned the clothes on Friday morning and never looked for them again. Wall attacked his credibility, claiming that Holeman had been asked about the jacket by Sheriff Lipps and had denied having it at the time. Holeman, echoing a response from Ray, did not remember any such a conversation. "There were so many talking to me, I don't know what I did say." Govert on redirect got Holeman to say again that the coat, with its tag, had been in his closet and possession ever since he wore them.

He was replaced by Silba Lawrence in an effort by Govert to clear the good name of his partner and tidy up the matter of that conversation in the lawyer's office when Seehorn was supposedly advised to leave town.

Govert began, "At the time of that conversation, I will ask you if, after Mr. Seehorn had stated what facts he knew, bearing upon the case, if Mr. Lancaster told him that he and Holeman had better get out of town."

Lawrence answered, "Not in my presence." Furthermore, he swore he had been present for the entire conversation and that they all left the office together.

Wall would not let it rest there and prodded Lawrence to say who left first from the private room where they talked. Lawrence could not remember who went first, and who was the last to leave. Wall suggested that Seehorn was last and had been threatened out of the presence of the others. He also accused Lawrence of changing his story. In the end, Lawrence could not swear that there had been no opportunity for such a threat to be made; only that it had not been done in his presence.[245]

The defense then entered their roadmap into evidence, as Defense Exhibit 2, over the objections of the State.[246] Then Govert called John Lier

---

[245] 30-5264, p. 1214.
[246] 30-5264, p. 1215; p. 1216 is the map.

to establish his Saturday route and timetable using the defense's map. Lier repeated his earlier testimony, including that he did not remember meeting anyone or of being passed by anyone, especially Ray Pfanschmidt.

Wall rose to question Lier. Had he been drinking some in town?

"Well, some, yes."

And had he taken some along for the drive?

"Yes, I had some in the buggy.… I didn't take any drink along the road."

Wall pointed out that "while you were taking a snooze on the road, whether any buggy passed you on the road, you do not know."

"No, sir, I could not say." Lier acknowledged that there were any number of little lanes and side roads a buggy could pull into and be out of sight, if they heard him coming.

Wall clarified, "All you mean to say is after you left town and after what you had been doing, whether anybody passed you on the roads or not you did not know?"

Lier: "That's all."

Witness dismissed.

Daniel Reeder was called by Govert and shown a pair of leggings, Defense Exhibits 5 and 6. He was asked if they were Ray's, and said they were, to the best of his knowledge as they looked the right color and had the same strap. He was allowed to leave the stand.[247]

Henry Brinkman came next. He worked for Mr. Reeder and was there for dinner on Friday night when Ray came. He too thought those were Ray's leggings, but the only time he really looked at them was when Ray walked into the room. The rest of the time they were all sitting at the table, or Ray was in another room. He was dismissed.

Govert called Esther's sister-in-law, Mrs. Hugh Reeder, who was with Esther on Friday evening and had noticed the leggings and the khaki suit. She had also been at "Father Reeder's house" on the Monday before, when Esther returned home after spending three or four days at the Pape's home. Esther had been under a doctor's care and for convenience was staying at

---

[247] 30-5264, p. 1221.

the home of Mrs. Pape, who lived only a block from the doctor's office.[248] Ray brought Esther back to her home about eight o'clock in the evening. Mrs. Reeder was also there on Wednesday when Ray came to visit, and she had been at the fire scene from about 9:00 a.m. until noon. By that day, she had known Ray a year.

"Can you state whether Ray Pfanschmidt was, at that time, of an emotional nature?"

"I hadn't seen him in such a manner." She continued, saying that at the fire Ray was very quiet, when "generally he had a good deal to say." At first she felt Ray might have taken it differently, but "when I thought the matter over, I understood how he felt about it because I had known some of his other folks before when they were in trouble."

Govert sought a description of Ray's relationships with his family, beginning with his mother. The witness said that Ray and his mother "seemed to be very devoted to one another;" with his sister: "he seemed to pet her; he seemed to favor her and pet her;" and of his father, "He always seemed to think what his father said and did was just right."[249]

Wall delved into just how well Mrs. Reeder knew Ray. She admitted that she had observed him sometimes with a view toward understanding his temperament. She watched him at Mother Reeder's funeral, but Wall pointed out that that loss was on a different scale. "You had never seen anybody during your whole life whose loss was as great as his was upon this occasion, had you?"

"No." She admitted that she was at first surprised that he did not manifest any emotion but denied that it was a subject of conversation in the Reeder household or that she talked about her concerns with her husband. Mrs. Reeder said that Ray said very little at the fire and had a "haggard and wearied look."

Wall shot back, "Whether that was caused by the loss or whether he had been up all night, you don't know, do you?"

"No, sir."

---

[248] 30-5264, p. 1224.
[249] 30-5264, p. 1227.

Wall finished by asking, "You are basing that entirely upon what you have heard people say about the stoical characteristics of the Pfanschmidt family, that is solely upon which you base it, is it not?"

"Why, I guess so."

After the noon lunch recess, Wall resumed questioning Esther's sister-in-law about her judgment of Ray. "You measured his conduct by what you know of his aunts' peculiarities?"

"Yes, sir, and the excitement too."

Wall, digging for more information about the leggings, uncovered something that did not suit him. Asked wasn't Ray dressed on Friday night the same as the last time she saw him, Mrs. Reeder disagreed and confirmed Ray's story. "On Wednesday night he had on his blue serge suit."

Wall asked if she visited with Esther and Ray in the other room. Mrs. Reeder said that she did, for a time, "[w]ell, not so very long, perhaps fifteen minutes; but not talking all that time; we were at the piano." Another bittersweet picture emerged of the last happy evening the young couple would have.

Mrs. Reeder agreed that there was little discussion after the fire, with nothing said about its possible origins or any suspicions Ray might have. It seemed not to be the time for much conversation. She was dismissed.[250]

Henry Geisel came to be questioned. He learned of the fire on Sunday morning about half past three. He quickly phoned some relatives and, with his son, drove a one-horse buggy the seven and a half miles to the farm, arriving in about an hour. He met Miller and his mule team about two miles from the farm.

When Geisel and son, Elmer, arrived, nothing had been done. The east part of the house was burning freely, and the flames were leaping skyward two or three feet above the cellar. The heat was so intense that no one could approach the foundations. The tin roof had fallen, split at the joints from the heat, and had a "red-hot appearance." The Geisels organized the men, who carried water and poured it on the tin for about an hour. It took until about 6:30 a.m. before the flames died down in the cellar. Eventually the

---

[250]  30-5264, p. 1234.

fire cooled enough for the men to put a plank across the flattened roof along the east side and stand on that board to shovel the bricks from the collapsed flue off the top of the tin roof.

Geisel was called to investigate tracks found in the barn lot. He had already lit a lamp to look for buckets or "anything to pack water with," and then handed that lantern to somebody, who took it to the barn lot. He was not sure who he gave it to.

Govert revisited the ground conditions. Geisel answered that it had rained enough to settle the dust, but there was no mud in the barnyard, and there was no evidence of any mud in the preceding twenty-four hours. Govert was strengthening the idea that the suspicious shoe imprint was already a week old when the fire started.

Geisel followed the tracks and found, "There was continuous driving." He saw a swerve in the trail leading out of the barn lot that veered toward the hitching post, but no evidence of the horses stopping. Even in dim light, it would be easy to spot the disturbance in the ground left when eight horse hooves shifted about, stomping or pawing or moving to ease the waiting.

Geisel claimed he examined the hoof prints "just as close as I could" but did not see any peculiarity about the print, only that the horses were "shod all 'round."[251] Geisel said of the wheel tracks, "Well, I would say it was a rubber tire that had been wore just a trifle. It was a three-quarter or seven-eight's tire with the pointed part which had been worn a little." The track "was concave at the bottom just the same as any round edge on anything would make." And he judged that steel tires, especially on a short turn, had a tendency to throw out more dirt at the edge of the track than a rubber tire would.

Geisel told Govert that he had known Ray ever since he was born, and the family for that same length of time. To him, the boy appeared to be suffering grief. Govert invited him to describe Ray's behavior further.

"Well, he had very little to say, and when you did say a word or talk to him he began to fill up and walk away from you and seemed as though

---

[251] The horse was fitted with four shoes, rather than only two on the front feet.

he could not talk any more. He would get right away from you. This he did from time to time."[252]

The attorney wanted to know if that grief would be apparent to the ordinary observer. "No, it would not be."

What was the tendency of the Pfanschmidt family generally, in reference to showing emotions?

"Well, they don't do that," said Geisel.

By Monday, September 30, when Geisel returned to the farm, he estimated that at least fifty automobiles and between three hundred and four hundred buggies and teams had passed along that stretch of road. He watched Strumpfer handle his bloodhounds, but he saw a far different picture than that told by the prosecution. He told the jury that Strumpfer went to the box, removed it, and "he caught the dog right back of each ear and shoved his nose right down to the track and told him to take it; he repeated that possibly three or four times.... He shoved his nose right down in the track ... he shoved it down enough to blur the track."[253] Geisel thought the dog acted as though he was being hurt. He did not know if the track was re-covered by the box; nor did he see the other dog ever given the scent.

On Tuesday he went back to the farm with Fred Pfanschmidt and the attorneys to measure that track, but "it could not be measured in the condition it was.... It was destroyed."

Geisel agreed that Strumpfer got out at each crossroad to check for the trail before putting the dog back into the car. He said the dog handler only walked about a quarter of a mile initially, which differed greatly from Strumpfer's own estimate. When they passed Geisel's lane Strumpfer did not take his dog out of the auto. Since that entrance was not checked, there was no verification for Ray's story that his team turned there on Friday night; nor was it proven false.

Geisel was waiting at the camp to see if the dogs trailed there. When they arrived he saw only a single dog trailing. He watched as that dog went to the north side of Ray's buggy, then to the big tent, then came out and

---

[252]  30-5264, p. 1242.
[253]  30-5264, p. 1245.

visited the next tent, then went on east about two hundred feet toward the pasture on Twenty-Fourth Street, and then came back to the buggy. Eventually the dog went to the horses and circled and sniffed around and came to a halt beside one of them.

Did the men trailing look at the feet of the horse the dog stopped at? "Not to my knowledge."

On Thursday, October 3, 1912, Geisel went back to Ray's camp, gathered up all the clothes that he could find, and delivered them to the defense attorneys, where the clothes were sealed up and put away. Later the box was opened and each piece was marked with a "+ G" ("Plus G"). Govert pulled out clothing: Defendant's Exhibit # 7, trousers; #8, trousers; #9, a coat with the Bull Moose pin; and #10, a shirt. Geisel identified them all, plus the leggings, and said they were in the same condition as when he marked them.[254]

Geisel thought that the Pfanschmidt family relations were normal. "I always thought they were affectionate," and that Ray and his father "got along better than the average father and son." The State was objecting to these statements but was overruled.

Wall took Geisel for cross-examination[255] and began by chipping away at this assessment of family relations. Under questioning, Geisel admitted the last time he visited the family farm was about a month before the murders on the day of the Old Settler's Picnic in Payson. Ray was not there when he stopped.

Wall wondered if Geisel knew that Ray's father had been "compelled" to bail him out financially, and if this might have affected their relationship. Geisel did not know anything about their money situation except that Charles had "assisted" Ray. Wall asked if perhaps the father-son relationship was good only as long as Charles was helping Ray, but Geisel held firm. "I never knew of any hard feelings between Ray and his father." Then he admitted he had never in fact talked to Charles about this. "No, I never had occasion to."

---

[254] 30-5264, p. 1251
[255] 30-5264, p. 1253.

Geisel testified that he had mentioned something to Charles about his good relationship with his son, and Wall pounced. Why did he say that? Did he mention it to anyone else—anyone alive today? What was the occasion of the conversation? Which summer month was it that this happened? What brought it up? Did his wife hear it? Geisel could not recall particulars.

Wall wanted to make plain the idea that Geisel's opinion of Ray's relations with his father came from the time prior to the Old Settler's Picnic but that he hadn't seen them together much since. Then Wall got specific, "You hadn't heard of him kicking his mother after that because she refused to give him money?"

"No, sir."

"You had not heard that he had a violent quarrel with his father because he would not give him any money?"

Objection! "There is no evidence to that effect." Sustained.

"Well, do you know what difficulty, if any, that Ray had had with his father at the Old Settler's Picnic?"

"I do not."[256]

Nor did anyone else ever offer any testimony about this alleged quarrel at the picnic.

Wall next accused Geisel of following Archie Pape after he testified for the prosecution; of interviewing the teacher, Miss Smith, at her home; of going to the saloons to check on stories; and of doing everything he could to help the defense but not cooperating with law officers.

Geisel replied that the sheriff wouldn't talk to him, and added, "If I knew anything to tell them, I should certainly have told them." Wall quizzed him extensively about which officers he did or did not talk to. Geisel denied that the sheriff ever spoke to him or warned him not to put anything in the way of the investigation.

Wall wanted to know how he knew the dogs were coming to the camp, and Geisel replied that C. C. Pfanschmidt, his father-in-law, had informed him. Wall exploited this trip to the camp. If he wasn't expecting

---

[256] 30-5364, p. 1258.

the hounds to track there, why even go? Wall asked him if the clothes were taken at the behest of the defense attorneys.

Wall was rapidly firing questions until Geisel finally interrupted him, "I would like to answer a question, if you would let me."

Wall backtracked, and Geisel finally said that it was his own suggestion, not the attorneys, to fetch the clothes from Ray's tent. And furthermore, the sheriff never asked him for those clothes, not at any time. Geisel said he had the clothes at home for about a week and had never been asked.

Wall then wanted to know if Ray had access to Geisel's house during that week, but Geisel said Ray was never there.

Ray's wardrobe was sealed up and given to the attorneys and only opened two or three or four weeks ago and marked. Geisel said he had kept a list but neglected to bring it to court. The clothes were found lying about the tent; some had been worn and were soiled. The clothes were removed before Ray had been arrested, and there was no impediment to anyone who wanted to enter the tents. It was basically "free access."

Geisel said that he did not consider that the clothes might be used for Ray's defense, and he did not know there was a Bull Moose pin on the coat until he got it home. Geisel repeatedly said that no one asked for the clothes and that he gave them to the lawyers just because he didn't want to keep them any longer.

Wall scattered his questions among many topics. How long was Geisel at the fire before Ray arrived? Geisel thought it was an hour or maybe a bit less. Then Wall went on to the tracks, the weather, the ground conditions, the barn lot conditions, and lastly to the bodies.

Geisel was clearly uncomfortable and would only admit to "glancing" at the bodies. He said when they were discovered he went to a telephone and called Dr. Gabriel in Payson to ask what he should do. During the call, Geisel asked his opinion, and Dr. Gabriel told his friend that it looked like foul play.

Wall sharpened the tone of his questions. What about a conversation with William Peter at Melrose Chapel the day after the fire? "Do you remember saying to him upon that occasion, that when you discovered those tracks in the yard, 'It was just like sticking a knife into you'?"

Geisel failed to remember that remark and further denied Wall's assertion that he waited until Ray showed up in a steel-tired buggy to give an opinion that the tracks were made by a rubber-tired one.[257] Then the two argued on the stand about undercut buggies. Wall claimed they all have steel tires; Geisel countered that Dr. Nickerson had a rubber-tired one.

The argument progressed to the barn lot, questions coming in rapid succession: Was there seepage from the water tank that collected in the lower center part that could make a mud puddle? Was it dusty?

"What color was the dirt?"

"Black loam over yellow clay."

Were there any cinders? When did he see Ray last before the fire?

"Thursday noon."

After three hundred or so questions, Wall gave Geisel back to Govert for a few more questions. The defense wanted Geisel to say clearly that the buggy did not leave the lane or get on the sod near the hitching post. Then Wall resumed the fight, but nobody gained any ground, and Geisel was dismissed.

Mrs. (Ben) Opal Holeman was called to the stand. She talked about the suit Ben borrowed from Ray[258] and identified one jacket as the one that had been in their closet. "I think that is the same one; it is like the one that he wore that Thursday night and been wearing ever since."

Ray's cousin Elmer Geisel arrived on the stand, and the same ground was covered yet again. One new thing was added when Elmer said Ray helped carry water and take off the roof. "Yes, sir, we were both working there just like the rest of them."[259]

Elmer sometimes stayed with Ray's family for several months at a stretch and knew them well. Asked about Ray's demeanor at the fire, he said, "He acted like he was kinda stunned like; that is the way he acted to me.... He did not talk; he would begin to talk to you a little bit, and just kinda swallow and walk away from you." This was not customary behavior for Ray.

---

[257] 30-5264, p. 1275.
[258] 30-5264, p. 1279.
[259] 30-5264, p. 1286.

Wall was intense on cross. He followed the same lines of questioning, hammering against Elmer about the family relationship dynamics, the tire tracks, and how much the family had discussed the case in order to correlate their stories, especially about the rubber-tire tracks.

Elmer said he had discussed evidence with the attorney on that Monday morning when the bloodhounds came. While this did not prove Ray lied about the date he hired lawyers, it did tend to lead toward that conclusion, regardless of the fact that Govert was attorney for the Pfanschmidt family and in any event would have been consulted to settle the estate.

Govert called Wilber Meyer to the stand. Meyer agreed on rubber buggy tires, thought the turn could have been made by a regular piano-box buggy, and said Ray's team was similar to several others in the area. Wall quizzed Meyer about the markings on Ray's team, as well as his relationship to Ray. "Mrs. Pfanschmidt was an aunt to my wife." Wall grilled him with little result, and Govert finished by asking simply if there was any mud in the barn lot that day. Meyer said no.

Court was adjourned for the weekend.

# Chapter 23

# Possible Perjury

## Monday, April 14, 1913

When court was called to order on Monday, Wall asked to put Henry Geisel back on the stand.

Wall had tired of failing memories, and this morning he was intending to set the basis for a perjury charge. He asked politely if Geisel knew Walter Heidbreder of the State Street Bank, and if he remembered having a conversation with that gentleman in reference to Ray's attitude toward his father.

Amid strident defense objections, Wall said, "I will ask you if you did not say there to Walter Heidbreder that Charles A. Pfanschmidt, the father of Ray Pfanschmidt, had come to you and said that he could do nothing with Ray; that the way Ray was carrying on, it would break him; and if he did not ask you to speak to Ray and say to you that no matter what you might say to Ray it would not hurt his feelings or that in substance?"

Geisel replied, "I did not." Wall dismissed him. But it was not to be the end of that particular issue.

Govert called Deputy William Schaeffer to question him about the axe head found in the ruins. He reported that he asked Dr. Erickson to examine the spot on the blade. Dr. Erickson was called and said he took a scraping from the spot, treated it with water and glycerin, and found well defined blood corpuscles under the microscope.

Dr. Center, next on the stand, reported that when he examined the pants from the vault, the spots were red in the fingerprints near the hip pocket but a darker red on the spots found elsewhere. Once the varying red colors of the stains had been established, the defense called in their expert, J. Robert Zeit of Northwestern University Medical School in Chicago, a professor of pathology and bacteriology.

Govert and Dr. Zeit explored the composition of blood and especially how it reacted when exposed to air. Zeit said that within a matter of hours blood would turn purple and then brown. If moisture was present, it would turn brown even faster. Govert leveled a blast at the prosecution. "In case, Doctor, small drops of blood were found on khaki or a cloth suit made of khaki and are, at the time of being found, purplish red in color, state whether in your opinion those drops could have been placed upon that suit in excess of five days before the time when found in that condition?"

Zeit delivered his opinion. "If they were glossy purplish clots of blood, I would say that they are less than six days old."

Govert next inquired about the effect of heat on blood. Zeit said that after 170°, blood corpuscles would be "fixed" so that water could not dissolve or remove them. He went on to say about the blood from the axe, "It has been exposed to less than 170° if it can be removed from the film [surface] ... the heat to destroy wood would destroy and incinerate all blood." It would be "inconceivable" for any blood to remain after such a fire.

Just to be sure everyone understood, Zeit said, "If red corpuscles on this axe could be removed by dissolving in water the heat to which it was exposed could have been no more than 170°. This axe looks as though it had been heated to much more than that; it is black—it must have been exposed to high heat, to a heat I should judge, from what I see here, that would destroy all blood."[260]

Govert expounded upon this point for a few more questions and then gave the witness to Wall. Wall drew out the information that Zeit had

---

[260] 30-5264, p. 1319.

testified in numerous court cases and was paid $250.00 for his testimony. Wall explored the idea of what color "brown" was; if Zeit had ever actually put blood on an axe blade and heated it till the handle burned out of it; if the color of the cloth made a difference to the coloration of the blood spot. He asked if an axe blade, entirely covered in blood for a day, was then covered in rubbish and the handle burned out if there might not be some measurable blood left. Zeit held true and said that the entire metal axe head would heat up enough to destroy the blood. But the witness was forced to admit that he, himself, had not performed an experiment with a bloody axe. Wall picked and poked at him about his experience, but Zeit was careful and hard to trap. Govert, on redirect, helped him say that anyone with fairly good eyesight could tell the difference between old and new blood, and that the heat from the fire should have destroyed any blood on the axe head.

Govert recalled Dr. Center, who agreed that the blood on the axe head could not have been there when the axe went through the fire. Wall tried to mitigate this testimony with only minor success. Dr. Knox was recalled and agreed that the blood could not have come through the fire on that axe head.

Wall, in the face of unanimous agreement by the physicians, invoked the possibility of divine intervention. "Providence sometimes interposes things that the medical man cannot explain?"

Knox answered, "Provided you grant that Providence has anything to do with it."[261]

While not entirely out of the range of possibility, it remained an unexplained oddity, something either arranged by God, or contrived by man.

Aunt Elizabeth Petrie, sister of Charles Pfanschmidt, who now lived with her father, C. C. Pfanschmidt, on South Twelfth Street, took the stand. Mrs. Petrie recalled how three weeks before the fire, Ray's father spent the night in town with C. C. before a trip to Missouri, and Ray came that night to visit them. She rated their relationships as more affectionate than usual.

---

[261]   30-5264, p. 1338.

Govert led her to talk about Saturday, the day before the fire, when Ray arrived in the evening dressed in khakis, and changed, "as he always did, when he was at our house," putting on a brown suit. There was no blood on that khaki suit, which remained under her bed until Ray and Mrs. Cook (Mrs. Petrie's sister) came and took away both the suitcase and a box a week later.[262]

Govert asked if anything was said to her son, Howard Petrie, about going to Ray's camp for the night. The State objected vehemently, and the jury was excused. Eventually the court overruled the objection, and she was allowed to say that Howard did ask permission to accompany Ray to his camp for the night. Then she was not allowed to say what answer she gave to that request.

The previous time she had seen Ray was on Thursday morning, September 26, when he came and again changed clothes. He arrived that time dressed in a blue serge suit, the same one he was wearing here in court, and with a light gray raincoat and a stiff hat. He changed out of the blue suit and into khakis. The khaki suit he changed into that Thursday was the one he had left there the Sunday before. Mrs. Petrie knew this because Ray always left his clothes in the closet in her room.

Under oath, she stated emphatically that the blue suit and gray raincoat were in her room on the Saturday morning of the fire. So, it seemed, Ray could not have been wearing them at the works as the State charged. But by this time, perhaps the jury was either no longer interested in Ray's wardrobe or were hopelessly confused.

Govert brought out State Exhibit #11, a pair of khaki trousers, and Exhibit #12, a khaki coat, and asked if they were the ones that had been left with Mrs. Petrie. "In my opinion it was, it was one just like it."

Govert asked her if there had been any conversation on Saturday night about Ray's people coming to town the next day, but the State immediately objected, calling it immaterial and hearsay. The jury was again excused, and this time the court's ruling sustained the objection. That line of questioning would not be allowed.

---

[262] 30-5264, p. 1342.

Not to be deterred, Govert asked Mrs. Petrie if she said anything to Ray about going home that night. The State objected while Mrs. Petrie was nodding her affirmation on the stand. The State objected to her affirmative nods, and the court sustained the objection and said the witness must not answer this question.

Govert circled again, asking if Ray said anything about going to Cottrell's for a letter. Objection. Sustained. Govert asked if anything was said about what Ray's mother would do if they did not come to town on Sunday. Objection. Sustained.

Govert asked how Ray seemed. "He acted just like he always did," was Mrs. Petrie's answer.

She then spoke of Ray whipping his horses on the way to the fire. When Govert asked her what she said to Ray concerning his driving, Mrs. Petrie seemed reluctant or perhaps embarrassed to answer. "He was driving so fast. Must I tell you what I said?" The court answered: "No."

Mrs. Petrie told of Ray's tears, saying that he came into the smokehouse where she was and "laid his head upon some boxes or things piled up, and was crying, sobbing." She told him to brace up. "Why, he sobbed a little while, then he raised up, wiped the tears out of his eyes, braced himself, and swallowed two or three times and went on out of the summer kitchen.... I mean out of the smokehouse, to where the men were."[263] Govert asked if he appeared to be suffering from grief, and Wall objected. An incensed Govert replied, "I think every witness on behalf of the State answered that question!" The objection was overruled by the court. Mrs. Petrie was allowed to say that Ray looked like he was grieving. And that she had suggested he spend that Sunday night at the Reeders.

Govert asked Mrs. Petrie if, on Wednesday before the fire when Mathilda and Blanche were at her house, Blanche took any of Ray's clothes home with her. The State objected, and the jury resignedly rose, being once again excused from the room. After discussion, the court overruled the objection, returned the jury, and Mrs. Petrie explained that Blanche did leave with some of Ray's clothes, which she took home to wash. It appeared

---

[263] 30-5264, p. 1349.

family relations were good enough for the sister to volunteer to help her brother by doing his laundry.

Govert was curious about what kind of food Ray was given at home, referencing the Viehmeyer remark that Ray was used to "coarse cooking." Mrs. Petrie said the food at his house was "very good." And she said that the day after the fire, Ray "was lying on the couch sobbing and crying."[264]

Wall arose to dismantle this sympathetic version of Ray. Did Mrs. Petrie's father see Ray crying? No. Wall pursued the idea that only Mrs. Petrie had seen Ray crying. Where exactly was her father while this was happening? "I do not know; he was in the house someplace, but I could not say where he was.... Father did not always just sit in that one room, you know."

Mrs. Petrie refused to back down from her testimony. She denied hearing any conversation between Ray and her father. "I went in there and talked to Ray a little while and went about my work."

After Monday lunch recess, Wall resumed questioning and established that Mrs. Petrie was not at the fire for long. She rode part way home with Mr. Peter, got out at Twenty-Fourth Street and Harrison, walked to Twenty-Second and State, and caught a streetcar from there to her home. Wall then switched tactics, becoming more conciliatory toward the witness. Mrs. Petrie acknowledged that she was indeed terribly grief-stricken, both then and now, and could hardly testify or think about it without manifesting grief.

Wall led her to the gathering on Saturday after the Herrs had arrived from Wichita to visit at C. C.'s house. Wall was curious, asking if Ray had a closet of his own for his clothes. Mrs. Petrie said, "No, he kept them in where I keep my clothes. He just threw them on the table in my room and I would put them away." But the blue suit he hung in the closet.

On Sunday, Mrs. Petrie said, she took a khaki suit from the suitcase under the bed, which also held "different clothes; there was some shirts, and socks and ties and all different kinds of clothes, I could not name all the articles there; there were quite a few things in there." Wall wondered how many clothes Ray kept in her closet. Mrs. Petrie answered, "Sometimes

---

[264] 30-5264, p. 1354.

there was only one there, sometimes two, just as it happened as he came and changed them." He only kept the suits in the closet that held both her clothing and her son's; the other clothes were left in her room.

Mrs. Petrie acknowledged that she not only lived with but took care of her father. She admitted she wasn't home all the time every day and that Ray had access to the house and the closet. He could come and go, and change, pick up, or leave clothing as he wanted. Mrs. Petrie explained that the house was locked when everyone was gone, so she doubted Ray could have come in when the house was empty.

Then Wall asked if Ray had expressed as much emotion at the fire as he had in this trial. The defense objected powerfully "to the entire line of examination as being manifestly objectionable." The court sustained the objection. Wall, with a glint in his eye, asked Mrs. Petrie if Ray showed more emotion at the fire than he did on the stand. This time the shouted objection was overruled, and Mrs. Petrie answered, "He manifested more."

Wall wondered then why Mrs. Petrie looked at the suit left in her room. "My father sent me up … to see if there was any stains of any kind on it." Wall pressed. What kind of stains were you looking for? After more disputes, the court sustained the objection for not being cross-examination. But the jury and the audience got the clear picture that Ray's own grandfather had sent her to look for blood spots.

Govert got the last word with her. Mrs. Petrie knew that blue serge suit was definitely at the house on Monday because she had sent it to Weems Laundry to have it cleaned and pressed.

Witness dismissed.[265]

Lancaster called Mr. Chris G. Weisenborn, owner of the pasture at Dick's Farm that the bloodhounds had visited. He explained that it was his custom to keep one gate wired shut and the other locked with a padlock, leaving the key with the railroad guard. He admitted he would not know if the gate had been left unlocked.

Govert put Ray's eighteen-year-old cousin Howard Petrie on the stand to confirm Ray's wardrobe changes. Howard told the story of Ray arriving

---

[265]  30-5264, p. 1376.

at his grandfather's house in the khaki suit and an old black raincoat, which was left in C. C.'s barn. He watched Ray change into the brown suit upstairs, putting his khaki clothes in the suitcase and shoving it under the bed.

Howard confirmed that Ray asked him to spend the night and that he talked it over with his mother. He was allowed to say that he refused the invitation, but due to the State objections, he could not say why. He was permitted to say that Ray left him at Twelfth and State headed downtown but was not allowed to say that Ray went looking for a letter.[266]

Howard reviewed which pieces of Ray's clothing were left at his house and when. He admitted to wearing the light-colored raincoat for about three hours on Friday night and returning it to the closet, where Ray picked it up on Saturday night. Howard reported that Ray's team of horses was fresh and anxious to go when Ben brought them to C. C.'s house on the way to the fire. "They would not stand when he brought them down at our house; Ray went around and held them while me and Ben Holeman took the side curtains off."

How did they start off from the house? "Fast; Ray stood up in the buggy with a whip and gave each of them a cut with the whip," replied Petrie.[267]

He remembered time spent at the Pfanschmidt farm that summer, often for a week or two at a stretch. Govert asked if the family members were affectionate, and in a perfect example of the clan lack of effusiveness, Howard answered, "They were."

Howard saw Ray crying on the sofa in the sitting room on Monday but said that when Ray noticed, "He jumped up and sat up so I would not see him." Wall tried to stop the momentum, asking Howard, "Did he seem to think more of his mother than you did of yours?" Howard, recognizing a hazardous question, answered, "That would be pretty hard to say."

Wall wanted Howard to admit that he was too worked up about the fire that morning to really notice the team, but the boy stood his ground. Wall reversed and tried to lead him to say that the horses were so fresh,

---

[266] 30-5264, p. 1383–1385.
[267] 30-5264, p. 1388.

they must not have had distemper. Again, Howard was steady: "They had this summer."[268]

Wall focused on the side curtains; was Howard sure they were up? He was. Wall besieged him for another couple dozen questions and then released him. This was the first piece of testimony that could tie together the late-night sighting of a buggy like Ray's with the side curtains in place, and it contradicted Ray's own testimony.

Govert called Mrs. Fred Keim, Howard Petrie's sister, to the stand. She witnessed Ray's khaki suit exchanged for the brown one on Saturday night and heard Ray request Howard spend the night, along with his mother's refusal. Govert said, "You may state whether or not the reason assigned was because of a cold from which the boy was suffering."

The State objected and was sustained. Nonetheless, Govert had managed to introduce a plausible reason for the refusal and one that had nothing to do with Ray's character or his relations with the family. Mrs. Keim was more forthcoming than her brother when questioned about family affection. She said of Ray and his mother, "They seemed to think the world and all of each other."[269]

Wall established that Mrs. Keim lived on State Street and had been married for five and a half years. Then he pressed her about the family relationships: if she ever even noticed the feelings between them before this trial; if she ever commented on it; and if she had discussed her testimony with the attorneys or anyone else.

Wall asked if she remembered when Mrs. Pfanschmidt bought a piano for Blanche and if she had seen Ray and his sister together after that. Wall challenged her to remember exact times, but she could not. He quizzed her about the Old Settler's Picnic conversation between Ray and his father, but Mrs. Keim only recalled seeing them together; no other details. Finally she was excused.

Govert replaced her with Mrs. (Walter) Ida Cook, another sister of the slain Charles, and aunt to Ray. She, her husband and Miss Reeder were

---

[268] 30-5264, p. 1393.
[269] 30-5264, p. 1398.

with Ray after the funerals. Ray "cried real hard….he cried just as hard as anyone could cry." Govert asked her if Ray said he had wished he'd burned up with the rest of the family, and the State objected emphatically, calling it a "self-serving statement." Objection sustained.

Wall asked if everyone at the funeral wasn't sad and crying. Mrs. Cook countered, saying that it was the usual thing to find little public emotion in the Pfanschmidt family. In her opinion, they were private with emotions. Wall probed, "Did you see [Ray] out at the graves when they were lowering the coffins into the graves?" "I did not see him then," Mrs. Cook answered.

Wall went even deeper, "You were familiar with his peculiarities to some extent, were you not?"

"I do not know what you mean by his 'peculiarities.'"

"You could tell from what you knew of him when his grief came and the cause of it?"

Mrs. Cook replied, "He was just about like his father always was."

"Whether or not he shed tears at Mr. Niekamp's from grief or from remorse, you did not know, did you?"

"I think it was from grief."

"You are just giving us your judgment, are you?"

Mrs. Cook said simply, "I could not tell from anything else."

"You did not know, of course, of your own knowledge what it was that impelled him to cry upon that occasion?"

"I think Ray felt like the rest of us did."

Did Ray know at the time he cried that people were "sort of connecting him with the fire in some way?" Mrs. Cook did not know what he knew. Wall finished with a flourish. "You don't know whether that was what was making him cry or whether something else made him cry upon that occasion, do you?"

"No."

Charles Ellerbrecht was called by Govert. He agreed that he sold Ray four suits (coat and trousers) and three shirts, all khaki, and identified the clothes offered as defense exhibits. Wall had a turn asking if he had seen these clothes before. Ellerbrecht admitted he had seen them at the attorney's office last week, but he only remembered seeing two coats at that time.

Wall, seeing opportunity, asked, "There are three of them now?"

"Yes, sir, I don't remember seeing but two," Ellerbrecht answered.

They agree that these coats were only made in Chicago by a particular manufacturer. Then Wall asked, "Can you state whether that is the coat you sold to them, or whether it is the coat a detective might have brought from Chicago and brought down here?"

"They may have done that, and I could not tell any different," answered the clerk.

In parting, Wall asked if Ellerbrecht was related to Ray. "His mother is a cousin of mine."

Henry Niekamp appeared on the stand, and Govert herded him through testimony of bringing Ray's clothing to the attorneys and marking them for identification. Govert had to point out the mark because the witness at first could not find it. Wall, in turn, discovered that the clothing was taken to the attorneys about a week after the fire, but the marks were added only about "two or three weeks ago."

Wall and Govert traded this witness back and forth several times. Niekamp admitted that the clothes were wrapped and sealed when they were originally delivered to the attorneys. Wall wanted to know how they were sealed. He was told that they were put in a box, wrapped in plain white paper, and sealed with "some sticky stuff."[270]

Lancaster brought Ray's uncle Walter O. Cook to the stand. Cook added little, agreeing that Ray broke down in the carriage after the funerals and again at the house. He was there when the clothing was taken to the attorneys and said that an itemized list was made before the clothes were boxed and sealed. When the box was opened later, the clothes were marked with a Plus N (+N). Mr. Cook then identified Exhibit #12, coat, as one of those coats originally delivered to the attorneys.

Govert asked if Cook had made his own measurements of Ray's buggy wheels. He answered affirmatively, saying the distance between them varied

---

[270]  30-5264, p. 1416.

by about two inches depending on whether you took the measurement at the top of the wheel, across from the axle, or at the bottom of the wheel. Cook also experimented with the buggy's turning radius just a few days after the funerals. His turns varied between five feet at the shortest (keeping the rub iron continuously against the tire) and seven feet at the widest. Cook also testified that there were no spots on the seat or cushions in the buggy; nor were there any spots on the floor boards or the top when he examined it at Joe Eakins' home.

Wall immediately wanted to know if Cook was looking for blood spots. Ray's uncle said he was just examining it. Wall prodded him about what he was looking for, but Cook maintained that he was just looking.

"You weren't looking for tobacco juice on the buggy, were you? You were looking for blood spots on that buggy, weren't you?"

"If there were any there, I surely would have seen them," said Cook.

Wall then implied that Cook's reason for examining the buggy was solely to testify in this trial. The buggy had been kept at Fred Pfanschmidt's place, and there was quite a crowd on hand, including Mr. Cook, Fred Pfanschmidt, A. W. Meyer, Henry Geisel, Jesse Dooley, and attorney Lancaster, for the buggy turning trials.

Wall accused Cook of leaving court after Archie Pape testified against Ray to track down Pape's woman friend and check Archie's story. Cook replied, "I suppose so." Wall chided him for doing everything he could in order to help Ray. Finally, after 191 questions, Wall turned him loose.

Govert asked in rebuttal, "Mr. Wall referred to the time when Archie Pape testified in court and you and Mr. Geisel went out to see the party referred to; I will ask you whether or not you knew that Mr. Wall's detectives were watching you?"

Over the State's objections, Cook answered, "I did not."[271]

Wilber Meyer was called and confirmed the turns measured in the buggy experiment and gave a lot of measurements. In his opinion Ray's buggy bed was actually wider than most regular, or piano-box, buggies. Ray's Viehle brand buggy was twenty-four inches wide across its box, and

---

[271] 30-5264, p. 1438.

most piano-box buggies were only twenty-two inches wide; the norm for buggy wheels was a forty-four inch diameter. He also thought Ray's wheels were straight, not worn or "dished." Wall did not cross-examine him.

Dr. H. O. Collins was recalled by the defense. Govert was attempting to show that the Pfanschmidts paid for the autopsy, but even though Fred Pfanschmidt offered payment, Dr. Collins did not see him consult Ray; and none of the doctors had actually submitted a bill for payment.

Govert called Uncle William Abel to the stand and asked if he went back to the jail to see Ray on Monday in response to Ray's request to speak with him. Objections flew; the State called it hearsay and completely self-serving. The jury was roused from their chairs and again sent from the room while things were hashed out. Eventually the court sustained the objection, and the jury filed back into their seats. The commotion left Abel flustered.

Govert said, "State on that occasion whether or not Ray Pfanschmidt refused to tell you what he knew about the Pfanschmidt fire."

"He did not refuse; no."

Objection was made by the State. The court ruled that the witness could not detail the conversation and instructed that the attorney's questions must be phrased so that they can be answered by yes or no.

Govert obliged, and asked, "Did he, at that time, Mr. Abel, on Monday night in question refuse to tell you what he knew about the Pfanschmidt fire?" Abel was confused and answered first that Ray did not refuse, and then answered three times to the same question that Ray did refuse. Govert kept on asking, calling forth a State objection. The court asked directly, "Did he refuse?" Muddled, Abel answered wrongly, "Yes, sir."

Frustrated, Govert asked yet again, and the sound of laughter disrupted the courtroom. The judge, with parental overtones, said, "I do not want any more laughter in the courtroom this afternoon. I mean exactly what I say." And he again instructed Abel not to say what had been said.

Govert asked to have his last question stricken and then asked Abel once more if Ray refused to tell what happened. Abel again misunderstanding, replied, "Yes, he did."

"Did you ask on the Monday night in question, ask him to tell you about what he knew about the Pfanschmidt fire?" Govert's questions were becoming harder to follow.

Abel said, "No, sir."

The judge stepped in, "That is for what purpose?"

Govert replied, "To see if he understands the question."

"Ask him if he understands what the word 'refuse' means," suggested the judge.

Govert addressed Abel. "Did he, on that night, say that he would not tell you what he knew about the Pfanschmidt fire?"

The light finally dawned, and Abel belatedly answered, "No, sir."

Govert wanted to know if Ray said anything about being guilty or innocent, but prosecution objections were many and loud. The court admonished Govert, saying he was attempting not to comply with the instructions about a "yes or no" answer, and sustained the objections. Govert tried again, and again the State's objection was sustained.

Finally the judge questioned Abel: "Did he, upon that Monday night, confess that he perpetrated the crime with which he is charged? That may be answered 'yes' or 'no.'"

Abel answered, "No, sir."

Wall, not wanting to help clarify the contradictory answers, let him go.[272] Witness dismissed.

Mrs. Henry Niekamp, another sister to Charles, arrived as a defense witness. She held the family line; Ray was affectionate and then grief stricken. Wall ascertained that Ray stayed at their home until his arrest and that Mr. Niekamp was not around much except for meal times. Ray did not break down in his uncle's presence, so only the women saw him grieving. Wall, in a subtle and inspired turn of phrase, got her to agree that Ray's mother, father, and sister thought a lot of him ... but left behind the impression that this affection, while it may have been present, was perhaps one-sided, not equally returned by Ray.

---

[272] 30-5264, p. 1447.

Govert recognized the inference and in final redirect question sought to counter it. Mrs. Niekamp volunteered, "Well, I thought he seemed to think a lot of them; at least he always did when I was around."[273]

Mrs. Henry Geisel, another sister of Charles, came next to speak, She talked about the khaki clothing her husband brought to their house, and said she was the one who wrote the list before the pieces were boxed. She confirmed Ray's stories about being at Geisel's farm on Tuesday and Thursday before the fire and the work he did blowing tree stumps.

Wall tried to demolish her testimony, saying she couldn't know where the box of clothing had gone, except for what her husband said. She agreed. She was also forced to agree that she did not know if anything happened between Ray and his father after the Old Settler's Picnic. It seemed that none of the family had seen Ray and his father together in the three-week period between the picnic and the fire, which Wall had successfully pointed out with every witness. Something might indeed have changed their relationship, and no one would have been the wiser.

In an effort to counter one of the late-night supposed sightings of Ray's buggy, Govert then called Henry Rees, a contractor working on streets in Quincy. Rees had the contract for installing concrete paving on Vermont Street between Eighth and Eighteenth streets and detailed the progress of his work at the time of the Pfanschmidt fire. Govert wondered if it would be possible for a vehicle to drive down Vermont Street. Rees replied, "Not unless the barricades were removed." Vermont was closed between Twelfth and Eighteenth streets, which would seem to contradict the testimony by Archie Pape.

On cross, Wall heard what he was hoping for. The crew had made enough progress that half the intersection at Twelfth Street was passable except for some trestles, which were easily moved wooden sawhorses. All in all, Vermont was passable late on Saturday night. The witness was dismissed, leaving Pape's testimony plausible.[274]

---

[273] 30-5264, p. 1451.
[274] 30-5264, p. 1460.

Esther Reeder came back to speak again for Ray. She told sweetly of knowing Ray "all my life, but never real well until a little over a year ago." She remembered spending the night at the Pfanschmidt farm about two weeks before the fire during the time Charles was in Missouri. The last time she had seen Ray with his father, "Well, Mr. Pfanschmidt acted as if he was awfully glad to have Ray home, like they always had."

Govert asked Esther what Ray had to say about his guilt or innocence when she visited him in jail, but the State objected. That day in November was the only time Esther was allowed to visit Ray. After much arguing between Lancaster and the court, the ruling stood that Esther might not repeat on the stand anything Ray had said to her.[275]

Wall rose to question Ray's fiancée and asked if she was able "to be of any consolation to Ray" in the carriage ride home from the funerals. She said she was not able to do so.

"What did you do?"

Esther replied, "I just spoke to him about it and told him he must not carry on that way." Could the others in the carriage have heard everything? "Yes," she said.

Esther did not see him cry as the caskets were being lowered, only later in the privacy of the carriage. Wall wanted Esther to enumerate how many times she saw Ray manifest grief and to say if anyone else saw it. She could not come up with a number and finally settled on "three or four times." Wall asked where and when, but Esther had no details to deliver.

Wall pressed. "He was grief-stricken out at Eakins when you were picking out the rug, was he not?"

"I am sure I do not know."

"You were there and saw him?"

"I was."

"He was grief-stricken there when he got that dollar changed?"

"I did not see him get any dollar changed."

"When you went down to the camp and got the lap robe, he was grief-stricken then, was he not?"

---

[275] 30-5264, p. 1465.

"I don't know."

Finally the defense objected when Wall recited the same "grief-stricken" phrase in a question about fetching the revolver. The court sustained that objection.

Esther admitted that before she visited Ray in jail, she had talked to Mr. Petrie and visited State's Attorney Gilmer and the offices of Lancaster and Govert. Lancaster asked why she went to Gilmer's office and was told, "There was a mistake in the telephone message; we understood it was Mr. Gilmer that wanted to see us."

Daniel Reeder replaced Esther and explained they waited two hours in Gilmer's office before somebody arrived, and the mistake was corrected. They stopped by the defense attorney's for just a moment on their way to the jail, where Esther waited while her father first spoke to Mr. Schaeffer.

Reeder was asked if Ray said anything about his guilt or innocence, and the same battle between attorneys occurred. Ultimately, Reeder was prevented from answering the question, despite being asked four times in various ways.

Mr. Reeder was allowed to testify that Schaeffer asked him to advise Ray to confess and to say that Ray would probably get off with ten or twelve years if he did so. Reeder was dismissed, and court adjourned for the day.

# Chapter 24

# Evidence Questioned

## Tuesday, April 15, 1913

Govert opened the Tuesday morning session by attacking the credibility of informant Frank Viehmeyer. He called Ira Calkins, secretary of the Electric Wheel Company, who had known Viehmeyer for twelve or thirteen years. The attorney's first inquiry concerning Vichmeyer's "reputation for truth and veracity" met a State objection, and the jury was ushered from the courtroom yet again.

Govert told the court that he had not only this witness but a parade of twelve others lined up to say they wouldn't believe Frank Viehmeyer even under oath. The State objected, calling this line of examination "immaterial," and the objection was sustained. The defense would not be allowed to cast doubt on Viehmeyer's damaging testimony or on his veracity.[276]

This witness was dismissed, and the jury returned.

Dr. Center was recalled and questioned about some horrific details that bolstered the defense's version of the timeline. He was asked how long it would take fire to consume the missing portions of the unidentified stump of a body, if the attempt was made in an ordinary kitchen stove. Dr. Center

---

[276] 30-5264, p. 1477.

could not answer exactly. "The length of time would be elusive; I would say somewhere between five and thirty-six to forty hours."

What if the attempt to burn the body was made in some open space using coal oil and gasoline? He stuck to the same time range. Govert asked if, in his opinion, a single application of coal oil and gasoline would suffice. The State objected, but the court overruled. Dr. Center did not think one treatment would do it. "Because a single application of gasoline or coal oil, or similar substances, would burn off in a comparatively short time, and the fire would die out." He thought it would take a "continued application of such fuel." This opinion nicely supported the defense's theory that some fiendish person was working all Saturday to burn the bodies while Ray was about his business in Quincy.

On cross, Wall asked for more gruesome speculation. "My question is; if [parts] were cut off first and an attempt made to burn them one night, would the fire the next day of that house be sufficient to consume them?"

Dr. Center replied, "I do not know."[277] When Dr. Center was dismissed, he left behind images of bodies and body parts lying in the house all day, alone, unattended, and partially burned while the world went about its business on the road outside.

Govert brought Charles H. Williamson to the stand to testify that the roads near Payson last had mud in them one week prior to the fire. Ray's last admitted visit to the farm was a week earlier than the fire and coincided with the rain and mud.

Govert called G. W. Gray, the "second-trick operator at the CB&Q Railroad Passenger Depot," who was in charge of recording all the passenger trains that arrived during his shift, including their time of arrival. At midnight on the Saturday of the fire, the first train from the north was #55, which passed by Soldier's Home at 12:58 a.m. After much verifying and explaining, Gray testified that there were only two passenger trains coming from the north and passing the camp: the first at about 1:00 a.m. and the second at 7:15 a.m. He admitted he did not know or record

---

[277] 30-5264, p. 1481.

any freight trains passing in that timeframe. Govert had the record book admitted as a defense exhibit.[278]

Uncle Fred Pfanschmidt stepped to the stand to testify that he went to the fire with Roy Pfanschmidt, and Arthur Pfanschmidt and his wife. Govert managed to get into the record that Ray told Fred to talk to Gilmer and get the bloodhounds if they thought it would help. Then Govert took up with Fred the issue of uncovering the tracks, and the jury was escorted out while the court sorted out the nature of Fred's conversation with Gilmer and whether or not it was admissible.

Eventually, Fred was allowed to testify that following his conversation with Gilmer, which included the idea the dogs would *not* be useful, Fred told Ray they might as well take the protection off the tracks. Ray instructed his uncle to tell John Lier, the sometime Pfanschmidt hired hand, to do it. But Fred, who did not know Lier enough to recognize him, could not comply.

Fred also stated that Ray directed him to talk to Dr. Collins about an autopsy, and he did so. Fred was intending to talk to the attorneys "for all of us" on Monday morning but couldn't find them. After waiting futilely all morning at the lawyer's offices, he went back to "Charley's" and was there when the dogs came.

Govert paced him through the bloodhounds' escapades again, which provided a moment of levity. The *Journal* reported Fred's tale of what happened at Twenty-fourth and State streets when one of the dogs left the trail and went nosing around on State Street. Fred said, "It went down State Street to a saloon and got a drink and then came back to the corner and picked up the trail again." Lancaster, with a perfectly straight face, asked what the hound did after "getting a drink at the saloon," and the courtroom erupted into laughter. The judge relented, "I believe that we will give the jury a chance to laugh at that." And the jury and the courtroom and even Ray joined in the laughter.

Then Fred was allowed to correct his story to say the dog got a drink of water near the saloon. Fred's version of events had the dogs wandering

---

[278] 30-5264, p. 1490.

about at the campsite and included Strumpfer taking them into the tent and then back out and to the horses.[279]

After that, Fred returned to the farm with Govert, Geisel, and Beatty to attempt to measure the tracks. When they arrived, the box was no longer on top of the horseshoe print, and the tracks were by then too indistinct to measure. This was the day before the paraffin casts were made!

Since Ray was still a minor, as his guardian, Fred recovered from the Thos. B. Jeffery's Co. the $500 Ray had put down on the Rambler car, less about $28 freight. Once again, the conversation with Ray in the jail was broached, but the court stopped testimony, and the jury was once again led from the room.

Lancaster offered to prove by this witness that Ray had said to Fred, "Before God and man he was innocent of the crime charged against him and that the officers had been trying to get him to plead guilty and insisted that if he did do so he would get a short sentence and that it would be better for him and his family and save his estate; and that the officers had stated to him that whether he was guilty or not, they could prove him guilty."

The court refused the offer, saying the "great part of and practically all of it being hearsay."[280] The jury returned none the wiser.

Govert turned his attention to Fred's conversations with Willis Seehorn. Fred had brought Seehorn to Govert's office on Tuesday morning and had overheard Seehorn say Ray had come in about midnight and was in bed before the passenger train went by.

Fred Pfanschmidt still had to face Wall before he could be excused. They began at the fire scene. Fred said he was not familiar with Ray's buggy and only knew the one horse of his team, the "little mare." The attorney and the uncle argued then about tracks for forty questions or so before they moved on to when the attorneys had been hired. Fred said he and Abel both thought on Sunday night that legal help should be hired, but he did not speak to Ray about it. Wall asked if Fred heard Ray's grandfather tell

---

[279] *Journal*, April 15, 1913.
[280] 30-5264, p. 1502.

him to get attorneys, but the defense objected and the court sustained it, saying, "I do not think it is proper at all."

Fred, when asked if he expected the hounds at the camp, said, "To be honest, I was kinda looking for it." But he stolidly maintained he had not hired Lancaster on Monday. "It appears to me like it was Thursday when I says, 'The way the thing is going now, it looks like to me we ought to make some arrangement.'"[281] Fred also rejected the idea that the sheriff warned him not to let his attorneys hamper the investigation. Wall also questioned Fred about being coached on how to testify. He denied it.

Then Wall asked how many detectives Fred had hired.

"Well, it was off and on," Fred answered.

Wall said in exasperation, "Off and on don't tell us how many."

Fred thought it was probably three or four. Mr. Lund was one of them, but Fred didn't know the others; he left that up to the attorneys. Fred did say, "The first time I saw Mr. Lunt then I said to Mr. Lunt, 'I want you to get everything for and against.'"

Wall inquired if he got anything that he then gave to the officials. Fred did not know because Lund sent his reports directly to Govert and Lancaster. Wall was intrigued. Lund had been hired on Thursday only five days after the fire and was paid by funds from Ray's estate. Fred said he didn't get in the way of the investigation once he heard Ray was suspected, but he didn't really help either. He also did not tell his own father what had been found.

"As a matter of fact, is it not true that you concealed from your father everything that you had learned from the detectives hired by you to run down this case?"

Fred answered, "Practically all, I did." Wall doggedly forced Fred to say that C. C. "never got track or hunted anything else; he hunted this one case down; this one party."

"What party do you mean?"

"Ray," responded C. C.'s son Fred.

So, pursued Wall, why didn't Fred show him what evidence they had pointing to Ray's innocence?

---

[281] 30-5264, p. 1513.

"I don't know."

"Did you have anything to show him along that line?"

"I don't know.... There were a few things I could have told him." But Fred could not justify his failure to speak to his father about Ray's innocence.

Wall moved on to Ray's buggy, back to the tracks, and on to who said to take away the boxes and strings, and why. Fred maintained Gilmer said the tracks were useless, the protection was not needed, and the witness assumed full responsibility for the proposed exposure of the tracks. Wall now took up the subject of the gas can, and he discovered that Fred had finally picked up the dented can in December and had it in his possession still.

Govert returned to control the damage. He asked if Fred had ever impeded the investigation by the officers or by his father. Fred said, "Not intentionally." Govert fished a bit, asking if Grandfather Pfanschmidt was involved in the investigation in any way other than through hiring the bloodhounds. Fred did not know. Govert pressed. Did Fred hear of his father investigating anything else? Fred equivocated, "Personally, I will have to say no; but I am of the opinion that he did."

The State objected, asking to have that answer stricken, and it was removed from the record.

Govert asked whether the officers would consult with him, and Fred answered that the only official who would speak with him was Mr. Bumpster. Fred added, "You might say all along, and I tried to get some information out of them, talked to them; it seemed they didn't want to talk to me, and that struck me kinda bad."

Wall probed the subject of hired detectives. Fred was put in touch with a Mr. Tobie through Lancaster, and Tobie was responsible for hiring Lund. After further inconclusive discussion, Fred escaped the stand.

Govert put Ben Holeman back in the witness chair. Holeman reported that on Monday after the fire he picked up Ray's buggy and team at C. C.'s house and drove back to the camp along a route that went north on Twelfth Street. Once there he unhitched the buggy and tied the team in the wagon shed. On cross, Wall simply inquired if Holeman had any trouble getting through the intersection at Twelfth and Vermont. He didn't.

Fred Knollenberg, Ray's uncle by marriage, came next. Knollenberg said he heard talk at the fire connecting Ray to the trouble, and after consideration, suggested to Ray that he get an attorney. Later he returned home and called Lancaster at his own instigation.

On Monday he went to the farm again, along with Lancaster, in Mr. Flynn's automobile. He had had heard about the hounds coming and wanted to see them. Wall got Knollenberg to agree he had contacted Lancaster after telling Ray that there was gossip against him, but Knollenberg remained firm that Ray had not initiated any contact with the attorney.

Henry Geisel was recalled and remembered being present when the typed statement was read by Lancaster to Willis Seehorn, before Seehorn was asked to sign it. Geisel verified that Defendant's Exhibit #14 was that statement. He testified that the pencil marks on the pages were changes suggested by Seehorn and were made before he signed it in Geisel's presence.[282]

Wall, frustrated at being unable to shake Geisel's certainty that the statement was read to Seehorn, asked sarcastically if Lancaster read it as slowly as he talked. Geisel said he read it so anybody could understand it. Then Wall acidly asked if Geisel could swear that Lancaster read the paper exactly as it was written. Geisel could not state that, and he didn't remember the particulars of the statement.

Wall demanded to know how he could not remember particulars if he had been there. If he didn't remember particulars, how did he know it was the statement just identified? Geisel insisted that he only took Lancaster because he had a rig available and was not there to be a witness to the signing.

Witness dismissed.

Then, in some housekeeping matters, Wall asked that Fred Pfanschmidt be recalled because the State "had forgotten to cross examine Mr. Pfanschmidt" about a check the defense had entered into evidence.[283] After a few meaningless questions about the check that Ray had written in the amount of $500.00 for the Rambler car, Fred was excused.

---

[282] 30-5264, p. 1539.
[283] 30-5264, p. 1542.

The court then refused to admit Defense Exhibit #3, a map of the camp, since the tents and the vault locations were indicated by stakes but not proven and no longer present. The defense offered a coat, marked Exhibit #4, which was accepted over objections from the State. The same held true for the leggings (#5 & #6); trousers (#7); trousers (#8); a coat (#9); a shirt (#10); trousers (#11); a coat (#12); and the plat, #13, having been already admitted, they offered #14, the statement by Seehorn, to which there was no objection.[284] The defense also offered page thirty-two of the minutes book for the directors meeting of Quincy Parks and Boulevards Committee.[285] Over objections by the State, it too was admitted.

Then the defense called as an expert Paul Carroll, foreman at the H. Little Wheel company, and a worker in metals for some twenty-seven years. With the permission of the court, Carroll took the axe head over into the daylight near a window to better examine it. He said it "had been considerably heated.... One place shows it was on the verge of the melting point."

Govert asked him if one side of the axe could have been heated more than the other. Carroll agreed. "State whether or not that is the same side upon which there appears a sort of a brown and black stain or debris."

"Do you mean this rust stain?"

"Yes," answered Govert.

"Yes," echoed the witness.

On cross, Wall managed only to have him say that "that ax was so much thinner on the point, it got much hotter there." Witness dismissed.

Govert called Rolla E. Lynn, a blacksmith and foreman at the Collins Plow company. Lynn agreed that the edge of the axe "has been just hot enough that the steel melted and ran away from it."

How do you know? asked Govert.

"Well, from the scale, which has been formed on there."

Wall rather pointedly asked about Govert's ownership interest in the company for which Lynn worked. He next zeroed in on the amount of

---

[284] Seehorn's statement is on 30-5264, p. 1549.
[285] This page referenced Ray's proposal presented at the meeting.

heat it took to melt steel and implied that it was unlikely that a wood fire could do that,[286] but Wall made little headway. Wall asked Lynn if Govert also had an interest in the Little Wheel Works, where the previous witness worked. That answer was "yes." On redirect, however, it was determined that it was William Govert, father of the defense attorney, who was invested in these companies.

Esther was recalled once more by Lancaster, who asked if Ray was at her house on Thursday afternoon, the week of the fire. Esther agreed he was there for about three quarters of an hour, at about half past two.

The judge then requested that the State allow Exhibit 3, the map of the camp, into evidence, saying, "I would like the jury to have the benefit of the plat of these premises." The State agreed.

Whereupon the defendant rested.[287]

The end of defense testimony came with a lack of fanfare that sucked the air out of the room.

It was expected that Wolfe would ask for an adjournment for a day to prepare for rebuttal, but after a short conference, the State began[288] by calling Miss Esther Reeder yet again to the stand. Wall wanted to know if it was warm and comfortable in the Reeder home on the Friday night when Ray visited. Esther remembered they had a fire, and "it was warm enough; we all sat around the stove; it was probably sixty or seventy degrees." She was excused, left to wonder why the temperature mattered. It was not mentioned again.

Wall then called Walter Heidbreder of the State Street Bank to ask about a conversation Heidbreder had with Mr. Geisel in the week after the fire. "I will ask you if at that time and place Mr. Geisel, since the Pfanschmidt fire, told you that Mr. C. A. Pfanschmidt had come to him and said that he could not do anything with Ray; that the way Ray was carrying on would break him up; and if he did not ask him, Mr. Geisel, to speak to Ray, that no matter what he said to Ray it would not hurt his feelings, or that in substance?"

---

[286] End of Roll 30-5264.
[287] 30-5265, p. 5.
[288] *Herald,* April 15, 1913.

"He did," Heidbreder agreed.

Govert did not challenge the banker, although his testimony directly contradicted previous testimony by Uncle Geisel that such a conversation had never happened. The State's momentum increased when Claude Peter next created a bit of a stir by testifying that he had spoken with Henry Geisel after the fire and Geisel told him that seeing those tracks in the barn lot was "like sticking a knife in him."

Sheriff Lipps came next to tell a tale of Ray's tent. Frese, Young, Koch, and Buerkin conducted an experiment "last Sunday night" to see if the train lights could be seen from inside the tent. Lipps and Koch raised up the tent exactly as it was placed when Ray stayed there and remained until about 1:00 a.m., watching the passing of three trains.

The defense attorneys were now objecting to each and every question but being consistently overruled. Lipps and Koch reportedly waited in the tent as the first train went by, at about nine o'clock, headed east. It was followed by a second train going west, which matched the one in Ray's testimony. Wall wanted to know what part of the train could be seen from the tent.

"State to the jury whether you could see the headlight of that train as it went by."

"I could not."

"State to the jury whether you could see the taillight as it went by, the second train that went by."

"I could not."

When the Ely #55 went by, Buerkin was waiting outside the tent, while Koch, Young, and Lipps were inside. What could they see inside the tent? "Just a little light, like a flash."[289] He could only see the taillight when he left the tent.

Govert asked the court to strike all testimony in reference to this experiment, as "not rebuttal; immaterial, irrelevant, and not shown to have been made under similar conditions." The court overruled the motion.

Govert quizzed Lipps about the source of the tent. Lipps reported that it came from Hartman's on Ninth and Hampshire and was nine feet

---

[289] 30-5265, p. 16.

by fourteen feet (he thought) with about fourteen inch high sidewalls, but he did not know how thick the canvas was. Then under skillful cross examination, Lipps was forced to admit that the train light *was* visible inside the tent. "Yes, sir, I saw light there."

The position Lipps assumed in the tent was "sitting down on my haunches." They had no cots; and Lipps said he could hear the train, but not every car passing over the viaduct. Govert was incredulous. Could Lipps not hear the sets of wheels on the railroad cars passing over the steel viaduct twelve feet in the air? Lipps allowed how he could hear it but not distinguish the individual cars.

Govert pulled stingy details from the reluctant Lipps. The crowd of men waited outside until they heard the train whistle for the Fourteenth Street crossing and then he went into the tent "about as far back as the head of a cot would be." Govert spent one hundred questions on the sheriff before he released him, replaced by George Koch.

Koch agreed with everything Lipps had said, including seeing the "flash for a second or two" of the westbound train's headlight. According to Koch they knew the train had gone by because Buerkin told them from his post outside the tent. Koch saw three taillights on the train after exiting the tent.

Again, Govert wanted to know how thick the canvas was, but Koch also didn't know but thought the tent side walls were three feet tall. Koch said, under prodding, that he put his overcoat down and kneeled on it because the ground was dirty. Young took his turn next. He would admit to seeing no light ever—only a reflection of the headlight.

Young, like his two predecessors, agreed that the color of the blood spots on the clothing from the vault had not changed since last October. Wall asked Young point blank if he placed or had those clothes placed in the vault. Young denied this emphatically.

Over strenuous defense objections, Wall emphasized the validity of the physical evidence. "State to the jury whether or not either at your direction of your connivance or acquiescence that suit of clothes, which was taken out of the Frese vault, was placed there by you."

Young answered, "I knew nothing of the suit of clothes until it was taken out of the vault."

"State to the jury whether the blood stains found upon those clothes were placed there by you or anybody at your direction or with your acquiescence, connivance, or approval."

"They were not placed there. I knew nothing of them until I saw them when they were taken from the vault." Nor was Young responsible for the blood on the axe head.

Govert, when he faced Young, repeated the same question that prosecutor Wall asked Ray: "If you had put it there or known about it, you would have told about it upon the stand?"

Young answered, "I certainly would."

The witness resisted Govert at every point, refusing to say he saw the light of the train—only a reflection of it. Might it have reflected against the wall of the tent as Ray said? "It might have … but I saw it from the bottom of the tent."

Govert inquired, "Were you sitting in the same graceful position of body that the other witnesses were?"

"I was sitting on my heels, crouched down."

"And supporting yourself on either side with your hands?"

"No, sir."

"You were sitting there without any support at all?"

"Yes, sir."

"You were doing that for $25 a day and expenses, were you?"

Objection!

The court ruled, "He may show whether he was being paid by the day at this time. The form of the question is objectionable."

Young flippantly answered, "This was a part of the night, not the day."

Govert asked sweetly, "This was gratis, thrown in for good measure?"

"Yes, sir." He was excused.[290]

Henry J. Hartman was called to say that he purchased a tent from the auctioneer, Mr. Rump, at the farm sale when the remaining Pfanschmidt belongings were auctioned off by the executor of the estate. It was this tent Koch had borrowed for the train experiment. Wall put George Koch back

---

[290] 30-5265, p. 46.

on the stand to swear that he told Fred Pfanschmidt not to put his attorneys in the way of the investigation and that this conversation happened on Monday, when the dogs trailed to the camp. Over the defense's objections Koch was allowed to swear that he too was in no way responsible for any blood being put on anything or for putting the clothes in the vault.

Koch left the stand, and John Lier returned to tell of finding the axe head. Wall began by instructing Lier to tell the jury that very near the spot where he found the axe head he also found unburned combustible material. The defense objected strenuously and the jury members were excused from the room.

The judge said the question was "suggestive." "I will sustain the objection on the ground that it is leading and suggestive. Change the form of the question, and I will let you show the subject matter of it."

The jury returned. Wall asked what else was found near the blade. Lier said, over strenuous protests from the defense, "There was some cloth there that was not burned very bad ... there was a lot of jars and some potatoes."

Govert asked when the axe was found. Lier replied that it was just one day before this trial began, on the seventeenth of March, 1913. He was dismissed.

Fred Pfanschmidt was recalled and asked about the tent sold at the sale but said he could not be sure whether it was the sleeping tent or the supply tent. After further argument about a witness who was absent from the courtroom, the State rested the rebuttal portion of their case.

The transcript read, "This is all the evidence offered by the People and by the Defendant on the trial of this case."[291]

It was time for summations. The importance of these end pieces to organize the rambling content of the evidence into a coherent picture in support of either the theory of the prosecution, or, alternatively, of the defense, could hardly be overestimated. The entire outcome of the trial might rest on these orations.

---

[291]  30-5265, p. 53.

Counsel for the People asked permission to make three closing arguments to the jury, to which the defense objected. Specifically, the defense did not want Wall to make the last and therefore most powerful statement, saying he was merely a private attorney in the employ of Charles Kaempen assisting the People. The defense wanted the State limited to two arguments, made only by the State's attorneys.

Wolfe explained to the judge that he had requested Wall's help since he had held office only a few months, been a practicing attorney for only four years, and had never prosecuted a murder case. Mr. Wagner, assistant state's attorney, also had only four years' experience. In reply, Govert countered by saying that this was also his first murder case, and Lancaster had previously been involved in only one murder trial. As far as experience, they had been practicing for ten and twelve years, respectively, while Wall, in contrast, had been practicing since 1896, a far longer period.

The court denied the defense and ruled the State could make three arguments, the first by Rolland Wagner, assistant state's attorney, the second by Fred. G. Wolfe, state's attorney, and the concluding one by John E. Wall.[292] Wall would be the final speaker following the defense's closing arguments. There were no limits placed upon the length of the closing arguments.

This decision presented a distinct advantage to the State.

---

[292] 30-5265, p. 55.

# Chapter 25

~

# Closing Arguments
## "The Hand of God Almighty Pointing at the Gallows!"

### April 15–19, 1913

"With brilliancy and eloquence unusual in so youthful a practitioner, Rolland Wagner, the assistant to Mr. Wolfe, made the opening argument for the State this morning. Mr. Wagner has not been prominently identified with any case of the first magnitude here before, and has never had an opportunity for the display of his merit as a forensic orator. His castigation of the defendant ... was a masterly effort at denunciation."[293]

Wagner spoke through the morning, finishing after the noon recess. Ray at last displayed emotion, swallowing convulsively and biting his nails as he gazed continuously at the orator. One reporter proclaimed Ray almost in a hypnotic trance, his body movements mirroring, to a slight scale, the movements of Wagner as he spoke. Ray's relatives were also moved and could be seen shaking their heads at some of the arguments made.

Wagner began by thanking the jury for their close attention in this long trial and promising he would explain the evidence to them. He

[293] *Herald,* April 15, 1913.

read the indictment to the jury. Then he considered motive, and his first candidate was love. "Ray Pfanschmidt was engaged to Esther Reeder. He was dead in love with that girl, and that was a motive which would cause a man to do almost anything."

Poor Esther! She was horrified, embarrassed, and outraged to hear these words tying her to the motive for an unspeakable crime.

Wagner maintained that Ray lied to Esther's father about having money in the bank. In truth, according to the prosecution, he was indebted to the bank, losing money on his job, and in debt to the auto company and to Cottrell Hardware. He was having trouble with his father, as evidenced by the conversation with Mr. Heidbreder, and the letter from the bank demanding repayment of overdrafts would prove to be the last straw. Wagner read a copy of the letter mailed to Charles Pfanschmidt one day before the fire, maintaining that since the letter was never returned as unopened mail, Charles had received it and read it. He alleged that Ray, an expert on dynamite, used the clock, wire, and fuse to set the home on fire.

Wagner explained that Ray delayed leaving the Reeder homestead on Friday night while he was trying to decide about going to the farm to confront his father. Ray lied about his alibi at the lunch stand, as Mr. Clutch testified, although he had been there on a previous night and introduced himself as "Dynamite Pfanschmidt." Wagner told of Seehorn getting up, looking at his watch, and finding Ray's empty cot. He claimed that the defense was so frightened by this evidence they concocted a statement and Seehorn signed it without knowing what it said. Then the defense tried to make him leave town.

Wagner heaped disbelief upon Ray's story of seeing and hearing the train that night, citing the tent experiment which, in Wagner's opinion, proved Ray's claims to be impossible. He detailed the people who on Saturday morning saw Ray in a blue suit and enumerated Ray's demeanor and his stories about his broken watch. He called it a "likely story" that a fragile wire from a charging cord could withstand the force necessary to drag his watch to harm.

The drama escalated with Wagner's rhetorical question, asking where Ray was on Saturday night. "I say he drove home to the place where his dead father and mother and little sister lay cold and dead. There is where he went on Saturday night." Walter Dingerson saw him. "And Ray was driving slowly. Yes, he was driving slowly. Why, gentlemen? Because he expected to make a run for his life when he came back." He needed to keep his team fresh for the furious trip back to the city after setting the fire.

Wagner had a definite dramatic flair and a forceful presentation that carried the courtroom and held their rapt attention. At this point, the *Herald* reported, Ray began biting his fingernails.

According to Wagner, some of the many phone calls to the farm on Saturday were from Ray, wondering why the crime had not been discovered and why he had not been notified. "Gentlemen, there are lots of things that Ray forgot to cover up. He is a shrewd man, but the man never lived who does not leave something undone …"

Wagner went on to a detailed description of the soil in the barn lot and the tracks Ray left behind, casting aspersions on the relatives who saw nothing odd about that track. Waving the horseshoe, he asked the jury instead to follow the evidence of the "honest neighbors" who described the calk mark that matched the shoe on Ray's mare.

He claimed Ray expected the early awakening on Sunday morning. When Ben Holeman "bursts in and cries" for Ray to get up, Ray calmly told Ben to feed the horses, grease the buggy, and hitch the team. It was not the expected reaction to news of unexpected tragedy.

Ray's actions at the fire were completely unacceptable by the prosecution's standards. "Oh, gentlemen, I should think that it would have been a memorable morning: the house in ruins and the bodies lying in the ruins. Yet he knew where they were."

Wagner censured Fred Pfanschmidt for hiding the odd gas can. "Why in the name of heavens, gentlemen, hadn't that can been in evidence?"

He dwelt in depth on Ray's lack of emotional response and concluded that if any tears were shed it was from "remorse, not grief." To fortify this claim, Wagner cited Ray's undiminished appetite. "From the fire, Ray went to Reeders and he had dinner, and he went to his grandfather's and had supper, and there is no evidence to show that his appetite was not as good as anyone's there." Wagner simply could "conceive of no punishment fit for such a man."

That night Ray gave a bill to someone with the blood of his family on it; the experts had testified that it was human blood. Wagner asserted that from Sunday on, Ray had attorneys and was instructed not to talk.

He unfurled the bloody clothes to the jury and gestured to the mattress and the nightgown saturated with blood as mute testimony to the tragedy.

Wagner proposed that the story Geisel told about the dog stopping in a saloon at Twenty-Fourth and State to get a cigar was only part of the truth. He said Geisel went in to call the attorneys and tell them, "The dogs had struck a hot trail." He staunchly defended the accuracy of the bloodhounds in the Shaw case, saying that in Virden they followed the trail of the killer until he jumped a train. It was only later, filled with remorse, the killer returned and shot himself.

After lunch, Wagner resumed his summation. He contrasted the "poor old grandfather who seems at the end of his life" with young Ray, saying that it was the grandfather who hired the dogs, and the grandfather who said Ray had already hired attorneys by Monday. He alleged that the information gathered by Uncle Fred's detectives was never given to the officers or to the grandfather, because they were working to clear Ray, not simply to solve the crime.

He faulted Ray for stringing along the officers, promising to tell his story, then not following through on his word. Wagner disparaged Ray's selective memory. "He said he cannot remember what he did on the way home on Friday night. Oh, no, but he could remember how many cars were in that train."

Wagner reminded the jury that Ray never denied wearing those bloody clothes. Furthermore, the defense never refuted witness Crubaugh, who saw Ray headed back to camp at one thirty on Sunday morning. Wagner detailed to the jury how Ray was visited in his cell more than three hundred times by his attorneys, who "drilled him" until he could stand up to a cross-examination on the stand.

In a grand burst of drama, Wagner pointed his finger at Mr. and Mrs. Kaempen and reminded the jury of their interest and involvement. Mrs. Kaempen burst into loud sobs. He gestured to this "dear old grandfather," who also could not restrain his tears. He demanded that the jury fix a penalty upon the man who committed this atrocity "which will send him to the gallows."

"Gentlemen of the jury, I am going to ask you just one thing. If you determine this man is guilty, which he is, I ask you in the name of the people of the State of Illinois to give him the death penalty. I thank you."

Wolfe was next to address the jury. Three weeks ago, when he gave the opening address, he laid out at length what the State would prove. Now he contended that they had "made an honest attempt to prove it." After this prologue, he expended three hours hurling pointed accusations at the defendant.

The *Journal* described it this way: "It was the duty of Assistant State's Attorney Rolland Wagner to sum the evidence to a certain extent, but it was the duty of the State's attorney to dig to the very bottom of everything and bring out hidden facts which the inexperienced minds of the jury might fail to grasp. And this he did."[294]

Wolfe first dealt with the nature of "reasonable doubt," explaining that it was "not a little speck away back in your mind; it must be more than that." He reaffirmed the evidence that the Pfanschmidts were indeed dead. Then Wolfe listed in detail the defense testimony that had been contradicted, beginning with Mr. and Mrs. Cook, Mrs. Lizzie Petrie, Howard Petrie, and others and included Miller with his time confusion the night of the fire; Geisel's testimony; and Ray's wardrobe alibi.

"There's something funny about Ray wearing his old muddy trousers to see his sweetheart. He said he changed his shirt for grease spots on the sleeves. Where were his leggings from Friday evening until Sunday evening? What about the team, supposedly recuperating from distemper, which could make the run from the camp to Geisel's house in only forty-five minutes?"

Wolfe claimed divine intervention, saying, "This was the most carefully planned deed I ever heard of, and it seems to me like the hand of God has played a part in preserving some of the evidence by which [Ray] might be brought to justice."

---

[294] *Journal*, April 17, 1913.

The State's attorney maintained that the fire Ray attempted to set on Friday didn't go off, forcing him to return on Saturday to finish the job. Yet Ray's forethought in asking superintendent Love about crossing through the Home at night spoke to his preplanning.

Wolfe pointed to the wheel tracks as being too shallow for rubber tires and being of the right dimension for Ray's buggy. He expressed appreciation for the honest, God-fearing neighbors testifying against Ray, saying that they knew his relationship with his family was not so affectionate.

He offered a backhanded compliment to the defense attorneys. "He could not have selected two better than Govert and Lancaster to defend his case. They have put up a shrewd defense. Ray Pfanschmidt has told the best story I have ever heard for a man so guilty. I give him credit for it, but I know he has been schooled in what he said."

In Wolfe's version, Ray damaged his watch in the scuffle to kill the athletic Miss Kaempen. "The dead body of Emma Kaempen was found with portions of the stockings still on her limbs, which showed that she was not yet in bed. I believe Ray Pfanschmidt went out there that night with murder in his heart. I do not believe he wanted to kill Emma Kaempen, but he had to do this to cover his bloody tracks." In fact, Wolfe considered that Ray had picked Friday because it was the custom for Emma to be in Quincy that night. Ray was doubtless very unpleasantly surprised to find her at the farm.

A scornful Wolfe maintained that it was unlikely Ray would sleep all the way home in the buggy from Esther's on Friday night "with nothing on but a thin khaki suit. No overcoat and no lap robe?" At 2:00 a.m. on Saturday morning Ray's buggy was sighted in town. "Do you believe Archie Pape, a cousin of Ray Pfanschmidt, would lie to send this defendant to the gallows? Or do you believe Ray would lie to save his neck?"

As he continued his interpretation of the evidence, Wolfe pointed out that Ray's leggings were mysteriously missing from the tent between Saturday morning and Sunday evening, when they were returned. He pointed an accusing finger at Geisel for driving his rubber-tired buggy into the barn lot and crossing and recrossing the tracks in an effort to obliterate them, and firmly stated that Ray wanted the boards removed from the tracks to destroy them before the hounds could arrive.

Furthermore, Wolfe said, the message over the phone to Ray's mother was a plant because Ray knew everyone listened in on calls on the party line. Tallying still another way the telephone served Ray, he explained that the combination of the battery in the phone, along with the clock and the gas can easily could have been used to trigger the fire.

The bloodhounds were staunchly defended by Wolfe, who said that when Lancaster, Geisel, and Fred Pfanschmidt left the dogs at Twenty-Fourth and State they knew that the trail was headed to Ray's camp. He advocated the belief that innocent men did not hire attorneys before they were arrested, and he asserted that the reason Ray did not proclaim his tale of innocence before his arrest was that it would have given the State time to prove his story false.

The State's attorney reminded the jury that Ray never denied anything he reportedly said to the informant, Farley, although his attorney would have you believe that Ray knew he was a detective and was stringing him along. Ray thought Farley was a genuine crook, said Wolfe, and crooks do not "peach"[295] on each other.

Wolfe did not quite call Esther a liar but said her impressions of family relations reflected only a façade. "Gentlemen, wouldn't it have been a mighty unmanly thing for him to have shown otherwise when his intended wife was with him? Wouldn't it have been a highly improper act for him to have picked a fuss with his father at such a time, or to have indulged in other family quarrels?" He continued, "People as a rule do not air their family differences in the open."

The issues of Ray's troubles while attending college in Champaign, involving shooting "a certain party in the nose" and robbing his roommate were mentioned. Wolfe doubted Ray's claim that he carried a gun merely to protect his team from dogs and turned mocking when he spoke of Ray's plans to pull the plug on the Payson phone system and rob the bank there. "Yes, gentlemen, this wonderful little boy, with such undying devotion for his relatives, had planned such a robbery."

---

[295] Inform on each other.

In summation, Wolfe said, "Gentlemen, as we said at the start, this had been a circumstantial case, but I am just as well satisfied of this man's guilt as if I had seen him commit the act. For the protection of our homes, I ask for this man's life. I ask you to say that he is guilty and ask you to fix his punishment at death."[296] Wolfe took his seat.

There were nods and murmurs of agreement from the majority of the spectators. Just about 10:30 a.m. Govert began to speak for the defense, and the atmosphere shifted.

He set the stage by reading cases where the accused had been convicted on circumstantial evidence, where it seemed there could be no possible doubt; but, after their execution, these accused men were found innocent. The *Journal* expressed the opinion that this presentation was so powerful that even jurors convinced of Ray's guilt would now take a second look at their conclusion.

"A man who goes out and chops his parents to pieces doesn't do it for money. He does it because his mind is disordered. He is a fiend, unbalanced mentally." Govert then began to rebut the State's case against Ray.

It was obvious, he said, that a crime had been committed, but the motive as proposed by the State "has mighty little in it." And their evidence was certainly lacking, and, in the eyes of the defense, this evidence was either faulty—or contrived.

For a start, where were the huge blood spots from this horrific crime?

Govert held up and gestured at the clothes. "Here is where they cut out a spot, but they haven't shown the piece of goods cut out. There isn't enough blood on the clothes for a good nosebleed. Why not? Why, because the man who put the blood on them didn't want to spare very much from his person just then.

"Oh! The man who put the clothes made a bad job of it. I want to tell you that a man couldn't wring the neck of a chicken and not get more blood on him than that. And still they come here and say that this man with his ax struck down one after another of four people and then dismembered some of them. No man can believe that anyone can kill even one man with an ax and not get more blood on him than that."

---

[296] *Journal*, April 17, 1913.

And the leggings were vastly important. It was proven that Ray wore leggings on Friday night, yet the blood spots on the pants came six inches lower than that. "The man who put the blood spots on the pants forgot ..." was Govert's damning explanation. This one piece of evidence proved both Ray's innocence and that the bloody clothes were contrived, according to Govert's reasoning.

He reminded the jury that all the suits were accounted for immediately after the fire. Koch and Lipps found two and one half suits on Sunday morning, one suit was at the grandfather's house, and Ben Holeman had the other coat. But by Thursday, four days later, when Henry Geisel went to the camp there were only one and a half suits. Where was the other suit Koch and Lipps had seen on Sunday?

And there was that interesting coincidence that *one day* before the trial began, after the ashes of the home had been dug over until even little rings were found, here comes a man with an axe with blood on it. The defense proved that it only requires heat of only 170° for blood to adhere to steel. "Still they bring it in to pass a noose about that boy's neck. Better be it by far and more righteous that the noose be passed around the neck of the man who is responsible for anything of that kind."

Govert declared that when Ray saw the gas can at the fire, he pointed it out as anyone would do. He faulted Young for not collecting it and restated the conflicting evidence about whether it was said to be a "strange can" or a can in a "strange location." One of the "honest" neighbors, Moritz Lier, heard Ray say that it was a "strange location." It was the law officers who had put a twist to Ray's words, claimed Govert.

"And if it was one that he knew came from the Frese place, why would a bright boy like he is tell the officers about it?" And why didn't the Lier boys, who were familiar with the farm, notice that it was a strange can?

And about the clock, "this insignificant piece of battered wheels," which was kicked around for days? Where is the clock's dial? "There is not a thing to connect this clock with this fire whatever."

Govert claimed that the horseshoe tracks in the barn lot mud were made a week before the fire and then covered and preserved by dust, only to be uncovered by Mr. Plank and his air pump. He rebuked the State for "diatribes" about the Pfanschmidt relatives who stood with Ray, saying that the entire county knew Geisel for an honest and upright man and Mrs. Petrie a "faithful and true woman."

The *Herald* wrote, "Govert ridiculed the bloody dollar-bill evidence, making the crowd in the courtroom laugh with his biting sarcasm." He ridiculed Seehorn, asking if Ray had killed his family on Friday night, how then did it make sense that he would he wake up his tent mate to document his late time arrival? And, by the way, did Seehorn sleep with his boots on, so that he could roll over and strike a match to see his watch? And how did Seehorn know more on the stand now than he did that day last October when he and Lawrence and Holeman first made statements?

About Clutch and the lunch stand, Govert explained that the walkup window was small, and Clutch could not always see who was ordering a sandwich. "We have been accused of putting up a story for that boy to tell, but if I had, I would have made it agree with other people's stories."[297]

Govert called attention to the fact that "every man or woman" who passed the house on Saturday smelled burning flesh. And where were the missing parts of Charles? Govert reasoned that it was clear that someone was in there burning bodies in a stove all day on Saturday, while Ray was accounted for in town. All that work would have taken time. "Do you think one man could have traveled that far and done all that work in the short space of two hours?"

He carefully reminded the jury that the witnesses did not ever see Ray that weekend, only a team that resembled his. It was simply not possible to drive twenty-three miles and burn a house down in an hour and a half, as was supposed for Saturday night. He repeated that only one person noticed anything at all different about Ray on Saturday, and a man who had killed his father, his mother, and his sister, no matter how little emotion he may show, could not go about among his friends and show no trace of it.

Bitterly, Govert elaborated on the many prosecution exaggerations and distortions. "It would not have mattered what that boy had done that day, they would have interpreted it as evidence of his guilt."

[297] *Herald*, April 18, 1913.

The attorney concluded with an eloquent plea to release Ray to "breathe the free air" and to face down this terrible crime, and to eventually bring to the courtroom the true killer.

Govert was finished.

On April 17, the *Herald* noted in the "Tales of the Town" column, which was next to the story about the closing remarks, and tucked between an offering of dress gingham for nine cents a yard and the Halbach-Schroader Co. Wool Skirt Sale, that "George Govert is ready for the rest cure. His strenuous and long continued work in the trial has run him down physically. It seemed really a hard exertion to make his speech before the jury."

Besides taking a physical toll on the participants, the trial had also split relationships and would influence the area in unforeseen ways for years to come, as evidenced by this quote from Govert in response to Wolfe's charge that Govert manufactured evidence: "No man can say of me what Mr. Wolfe said here yesterday and not realize that he is not to be forgiven."

As soon as Govert concluded, Lancaster rose to plead for Ray.

"Emery Lancaster, rising yesterday to heights of oratory stepped into the place before the jury left by his partner and upon the foundation laid by Mr. Govert's calm analysis of the evidence and incisive reasoning and appeal to the sense of Justice of the jurors, Mr. Lancaster began the erection of a fabric of sentiment blended with facts as he saw them of fiery appeal and dramatic condemnation. So appealing was the plea of Mr. Lancaster that it drew tears from the eyes of men and women in the audience who had not displayed emotion before during the trial. He swayed the crowd as easily as though all had been friends of his client, instead of a crowd perhaps impartial, perhaps biased in their opinion but certainly not as a whole favoring the young defendant in the case."

Lancaster asked the jury to consider the feelings of all involved. Even the attorneys, he said, were not in the case for solely professional reasons. "Indeed, were we not retained to clear the name of this innocent boy, our feeling would prompt us still to stand beside these devoted relatives in an effort to show the world how cruelly it has judged this boy." Lancaster detailed his own long friendship with the deceased Charles Pfanschmidt and his respect and admiration for the relatives standing by Ray.

He addressed the family of the slain Emma, saying, "I have but the kindest words and the truest sympathy for Mr. Kaempen and his sorrowing family. He has always been a friend to me. He is doing what he thinks is right in this matter. He seeks only justice and the infliction of the proper punishment upon the man proven to be guilty of slaying his daughter. Mr. Kaempen would be the first to say to any of you, even as we say it, 'Men, do your duty.'"

Mrs. Kaempen's sobs were heard amid the stillness in the room.

Lancaster condemned Ray's treatment in the jail. He was irate that Ray was denied family visits yet subjected to repeated interrogations by assorted detectives from three states. "Gentlemen, never before in the history of this county has such outrageous treatment ever been meted out to any human being. Sixteen to twenty hours each day locked in a tiny cell where the sunlight never penetrated ... And Ray, from the kindness of his heart, has not offered a word of criticism upon the stand for all they did to him." The officers repeatedly told him that if he didn't [confess and] get it off his mind he would go crazy. "Well, he had gotten it off his mind on the witness stand, where he should do so. And is he crazy?" asked Lancaster.

The *Herald* reported that Fred Pfanschmidt was in tears, and so were the aunts. Many more hands among the courtroom listeners held handkerchiefs. "Ray was greatly moved and his lips quivered, but even in this moment of emotion tears did not come to his eyes." Miss Reeder was bent over sobbing bitterly, with her friends about her. Finally she had to leave the room to weep privately in the ladies' retiring rooms as Lancaster paid tribute to her loyalty and devotion.

Lancaster castigated the people put into the jail to trick Ray and said Viehmeyer was not put on the stand because Lipps knew the people of Adams County would not tolerate the idea of a stool pigeon.

He pointed out that the exact time of the fire was in question, and even using "five gallons of gasoline would not have consumed that house in the twinkling of an eye, but it would have started the flame that destroyed the home."

Lancaster explained how the State's own witnesses contradicted each other on the timing of the fire. If Miller was right, the fire was burning

Saturday night even before Ray left Seventh and Maine with his team. With a glint in his eye he mockingly reminded the jury that the State had called their own witness "Mysterious Miller" when they didn't like his testimony.

He clarified that although Dingerson saw the same team that he had seen the night before, it was not Ray's. Nor could Ray fly from Sixth and Maine streets at eleven fifteen to start a fire at the farm that could be seen by Miller at eleven thirty. Only the officers saw any peculiar markings on the horseshoe track, and they only found the marking after they got down in the dust blowing away debris to find a track from the previous week. He pointedly asked why the prosecution didn't introduce the paraffin casts of the tracks and claimed that they did not dare to because they would not match the testimony!

Lancaster inquired of the jury just what it was in Ray's behavior that could make them want to hang him. Was it that he'd said he had to put his shoes on that Sunday morning? Was it because he wanted to use an automobile to get there faster? What *should* Ray have done?

"Who would be the best able to tell whether Ray showed emotion, Pete Lott, who never saw the boy before, or Esther Reeder, who has known and loved and gone with him and knew every feeling which affected his heart? … Suppose the boy had broken down with grief? The first thing the State would say was that he had a nervous breakdown."

Lancaster painted a compelling and detailed picture demonstrating that once Ray came under official suspicion, he was left with no acceptable course of action. The attorney strongly criticized the State for slandering Mrs. Petrie, who had been like a mother to Ray since the tragedy. He itemized all Ray's khaki suits and explained again how they were accounted for on Sunday morning, reminding the jury that they were not bloody. "Oh, I tell you. Those clothes found in that vault were not bloody from those bodies found in that fire." But Lancaster stopped short of naming a culprit for the fabrication of evidence. He ended with an impassioned and eloquent plea for Ray's life.

Wall followed with the State's summation.

Attorney Wall, who was as persuasive and even more dramatic than Lancaster, began his "supreme efforts to send the murderer to the gallows" by describing a vivid picture of the crime as he imagined it to have happened.

"I can see that little house there in the calm, still moonlight. The night breezes play softly about it, whispering among the trees and gently stealing in at the open window … then enters the murderer, his bloody ax raised for the blow. With his flashlight he steals up the stairs, making never a sound. He enters the room where his aged father lies sleeping. By means of the flashlight he finds the location of the bed and the still form upon it. The ax descends and the hot blood spurts forth on the murderer's hands and face. My God, how hot that blood is. It burns my hands like molten metal, yet I must go on.

"I must get into that next room and finish the job. Here lies Mother; her sweet, kindly face shows plainly in the little circle of light. Down comes that terrible ax and again the blood spurts forth, hotter this time, a thousand times than that of the father as it falls on his face and hands.

"But now I must rush on, thinks he. I have killed Father and Mother without jarring the beds. I can kill sister, Blanche, and Miss Kaempen while they sleep also. But hark, suppose one of them should awaken and flee—escape through the window, or scream. My God, I cannot think of that now. One blow and poor little Blanche's life is snuffed out like a candle flame.

"But what, Miss Kaempen is awake. She rises and struggles with the fiend. She feels his bloody hand and knows that she must fight for her life. Ah, what a struggle, once, twice, thrice. At the third blow the ax cleaves her skull, and with a groan she sinks to the floor."[298]

Wall detailed the wiring of the clock, the covering the bodies with oil, and Ray's rush back to town in a frenzy. "The very heavens were streaked with blood. The clear moon, riding high in the sky is gory while the stars seem to be drops of blood, saying, 'We know your crime …' The branches of the trees look like demons ready to reach down and grab him …

"Shall we stand and not deliver this man to justice? The safety of your homes, your wives, your children depends on giving this man justice. Look

---

[298] *Journal*, April 19, 1913.

there, against the sky is a great scaffold and the hangman's noose. Far back and towering far above it are the still shadowy forms of those four poor murdered souls, while above I see the words, 'Justice, Justice, Justice,' and the hand of God Almighty pointing at the noose."

# Chapter 26

~

# The Verdict

## Saturday, April 19, 1913

After wrangling over final instructions to the jury, the case was given into the hands of the twelve men on April 19, 1913, at three twenty-five in the afternoon, and the courtroom cleared.

At six thirty that same evening a verdict was agreed upon.

At seven forty-five that evening it was read to the court.

When the sheriff came to escort Ray back to the courtroom to hear his fate, the boy said simply, "All right," the very same words he had uttered at the time of his arrest. He entered the courtroom from the deputy's room a mere fifteen minutes before the jury filed in. Ray sat flanked by Emery Lancaster on his right and George Govert on his left. Fred Wolfe and Rolland Wagner were at the State's table, facing the bench.

The courtroom that had been packed beyond capacity for the trial was now nearly deserted. Only the attorneys, officers of the court, and a few newspapermen made up the scant audience. The two Kaempen men were the sole relatives present.

Amid terrible suspense, the verdict was solemnly handed by the foreman to the bailiff and then passed to the judge and then to the clerk. The hush was dreadful.

Ray Pfanschmidt sat unmoved while clerk Erde Beatty read the verdict. Guilty!

While others present at the time sat almost breathless, the youthful defendant seemed perhaps the most indifferent man in the room. When the clerk read the second half of the verdict, which fixed the penalty at death, there was not the least sign of a tremor from the defendant. Ray's habitual mask remained in place for the time being, but it would slip away later in the dark despair of his cell. Then the other residents of the jail would report hearing sobs from the convicted boy's cell for two nights running.

Bitter disappointment was displayed on the face of Govert and to a lesser extent, Lancaster.

A pin dropped on the floor at the time the verdict was read could have been heard in the farthermost recesses of the room. The attorneys for the defendant for a moment were dumbfounded. The silence was only broken when Govert arose and said, "If the court please, we enter a motion for a new trial." Judge Williams, after thanking the jurors briefly for their work, announced that he would hear arguments on May 6.

The *Journal* reached some of Ray's relatives by phone. No one would say anything, except C. C., Ray's "dear old grandfather," who was quoted as saying, "May God have mercy on that boy's soul."

The prosecution was elated, basking in the guilty verdict, sure that justice had been done and Ray would hang. The stubborn defense team had other ideas. The judge set a date about three weeks distant to hear arguments concerning the appeal.

Ray, meanwhile, was led back into the familiar, desolate gloom of the jail.

# Section III

# Days of Defeat and Strategy

# Chapter 27

# Justice Revisited—Verdict Reversed

## April 1913–October 1914

There was no good news for Ray when his hearing for a new trial concluded. Since Judge Williams, the presiding judge from the original case would also hear the motions for retrial, it was unlikely from the start that the defense could convince him that he had made errors only a new trial could remedy. As he had done repeatedly, the judge denied all defense petitions. Sentencing was set to be pronounced in July, and the boy would be executed within twenty-five days of that date.

In the way things have of going from bad to worse, by the end of May Ray's troubles deepened. Given the death sentence he was living under, it probably didn't matter too much when prosecuting attorney Wall and his private employer, Mr. Kaempen, brought suit against Ray's inheritance.

The suit claimed that since he was guilty of murdering his parents and sister, Ray was not entitled to inherit the farmland, and they asked the court to partition the farm, which was held and deeded in two legal parcels. The suit would leave Ray only one half of the parcel of eighty-four acres, which was granted directly to him upon the death of his mother (through the estate of his maternal grandfather). The second half of the parcel, consisting of forty-two acres, would have gone to Ray's sister,

357

Blanche. With Ray's conviction, the attorneys claimed that parcel now reverted to C. C. Pfanschmidt, paternal grandfather, along with all the rest of the acreage.

In a further convolution of things, C. C. quitclaimed his forty-two acre share of that parcel to attorney Wall, and Wall in turn had quitclaimed two thirds of that share to his employer, Kaempen. The remaining one third of this share would be sold to pay Wall's fees for the case. In addition, there were eleven other living Pfanschmidt and Abel relatives that the suit claimed were each entitled to one eleventh of the remaining land.

Ray had already mortgaged the contested land in the amount of $8,000 and paid the money in equal halves to his defense lawyers and to Uncle Fred Pfanschmidt, Ray's guardian at the time. Now the court must decide who actually inherited the land and if Ray had mortgaged property he did not own.

While the land case dragged on, the time for Ray's official sentencing on his murder conviction arrived in July 1913. It was erroneously reported in the area that Ray would hang in July, but in fact this was the time at which Judge Williams would officially pronounce the death sentence and fix the execution date.

On July 12, the Reeder family—Daniel, Esther, and daughter-in-law Mrs. Hugh Reeder—departed Quincy for Spokane, Washington. In an effort to spare Esther the awful prospect of being in the city when Ray was hanged, Daniel took her West. He announced plans to remain for the winter well away from the furor.[299]

July was also the time the defense would begin the appeal process with a filing to the Illinois State Supreme Court. Their brief was ready to be submitted and would ensure that Ray lived at least a few months longer. Local barristers were supremely confident that the guilty verdict would stand—that the trial had been error free and that the Illinois Supreme Court would refuse to hear the case.

Meanwhile, at sentencing, Ray stood straight-backed before the bench and looked Judge Williams directly in the eye. When asked if he had

---

[299] *Journal,* July 12, 1913.

anything to say, he replied clearly, "I am innocent—not guilty of this charge." It was the clearest and most potent denial he had made to date.

And it came very, very late!

Judge Williams reiterated from the bench that Ray had received a fair trial and a just verdict. He then set the execution date for October 18 between ten o'clock in the morning and four o'clock in the afternoon and ended with the traditional words, "May God have mercy on your soul."

The *Journal* reported that Ray blushed slightly when the death sentence was passed and began a "hasty conversation with his aunt, Mrs. Cook, who was the only relative present ... the slight coloring soon passed from his face as he talked to his aunt. He smiled frequently and there was nothing about him to indicate that the death sentence has just been pronounced ..."[300]

Two days after the verdict, an article appeared in the *Journal* telling of prisoners in the jail singing to entertain themselves. On this particular day, July 10, the vocals continued all morning and into the afternoon. The songs "with something in that resembled harmony" could be heard over the entire courthouse square and included, "The Trail of the Lonesome Pine." Ray did not sing. "Pfanschmidt takes no part in the singing at all, but he is a mightily good listener. Pfanschmidt absorbs every sound made by the other prisoners and appears to enjoy immensely the singing of the others. Whether he would like to sing or not is not known. But it is known that the indifferent attitude which he assumes when led into the courtroom is discarded in the cell for his original nature."[301]

A month later, the inmates of the jail were again mentioned in an article, reflecting longingly about the coolness of the cells in contrast to the sweltering heat Quincy suffered in August. Ray, back in solitary, was at least spared the "grilling" by detectives that regularly occurred before his trial. The only visitors he was allowed were family, and they visited rarely. Otherwise he was kept in isolation.

Also, in August, another rarity occurred. The Quincy jail, for the first time in its history, held three men charged with murder. Along with Ray, the

---

[300] *Journal,* July 8, 1913.
[301] *Journal,* July 10, 1913.

jail held Henry Mapes, wanted for a murder at Meyer, Illinois, and James Robinson, charged with killing William Sheehan at Marblehead.[302]

By September it was apparent that the execution of Ray's sentence would not occur as scheduled. The wily defense attorneys were waiting until the last possible moment, which was October 8, the day the Supreme Court convened, to file their appeal brief. The timing of such a late filing ensured that the court would not be able to examine the case until its winter session. Illinois law provided that a man could not be hanged while appeal was pending, so until the court could consider and rule on whether it would hear the case, Ray remained safe from the noose.

The *Journal's* opinion was this: "Well-versed lawyers who followed the trial of Pfanschmidt do not consider him [having] the least chance of securing a new trial. They hold that the decisions of Judge Guy Williams in every point at issue came as near being perfect as is possible for the most astute lawyer to make."[303]

Ray reached his one-year anniversary in the jailhouse as his appeal was filed. As his hanging date arrived and passed, the newspapers filled with optimistic opinions that the verdict would stand. Then, in a glimmer of hope for Ray, the Illinois High Court agreed to hear his case.

In November, the lawsuit concerning the distribution of the farm came before the court, and Govert appeared to argue on Ray's behalf. He rightly stated that "State laws allow the property to descend to the son regardless of conviction of a crime for this purpose."[304] Govert prevailed. His argument was the basis for a verdict that prevented the partition of the farm and gave it all to Ray.

But the other side would not go quietly. They copied a page from Govert's game plan and immediately appealed the decision, backed by Ray's grandfather. This appeal would also go before the Illinois Supreme Court.

Ray spent his second Thanksgiving behind bars, thankful to be alive, while his attorneys prepared to argue for his life before the state's highest

---

[302] *Whig*, August 6, 1913.
[303] *Journal*, September 27, 1913.
[304] *Whig*, November 5, 1913.

court. In early December, as arguments were finally scheduled, the *Whig* blasted the headline "Pfanschmidt Case Set for Unlucky 13th."[305]

According to procedure, each side would have one hour to present arguments before the high court. State's Attorney Wolfe would lead the prosecution assisted by Wall, while Govert and Lancaster would split the other hour between them. The defense alleged in their lengthy brief that there were many errors in the trial, including not allowing the change of venue; admitting improper evidence such as that of the bloodhounds and the bloody dollar bill; the testimony of Ray's grandfather, which should have been inadmissible; and the use of statements Ray made to detectives under duress. In all, they had provided to the court a brief of 276 pages listing contested evidence and issues.

When the thirteenth arrived, State's Attorney Wolfe unexpectedly refused to argue the case—at all! He would later claim this was a strategy based on advice from the Illinois attorney general. The effect of this decision was to limit the defense to a single thirty-minute time period in which to present its case. As both the other lawyers, Govert and Wall, were unable to attend this session, Lancaster alone made the eloquent argument on behalf of the defendant.

In the courtroom Wolfe sat mute and watchful.

A decision was expected to be rendered by the court in February 1914. Meanwhile, Ray spent his second Christmas in jail, eating a dinner cooked by Sheriff Lipps's mother. Arthur J. Roy, assistant attorney general of Illinois and former Quincyan stopped in town to reassure the local folks that the court would uphold the original verdict. Meanwhile, Ray's other case, the suit to partition the farm was also making its slow way through the supreme court's appeal process. It was about a month behind Ray's more pressing matter.

On February 18, 1914, an article appeared in the *Whig* speculating about the ruling on Ray's appeal, which was expected shortly. The reporter pronounced that only the governor, Edward Dunning, could save Ray now by commuting his sentence of execution to one of life in prison. The hanging would likely take place in March, with Sheriff Lipps doing

---

[305] *Whig*, December 2, 1913.

the honors and pulling the trap. And in the paper's opinion, unless Ray confessed, the Pfanschmidt name would forever carry a stain.

Quincy was rocked on Saturday, February 21, by strong and unexpected words from the highest court in the State and discovered that Ray had been granted a new trial. The supreme court opinion, written by Justice Carter, listed seven errors as the basis for the decision. Beyond that, the ruling included wording which seemed to say that though there was enough evidence to hold Ray for trial, the application of a death sentence was not justified in this case. "The evidence, in our judgment is of such a character that the cause was properly submitted to the jury, but it fell short of justifying this verdict regardless of the errors heretofore considered."[306]

Ray, as always, presented a calm front when given the news. In an interview by the *Whig*, he was quoted as saying, "I knew from the start that I had not received a fair trial at the hands of the jury, for I am innocent of the crime as sure as there is a God above. I have all confidence in the world in my attorneys and am sure that all will turn out right in the end. Of course I am happy. Who wouldn't be when the gallows were looking you in the face? I am getting fat on the feed by the sheriff, and the decision will not make me sleep a bit better. I have never enjoyed better health and sweeter sleep."

Ray's grandfather was of an entirely different mind. In the same article, C. C. was quoted as saying, "I am not in a position to say whether I still believe the boy guilty of the terrible crime, and I do not want anything in the papers about me. I have never been to see Ray Pfanschmidt since he was arrested, and I do not want to see him now."

Govert and Lancaster reported feeling vindicated, convinced of Ray's innocence and confident of reaching a verdict of acquittal in the next trial. Wall was said to be surprised but unwilling to be part of any future trial. The other prosecutors reported they would begin at once to prepare for a new contesting of the charges. The only major figure who said nothing in public was Esther. She remained at home, guarded by her father. Speculation was that she was still "sweet" on Ray, but there was no confirmation.

---

[306] *Journal*, February 21, 1914.

But not all was settled by the ruling. The wording of the high court opinion was ambiguous and open to interpretation as to whether the court meant that the verdict was not justified by the evidence so Ray should have been found not guilty, or whether the defendant was guilty but the evidence did not justify the death penalty.[307] In either interpretation, the countryside was outraged.

Wolfe applied to the high court for clarification. There was no appeal of a decision handed down by the supreme court, but the State's attorney could and did request a review of the matter.

By March, Wolfe was asking the Adams County supervisors to appoint a second attorney to aid him in the retrial of Ray's murder charges. Wall was standing firm in his unwillingness to be part of a second trial, and Wolfe argued that since the next would take place out of town, it was impossible for him and his assistant to both be away while still attending to the duties of his office. Wall had carried the bulk of responsibility in the first trial, which weighed heavily in Wolfe's mind along with the fact that Wall's substantial salary had been covered privately by the Kaempens and so spared the city expense.

The county supervisors were already looking at ever-mounting costs in litigating this matter and seemed unwilling to commit more taxpayer money. The mandate for a change in venue would at least double and perhaps increase by three or four times the cost of a trial that had already set county records, reaching between $7,000 and $8,000 thus far.

Meanwhile, the local rumor mill ramped up its output. One of the wilder conjectures was that the defense would admit that Ray *was* at the farm on Friday but got there before his parents arrived home, and finding the place empty returned to Quincy for the night.[308] Then, on March 8, the *Whig* reported that there was a physician from the Payson area who saw the Pfanschmidt family on their way home from Payson that night, and also met and spoke with Ray on his way to the farm. This "star witness" was said to be waiting to appear at a new trial. These

---

[307] *Journal*, February 25, 1914.
[308] *Whig*, March 4, 1914.

newspaper stories did nothing to calm a countryside that was once again seething.

On March 4, 1914, the county supervisors finally voted to authorize a trial assistant for Wolfe. Everyone assumed and hoped it would be Wall, who was still out of town and out of communication. However, he returned to the city on March 17 and officially declined to be part of the second prosecution team. He would be difficult to replace.

This was also the week the circuit court adjourned its session and did so without Govert & Lancaster presenting their client's request for a change of venue. Even though mandated by the supreme court, such a request had to be filed by the defendant before the machinery of justice could act upon it. And, since this type of request could only be handled by a criminal court, the failure to file meant that the next period a court would be able to deal with such a request would be in May 1914. The defense had successfully stretched the timeline yet again.

Notice was delivered this same week that the suit for the partition of Ray's inheritance was also slated for arguments in the May term of the Illinois Supreme Court.

On March 18, a forceful letter arrived at the offices of the *Whig* from Payson doctor E. J. Gabriel, refuting completely the idea that he had any evidence to offer, and decrying the fact that friends and acquaintances were taking him to task for withholding evidence. He, being the only doctor in Payson, stated emphatically "that the article is without foundation in fact.… I know nothing about the purported facts as published in your paper. I make this statement and trust you will find space in your valued paper to give this statement due publication." And so they did.[309]

Ray, meanwhile, had become a prolific letter writer from jail. When Harvey Scott of Cottrell Hardware married Miss Winona Gill, Ray took the time to send them his best wishes. The Scotts must have shown the letter about, for the *Whig* article said, "Ray writes [in] a pretty hand, and the letter does not show the least signs of nervousness."[310] It did show that

---

[309] *Whig*, March 18, 1914.
[310] *Whig*, March 19, 1914.

he was keeping up with events outside his jail cell. It was not known if Esther was allowed to correspond with Ray, but it seemed unlikely that her father would allow any such communication after his guilty verdict.

As scheduled, arguments were made before the Illinois Supreme Court attempting to reverse the ruling of Judge Albert Akers, who had determined that Ray was entitled to inherit under the current state law—even if he had killed his family for that very reason!

The first anniversary of Ray's conviction had now also passed quietly. The *Whig* said that Ray was a favorite within the jail and had become a "strong friend of Sheriff Lipps and the attaches."[311]

In late April 1914, the supreme court turned down Wolfe's request to modify its ruling on the murder case but did change somewhat, the wording of that ruling. The court removed all general opinions about bloodhound evidence and limited its ruling to only this trial. It also removed some opinions written about the judge, and most tellingly, the court removed the final imprecise statement that said the verdict had not been supported by the evidence. Nonetheless, the court's ruling stood that a new trial should be granted.[312]

Things were getting serious and somewhat nasty as the prosecution geared up once again. On May 23, Wolfe brought evidence before the Adam's County Grand Jury seeking to indict Henry Geisel for perjury based on his testimony at Ray's trial. The charge involved that conversation reported by Walter Heidbreder, in which Geisel was said to have discussed the fact that Charles Pfanschmidt asked Geisel to speak with Ray about his poor financial habits. Geisel had denied, under oath, that the conversation took place.

Word of the coming indictment had leaked because Geisel was prepared and in the courtroom with his attorneys, Govert and Lancaster. He was released on his own recognizance. Wolfe had served notice of his intent to secure a guilty verdict even before the next trial could begin.[313]

---

[311] *Whig*, April 19, 1914.
[312] *Journal*, April 28, 1914.
[313] *Whig*, May 23, 1914.

In a curious side note, one of the jurors who had originally convicted Ray was himself arrested in early June for beating his wife. Charles Aldag was fined ten dollars in costs and assigned to a probation officer.[314] His wife "told a sad story of mistreatment.... She alleges that he has not been providing food sufficient for her sustenance. She declares that for two days she was forced to subsist on two slices of dry bread. Mr. Aldag denies this and says that he has provided liberally for his family. He said in his defense that his wife was weakly and not able to eat much."

At last, in change of venue hearing on June 8, 1914, Judge Albert Akers's ruling sent the Pfanschmidt case to Macomb for retrial. This hearing was the first time Ray had been out of the jail or seen the sun since his sentencing in July 1913. Ray, as always, managed to look dapper in a freshly starched shirt and his blue serge suit. The crowd in the courtroom was small and mostly female.

A *Journal* reporter checked the record of murder trials held in McDonough County, Illinois, where Macomb was situated, and judged the prospects favorable for the defendant. The little courthouse, built in 1869, had been the site of fourteen murder trials. Of these, two defendants were granted a change in venue; four were acquitted outright; one escaped, never to be caught; and seven were convicted. Of the seven found guilty, only one was sentenced to hang, and his sentence was later commuted to life in prison. The others received sentences ranging from five years to life. Certainly the prospects there seemed better for Ray.[315]

By the first of September, the populace was speculating whether Adams County would be the site of Ray's hanging if he was again found guilty. But that privilege had been lost along with the change of venue. Even if found guilty, Quincy would no longer be the location of Ray's gallows.

This month, the grand jury from McDonough County, as a legal formality, came to Quincy to visit Ray, who was ordered to be turned over to the Macomb sheriff on September 19. The State's attorney served Govert and Lancaster with a list of 111 potential witnesses against the

---

[314] *Journal*, June 2, 1914.
[315] *Journal*, August 21, 1914.

young man. In spite of this, it was expected that the next trial would take less time than the first one.

On September 29, 1914, the second anniversary of the tragedy quietly passed.

In October, the local papers began a campaign for readership loyalty during the second trial. The *Whig* claimed a slight edge, as their man "Pat" Keefe was the only reporter who had covered the tragedy from its beginning.[316] Ray had a subscription to the *Whig* sent to him in the Macomb jail.[317]

Wolfe, Bennett, and Wagner for the State and Govert and Lancaster, the defense team, met with Judge Harry Waggoner, who would preside over the case, and settled on October 6 as the start date for the trial in Macomb. The Bennett who was assigned to assist Wolfe also served as an Illinois state fire marshal in the same department as Mr. Bogardus, whose actions had created such difficulties in the first trial.

---

[316] *Whig*, October 1, 1914.
[317] *Whig*, October 6, 1914.

# Chapter 28

# The Second Trial

## October, 1914

Ray's second trial for the murder of his sister, Blanche, would proceed more swiftly and in a more professional manner than the previous one. In important ways that first trial provided a dress rehearsal that pointed out the pitfalls and problems needing to be addressed by both sides. The Illinois Supreme Court, by pruning the evidence allowed, saved innumerable arguments between the attorneys and shortened the amount of testimony, even with new witnesses.

Both sides had honed and refined their arguments, and some unexpected angles appeared. Animosity between the attorneys ran high on the courtroom floor, and points were hotly contested. Wolfe again elected to take a secondary role in the actual interrogation of witnesses, delegating this time to a Macomb attorney, Hainline, hired to assist in the case.[318]

The Macomb courtroom was less than one third the size of the previous venue and had room for only two hundred spectators. Judge Waggoner would not allow onlookers to stand, so the number of seats determined

---

[318] There is no official transcript of these proceedings available, which forced reliance on newspaper reports. Trial transcripts were only retained when an appeal was filed. No appeal was filed in this case.

the size of the audience. The warm October made the temperature in the crowded room almost unbearable, and the first juror selected collapsed from the heat. He had to be taken out into the cooler air to recover.

It wasn't long before the first scandal of the trial, involving Walter Bennett, the current fire marshal and Wolfe's assistant, hit the papers. Bennett had dispatched Deputy Fire Marshal D. N. Balzer to the Macomb area to canvas the locality. It was claimed that he was aiding the prosecution in seating a jury that would hang Ray. Bennett staunchly denied exploiting his office to aid the State.

By October 10, 1914, the jury was seated, and the trial could begin. It had taken fewer days, but an even larger pool of prospects to empanel this jury. A man's unwillingness to apply the death penalty on purely circumstantial evidence or the holding an opinion about Ray's guilt or innocence were the major impediments to being accepted. All the men eventually selected were from outlying areas of the county; all but two were farmers; all but two were married; and they ranged in age from twenty-one to fifty-eight years. None lived in major cities or represented business interests.

One crucial procedural difference, requested by the defense team and agreed to by the State, was to ban prospective witnesses from the courtroom until after they had testified. The defense was worried that hearing others testify would change their stories.

On the very day the State presented its opening remarks, prosecuting attorney Bennett appeared in chambers before Judge Waggoner to confess that he had, in fact, been using his deputy fire marshal to aid in jury selection. Since no official charge of jury tampering or illegal activities had been made, the judge dismissed the issue. There was nothing for him to rule on.[319] This incident clearly indicated the lengths to which the State was willing to go to gain a conviction. And it did lend credence to the defense's contention that those lengths might even include evidence tampering.

Wolfe delivered the opening remarks for the State, laying out the same scenario as before. His oratory stepped into "dangerous ground"

---

[319] *Whig*, October 10, 1914.

when he quoted a conversation that had been banned by the supreme court verdict, and the defense leaped to its feet with shouted objections. The court advised Wolfe to save this line of argument for testimony rather than opening remarks.[320]

This time the defense did not elect to waive its opening remarks. Lancaster made a powerful opening statement, perhaps learning from the previous proceedings, or possibly because there was no longer a need to guard defense strategy.

Public sentiment was much different in the new venue. There were reports in the paper that a fistfight was narrowly averted between a Payson resident who had traveled to Macomb for the trial and a local from the host city. The Payson man stated in no uncertain terms that Ray was guilty, while the Macomb man held out that it hadn't been proven so. An invitation was extended for the Macomb man to venture to Quincy and express that opinion … and receive a beating. The Macomb man apparently decided the trip was unnecessary and offered to initiate things immediately. Bystanders separated the two.[321]

Ray too had changed and seemed more actively engaged this time around. He sat attentively, making copious notes on a tablet, watching the speaker or the jury to see what reactions he could read. He held whispered consultations with his attorneys, but his usual posture was still relaxed, tilted back in his chair with one knee propped up against the defense table.

On the first Sunday of the trial, the jurors were taken to services at the First Presbyterian Church, where the minister had been requested to keep the topic clear of the court case. The sermon preached was about "Harvest Home." The sermon was an excellent one, but there was no pathos is it. In spite of that fact, however, three of the jurors seated directly in front of the pulpit wept like children. Many times they were required to use their handkerchiefs in an effort to stop the flow of tears that seemed to come spontaneously. It is believed that the men have taken keenly to heart the

---

[320] *Journal*, October 12, 1914.
[321] *Whig*, October 11, 1914.

responsibility that rests with them in this trial, and it is thought that the weight of that problem and not the service caused the tears. The other jurors sat quietly."[322]

On that same Sunday evening, Ray's spirits were unexpectedly lifted. Mrs. Joseph Eels "appeared at the office in the jail carrying a large bouquet of flowers, which she asked the sheriff to give to the prisoner. 'I thought that they might help to brighten his cell a little.' Ray was pleased. 'Someone has a kind thought for me,' was his comment."[323] The *Whig* further said that the woman was a "young widow," and the flowers were roses tied with pink ribbons and the stems wrapped in tinfoil. Ray was either a handsome, fresh-faced villain or a brave victim facing his accusers. In any event, he retained his appeal for the ladies.

The jurors were housed in less comfortable quarters and sent a request for more blankets for their cots, plus additional towels. Only one towel had been provided for the use of the twelve jurors plus the two deputies assigned to them.[324]

On Monday the courtroom was full, and the Pfanschmidt story again began to unfurl from the witness box. Testimony quickly moved through the appearance of the family on Friday evening in the village of Payson: all seemed well, everyone healthy. Timeframes were explored, and the fire was described, along with the grim discovery of the bodies.

Testimony for the State seemed powerful, as new witnesses offered their words. Henry Echternkamp of Fall Creek Township testified that to his eye, the prints left by Ray's team leaving the fire scene matched the tracks protected in the barn lot. In his opinion Ray did not seem disturbed or grieving at the fire as he introduced Esther to people. Schoolteacher Margaret Spindler at the first trial, now Mrs. Tearney (a.k.a. Tourney), said she thought the driver of that buggy that looked like Ray's rig was leaning forward in order to hide his face as her buggy passed his that Friday night.

The telephone again played a large part. Caroline Wand testified that while listening in on the party line, she heard Ray tell his mother he

---

[322] *Journal*, October 12, 1914.
[323] Ibid.
[324] *Whig*, October 13, 1914.

would be home that Saturday night. Miss Roberta Whitcomb, the night telephone operator on that Saturday night shift, testified she was unable to raise the Pfanschmidt family for Mrs. Kaempen despite several tries.

Mrs. Rose Hood added to her previous testimony by saying that Ray not only denied his folks had been murdered Friday night but said that the stock had been fed on Saturday, and that Ray further denied that he had ever planned on coming home that night, avowing instead that he was going to visit his uncle for dinner. John Lier clarified his previous statement to say that Ray had told him to remove the barriers protecting the tracks "for they have new evidence and will not need this."

There were many choruses of "I don't remember" when witnesses were asked about their testimony at the first trial now nearly eighteen months ago. Conversely, the attorneys benefited from the record of that testimony. Some witnesses' stories had changed slightly, and the defense effectively used those variations to create confusion on cross-examination. Redirect questions often had to be asked to get a witness back on track for the State.

Among the first to testify were familiar names: Harvey Groce, George Wagner, Albert Lawrence, William Long, Iris Spencer, Henry Schreck, Ben Lier, and Moritz Lier. Court adjourned for the day when the last Lier brother finished on the stand.[325] It was half past five.

All the witnesses for the State's case had now assembled in Macomb and were required to report each morning to the court clerk so that their whereabouts were known. There was a waiting room and a bailiff manning the door, calling one to testify and alerting the next on the roster. In this way, the proceedings moved along smoothly. A second bailiff guarded the door to the audience section of the courtroom, asking everyone who approached if they were to testify, and denying entrance to any scheduled witness.

On Tuesday morning, October 13, the State dealt with the details of the estate and land values. Grandfather C. C. Pfanschmidt took the stand for only a quarter of an hour, as most of what he had said in the first trial was no longer admissible. Unfazed, the senior Mr. Pfanschmidt tried to

---

[325] *Journal*, October 13, 1914.

add more commentary but was thwarted by defense objections. The old grandfather's emotional impact was severely curtailed in this courtroom.

Ray's cousin Walter testified that Ray nudged the body of his father and said, "There ain't much left of the old man, is there?"[326] When asked on cross-examination, Walter did not remember the conversation where he told Lancaster that Ray had helped gather evidence at the fire. This was a desertion by a family member.

The State brought Fred Schnellbecker and Hiram Blivens to say that Ray pointed out and named the bodies before they had been removed from the ruins. This, said the State, showed that Ray must have known where they were lying before they were taken out and identified. Surely only the killer would have that information.

This day, Judge Waggoner adjusted the noon break. Jurors had complained that an hour and a half was insufficient time to walk to their boarding house, eat a meal, and return to their seats without undue haste. The court agreed to allow a two-hour lunch break and make up the time by continuing one half hour later in the evenings.[327]

Before court reconvened, the defense, in a strategic move, presented an affidavit to the court saying that Ray's grandfather was prejudicial to their case; that he was antagonistic; that he would be called as a material witness for the defense and should be banned from the courtroom until that time. In addition, it was alleged that he was not as enfeebled as he pretended and would predispose the jury against Ray. The State said they would present a counter affidavit by the next morning.

When testimony resumed, Walter Dingerson came to the stand and offered the most damaging evidence so far.[328] The defense was unable to shake Dingerson's conviction that the buggy he passed that Friday night was Ray's, as was the one that he later identified for Sheriff Lipps.

However, the defense did make up some ground when Edward Lawrence, a blacksmith in Payson said that the sizes of No. 2 horseshoes could differ, and that Curry, the other blacksmith involved in the

---

[326] *Whig,* October 14, 1914.
[327] *Journal,* October 14, 1914.
[328] *Whig,* October 13, 1914.

investigation, had lost the measurements he took of the tracks. The defense contended to the jury that if the measurements had matched, they would not have been "lost."

A new witness, Arthur Bolles, an employee at the worksite, testified that he saw Ray early on Saturday morning wearing a raincoat, blue serge pants, and low black shoes and that later Ray returned in a new khaki suit. John Harris also testified to Ray's relaxed demeanor at the fire and to the odd shape of the horseshoe.

John Kaufman, who testified at the first trial that he saw someone about the Pfanschmidt farm on Saturday, said he had "refreshed his memory" and realized that the day really was Friday. He hadn't seen anyone alive at the farm on Saturday after all.

In the "what did he wear when" debate, Gustav Hutmacher also put Ray in a blue serge suit on Saturday morning. He was reinforced by Silba Lawrence, another of Ray's employees. However, Lancaster demolished this testimony by reminding Lawrence of his previous sworn statement. He also got Lawrence to testify that there were no clothes in Ray's buggy when he rode into town with him on Friday night. But three people this day spoke of Ray dressed in the blue suit on Saturday morning instead of his regular khakis.

On Wednesday, Esther Reeder was called as a witness but refused to answer personal questions concerning her relationship with Ray. Her father, however, did answer. When asked if she was still wearing his diamond ring, he said firmly that Esther was wearing "no ring at all."[329] It was not certain to what extent her private thoughts and wishes matched those of her father.

On this same day, C. C. Pfanschmidt was barred from the courtroom and listed as a defense witness. The State did not have their counter affidavit ready to present, so Ray's grandfather had to remain absent from his prominent place sitting at the prosecution's table.

In an odd occurrence, the foreman of the first jury, S. G. Sparks, died at his home in Quincy. He had been delirious for several days, and stories

---

[329] *Journal*, October 14, 1914.

circulated saying he regretted the guilty verdict in his ravings. His family, however, denied these stories.[330]

By this point, the defense had scored several critical points in their effort to prove Ray's innocence or toward establishing what they considered to be irrefutable and reasonable doubt.

The first came from Dr. C. D. Center, who stated his opinion that "there could have been no blisters on the body of Mrs. Pfanschmidt if the murder was committed on Friday night. Blisters were found on the body of the mother." The doctor said that blisters could not form on a body that has been dead for more than eight hours. Since the State contended that the killings were done on Friday, this seemed to point to someone other than Ray as the person attempting to burn the bodies on Saturday, since Ray was accounted for in Quincy. The State was left to propose that the contraption of the clock, wires, and gasoline that Ray contrived on Friday night failed to work but had managed to create enough fire and heat to raise blisters on Mathilda's body.[331]

The second boon to the defense was Judge Waggoner's ruling that a driving test concocted by Sheriff Lipps would not be allowed into testimony. The good sheriff had found a buggy and two small horses and duplicated Ray's supposed route from the Reeders to the Pfanschmidt farm, including a thirty-minute stop there, before heading back to Twelfth and Broadway. This entire trip was supposedly accomplished in eighty-four minutes—a surprisingly short length of time that would nicely support the timeline proposed by the State. But the jury would not hear of it in this trial. There was no report on the condition the following day of the team that made in eighty-four minutes, a journey that normally took two and a half hours.

A third and the most beneficial occurrence for the defense was testimony concerning the clothing from the vault. Dr. Center stated that "one of the spots near the top of the right hip pocket was dye." Not blood at all. The physician provided professional collaboration for the defense assertion that those bloody clothes had been concocted by the State.[332]

---

[330] *Whig*, October 14, 1914.
[331] *Whig*, October 15, 1914.
[332] Ibid.

Center also said that the blood spots were very small and not what would be expected from an axe murder as bloody as the wounds on the bodies suggested. "Most of the blood spots were drop size."[333]

Systematically, the defense demonstrated changes in testimony, such as Ben Holeman, who this time testified that Ray was wearing a blue suit on Saturday morning, while at the first trial had said Ray was dressed in khaki. Ray's lawyers successfully revealed the unreliability of human memory and fervently hoped the jury would not hang a man on such inconsistent testimony.

The day began as a repetition of the first trial, with witnesses detailing finding of the clothes, Ray's purchase of the khakis, the discoveries of the oil can, the tire tracks, and horseshoe prints. The courtroom was taken through familiar evidence recounting the happenings at the fire.

Then drama returned to the courtroom. Dr. Knox testified that the body of Ray's father had been disassembled using first a knife and then a saw before being burned. The doctor explained that cut marks were obvious on the portion of the body protected from the fire, which remained "more baked than burned."[334] He named blows to the head as cause of the deaths, and said that the bodies bled before they were burned. Knox raised the horrifying possibility that at least one head may have been completely severed before burning, possibly referring to Mathilda, as her body had a portion of neck remaining, which could have exhibited cut marks.

Joe Eakins's testimony helped show that Ray was affected by grief. Eakins testified about the Sunday evening visit by Ray and Esther at his home. "[t]he defendant and his sweetheart remained about two hours, and during the conversation the prisoner at times smiled, talked freely, and was jovial, while at other times he appeared dazed and stared at the floor, only to recover himself and again take part in the conversation."[335]

Lancaster reinforced this more positive picture of Ray, presenting the trip to the Eakins house as a business necessity for continuity at the job site and not a social visit. The time spent was only while awaiting the return

---

[333] *Journal*, October 14, 1914.
[334] Ibid.
[335] *Whig*, October 15, 1914.

of Holeman, who lodged at the Eakins'. Ray was also shown to be fond of the Eakins' baby. How could you love children and still murder your parents? the defense was tacitly asking.

In the midst of this, Waggoner was having troubles of his own. The *Whig* reported that the jurist was unable to calmly view the pieces of bloody evidence. "Judge Harry Waggoner could not stomach the sight of the bloody clothes … and refrained from glancing at the garments and bed clothing that were taken from the ruins at the Pfanschmidt farm. The court sat with his back to the table where the exhibits were lying, and it was noticed that a paper was thrown over the articles, probably because the judge did not relish the idea of looking at them."[336]

It was undoubtedly a relief to the judge, as well as the defense, that the admission of the supposed bloody dollar bill had been banned from this trial.

Meanwhile, Esther was in the city awaiting her turn on the stand. "Standing in the office of the State's attorney shortly after the noon hour yesterday, Miss Esther Reeder, sweetheart of Ray Pfanschmidt, saw the prisoner being escorted to the courthouse down Jackson Street, and gazing in his direction with deepest sincerity she exclaimed, 'I wish I could take his place.'"[337]

The trial continued.

The State produced its star expert witness, Dr. Ludwig Hektoen of Chicago, on October 15. New information from his testimony about the blood tests revealed that he had only been given the bloodstains to examine in March 1913. He admitted that fresher samples would have yielded better and more accurate test results.

In another startling turnabout, Willis Seehorn now swore to the truthfulness of his previously disputed statement. In the first trial, Seehorn had refuted the signed statement, saying in effect that it was not accurate. Now, however, he proved a good witness for the defense, putting Ray in the sleeping tent at the worksite between midnight and 1:00 a.m. Friday.

---

[336] *Whig*, October 15, 1914.
[337] *Journal*, October 15, 1914.

And in a stunning coincidence, the *Journal* published verbatim an article from the Illinois Law Review of Northwestern University, written by John Henry Wigmore, "The best authority in this country and England on questions of evidence." This article explained why the bloodhound evidence was excluded from the second trial. The author revisited the events of the crime and included this damning statement: "The rest of the evidence against [Ray] consisted of numerous trifles, more or less significant but too flimsy to support a charge of murder." He went on to say, after recounting the actions of the dogs, "Can anyone rationally take that for evidence worth considering? It may be singular, it may be startling, it may be suggestive, but will anyone soberly maintain that it is evidence fit to persuade us to charge with a five-dollar theft, much more to charge him with murder? Why do we dismiss instantly such a valueless clue—popular though it be in public credulity? Because it is built upon a series of assumptions, full of insidious opportunities for error."[338]

Wigmore listed those opportunities for error, including the lack of scientific knowledge as to how a bloodhound scents; how confused the trail must have been by the hundreds of visitors; and the admission that the suspect being trailed had been over that same pathway earlier in the day. His final pronouncement was this: "Unless the trail set is that of a person already known, then at its very best the trailing discovers merely some thing once present at the scene of the act and discloses nothing as to the identity of the person."[339]

If, as Bogardus originally testified in the excluded evidence, the dog was trailing the horse, it does not determine the driver of the buggy, much less when that horse made that trail, or if either was associated with the crime under investigation. The newspaper ended by expressing satisfaction that this evidence had been discredited.

The jury was not allowed to read the newspapers, but the countryside devoured them.

The parade of State witnesses began with Daniel Reeder; moved on to Everett Clutch, who said again that Ray was not at his lunch stand on

---

[338] *Illinois Law Review,* quoted in the *Journal,* October 15, 1914.
[339] Ibid.

Friday; worked its way through Harvey Sprick, the banker; the Cottrell Hardware credit manager; and all the same witnesses still allowed by the supreme court decision.

But the State was not without its own surprises. A new prosecution witness, William Childers, said he saw and recognized Ray and his buggy and team at Twelfth and Broadway about 2:00 a.m. on either Friday or Saturday night of the fire weekend. His story added credence to the reported sighting by Archie Pape. Childers was a mechanic who had stayed until midnight at his shop near Fifth and Jersey, working on a car belonging to John A. Stillwell. Walking home, near Twelfth and Broadway about 2:00 a.m., he saw Ray's buggy coming north on Twelfth Street. Childers said he had known Ray to recognize him for years and that the buggy did not have the front rain curtain up. Archie Pape was then called to the stand to recount his story of seeing Ray late Saturday night.

The emotional climax of the State's case came at quarter till five on Friday, when Esther Reeder took the stand. "Miss Reeder, dressed in a pretty suit of plum color and wearing a hat trimmed with a plume of the same color ... answered to her name at 4:55 p.m.... Miss Reeder's step was firm and there was no outward sign of nervousness as she walked to the witness chair. Only while being questioned by attorneys did she grip a handkerchief nervously, and while waiting for questions, bit her lips."[340]

Ray watched her intently, and the paper said Esther "gave the defendant a sweet, friendly smile as she passed him when leaving the witness box." But it was noticed in the courtroom that when asked about her arrangement with Ray, she used the past tense. "We *were* engaged."

The others who said their piece that afternoon included George Vasen, proprietor of the electrical store, who said that if indeed the clockwork hands were wired together, no current could be formed and no fire could be started. It was another point for the defense.

Finally, after calling seventy-one witnesses to the stand, the State rested its case about 10:00 a.m. on October 16.

---

[340] *Journal*, October 16, 1914.

# Chapter 29

# He Surely Can't Be Guilty

### Friday, October 16, 1914

Ray sat quietly throughout the short recess; then the defense rose to present its case. The progress of this trial was three times faster than had been originally projected.[341]

The defense began by calling chief of police Koch, followed by Sheriff Joe Lipps and Mr. Reeder. When Esther took the stand for the defense this time, she and Ray exchanged smiles. Her testimony described a grief-stricken Ray who was affectionate with his family. She contributed a new bit of information, recalling that when she visited the Pfanschmidt farm two weeks before the fire, Ray and his father had discussed the purchase of an automobile.[342]

From there, the defense called a parade of witnesses who testified to facts and observances that were almost exactly counter to the State's witnesses. Rubber-tired buggy tracks and shoes with no odd calk impression were two of the major differences, along with good loving family relations and reasonable financial dealings on the part of Ray and his family. The timeline of the events was also contested.

---

[341] *Journal*, October 16, 1914.
[342] *Whig*, October 17, 1914.

Both Elmer Geisel and his father, Henry, were called to testify. Elmer saw some tracks in their lane on Saturday morning that could have been made by the buggy of a sleepy Ray on his way home on Friday night, but this assertion was demolished handily on cross. Henry Geisel was still under indictment on perjury charges stemming from his first trial testimony when he denied a conversation with Mr. Heidbreder, the banker. But in this trial, Geisel could not be asked about that conversation, nor the letter concerning Ray's overdraft since that evidence was disallowed by the supreme court ruling. Nevertheless, Geisel was very careful and nervous on the stand.[343]

There was one verdict on this day in Ray's favor. The Illinois Supreme Court upheld a lower court ruling that Ray was entitled to inherit the property from his family. The partition suit had been argued through two terms of the circuit court; however, there was no law in place governing such a situation and nothing to bar inheritance, even if the heir was convicted of murder. The ruling of the court was final and could not be appealed. Ray at least had the money to pay his attorneys. Indeed, he had already done so.[344]

Back at the murder trial, the first witness on Saturday promised fireworks. The crowd was the largest thus far, with more than five hundred disappointed people turned away from the packed courtroom. Extra deputies were required to keep order and extra chairs were added until they completely circled the counsel tables and judge's bench.

The day began with the defense calling Dr. Thomas B. Knox, who testified that Detective Young told him he'd "put one over on Dr. Center when he made the latter believe that blood spots were on the youth's clothing found in the vault on the Frese place; that the spots were ink and had been placed there by the detective."[345]

The line of questioning and potentially explosive answers about evidence contrived or tampered with was the occasion for a lengthy and vitriolic battle. In due course, on cross-examination by the State, the doctor said he had not told anyone about the conversation, "possibly because

---

[343] *Journal,* October 17, 1914.
[344] Ibid.
[345] Ibid.

he considered it all a joke." He further admitted he had met with Lipps and Bogardus in Quincy "this very week" about his testimony, and they advised him to say it was all a joke.[346]

No mention was made of exactly what form their "advice" took, or just how courageous Dr. Knox was to give this testimony, as he had to return to Quincy to live and practice medicine.

Grandfather C. C. Pfanschmidt made his displeasure felt by requiring his daughter, Mrs. Herr, to remain with him at the Pace Hotel instead of being available at the courthouse as a witness. When the defense called her name, a deputy had to be sent to fetch her. C. C. did not want to give Ray any aid or support, but his daughter did eventually appear and, as before, testified in Ray's favor.

Other witnesses testified without change from the first trial. Arthur Lund, a detective from Burns Agency in Chicago was called to dispute the lunch-stand owner's claim that Ray was not there on Friday night. Some headway was made in assigning the creation of the track in the barn lot at a time there had been mud, which was one week before the fire.

The Sunday edition of the *Whig* ran a story that mirrored the alteration of attitude apparent in this trial. The State was already planning to push the other murder indictments if Ray was found not guilty. They were beginning to discount their ability to gain a conviction. The article mourned the loss of evidence and the lack of John Wall's oratory, and claimed "the noose has been loosened from the defendant's neck." The defense, it was believed, had established reasonable doubt in the minds of the jurors about the supposed bloody clothes.[347]

Then more evidence came to light adding weight to the defense's theory that those bloody clothes were contrived evidence, manufactured by the authorities. The clothes had been wrapped in a piece of the *Quincy Daily Journal*—a paper the family did not take at the farm; nor did Ray subscribe to any paper at his work camp; nor did the Reeder family. The use of this particular paper as wrapping paper did not seem to connect to Ray.

---

[346] *Journal*, October 17, 1914.
[347] *Whig*, October 18, 1914.

On the day of Ray's testimony the small courtroom was overstuffed with people; even after the lunch break more than four hundred were still waiting in lines but were denied seats. There was little floor space left, even in front of the judge's bench. It was announced that the next morning, the doors of the court building would remain locked until 8:30 a.m. to aid in crowd control.

The defense had called eleven witnesses before Ray began testimony on his own behalf on the nineteenth of October 1914. It was time for the defendant to take center stage.

"Up from behind attorney Lancaster rose the young defendant, and with a firm step he walked to the witness chair. His hand never trembled as Judge Waggoner administered the oath, and calmly he seated himself in the witness chair. He was dressed in a blue serge suit, a white plaited shirt, and wore a black bow tie."[348] He was clean shaven and his hair was neatly trimmed, having been attended to in the jail by a local barber over the noon recess.

The crowd, without the advantage of raised or staggered seating, shifted and bobbed, trying to get a look at the defendant. In a clear voice Ray spoke about his movements, his business plans, his whereabouts, and his wardrobe. He detailed in a consistent and concise manner where he'd been and what he'd worn. He was on the stand this day for about an hour and a half, and the courtroom was quiet and intent on his words and demeanor.

The *Journal* reported that, "As he passed from the room, time and time again was the remark heard, 'He surely can't be guilty for he couldn't act and talk like that.'" Nothing disturbed Ray's calm on the stand or betrayed the presence of any nerves at all.

On the second day of Ray's testimony, the crowd was again more than the room could hold, and there was much jostling. One woman fainted, and another was literally pulled out of her shoe in the crush. Two other women engaged in a hair-pulling contest for a place in the room and had to be separated.

---

[348] *Journal*, October 20, 1914.

The Macomb paper reported that there was much local sentiment for an acquittal or at least a hung jury and reminded their readers that the same sentiment was abroad in the populace when Ray was declared guilty at the first trial. In any event, this proceeding would not be the end of the situation, as the indictments for the murders of his mother, father, and Miss Kaempen were still pending. The paper quoted Govert as saying that in the event of a hung jury the trial would be held again in Macomb. "The State cannot ask for a change from this county and the defense won't," were his terse words.[349]

The paper also reported that another woman, Mrs. A. E. Nash, had sent Ray a bouquet of beautiful nasturtiums and dahlias to show her support. Mrs. Nash reflected the sentiment that the paper stated so well. The puzzle was this: "Could he have planned his story, drilled it into his mind until every detail was so real that it would withstand the terrific hammering to which it was subjected? That is a point on which public opinion differs and only one person knows in this case, and that is the defendant himself."[350]

With his story still intact, Ray was excused from the stand at 5:00 p.m. on October 20, 1914, after more than five hours of testimony.

By Wednesday, October 21, the *Macomb Daily Journal* said "bitter public opinion" had influenced the first verdict, and, "Public opinion, like a great tidal wave, is erratic, irresponsible, and irrepressive. Public opinion was responsible for the crucifixion, the greatest of all crimes, and since time was counted it has been the foundation for wrongs without number.... Public opinion in Adams county was bitter against the defendant; the officers recognized it and catered to it.... And now, like a great tidal wave, public opinion has changed ... part of this is due to a belief that some of the evidence against the boy was manufactured at the former trial; the axe, with which the crime was alleged to have been committed was produced at the former trial, but not at this trial, for the reason that it looked too much like manufactured evidence, whether rightly so or not."[351]

---

[349] *Macomb Daily Journal*, October 20, 1914.
[350] Ibid.
[351] *Macomb Daily Journal*, October 21, 1914.

Court convened at nine o'clock for last-minute details and testimony, but by eleven o'clock both sides had concluded. Closing arguments began at eleven fifteen.

Bennett began the State's closing arguments, defending the admissibility of circumstantial evidence, citing law, and quoting cases that admitted shoe tracks and circumstantial evidence and ended with convictions. He paced back and forth in front of the jury as he built his case and tore down the defense. He finished at five thirty, garnering great reviews for sincerity. "The people of the State of Illinois may rest well assured that the duty delegated to attorney Bennett was well and fully performed."[352] Compared to reviews of the closing statements in the first trial, this seemed faint praise indeed.

Through it all, Ray "sat behind his counsel, seemingly as unconcerned as though he was but an uninterested spectator, instead of the one to whom the words of accusation were addressed."[353]

Public opinion seesawed as the two sides analyzed, explained, and justified their respective cases. The State reviewed evidence, lauded Esther, and was understanding about the Pfanschmidt family wanting to protect—untarnished—the family name. Bennett thanked God for sending the rain that made the tracks, and he defended the State's case. "Save the Family Name… this is why the uncles and aunts are trying to save this defendant—and I don't blame them. It is proper to do this to a certain extent, but beyond that, they transgress upon the laws of justice and of God."[354]

Govert took the floor promptly at 9:00 a.m. on Thursday. He ridiculed the idea that money was adequate motive for a son to murder a father, especially a father who had always backed that son. He declared there was no chance the charge of murder had been proven; in fact, the only thing the State could hope to obtain was an arson charge, but that was not true either. He became indignant at the cold, indifferent portrait of Ray painted by the State. He accounted for the clothing, named Young as the planter of

---

[352] *Journal*, October 22, 1914.
[353] Ibid.
[354] Ibid.

contrived evidence in the vault, and claimed the true object of the family was not to save the family name but to "save our innocent boy."

Govert spoke for only two and a half hours, an unusually brief time for him.

After lunch, attorney Hainline took up the prosecution's case. He denied tainted evidence and returned to motive, naming Ray as the only person to gain from this crime; he recounted the timeframe; pointed out discrepancies in the defense account; and argued that the family, by coming here, were not proclaiming Ray's innocence but trying to keep a skeleton out of the family closet. Battling a cold, he was still forceful and methodical in his review of the case.

On Friday, the twenty-third, court resumed a bit late because a juror had been "suffering for the past several days with stoppage of the bowels. His condition this morning was such that it was thought for a while court could not convene, but he recovered sufficiently to take his place in the jury box with the other eleven men."[355] The prospect of losing a juror at this late hour was too dreadful to contemplate.

About 9:40 a.m. court began, and by four o'clock Hainline was finished and Emery Lancaster began for the defense. The courtroom was filled to overflowing with a crowd waiting to hear Lancaster's oratory. He obliged by shredding the State's arguments while keeping close to the facts. Lancaster listed evidence referenced by the State but not provided in the trial, including the crude tracing of the horseshoe and the paraffin casts made after being fitted with the shoe from Ray's mare. He impeached the State's witnesses, decried their version of motive, and accounted for all of Ray's clothing. He pleaded persuasively for justice for the young man.

As the *Journal* reported, "For an hour and a half, at which time court adjourned for the day, he kept the audience spellbound with his wonderful flow of oratory and the keen logic and earnestness of his plea. For one hour and a half Mr. Lancaster, with arms extended toward the jurors, head thrown back, and perspiration streaming down his forehead, pleaded with the twelve men who sat in judgment ..."

---

[355] *Macomb Daily Journal*, October 23, 1914.

Lancaster reminded jurors that under the law Ray was considered innocent from the moment the trial began and must be proven guilty. He hammered the circumstantial evidence not on its legality but on its lack of weight. "Mere suspicion will not do. There must be a chain woven link by link, and welded so strong that there is no weakness in them as single units or taken in its entirety. When you find that chain of evidence so strong, gentlemen, then and then only, will you have the right to lay aside the presumption of innocence and return a verdict of guilty."[356]

Even as Lancaster was speaking, a *capias*[357] was delivered to the local sheriff, assuring that Ray would be immediately rearrested in the event of a "not guilty" verdict on the charge of murdering his sister. The State was hedging its bets.

After Lancaster finished, defense attorney Flack spoke. "Flack always rated high as a pleader before a jury, was at his best and in a voice of thunder he scored the officials of Adams County and the detectives who have assisted the State in the preparation of this case. With his face as pale as death and with a voice that fairly shook with anger, he denounced the sheriff, the State's attorney, and the other officials of Adams County for what he termed the 'persecution' of the defendant."[358]

Flack built up Ray's character, citing his business respectability and clean living. He asked the jurors to remember times they themselves had been so stunned they couldn't cry but wished they could. He accused the officials of planting the bloody clothes. He eloquently reminded the jurors of the weight of their responsibility and the lives that hung on their decision.

The local lawyer rallied the Macomb men to indignation speaking of the ill treatment the Macomb witness had received at the hands of the prosecution. He said the jury had a right to resent how "Honest Dutch Joe," the horseshoer, had been sneered at and misquoted by the prosecution. He labeled it a "damnable conspiracy" to convict Ray and declared that the marks of it were plain. Flack accused Wolfe of knowing

---

[356] *Journal,* October 24, 1914.
[357] The literal meaning is "that you take." Several writs and processes commanding the defendant be taken into custody are known by this term.
[358] *Journal,* October 24, 1914.

that Young planted the bloody suit of clothes, causing Wolfe to jump to his feet in angry objection.

Finally, Judge Waggoner admonished Flack for going too far. Flack, undeterred, switched his attack to Mr. Kaempen, employer of private investigator Young, and accused him of knowing about the planted evidence. Flack said of Ray, "If there was ever a thing that showed his innocence clearly, it is the strength and health given him by the Almighty to withstand the taunts and jeers of his former friends and neighbors throughout these past two years. Only one thing has kept him from breaking under the strain of it, and that is his innocence."[359]

The aid of the Almighty was claimed by both sides in this case—with conflicting expectations.

Attorney Wolfe spoke last for the prosecution, his presentation interrupted numerous times by defense objections. On each occasion Judge Waggoner allowed Wolfe to proceed, and Wolfe soldiered on. "People who have heard him talk before say that today's plea was by far the most masterful and scholarly that he ever made."[360] Compared to the accolades given the other speakers, this seemed paltry praise.

Wolfe attempted to punch holes in the defense's timeline and show Ray unaccounted for on Friday night for two hours. He tried to boost the State's credibility, claiming that if the State witnesses were lying about their timelines it would have been foolish not to have made a more effective story.

Wolfe pleaded for justice, hammered on the evidence, and claimed any dye spots found had bled from the red string necktie found with the clothes. He maligned Dr. Knox for not coming forward sooner, if indeed his story was even true. He systematically refuted the defense assertions point by point.

His last words to the twelve men of the jury were, "We selected you because we thought you would do the square thing, not only to the people but also to the defense. It is not Adams County that is trying to take the life of this boy, but it is the great State of Illinois. After hearing the instructions,

---

[359] *Journal*, October 24, 1914.
[360] Ibid.

and you are convinced this is the man who struck the fatal blow to Blanche Pfanschmidt, then it is your duty to inflict the extreme penalty."[361]

The judge read a few short instructions, and the jury retired. They were instructed to deliberate until ten o'clock on Saturday night, take Sunday off if they had not reached a decision, and begin again on Monday.

Eventually, after twelve ballots, at 10:45 a.m. on Monday, October 26, 1914, the jury returned their verdict: "Not Guilty."

The twelve men polled eight to four for acquittal on the first ballot, and fewer than forty-nine hours after being sent to deliberate, they were agreed. After setting the record for highest attendance at any local trial, there are only six spectators in the courtroom to hear the decision. The defendant himself was not present.

Bailiff Fred McKee carried the news to Ray, and the paper later reported, "when he told him that the verdict was in his favor, he did not make a reply of any kind; not a muscle changed nor an eyelid flickered as he received news such as falls to the lot of man but seldom."[362]

On hearing the verdict, Sheriff Lipps immediately handcuffed the boy, put him in an auto, and hurried him out of town to the train station at nearby Colchester, Illinois, where they boarded a train to Quincy. The Macomb paper thought it an odd and unflattering response. "The move on the part of the Adams County sheriff was a queer one and looks to have been done for effect to prejudice people against this city by giving out the impression that mob violence could have followed had he not been spirited away. If so, it was a case of bluff only, for there was no feeling whatever against the defendant."[363]

Ray had never worn handcuffs during his stay in Macomb for the trial.

Uncle Fred Pfanschmidt, speaking in Macomb, said simply, "We all feel happier. Ninety-five percent of the people here are pleased, and that percent in Quincy will be displeased when they learn of the result."[364]

---

[361] *Macomb Daily Journal,* October 24, 1914.
[362] *Macomb Daily Journal,* October 26, 1914.
[363] Ibid.
[364] *Journal,* October 26, 1914.

The cost to Adams County climbed ever higher with this failed trial. The circuit clerk's records in Macomb showed $4,105 paid in witness fees and jury costs; attorney Bennett received $2,000; $650 would go to Dr. Hektoen for his travel and testimony; and there were other expenses. The final estimate for the cost of the second trial was $8,085.50. It was far more than the $6,700 dollars for the original courtroom contest, which by itself represented nearly one thirteenth of all the taxes levied by Adams County that year. The total outlay for prosecuting Ray approached $15,000, and the case was not finished yet.

In the larger outside world, there were also people fighting battles for freedom. World War I had been raging between Germany and the allies for thirteen weeks, and in Mexico, Pancho Villa was fighting a guerrilla war.

In Quincy, Ray was met by a crowd at the railroad station. He was hustled off a rear car and rushed across the platform, through the building, and into a waiting police "auto wagon," accompanied by Sheriff Lipps, State's attorney Wolfe, Deputy Coens, and three newspaper reporters. Fewer than ten minutes after leaving the train, he was back in his dark cell in the depths of the county courthouse where he was greeted by shouts of welcome from the old timers in lockup.

Probably feeling oddly at home, Ray offered cigarettes to those around him and blew smoke rings with reporters and the sheriff. He expressed his appreciation for the people of Macomb and their treatment of him and his family. "Of course I liked the verdict ... I was pretty sure it would be that way. I knew that was the only verdict that could be returned that would be right and just."[365] He expressed displeasure only once, when he told the sheriff that it was a "dirty trick" not to allow him to say goodbye to Esther in Macomb. Ray seemed especially pleased that the news had been printed in an extra edition and hoped to have a copy brought to the jail to read.

---

[365] *Macomb Daily Journal*, October 27, 1914.

# Chapter 30

# "A Wonderful Lot of Nerve"

## October 1914

Tom Post, the jury foreman in Macomb, was quoted in an interview: "I couldn't see where they showed enough evidence to convict that boy, though. None of the rest of the boys could figure out where he had time to get out there that Friday night, kill those four people, and then burn a part of one of them up and get back to Quincy. By George, I don't see how it could be done. Innocent or guilty, that boy has got a wonderful lot of nerve."[366]

Ray's nerve would be tested while he awaited a third trial for either the murder of his father or Miss Kaempen. The indictment for killing his mother had been *nolle prossed*[367] some time ago. There was talk that a defense appeal might be made to the supreme court to quash the remaining indictments, since the same evidence, already judged insufficient for a guilty verdict, would have to be used in the next trial. The State maintained that there should rightly be another trial since the charges involved separate attacks, one on each victim, and therefore warranted separate trials.

---

[366] *Macomb Daily Journal*, October 27, 1914.
[367] *Nolle prosequi* is a statement to the judge by the prosecuting attorney that a charge will not be prosecuted, usually because the case cannot be successfully proven or the prosecution is convinced of the defendant's innocence.

The state supreme court, when it issued its ruling granting the original appeal, included a second mandatory change of venue if other charges were later brought to trial. The ruling meant that neither Quincy nor Macomb could be the location of any further proceedings. Once again an out-of-town trial would add a great burden to Adams County taxpayers.

All in all, the prosecution preferred this clean acquittal to a hung jury, which would have mandated a retrial in Macomb. Wagner said they would look for a larger town for the next field of battle, contending "that a town and country made up quite generally of farmers with conservative ideas is prejudiced against capital punishment and in favor of an accused person to the extent that the prosecution does not get a fair shake."[368]

At the scene of the tragedy, the ruins remained essentially unchanged from that haunted night two years past. In the basement there were still parts of a kitchen stove tumbled amid the foundations debris and bits of daily life remained. Hundreds of people visited the scene as a result of the trial in Macomb. The pump on the well still produced water when the handle was given a few cranks, but there were obvious signs of neglect: "hinges growing rusty and boards warping in a manner that denotes how, after all, use preserves and idleness decays. Even the trees in the orchard in front of the buildings show the absence of the hand of a man, and true indeed is the lesson that even nature, with all of her glories, if left to herself, will show a shabby appearance, indeed, when compared to the works of man and nature combined."[369]

The next dramatic development was a threatening "Black Hand" letter sent to Sheriff Lipps, postmarked from Macomb. The handwritten letter said simply: "Beware of your life and treat that boy with care," and the words were accompanied by a pencil drawing of a hand, shaded and completely filled in.

The instrument called a black-hand letter was mentioned as early as the 1750s and by the 1880s had become a common tactic employed in Italian-American communities in major cities to frighten and control people. It

---

[368] *Journal,* October 24, 1914.
[369] *Journal,* October 26, 1914.

was used by a terrorist organization in Serbia, reportedly responsible for assassinations of several members of the royal family and linked to the causes of WWI.

Gangs using this tactic delivered threats through letters consisting of a crude sketch of a human hand drawn and colored in black. The hand often clutched a knife dripping blood and usually included a demand for monetary payment. One of the most famous victims of this type of extortion was the great tenor Enrique Caruso, who paid a $2,000 black-hand demand. Receiving a second letter demanding $15,000 he called the police, who arrested two Italian-American men and retrieved the payment. This practice was common in Chicago, where in 1911 a man known only as the "Shotgun Man" extorted money using this method and killed some fifteen people. The use of black-hand tactics would fade as the 1920s began.

Sheriff Lipps staunchly declared himself completely unconcerned by the threatening letter and cordially invited the writer to Quincy for a personal visit. Analysis of the letter's handwriting showed it to be well written and likely penned by a man, though it was at first thought that one of Ray's many female admirers might have sent it. That idea was dismissed.

Attorney John Wall and Judge Epler were still investigating prospects for a last-ditch effort to block Ray's inheritance. They hoped that the state high court ruling meant Ray could only inherit through a trust that would deny him access to the property. But the Illinois Supreme Court held that there was no legal bar to Ray inheriting directly. Their ruling determined that the matter rested directly with the state legislature, which had authority to enact laws preventing similar cases in the future. Judge Epler was at work on just such a law. But the fact remained that such laws could not affect Ray.

One day before the deadline of October 29, Epler filed notice requesting a "rehearing" on this issue before the Illinois State Supreme Court. Although there was no possibility for an appeal, a rehearing might be granted. Epler had forty-five days to file his petition.[370] Ironically, with

---

[370] *Journal*, October 30, 1914.

his acquittal, Ray was not a murderer in the eyes of the law, and so stood to inherit in any event. At his third trial the State would seek to change his status once more.

Back in the county jail, Sheriff Lipps again cracked down on Ray's visitation. In a seemingly mean-spirited response to complaints from unnamed sources about Ray's treatment, the family's access to Ray was curtailed. The papers reported rumors that Ray might be charged with arson if the State failed to prove murder. This, however, had no weight, as there was also no law in Illinois prohibiting a man from burning his own property.

News coverage swerved still further into sensationalism, mystery, and pot stirring. On November 4, 1914, the *Journal* ran a confusing story about two women, one of whom may have seen the killer that fatal night. No names were mentioned in the story. It was reported that a "mystery" woman called the sheriff shortly after Ray's original arrest and asked to see the prisoner. She showed up at the jail a day late for her appointed visit but was granted access anyway. "It's not him. He looks something like him, but his eyes and cheekbones are different," one of the deputies reported overhearing her say to herself upon exiting the jail. When questioned by authorities, she refused to explain the meaning of her statements.

Detective Young began following the woman, to no result. Later in the week, she turned the tables and followed him. Young later saw her in "deep conversation" with private detective Lund, who had been employed by the defense.

The State believed she was hiding evidence. The woman was "landlady of a resort," a euphemism for a bordello. The prosecution sent a detective, who entered the house and started a commotion that resulted in a police raid. The woman was then arrested and interrogated, but no useful or damaging information surfaced. Before leaving for a trip to Peoria, the same woman made a deposit in a local bank and remarked that she would be well paid for her services in the Pfanschmidt case. Upon her return she was questioned about the money and replied that she had been saving it and it was mostly coins. The bank cashier contradicted her claim, saying the deposit was all in currency bills, not silver.

When hauled before the grand jury, she changed her tune and said that she had gotten the money for helping a "resident of a small Illinois town near here ... clear himself of some trouble he is supposed to have been inveigled into." The grand jury believed her and released her, with no further details made public.

Enter Woman Number Two. This woman was heard to say that she had overheard Mystery Woman Number One say Ray had come to her house after the crime to wash the blood off his hands. Woman Number Two was involved in a divorce proceeding in circuit court and said she was willing to speak to authorities so as long as her attorney was present. However, she then became unreachable and rumor was she had left town.

The authorities disbelieved that story and contrived to have a bicycle delivery boy arrive at her door with a personal telegram. Although she did not come from the house, she almost immediately telephoned the wire company, asking for her message. She was brought in for questioning but refused to give any answers except "abusive utterances against the detective."

Mystery Woman Number One lived in Quincy but at a distance from the route Ray was supposed to have traveled. There was speculation that her story might be true and that Ray had paid money to clean up at her place. The paper speculated, "This seems more credible when taken into consideration the character of the women involved." Money had appeared in her account a few days after Pfanschmidt's arrest; but Ray seemed cash poor, and an extra stop would mean the trip time from farm to Ray's camp would be stretched even further.

Still other rumors said that the bloodhounds trailed into the empty field within sight of Ray's camp because Ray removed insurance papers from the house before burning it and buried them in that field for later retrieval.

This last bit of nonsense was rounded out by a rumor that slain schoolteacher Emma Kaempen had written letters to her father telling of bad blood between Ray and his father. Mr. Kaempen himself had the grace to deny that directly.[371]

It was time for trial number three.

---

[371] *Journal*, November 4, 1914.

# Chapter 31

# Trial Number Three

## January 1915

P rinceton, Illinois, a small town one hundred twenty miles southwest
of Chicago was originally settled on the open rolling farmland in the
1830s by pioneers from Massachusetts. It was here that a preacher, Owen
Lovejoy, had operated an important stop on the Underground Railroad,
moving slaves to freedom during the Civil War. The town was also on the
Burlington & Quincy Railroad line, a definite consideration when looking
for a site for Ray's next trial.

In spite of numerous attempts by the defense to have the remaining
charges dismissed, Judge Davis set the date for proceedings to begin on
Monday, January 25, 1915. Ray would now have to defend himself against
the charge of murdering the schoolteacher, Miss Emma Kaempen.[372] This
trial would be far different than the preceding ones.

Two Princeton area attorneys, L. M. Echert of that city and O'Hara
of Carthage, Illinois, would assist in the prosecution. This numerical
imbalance between the two sides called forth protests from Govert and
Lancaster. Wolfe countered, saying the experience of years of practice by

---

[372] *Bureau County Tribune*, January 20, 1915.

the defense more than balanced the scales. The defense was being helped by a single local attorney named Spaulding.

On Monday court convened at 1:30 p.m., and by 2:30 the jury box was filled with sets of veniremen to be examined, twelve at a time. The prosecution laid out its case and said they wanted men who were not opposed to inflicting the death penalty. Of the first twelve prospects, four men were accepted. It would prove to be a far simpler thing to seat this jury than in the previous two trials: four men were accepted on Tuesday, four more on Wednesday, and the final four late on Friday.

On Saturday, January 30, the day was taken up by the opening statements from both sides. Wolfe began and spoke until after lunch, at which point Lancaster took up the oratory and held forth until adjournment at 4:55 p.m. The case was recessed until Monday.

On that day sixteen witnesses were called and examined by Wolfe and O'Hara, while Govert handled cross-examinations. At one point the packed crowd reacted to testimony with laughter, but Judge Davis was quick to rap his gavel and threaten to clear the room if order was not maintained. One new witness, Ralph Irkey, a farmer from near Melrose Chapel, recounted seeing scratches on Ray's face, the first ever mention of such a thing. No one else had ever mentioned any wounds on Ray, and on cross-examination the weight of this testimony vanished.

At the close of the first day's testimony, the Princeton paper noted, "So far there has been no evidence presented that would make it appear that the State had a case at all, but there are still many witnesses to come, and what will be brought out remains to be seen."[373] It was not exactly a ringing endorsement for the prosecution.

A week later, the reports were the same. Although the evidence was more tired than captivating, the case drew consistent crowds. A press of people would wait for the doors to open, jostling to gain seats and fill every inch of standing room. At noon recess, the courtroom would be completely cleared, the process reenacted after lunch.

---

[373] *Bureau County Tribune*, February 3, 1915.

As usual, Ray generated great interest among local women but remained unruffled. One local reporter wrote, "The defendant is holding up well in spite of the strain that he must be laboring under during the progress of the trial. He listens intently to the testimony that is given by all of the witnesses and seems to be cheerful at all times. He sits with the attorneys at their table and consults with them at intervals regarding certain phases of the case."[374]

The State's case was substantially weakened by Judge Davis's ruling that none of Ray's financial dealings before the murder could be introduced. This effectively destroyed the central support in the State's theory of motive.

It had been highly anticipated that a new witness, Harvey Six, a snitch from Joliette State Prison would provide exciting and damaging testimony against Ray. Six was invited to tell his story with the jury tucked away, safely out of earshot, so the judge could rule on its admissibility.

Six told a tale of happenings during some jail time shared with the defendant. In this account, Ray had instructed Six to go to the state of Kansas after Six was released and mail an anonymous letter to an unnamed person, which would include a concocted confession to the murders of the Pfanschmidt family. Six told of Ray being willing to pay up to $1,000 each for two witnesses who might swear that Bogardus put the blood spots on the clothes found in the privy. After Six's testimony was completed before the judge, but before a ruling could be handed down as to its admissibility, the prosecution changed their mind.

Almost unbelievably, attorney O'Hara rose, and "asking the indulgence of the court, explained that the convict had been introduced as a witness for the State because he had recently turned State's evidence in an arson trial, thereby causing the conviction of two of his accomplices, one of whom had later confessed. For this reason the State believed that Six was a truthful man and that he should be used by the State in this case. Attorney O'Hara, however, expressed himself as having no confidence in the story of the convict and said that he would take the responsibility to the people of Adams County in order to relieve State's Attorney Wolfe of censure in the

---

[374] *Bureau County Tribune*, February 10, 1915.

matter. O'Hara asked that the court therefore allow them to ask that the witness be withdrawn. The court agreed and the witness was accordingly taken back to the jail to finish his own sentence."[375]

Six later gave an interview from his jail cell, but even the newspaper reporter judged him less than credible. This last story did not match details Six had supplied under oath.

The trial ground on, and a serious game of witness strategy played out between prosecution and defense. The State had withheld one of their strongest witnesses—Detective Young—keeping him in reserve to be a rebuttal witness against Ray's testimony. What they could not know was that, in this courtroom, Ray would not take the stand. With nothing to refute, Young's potentially damaging testimony remained unheard. The prosecution's strategy had backfired.

As closing arguments neared, Judge Davis issued strict instructions that the attorneys must limit themselves to the facts as presented in this case during their summations and warned that straying outside those limitations would not be allowed. He also instructed the jury to draw no conclusions from the fact that the defendant did not take the stand.

Closing arguments, though eloquent, were short. Much testimony from the previous trials had to be left unspoken, and large pieces of that evidence had been ruled inadmissible. The prosecution's strategies failed, leaving still other stories untold.

Ray's fate was soon handed over to the twelve men in the box and was quickly decided.

When Ray entered the courtroom to hear the verdict, the room stilled. As usual he hung up his hat and overcoat and took his customary seat at the table with his attorneys. "His face did not betray any great emotion, his expression rather one of great weariness rather than of disheartenment. It had been a long trial, but he rested secure in the knowledge that if the verdict was against him, his lawyers would appeal the case to the supreme court."[376]

---

[375] *Bureau County Tribune*, February 10, 1915.
[376] *Bureau County Tribune*, February 24, 1915.

Judge Davis ordered the jury brought in, and tension climbed. The faces of the men gave little away. They seated themselves and declared they had reached a verdict. The stillness made the crackle of the paper holding the verdict seem overly loud.

The judge read in a quiet voice, "We the jury do find the defendant, Ray Pfanschmidt, not guilty."

February 24, 1915, one simple headline read: "Pfanschmidt Free." On the first ballot on Wednesday night, the jury polled ten for acquittal, one guilty, and one not voting. By the fifth ballot, the jury was unanimous in favor of freeing the accused. This verdict matched public sentiment that the evidence was one-sided, in favor of the young man.

Judge Davis thanked the jury, dismissing them. Whereupon Ray rose and walked over to warmly thank each of the jury members and shake his hand. Then he was taken back to his cell to stoically await the calling of yet another trial on the remaining count hanging over him. As it turned out, this would not happen.

Finally, the state's attorney gave up the hunt for a guilty verdict.

After a further few minutes in the courtroom, while Wolfe officially negated the last charge, Ray was freed. He was informed that he would not be rearrested as long as he kept his distance from Adams County.

In order to avoid public demonstrations, Ray waited in the jail throughout the afternoon and then, accompanied by his attorney, preceded by a roundabout route to the train station where he bought a ticket to Peoria. Ray displayed courtesy to the city that acquitted him. The local paper reported, "In speaking of his trial here, Ray expressed his gratitude to the people of Princeton and to the officers of the county for the great consideration and fairness which they had shown him. Especially he was enthusiastic in regard to the strict observance of justice in the proceedings of the court, stating that Judge Davis had shown a knowledge of the law which put to shame some of the other jurists who had been concerned in the two other trials. He could not refrain from speaking several times of the quarters and feed which he received at the jail. He said that in comparison to the cell he occupied at Quincy, his quarters here were palatial and that since coming to Princeton he had gained several pounds in flesh."

It was also reported that there were numerous women awaiting him with dinner invitations when the acquittal was announced.[377]

It would be nice if the story could end here, with Ray reclaiming his fiancée and restarting his life, but that was not to be. Other things awaited Ray, including further brushes with the law.

*Sketch of Ray based on a photo at the time of the last trial*

Original art courtesy of Grant House.

---

[377] *Bureau County Tribune*, February 24, 1915.

# Epilogue

Ray may have been free, but he had spent most of the past three years of his young life behind bars. He emerged almost without assets, nearly without family, and entirely at loose ends. Everything he had known had changed. He packed his scant possessions and moved to Wichita, Kansas, where Walter and Minnie Herr offered him their hospitality.

In a not totally accurate statement, Ray would later say, "I was only a kid when arrested. It was the first time I was in trouble. After nearly three years' slavery in jail, during which I was treated like a man convicted, my mail censored, and numerous attempts made to make me confess, it was like a new world to me when I was freed. I had grown from youth to manhood in jail."[378]

In March 1915, his staunch supporter, Uncle Fred Pfanschmidt, found himself in court to answer a charge of having "immoral relations" with one Pearl Whitlock. The charge was dismissed when she admitted consorting with three or four other men.

In May, the old lion of the family, C. C. Pfanschmidt died at home, where he had been convalescing from an operation. He was healing nicely until he was afflicted with a bout of hiccups that would not stop. Fifteen years ago he had suffered from uncontrollable hiccups and successfully emerged from it, but this time he would not.

---

[378] *Journal*, February 1, 1918.

In his will, Grandfather Pfanschmidt bequeathed to Ray the sum of one dollar, from an estate estimated to be worth $50,000. Other family members and friends were the main beneficiaries. His last living son, Fred, was away at the time, on a trip to take his ailing daughter, Lillian, to the dry healing air of the West.

Ray, who would not mourn his grandfather, had not been completely abandoned by his clan. Along with the Herrs, cousin Howard stayed a faithful supporter. In July 1914, Howard Petrie had married and in the process put the Pfanschmidt name in the paper again, this time in conjunction with an almost amusing incident of attempted bribery.

According to the newspaper,[379] Howard encountered a fair amount of difficulty obtaining a marriage license. The first problem was ascertaining the bride's name. She was born Helen Bartholomew but had been adopted by Mr. Valentine Keim of Melrose. This provided a dilemma concerning the proper surname for a license, but her current name was eventually settled on, with advice from the county clerk issuing the permit.

The second difficulty was that Howard had not yet attained his majority and needed the consent of his mother, Elizabeth Petrie. This was so embarrassing to Howard, who did not want his age publicized, that he offered the princely sum of fifty cents to induce the deputy to keep that piece of information from the public record. However, County Clerk Elmer Mutz emphatically declined to comply. The license was issued, but publicity resulted. The wedding was later performed in the home of Rev. I. W. Bingaman, pastor of the Luther Memorial Church.

Just more than a year later, in 1915, Howard and his new wife moved to Wichita, where they would make their home near cousin Ray. By July of that year, the *Journal* reported that according to Ray, both young men were employed by a tea and coffee company.[380]

About this same time, Esther Reeder's father died, leaving her to live with her brother, Hugh, and his family. She had enrolled in the city college and would manage to put her life back together.

---

[379] *Whig*, July 1, 1914.
[380] *Journal*, July 21, 1915.

Things stayed quiet for the last part of the year, but Ray just couldn't stay out of the newspapers. He wrote a nice note to the city of Macomb extolling the virtues of the Sunflower State and mentioning that he was in the landscaping business there.[381] But in November he was taken to task by the alumni of the University of Illinois for falsely claiming in his advertising to have graduated from that institution.

Ray was in the Quincy paper again in January 1916 when he returned to finalize the family's estate. He also made one final attempt to speak with his sweetheart. A week after a heavy snow and before leaving the area, Ray again traveled the well-known road to Melrose seeking Esther. She could not or would not face him and hurriedly left by a back door while Ray was at the front of the home asking to speak with her. She crossed a snowy field on foot to reach safety at a neighboring home, only to be followed by the determined Ray.

At this doorway, the hopeful young man was greeted with the declaration that Esther would not speak with him. Ray, unwilling to be denied, asked if that was her desire, or simply her family's. "It is both" came the reply, and Ray was forced to return to Kansas with a heart as cold as winter.[382]

Esther Reeder went on to graduate in 1917 from the dramatic arts department at the Quincy College of Music, as a pupil of Mrs. George Hartung. She was deemed a gifted elocutionist and was lauded in the papers as one of Quincy's most popular readers. After her graduation she was listed as part of the faculty and attended the summer session of the Columbia College of Expression in Chicago in the fall of 1917. Her heart seemed to have recovered from her alliance with Ray, for while there she met and fell in love with Frank Purcell of Mt. Sterling, Illinois. Their wedding was celebrated in Chicago in 1919.

Ray likely kept abreast of these developments. Since Esther had been named by the prosecution as part of Ray's motive for murder, it is tempting to consider her influence on his actions yet again. A scant two months after

---

[381] *Whig,* October 28, 1915.
[382] *Journal,* October 26, 1916.

being rejected at the Reeder Farm, Ray was under arrest in Kansas, this time for stealing and selling automobiles.

According to the Wichita papers, Ray was tied to a ring of automobile thieves that crossed state lines into Oklahoma and were involved the theft of motor cycles, and auto parts. Ray apparently recruited a young man living in his apartment building in Wichita, and this young man's mother was only too happy to detail his troubles to authorities. She reported that she had trouble most nights getting her son to leave Pfanschmidt's apartment before midnight, and she greatly distrusted Ray's influence. The young man, named Harold, said Ray told him he had a supply of tires brought in from Arkansas City and Oklahoma, for which he needed to find customers. Harold, who claimed not to know the parts were stolen, was enlisted to procure buyers.

The authorities in Kansas hoped to use information from this lad, who was ten years younger than Ray, to connect Pfanschmidt with the large and ever growing problem of organized car theft rings operating in the Midwest. Ray was arrested and charged with two counts of grand larceny for stealing autos.

For one of the stolen car deals, a third party "goat" was recruited to legitimize the transaction. Ray told this man, Neil Stimold, that he wanted to purchase a car. A few days later another man, also believed to be part of the theft ring, approached the "goat" Stimold and said he had a car for sale. The unsuspecting Stimold set up a meeting between Ray and the supposed seller. At that time the phony sale took place, allowing Ray to later claim that he purchased the stolen car from Stimold.[383]

Even after this arrest, Walter Herr and family stood by Ray, signing a bond for his bail. When he was indicted on a second count, Ray engineered a deal in which he agreed to enlist in the army instead of being jailed while waiting to face these charges. Ray was escorted to a recruiting office where he did obtain a draft card, but was judged unfit for duty by the criteria of the day. The remaining prospect was imminent jail, and Ray, unwilling to

---

[383] *The Wichita Daily Eagle*, May 19, 1916.

face another trial, skipped town.[384] The Herrs were left with his bond of fifteen hundred dollars on their signature.

*Photo of Ray's draft card*

Ancestrydotcom.

Ray fled to Kansas City, Missouri, where he lived quietly for about ten months. His only brush with the law was a speeding ticket, which did not tip off the authorities that he was still wanted in Kansas. Perhaps it was a need for cash or excitement or simply to feel alive, but something triggered his reckless behavior again. Ray and his roommate stole three tires from the Ford Livery Service garage where he had been working as a taxi driver and living off reported earnings of $18 per week.

This arrest involved an exciting high-speed car chase through the downtown section of a Kansas City darkened by a ban on street lights, ordered by President Garfield in aid of the war effort. Ray was soon captured, although his roommate escaped. True to form, Ray tried to bribe the arresting officer on the way to the station.

It didn't work.

---

[384] *Wichita Daily Beacon*, January 23, 1918.

The policeman offered the opinion that Ray should be grateful it was too dark for the officer to see to shoot. Ray reportedly answered, "I'd have been better off, I guess."[385]

Finally, Ray pled guilty to something. With fewer than three years of freedom since his last acquittal, he was sentenced in January 1918. At his hearing, the judge asked, "Haven't you anyone that cares for you—anyone that you, if not for your own sake, could do right for?"

Ray answered, "I did once."[386]

Despite trying to engineer a last-minute plea for clemency, Ray was sent to the Missouri State Penitentiary in Jefferson City, where he became Inmate #20481. He served time from March 15, 1918, until May 15, 1919, when, having earned early release through good behavior, he was discharged.

Various reports surfaced in later years in the Quincy papers. One claimed Ray was killed by the Mafia in New York in 1932. Another that same year, from an unidentified family source, said Ray had settled down after being freed the last time, married a preacher's daughter, and was raising a family with his wife, a former schoolteacher. This last report was confirmed to the newspaper by Emery Lancaster, Ray's former attorney.[387]

One can only hope that was true.

---

[385] *Whig*, January 22, 1918.
[386] *Journal*, January 16, 1918.
[387] *Quincy Herald Whig*, December 27, 1932.

# Postscript

Over the course of my research I have decided often about Ray's guilt or innocence—reversing myself each time. I invite you to reach your own conclusions. Bear in mind that some people had to be telling untruths. You must decide for yourself who told lies under oath.

Please visit http://liestoldunderoath.com for more information and to answer this question:

*If you had been on the jury, would you have voted Ray "guilty" or "not guilty"?*

I'll post a tally.

—*Beth*

# Selected Resources

The bulk of the information in this book came from the local newspapers and from the trial testimony and appeal documents:

The *Quincy Daily Herald*

The *Quincy Daily Whig*

The *Quincy Daily Journal*

The *Macomb Times*

The *Daily Illini*

The *Princeton Times*

The *Ellsworth Reporter*

The *Payson Times*

The *Wichita Daily Eagle*

The *Wichita Beacon*

The signed transcript of the Coroner's Inquest on file at the Adams County Courthouse, Quincy, Illinois.

Trial information permanently on file at the Illinois State Historical Society, Springfield, Illinois.

## Books and periodicals:

*Farm Machinery Illustrated*, Midland Publishing Co., St. Louis and Kansas City Edition, vol. 269, December 1, 1896.

*Farm & Home Plat Directory*, Adams County, Illinois: Farm & Home Publishers, Ltd., 1997.

Quincy City Directory. 1912.

Atlas & Plat Book, Adams County, Illinois. Published by Rockford Map Publishers Inc., 1975.

Atlas of Adams County, Illinois, published for the *Quincy Journal* by the World's Atlas Company, circa 1912.

Cemeteries of Adams County, Illinois, Vol. I, Great River Genealogical Society, 1987.

Adams County Atlas, 1872.

David Wilcox, *Quincy & Adams Co. History and Representative Men, Volume II*. Lewis Publishing Company, 1919.

United States Federal Census Records, 1910.

United States Federal Census Records, 1920.

McCall Patterns for Spring & Summer 1912, Catalogue #15.

*The Practical Stock Doctor, A Reliable Common-sense Ready-Reference Book for the Farmer and Stock Owner*, edited by Dr. George A. Waterman, professor of veterinary science, Michigan State Agricultural College: F. B. Dickerson Company, 1912.

Hon. William H. Collins and Mr. Cicero F. Perry, *Past & Present of the City of Quincy and Adams County, Illinois*. The S. J. Clarke Publishing Co., 1905.

Carl Landrum, *Historical Sketches of Quincy Illinois*, revised edition, 1986.

Pictorial Quincy, Past and Present (Commemorating the 50th Anniversary of the Lincoln-Douglas Debate, Quincy, Ill., Oct. 13th, 1858). Emmet Head & Willis Henry Haselwood, editors and publishers, Quincy, 1908.

## Websites

www.ancestry.com—to research family connections.

www.measuringworth.com/calculators—useful for converting values to present-day dollar amounts.

www.crimezzz.net/serialkillers/M/MOORE_henry_lee.htm—serial killer crime index.

http://www.phrenology.org/intro.html—for more on the history of phrenology.

www.ilgenweb.com—for pictures and information about farms in 1912.

http://archive.quincylibrary.org—QPS Public Library, for online copies of the Quincy, Illinois, newspapers.

http://www.candlepowerforums.com/vb/showthread.php?s=fe2c7b88 4eb0241fbe9c00abb3e7026c&t=3947—for information about the history of the flashlight.

www.rootsweb.com—for genealogy research.

www.greenmountqcy.com—the website of Greenmount Cemetery.

www.lectlaw.com—for information regarding citations of bloodhound evidence.

88975031R00257

Made in the USA
Lexington, KY
20 May 2018